ARISTOTLE'S *POLITICS*

Critical Essays on the Classics
Series Editor: Steven M. Cahn

The volumes in this series offer insightful and accessible essays that shed light on the classics of philosophy. Each of the distinguished editors has selected outstanding work in recent scholarship to provide today's readers with a deepened understanding of the most timely issues raised in these important texts.

Plato's *Republic*: Critical Essays
edited by Richard Kraut
Plato's *Euthyphro*, *Apology*, and *Crito*: Critical Essays
edited by Rachana Kamtekar
Aristotle's *Ethics*: Critical Essays
edited by Nancy Sherman
Aristotle's *Politics*: Critical Essays
edited by Richard Kraut and Steven Skultety
Descartes's *Meditations*: Critical Essays
edited by Vere Chappell
The Rationalists: Critical Essays on Descartes, Spinoza, and Leibniz
edited by Derk Pereboom
The Empiricists: Critical Essays on Locke, Berkeley, and Hume
edited by Margaret Atherton
The Social Contract Theorists: Critical Essays on Hobbes, Locke, and Rousseau
edited by Christopher Morris
Mill's *On Liberty*: Critical Essays
edited by Gerald Dworkin
Mill's *Utilitarianism*: Critical Essays
edited by David Lyons
Mill's *The Subjection of Women*: Critical Essays
edited by Maria H. Morales
Kant's *Groundwork on the Metaphysics of Morals*: Critical Essays
edited by Paul Guyer
Kant's *Critique of Pure Reason*: Critical Essays
edited by Patricia Kitcher
Kant's *Critique of the Power of Judgment*: Critical Essays
edited by Paul Guyer
Heidegger's *Being and Time*
edited by Richard Polt
The Existentialists: Critical Essays on Kierkegaard, Nietzsche, Heidegger, and Sartre
edited by Charles Guignon

ARISTOTLE'S *POLITICS*

Critical Essays

Edited by
Richard Kraut
and
Steven Skultety

ROWMAN & LITTLEFIELD PUBLISHERS, INC.
Lanham • Boulder • New York • Toronto • Oxford

ROWMAN & LITTLEFIELD PUBLISHERS, INC.

Published in the United States of America
by Rowman & Littlefield Publishers, Inc.
A wholly owned subsidiary of The Rowman & Littlefield Publishing Group, Inc.
4501 Forbes Boulevard, Suite 200, Lanham, Maryland 20706
www.rowmanlittlefield.com

PO Box 317
Oxford
OX2 9RU, UK

British Library Cataloguing in Publication Information Available

Library of Congress Cataloging-in-Publication Data

Aristotle's Politics : critical essays / edited by Richard Kraut, Steven Skultety.
p. cm.—(Critical essays on the classics)
Includes bibliographical references and index.
ISBN 0-7425-3423-5 (cloth : alk. paper) — ISBN 0-7425-3424-3 (pbk. : alk. paper)
1. Aristotle. Politics. 2. Political science—Early works to 1800. I. Kraut, Richard, 1944– II. Skultety, Steven.
JC71.A7A77 2005
320'.01'1—dc22

2005011159

Printed in the United States of America

™ The paper used in this publication meets the minimum requirements of American National Standard for Information Sciences—Permanence of Paper for Printed Library Materials, ANSI/NISO Z39.48-1992.

Contents

Acknowledgments

Stephen Taylor Holmes, "Aristippus in and out of Athens" originally appeared in *American Political Science Review* 73, no. 1 (1979): 113–128. Reprinted by permission of Cambridge University Press and the author.

Stephen G. Salkever, "Aristotle's Social Science" originally appeared in *Essays on the Foundations of Aristotelian Political Science*, eds. Carnes Lord and David O'Connor. (Berkeley: University of California Press, 1991). Reprinted by permission of University of California Press.

John M. Cooper, "Political Animals and Civic Friendship" originally appeared in *Aristoteles' 'Politik': Akten des XI. Symposium Aristotelicum*, ed. Günther Patzig (Göttingen: Vanderhoeck & Ruprecht, 1990). Reprinted by permission of the author.

Malcolm Schofield, "Ideology and Philosophy in Aristotle's Theory of Slavery" originally appeared in *Aristoteles' 'Politik': Akten des XI. Symposium Aristotelicum*, ed. Günther Patzig (Göttingen: Vanderhoeck & Ruprecht, 1990). Reprinted by permission of the author.

Fred D. Miller, "Property Rights in Aristotle" originally appeared as chapter 9 of Miller's *Nature, Justice, and Rights in Aristotle's Politics* (Oxford: Oxford University Press, 1997): 309–331. Reprinted by permission of Oxford University Press and the author.

Jeremy Waldron, "The Wisdom of the Multitude: Some Reflections on Book 3, Chapter 11 of Aristotle's *Politics*" originally appeared in *Political Theory* 23, no. 4 (1995): 563–584. Reprinted by permission of Sage Publications.

Dorothea Frede, "Citizenship in Aristotle's Politics" has not previously been published. It is a revision of "Staatsverfassung und Staatsbürger" that appeared in *Aristoteles: Politik*, ed. Otfried Höffe (Berlin: Akademie Verlag, 2001): 75–92.

Jonathan Barnes, "Aristotle and Political Liberty" originally appeared in *Aristoteles' 'Politik': Akten des XI. Symposium Aristotelicum*, ed. Günther Patzig (Göttingen: Vanderhoeck & Ruprecht, 1990). Reprinted by permission of the author.

David Keyt, "Aristotle and Anarchism" originally appeared in *Reason Papers* 18 (1993): 133–152. Reprinted by permission of the editor of *Reason Papers* and the author.

Josiah Ober, "Aristotle's Natural Democracy" has not previously been published.

Introduction

ARISTOTLE'S *POLITICS* IS WIDELY RECOGNIZED as one of the classics of the history of political philosophy, and like every other such masterpiece, it is a work about which there is deep division. Some of its readers think that it poses some of the deepest problems about political life, and that many of the answers it proposes to those questions continue to have great merit. Other readers, by contrast, think it is valuable only or primarily as a text that is reflective of its time and place; we can absorb from it the political outlook of one aristocratic thinker of the fourth-century Greek world, but that world differs so much from our own that Aristotle's ideas cannot be revived or reformulated in a way that has application to our own times. Probably most readers of Aristotle, especially those who are just beginning to come to terms with this text, fall somewhere between these two poles. They are uncertain whether his *Politics* has any contribution to make to contemporary debates about political life and political theory. It is the aim of this volume to sharpen this issue. Each of the essays that it brings together is addressed, implicitly or explicitly, to the question whether Aristotle's thinking has some applicability to ongoing debates in contemporary political philosophy.

The title of Aristotle's work—*Politikôn*—gives its author wide scope, for it indicates that its subject has to do with all matters that pertain to the *polis*—alternatively translated "city," "city-state," or "state." There were perhaps about one thousand such communities in the Greek world in which Aristotle lived, some of them containing no more than a few thousand citizens (though Athens was a monster of about 40,000 adult male citizens and a much larger number of non-citizens). At the Lyceum—the school he established in Athens, and which he oversaw during the last twelve years of his life—he supervised the composition of studies of the political systems of 158 of these *poleis* (plural of *polis*)—all but one of which (the *Constitution of Athens*) have been lost. It is debatable whether Aristotle himself was the author of this work, but in any case the person who wrote it seems, in many instances, to think about politics in a way that was influenced by Aristotle's own outlook. That Aristotle took such a deep interest in studying the multiplicity of political systems in the Greek world testifies to his conviction that political philosophy should be rooted in a wide familiarity with the institutions of one's own time and their historical development. To philosophize in an Aristotelian fashion about politics is to bring empirical and historical understanding into contact with philosophical ideas.

Those philosophical ideas, in Aristotle's case, are set forth in one of his major ethical treatises: the *Nicomachean Ethics*. It presents itself as a study of the ultimate human good, and it gives the name *politikē* (translated "political science" or "political expertise") to the branch of human knowledge that is addressed to that subject matter. This means that Aristotle would have no objection to giving to the work that has been named his *Nicomachean Ethics* the alternative title, *Politics*. It is a treatise addressed to future political leaders, and its aim is to tell them what they need to know about the ultimate good, so that they may then proceed to apply these philosophical ideas to the concrete circumstances of their own political communities. The importance of combining the theory of well-being outlined in the *Nicomachean Ethics* to legal systems is emphasized in the closing chapter of that work, which serves as an introduction to the *Politics*, and contains an overview of some of its major topics. In effect, then, Aristotle presents what we call the *Nicomachean Ethics* and the *Politics* as a single, two-volume study, a whole that would appropriately be called *Politics*. The first volume contains Aristotle's ideas about all of the factors that constitute a well-lived human life—chief among them the development and exercise of good states of character (*ēthē*: hence the title of this work); and the second volume offers a study of legal systems, which, Aristotle insists, have a profound effect on character. To understand the *Politics* fully, then, we must treat it as the completion of the project initiated in the *Ethics*. Aristotle's views about good social interaction—as exhibited in just relations and friendships—and about the external goods needed for living well (wealth and honor, for example) are especially important for his discussion of political institutions.

Having studied in Plato's research center (the Academy) for twenty years, Aristotle could not have been indifferent to the political philosophy of Plato's *Republic*, *Statesman*, and *Laws*. His most direct encounter with Plato as a political theorist occurs in Book II of *Politics*, where he subjects the social schemes of *Republic* and *Laws* to scrutiny and criticism. He is deeply opposed to Plato's most radical proposals—the abolition of the traditional family and of private possessions, and the extreme unification of civic life that is the goal of these institutional innovations. But, in a way, Aristotle was deeply influenced by Plato's way of thinking about politics, and especially by the progression of thought that leads from *Republic* to *Laws*. Plato's political project in the *Republic* is to reshape civic life by depicting an ideal community that is thoroughly informed by a deep understanding of what is good. In the *Laws*, he proposes a more practicable way in which a community can be guided by rational discussion and sound philosophical understanding. Aristotle's political project may be viewed as a more thorough extension of this same line of thought: his assumption is that every political community, no matter how badly governed, can profit in some way by receiving the guidance of leaders who have developed a philosophical understanding of human well-being. Political science must therefore consider not merely what the best possible constitution is, nor merely the best and second-best, but the entire range of political systems that are on offer. In each case, it will be found that there are possibilities for amelioration. Political theory must in this way ally itself with empirical political study, if the world is to become a more suitable home for human flourishing.

Can Aristotle's vision of the proper tasks and ambitions of political theory be applied to our world? Emphatically not, according to Stephen Taylor Holmes. He takes to task some of the most prominent philosophers of the twentieth century—Karl Popper, Hannah Arendt, and Leo Strauss—for ignoring the concrete political circumstances that made Aristotle's political project a live option in fourth-century Greece. The social world, Holmes argues, has been transformed, first by Christianity, and more recently by capitalist modernity, into a highly differentiated and pluralistic assortment of roles and institutions. It is no longer the case, as perhaps it might have been in the small city-states of Aristotle's time, that citizenship is the primary social role, or that the study of politics encompasses all that is of value in human life. For Holmes, Aristotle's political writings raise no issues with which contemporary thinkers can profitably engage, because our social world is so entirely different from his.

An entirely opposed point of view is taken by Stephen G. Salkever, who argues that Aristotle's conception of social science has greater resources for understanding than do two alternatives that are widely accepted today—one of them an empiricist approach that applies the methods of the physical sciences to the study of political phenomena, the other an approach that sharply distinguishes biology from culture and seeks to interpret the meanings of (rather than predict the ways of) social institutions, though without standing in judgment over them. Salkever argues that Aristotle provides a valuable alternative to these approaches by conceiving of political science as both evaluative and empirical, and by taking human beings to be social creatures with a "profound biological need for an institution that will shape our desires into healthy patterns."

Both Holmes and Salkever emphasize the importance, in Aristotle's political philosophy, of the thesis that human beings are political animals—a statement that appears several times in Aristotle's *Politics* and *Nicomachean Ethics*, but is explained and defended most fully in *Politics* Book I, chapter 2. The aim of John M. Cooper's essay is to focus in greater detail on this central component of Aristotle's thought and to uncover the assumptions about human values and human nature that lie behind it. Cooper's treatment of this issue leads him to the conclusion that for Aristotle the members of a political community are necessarily attentive to questions about the character of their fellow citizens, and that the common advantage that unifies them, however weakly, is not a mere sum of their separate interests, but a single collective good that is shared by all in common.

Book I of Aristotle's *Politics* is renowned not only for its explication of the thesis that human beings are political animals, but also for its extensive treatment of the question whether slavery is a just and natural institution. We who read the *Politics* today cannot but be chilled by Aristotle's efforts to defend slavery on the grounds that some people are natural slaves—and by the use of this text to support slaveholding in modern times. Our reaction should make us ask how philosophers who devote themselves to ethics can go so badly astray, and it is tempting to answer this question by appealing to the interests that a defense of slavery protected. Aristotle, in other words, was oblivious to the evils of slavery because his leisured way of life (he of course did not have to work for a living) required slave labor; self-interest kept him from recognizing the evils of this institution. But does that way of reading him survive scrutiny? Malcolm Schofield argues that it does not. He points out that Aristotle never claims that most of those who had the legal status of slaves were in fact *natural* slaves and argues that this empirical generalization is not relevant to Aristotle's project in *Politics* Book I. Aristotle is writing in opposition to Plato's idea that ruling is always the same relationship, wherever it is found—whether it is the rule over a child, or a woman, or a free person, or a slave. To show that Plato is wrong about this, it suits Aristotle's purpose to point out that if an adult is naturally deficient in reason—so much so as to be permanently childlike—then it is in his interest to be ruled as a slave. That way of justifying slavery can be used to show that nearly all of those who have the legal status of slaves are *not* in fact natural slaves, and that their enslavement is therefore contrary to their interests and unjust.

One of the major questions of political philosophy has to do with the allocation of property rights and the proper distribution of wealth. In nearly every society, some have more resources than others; and one of the most common uses of legal systems is the enforcement of property rights, and therefore the perpetuation of inequality. The division of the *polis* into rich and poor was something that every one of Aristotle's contemporaries was acutely aware of, and strife bordering on warfare between those who had abundant resources and those who had few was ubiquitous. This theme carries through Books III to VI of the *Politics*, but it is in Book II that he most fully considers questions about why people should have their own resources and whether the *polis* should equalize them. Drawing primarily on that material, Fred D. Miller Jr. attributes to Aristotle a theory of property rights that rests on a conception of human well-being. It is good for a human being to have material resources, and for control over those resources to rest with the individual and to be protected against collective re-allocation. So understood, Aristotle offers a conception of the value of property that differs radically both from that of socialism and that of laissez-faire liberalism.

Book III of the *Politics* turns to another fundamental question of political theory: Who should rule? Or, as Aristotle puts the question in III.10—What part of the polis is to have authority: the many? the wealthy? those who are virtuous? the one who is best? He struggles with this question for the remainder of Book III, and his discussion of political change and stability in Books IV through VI work within the framework of distinctions drawn in Book III. Chapter 11 of Book III stands out for the simple but profound point it makes: that any answer to the question, who should rule? must make room for the possibility that collectives can be superior to single individuals. A group of people might, by pooling information and ideas, have greater wisdom than any single person. Jeremy Waldron's essay explores the ways in which this basic idea can be exploited for the defense of a democratic politics that relies heavily on deliberative give-and-take. He points out that Aristotle's method for doing philosophy—sometimes called the dialectical or "endoxic" method ("endoxic" because of its use of *endoxa*, common or reputable opinions)—requires the synthesis of the views of the many and the wise, and not the mere counting of noses. Analogously, Waldron suggests, a healthy political community does not require unanimity among citizens; it only requires that each member contribute usefully to public discussion and the formation of a political will that combines the partial insights of each component of the community. Waldron also notes that political speech, as Aristotle conceives it, does not necessarily play a divisive and manipulative role in human interaction. In this respect, Aristotle's approach to politics provides a radical alternative to the one developed by Hobbes.

Waldron admits that he is developing Aristotelian themes in ways that may go beyond conclusions that Aristotle himself was willing to draw. Dorothea Frede's essay complements this concession by drawing our attention to several obstacles to treating Aristotle as an unequivocal advocate of the wisdom of the multitude. Some of his ideas lead him to the conclusion that certain exceptional individuals have what is in effect a right to rule over others: such individuals have a talent for ruling that exceeds even the combined understanding of many. Frede also notes a recurring theme in Aristotle's writings that makes it impossible to absorb him into a liberal or democratic framework: he holds that those whose daily work is intellectually routinized and commercial (*banausoi*: vulgar craftsmen) will not develop the skills of reflection needed for political decision-making and therefore do not deserve a place in the authoritative decision-making bodies—assemblies and courts—of the *polis.* As Frede says, Aristotle "accepts as inevitable the social distinctions that assign to one class the 'necessary labor' that gives the 'higher and better' the freedom to develop and employ their talents, be they political or philosophical or artistic. There cannot be a ship without plain oarsmen, and plain oarsmen never act as officers." But she then poignantly raises the question whether Aristotle accepted hard truths that we who live in a democratic age would rather not face. "Life in modern mass-societies has the soothing effect of making all but invisible what every member of the upper crust in a Greek polis could not overlook: that their comfort depended on the hard labor of those who were less fortunate than they were themselves."

Aristotle's credentials as a political thinker are severely tested in the essay of Jonathan Barnes, who goes so far as to classify him as a "totalitarian" thinker. His charge against Aristotle is that he fails to address the fundamental question of political life: Which matters should be treated as political questions, that is, as questions that the state may properly regulate without going beyond its proper authority (being, in other words, *ultra vires*)? It is not anachronistic, Barnes argues, to expect Aristotle to put this question on his agenda, for questions about the jurisdiction of those who hold political offices appear in such authors as Sophocles and Plato. Yet Aristotle systematically evades it, Barnes complains. He comes closest to addressing the issue in his discussion of democratic liberty, but just when we would expect him to assess the democrat's demand for a minimum of political interference, Aristotle changes the topic to "who should rule?" rather than "over what matters should there be rules?" Barnes proposes that metaphysics underlies Aristotle's totalitarian tendencies: Aristotle assumes that political authority should be as extensive as feasible because he conceives of human beings as mere fragments of a larger whole. We are, by our very nature, political: that is, we are defined as components of the political community. From this starting point, it is natural to infer, without further argument, that in every aspect of our lives we are to do as the *polis* directs.

Barnes calls Aristotle a "totalitarian" because he regards every aspect of human life as subject to the oversight of the *polis.* But whether this term (or even a somewhat milder one: "authoritarian") is appropriately applied to Aristotle should depend, at least in part, on where he stands regarding the legitimate use of coercion and violence. It would be odd to call a thinker "totalitarian" (or "authoritarian") if he opposes the use of coercion, or thinks that the threat of punishment against citizens has no place in well-governed regimes. That Aristotle adhered to such principles is the principal thesis of David Keyt's essay. He argues that Aristotle has a strong affinity to philosophical anarchists—that is, to thinkers who believe that coercion is inherently objectionable; that it should be used as little as possible; and that it will be absent from satisfactory human relationships. Aristotle's antipathy to the use of force in social relations, Keyt holds, has metaphysical roots: Nature is a strong unifying agent, and there is an inherent weakness in things held together artificially through force. Like Waldron, Keyt emphasizes the radical opposition between Aristotle and Hobbes: He contrasts Aristotle's conviction that willing cooperation is the social glue that best holds political communities together with Hobbes's insistence that only force and the threat of force can prevent political societies from deteriorating into anarchy.

Keyt observes in a footnote that the ideal political community depicted in *Politics* VII–VIII is an "egalitarian democracy." That point is fully developed and placed at the center of the interpretation proposed in Josiah Ober's essay. He argues that we should read the *Politics* as a cohesive whole, one that culminates, in its final two books, in a conception of the best constitution as one devoted to the excellence and well-being of the entire citizenry. Ober thinks that it can be called both an aristocracy and a democracy—an aristocracy because all citizens are educated to bring out what is *best* (*aristos*) in them, but also a democracy because all citizens, having been educated, participate equally in ruling. Such a democracy can be called "natural" because, like seeds of an oak tree that must be nurtured before reaching their full potential, we humans fully emerge as reasonable and reason-responsive beings only when political institutions encourage such growth. What Ober finds particularly appealing in Aristotle's approach to politics is its emphasis on the importance of both nature and history. Kingships, Aristotle notes, were once common, but political ability is now more widely shared, because our innate potentialities are beginning to emerge; and so oligarchies and democracies—often in mixed forms—have become the most common kind of rule. If we can learn from the failures of such cities as Athens and Sparta, and also from the insights of democratic practices (the wisdom of the multitude under favorable conditions, and the stability achieved by extending citizenship widely), we can educate and give equal political power to every citizen. Ober cites anthropological evidence that there is a natural tendency for democratic practices to emerge, and concludes that "if we are willing to expand Aristotle's frame, by assuming that virtually all humans come into the world with the potential to become fully featured political animals in an Aristotelian sense, his core argument could provide the jumping off point for a democratic political theory that moves well beyond the familiar late-twentieth-century frameworks of analytic liberalism and communitarianism."

Aristotle, these essays make clear, cannot be read with indifference by anyone who cares about politics and political theory. Like us, he lived in a democratic world, and so he is absorbed by questions about the strength and weaknesses of various forms of democracy. The Greek *polis*, as Holmes insists, cannot be replicated today. But what are we to make of democracy today? One cannot entirely leave that question aside, when we try to understand Aristotle's *Politics*. Looking at our democracies from his point of view can be as illuminating as looking at the *polis* from ours.

Abbreviations

Works by Aristotle

An. Post.	Posterior Analytics
An. Pr.	Prior Analytics
Ath. Pol.	Constitution of Athens
Cael.	On the Heavens
Cat.	Categories
De An.	De Anima [On the Soul]
Div. Somn.	On Divination in Sleep
EE	Eudemian Ethics
Gen. An.	Generation of Animals
Gen. et Corr.	On Generation and Corruption
Hist. An.	History of Animals
Mem.	On Memory
Meteor.	Meteorology
MM	Magna Moralia
Mot. An.	Movement of Animals
NE	Nicomachean Ethics
Oec.	Economics
Part. An.	Parts of Animals
Phys.	Physics
Pol.	Politics
Rhet.	Rhetoric
Somno.	On Sleep

Works by Plato

Euthd.	Euthydemus
Rep.	Republic

1

Aristippus in and out of Athens

Stephen Taylor Holmes

1.

SURPRISINGLY ENOUGH, numerous assumptions underlying contemporary, including neo-Marxist, approaches to the problem of political legitimacy are still essentially Greek. For this reason they are also essentially anachronistic. Almost without our noticing it, they have been worn out by time. More precisely, their contemporary relevance has been subtly and irrevocably undermined by the gradual shift first to the medieval and eventually to the modern type of European society. In this chapter I shall focus on two now-obsolete, though still enticing, premises of Greek political thinking: (1) that the state can be "humanized" as a dialogue, family or emotional communion with a "true" and therefore unifying purpose, and (2) that individuals, being thoroughly "political animals," can fully realize themselves in political participation. Not utterly implausible for the *polis*, it will be argued, both ideas lead to personal and governmental deformations when "revived" in highly differentiated and rapidly changing modern societies.[1]

Indeed, the Greek claim that all spheres of life should be subordinated to politics cannot be translated into a modern European language without divulging its contemporary irrationality. For us, such a claim seems to stand or fall with the patently absurd assumption that politics (and the absurdity stems from what "politics" now implies) can solve all human problems, indeed that it can bear the entire burden of making people happy, free, and in touch with themselves. Although this promise may have made some sense in a small city-state or *Gemeinschaft*, it is clearly out of step with the structural realities of a large modern society or *Gesellschaft*. Nevertheless, its stubbornly persistent influence on and attractiveness for much contemporary political theory can hardly be denied.

Verbally, of course, it is possible to defend the "timeless validity" of the works of Plato and Aristotle.[2] For instance, it may seem decisive that both ground political "legitimacy"[3] in forms of "participation" and "representation." Yet the prima facie modernity of these ancient ideas is deceptive. As a matter of fact, the basic moral claims advanced in the political writings of Plato and Aristotle are inseparably linked to descriptive postulates about the institutional framework of the city-state. As might be expected, the polis-bound connotations of these claims are irreconcilable with the structural realities of political participation, representation and legitimacy as they began to stabilize themselves in eighteenth-century democratizing bourgeois contexts, and as they continue to exist, precariously to be sure, in constitutional-pluralist societies today.

Not unpredictably, the indiscriminate use of a single set of concepts to elucidate such widely divergent situations as the ancient and the modern has produced a disorienting lack of focus in the philosophy of politics. It is my conviction that a cautious appeal to the idea of modernization developed by the pioneer social theorists of the late nineteenth and early twentieth centuries can help us correct the conceptual displacement at the root of this trouble. On the basis of a theory of social evolution borrowed selectively from Durkheim, Simmel, and Weber,[4] it is possible (I believe) to make a strong case for the following thesis: the totalitarian insistence that government should be everywhere and that politics can solve all of humanity's fundamental problems is *both* alluring *and* irrational because it anachronistically echoes the Greek identification of the political sphere with total society.

In defending this thesis, I will first explain how my argument can be understood as a response to the three writers whose works have dominated the postwar discussion of Greek politics and political theory. This will allow me to suggest, in a preliminary fashion, how a general theory of social evolution can provide descriptive orientation for normative discussions of political principles (part 2). I will then go on to state, in cursory fashion, what I take to be Aristotle's (and to a lesser extent Plato's) fundamental ideas about political participation and representation. The ethical doctrines found in the classical texts of Greek political philosophy, or so I try to show, are inextricably bound to the empirical premise that society can be adequately grasped as a "whole" made out of "parts" (3). I next examine some of the arguments advanced by Aristotle in support of his notorious principles that the city is "prior" to the citizen and that man is an essentially "political animal" (4), recalling briefly some of the special characteristics of the classical *polis* which lent a degree of everyday plausibility to these seemingly abstruse philosophical claims (5 and 6). Finally, I suggest the precise way in which, due to a special set of institutional transformations in the West since the end of antiquity and especially since the inception of the modern or "bourgeois" age, this whole/part schematization of society has become obsolete (7). As a direct consequence of this gradual yet dramatic structural change, or so it will be argued, the principles of Greek politics become flagrant and despotic archaisms when transported, even with the best of intentions, into the institutional context of modern society (8).

2.

Paradoxically, the inherent difficulty of acquiring a satisfying overview of Greek politics and political philosophy, as well as of their relevance today, seems to have been exacerbated by the work of three brilliantly controversial (and distinctly non-Marxist) exiles from Hitler's Reich. To be sure, there are vast discrepancies of tone, purpose, and political commitment separating Karl Popper's *The Open Society and Its Enemies*, Leo Strauss's *Natural Right and History*, *The City and Man*, and *On Tyranny*, and Hannah Arendt's *The Human Condition*. Simplifying slightly, we can formulate the basic disagreement in the following way: while Popper views totalitarianism as *a return* to Plato and Aristotle, Strauss and Arendt view it as the grim consequence of having *turned away* from the two greatest philosophers of classical antiquity. Underlying this formidable conflict of opinion, moreover, is a profound disagreement about the contribution of modern "scientific" rationality to contemporary social and political life. But these startling differences only emerge so sharply because of a background of shared and unswerving belief. Each of these books was written in the conviction that the study of Greek theories concerning law, politics, and society, far from being dusty antiquarianism, is of decisive importance to those facing the tragedies and troubles of twentieth-century civilization. Popper, Strauss, and Arendt (and given the European experience it is easy to see why) all agree that the fundamental political problem of our age is totalitarian autocracy. And their shared concern for the Greeks is motivated by the compelling need to evolve an adequate understanding of the threat to the democratic West posed by the total state.

To these common concerns most of us would not object. To a large extent we share them. The dramatically clashing conclusions, however, should serve to make us wonder. In reconsidering the basic claims found in the books listed above, the nonpartisan reader is struck by their authors' common and unmitigated indifference to that tradition of empirically oriented social theory which has contributed so much to our understanding of the *specifically modern conditions* under which Greek philosophy has become archaic and totalitarianism has become the threat to humanity it is. The methodological premise underlying my own argument is as follows: the difficult and constantly recurring problem of the relation between Greek political theory and the modern total state can only be clarified if placed within the context of a theory of the structural and institutional evolution of Western society. As I will try to explain below, the theories which I consider most helpful in this regard tend to interpret social evolution primarily as a process of increasing structural differentiation. All three of the authors in question have systematically neglected theories of this type.

Take Popper, for example. His exuberant indictment of Plato as a totalitarian and protofascist is devastating but unconvincing. Popper's critics, however, have gone astray in struggling to exonerate Plato from the charge that he favored a closed, collectivist, and regimented state. The glaring weakness of *The Open Society and Its Enemies* is not Popper's characterization of Plato (though this has its flaws), but rather his strange assumption that modem liberalism could have been anticipated by Lycophron, Alcidamas, and others to whom we find it solemnly attributed. Plato was doubtless more strongly attached to the *stratopedou politeia* or "garrison state" than certain pro-democratic Athenians. But there is no evidence that even the most vehemently anti-Spartan party was "liberal" in the modern sense.[5] Modern liberalism, as I will suggest in a moment, could only arise after the prior emergence of a theologically interpreted religion, a completely monetarized economy, and a political sphere robbed by nonteleological science of any chance to gain legitimation by an appeal to "natural purposes." As a consequence, liberalism could not even have been articulated as a coherent position in classical Greece, in a society with both a civic religion and an economy submerged in a surrounding nexus of political and military norms, and where there was a widespread belief in some kind of "natural law" capable of lending moral legitimacy to the regime. As a consequence, and in spite of all the Popperian efforts of Eric Havelock, ancient advocates of full-scale participatory democracy cannot be considered "liberal" in any meaningful modern sense.[6]

The elementary characteristic which Simmel, Durkheim, Weber, and their more recent followers have attributed to the modern social order is a high degree of social differentiation or the growing autonomy (and, hence, roundabout interdependence) of a number of distinct interaction contexts or channels of communication such as religion, science, art, law, economy, politics, education, and intimate family life.[7] I will return to this—I believe—decisive analysis below. For now, let it suffice to recall the following: in antiquity the only rigorously defined cleavage (besides those of class) commonplace in discussions of the structure of society seems to have been the breach between publicity and privacy, *ta koina* and *ta idia*, the agora of discussion and the agora of exchange. Roman epicureans were referring to a similar split when they distinguished the *res publica* from the *hortus conclusus*. In modern society, on the other hand, it would be ludicrous to suggest that whenever people withdraw from political activity they must (by definition!) sink into "solitude" or egoistic self-seeking. The old binary schema public/private, in fact, is simply too crude to help us understand ourselves. There are (and quite explicitly in the West) plenty of nonpolitical avenues of *social* interchange, and we take advantage of them every day. It is, in fact, the rather improbable evolutionary emergence of a pluralistic and "centerless" *communicative* network which lends plausibility to the modern liberal notion of "negative freedom," and especially to the idea that human beings should be free not to participate in politics. For instance, the right to *publish* scientific hypotheses, emphasized by Mill, is obviously not meant to shelter Epictetus' *interior domus*.[8] Its value lies rather in its capacity to help preserve *a channel of social communication* from repressive politicization and control.

Totalitarianism, by contrast, whether Hitler's *Gleichschaltung* or Lenin's "democratic centralism," always involves *an attempt at the coercive politicization of diverse arteries of social interaction* such as the unions, the press, the police, sport, science, law, art, family life, education and, of course, the economy (Linz, "Totalitarianism and Authoritarian Regimes"). This is what Franz Neumann referred to as "the destruction of the line between state and society" (*The Democratic and Authoritarian State*, p. 245). And, in spite of much talk about "atomization," the capacious maw of the total state wants to swallow "subsystems," not granular individuals. Thus, the murderous brutality which accompanies fascist and communist regimes probably results—at least in part—from the factual discrepancy between a pluralistic infrastructure and a tightly integrated or unified political ideal. Since there was no such discrepancy in Greece (and here lies my objection to Popper), there could not have been any Greek totalitarianism, just as there could have been no Greek liberalism. The "line between state and society" did not yet exist, and thus could neither have been defended nor destroyed. This structural claim, it seems to me, provides an excellent starting point for a fresh understanding of Benjamin Constant's neglected thesis (n.1) that transplanting the principles of ancient liberty into modern society inevitably produces tyranny.

Hannah Arendt and Leo Strauss seem to have had but little sympathy for each other's approach to Greek political theory. As suggested, however, the surface discord here conceals an underlying agreement, or at least a shared obsession with the "quarrel" between the ancients and the moderns. Both Arendt and Strauss, perhaps under the influence of Martin Heidegger, interpreted the self-destruction of the ancient world and the eventual transition to modern society as signaling a lamentable "loss" of depth and fullness. While Heidegger often speaks in this context of a "forgetfulness of Being," Arendt tends to view modernity as tragically marred by a forgetfulness of Aristotelian *praxis*, while Strauss views it as the sad product of amnesia about Platonic *noēsis* and especially about the intellectual grasp of "natural law" and humanity's highest Good.

The bizarre implication of all this is that modern society is based on a "mistake" or error of attitude, for example, on the hubristic "misinterpretation" of nature as a field to be exploited rather than a fount to be adored. One amusing claim found in Strauss's work is that the ancients entertained modernization (including Galilean science) as a hypothetical future on which to embark, but rejected it because they knew it would make them unhappy (*On Tyranny*, p. 190). What concerns me here is not so much this particular claim, but rather the assumption implicit in it and in fact underlying much of Strauss's thought: that the fundamental difference between antiquity and modernity can be traced to *a shift in attitude* or in the general climate of opinion. In other words, Strauss deliberately slights those *structural and institutional transformations* which make it rather pointless to place an ancient "regime" next to a modern one and solemnly ask, which is better?[9] Because ancient and modern systems of government present solutions to very different problems, of course, such direct "evaluative" comparisons are notably unilluminating. Strauss, no doubt, would reject my premise here, asserting that the problems confronting the ancients and the moderns are *indeed* different but not so different as I suggest, human nature having remained essentially the same. Be that as it may, my less controversial claim is only this: by associating, for example, Nazism with modern scientific detachment,[10] Strauss has helped promulgate the myth that twentieth-century autocracy is *basically* a result of our having stopped brooding over old books and having therefore forgotten the ancestral pieties. At the very least, it seems clear, this line of thought has deflected theoretical attention away from the possibility of an alternative hypothesis: that modern "totalitarian" regimes rely for ideological legitimation on a diffuse rancor against modernity and on an anachronistic nostalgia for the integrated and heavily politicized life of the Greek city-state.

Something similar can be said about Hannah Arendt. Unlike Strauss, of course, Arendt places her analyses of Greek politics and modern totalitarianism within the context of at least a rudimentary theory of social evolution. Modernization, she claims, can be summed up as "the rise of the social," the disappearance of political life and the atomization or privatization of the public sphere (*The Human Condition*, pp. 38–49). Isolation, "massification," and the loss of civic spirit are the immediate preconditions for the emergence of totalitarian "movement-regimes," or so she claims (*The Origins of Totalitarianism*, pp. 305–26). Now there is no question of doing full justice here to her intricate analysis. My concern is simply to point out that by linking totalitarianism so closely with "the loss of the political," Arendt too has been forced to neglect the plausibility of Benjamin Constant's thesis that the most appalling form of modern tyranny may actually contain a distorted echo of ancient freedom. She could have corrected this blind spot, I believe, if she had replaced her simplistic theory of the "rise of the social" with a theory more adequate to the increased structural differentiation of modern society. This possibility, in any case, is the one I will try to sketch out below.

As may be clear from these all too brief remarks, my sympathies are divided among Popper, Arendt, and Strauss. Against Popper, I agree with the latter two that Plato and Aristotle were not totalitarians, although I justify my agreement here by the argument that liberalism is a specifically modern development, parasitic on the highly articulated and centrifugal character of the modern institutional order—and that there were not and could not have been any "Greek liberals" (though there were "democrats" in a variety of senses) for Plato to attack, just as there was no highly differentiated society which he might have wanted to "unify" by mass mobilization and terror. On the other hand, I would like to emphasize with Popper, and without much regard for the piety toward Greece informing the work of Arendt and Strauss, that there is a totalitarian potential inherent in the basic principles of Aristotle's and Plato's political philosophies—a potential only fully unleashed in the industrial-bureaucratic nation-state, but which was already perceptible as a threat in early post-Reformation Europe. This, I believe, explains liberal "forgetfulness" toward Greece (the kind we find in Locke, Montesquieu, Adam Smith, and James Madison and which thus has nothing to do with ignorance of the past), and even encourages more. In this case too, however, I am far from being in complete accord with Popper, for I discern totalitarianism not in the texts of the *Republic*, the *Laws*, and the *Politics*, but only in the imprudent importation of doctrines there espoused into the context of a highly differentiated modern society.

The general methodological premise underlying my argument thus far might be reformulated as follows: the normative claims of political philosophy, so I believe, can never be understood from behind a self-imposed veil of ignorance, but rather must always be interpreted in light of historical information about the institutional order within which these claims are to be enforced. My more specific assumption is that an account of the increasing structural differentiation of modern society provides an illuminating framework for discussing the old and vexing question of the relation between Greek political theory and modern totalitarian autocracy. We are now in a position to examine this claim in greater detail.

3.

As I have said, the basic moral doctrines unfolded in the political writings of Plato and Aristotle seem inseparably linked to a series of "side premises" about the organizational structure of the city-state. I now want to examine what I take to be the most important of these auxiliary hypotheses. It is expressed most clearly in Aristotle's claim that "the polis is a compound like any other whole made out of parts, and these are the citizens who compose it."[11] The assumption is that society can be adequately grasped through the conceptual pair of "whole" and "parts."

It seems a pardonable oversimplification to locate the basic principle of Greek politics in the idea that totality is prior to individuality or that the *polis* is prior to the *politēs* [citizen]. Such an idea, moreover, was no monopoly of pro-oligarchic philosophers like Plato and Aristotle, though it certainly received its historically most notable formulation through them. Even in democratic cities like Athens, the institution of ostracism revealed to what extent citizens had no "subjective rights" against the city.[12] This idea was formulated in a plethora of ways. Aristotle claimed, for example, that human beings are fundamentally political animals and that they can fully realize themselves only in political participation. He also said that politics is man's essence, that political science (*hē politikē*) studies everything of human value and that all spheres of life should be subordinated to political concerns. Even that "protoliberal" Pericles seems to have had this idea: "We do not say that a man who takes no interest in politics is a man who minds his own business. We say that he has no business here at all."[13] These ideas all culminate in an emphatic subordination of individual rights to civic duties. And after all, how can individuals fear being impinged upon by their own essence? Why would they seek a "right" to lose their community?

In recalling the two principles that the *polis* is prior to the *politēs* and that rights are subordinate to duties, I have yet to say anything specific about social structure. Nevertheless, both claims (at least as Plato and Aristotle make them) seem to depend on the assumption that society can be accurately described as a "whole" made out of "parts." Indeed, the city-state appears to have been commonly conceived as an encompassing totality or ensemble of which the city dwellers were thought to be the constituent elements or living parts. Only in the light of this "empirical" premise, in any case, is it possible to understand the kind of "participation" glorified by Plato and Aristotle.

Plato, it cannot be denied, was an enthusiast of political participation.[14] But what did this imply? In Plato's "fully just *polis*," each individual plays his or her part, attends exclusively to a rigidly prescribed task, and stays unobtrusively in place. Participation, as Plato admired it, was not collaboration in group decision making, but rather *to ta hautou prattein*,[15] simply to do that which belongs to one's *part*. Furthermore, if we abstract for a moment from Plato's appeal to the timeless Forms (which I cannot consider here) we will see that his most persistent complaint against "injustice" is that it is dysfunctional. He blames it for splintering *homonoia* (being "of one mind," "in agreement with oneself"), both civic and personal, necessary for coordinated action. And *homonoia*, like its close kin Platonic justice, requires everyone to do an assigned chore.

For Aristotle too, political participation demanded that an individual's existence be ingredient in the *polis*, or, in Constant's words, *englobée dans l'existence politique* ("De la liberté des anciens compare a celle des modernes," p. 557). The statement that "the *polis* is prior to the individual"[16] stands at the opening of the *Politics*, and that book is full of arguments to the effect that "we must not suppose any one of the citizens to belong to himself, for they all belong to the *polis* and the care of each is inseparable from the care of the whole."[17] Participation in the mixed constitution or *politeia* favored by Aristotle has a great deal more to do with collective deliberation and policymaking than does the chore-minding of Plato's ideal city. Nevertheless, both regimes are conceived to be all encompassing. Both, for example, are compared to bodies from which one cannot (successfully) detach a foot or hand.[18] For the "part" played by the morally enmeshed individual, both Plato and Aristotle use *to morion*, a word closely related to *moros* and *moira*, one's appointed and fore-ordained destiny.[19] The background implication, about which much could be said, is that political portions are somehow allotted to individuals on the basis of incorrigible nature. And the unchallengeable messages sent by nature (for example, information that someone has a cobbler's or a guardian's soul, is a natural ruler or slave) are ultimately concocted to reinforce the whole/part interpretation of society. This is the case, so Plato (for example) believes, since the kind of soul I indelibly have can only unfold its potential in the context of a beehive division of labor.[20] The "physical" ascription of roles lets polis-dwellers know that they had better participate, had better stay piously inside the *polis* just as any other part must selflessly adhere to its embracing whole.

Now, one of the ideas in the classic texts of Greek philosophy which at first seems quite similar to "representation" turns out to be as unlike its modern counterpart as *to ta hautou prattein* is unlike participation at the polls. It too depends on the whole/part schematization of society, and especially on the direct corollary that "in all things which form a composite whole and which are made up of parts . . . a distinction between the ruling and subject element comes to light."[21] Conjoin this premise to the further claim that "a *polis* or any other systematic whole is most properly identified with the most authoritative element in it"[22] and you have a Greek idea of "representation" which both Plato and Aristotle seem to have thought a powerful device for legitimating the hierarchical order of society. They both tried to make rigid stratification acceptable, of course, by comparing the city to the soul, and then reminding us that "reason" must surely rule over the passions and appetites because it is "higher" than they are. The basic political idea, in any case, was that the worthiest members of the polity, the *maiores partes,* "represent" the whole in the sense that they embody the essential qualities of the polis-dweller to the highest degree. The plausibility of Aristotle's *pars pro toto* identification of the *politai* or full-fledged citizens with polis-dwellers in general depends directly on this "hierarchical" interpretation of the city, whereby the topmost elements of the unified status-pyramid "sum up" the ordered ladder below.

Even when we ignore the shadowy relation between citizens and noncitizen metics or slaves, and concentrate instead on authority relations within the citizen-body, Aristotle seems to justify "representativeness" in a similar fashion. Behind his preference for the constitution called *politeia* (the best regime possible under actual conditions) lies the idea that middle-class citizens *should* dominate the city since they can avoid the ingrained hubris and contempt of the wealthy as well as the ground-in servility and envy of the poor. Thus knowing how to rule and be ruled in turn, they *represent* the "best" in man, the ability to live and act according to "the mean."

4.

As should now be clear, the claims of Aristotle's *Politics* which interest me most are the notorious ones: that the *polis* is prior to the individual, that human beings are born for citizenship in a city-state, that ethics and politics coincide or that "political science" studies everything of human value. As has frequently been noted, these claims all sound wildly implausible to modern ears, and so the first thing to do is to try to explain exactly what made them seem convincing to Aristotle. The *Politics* begins, as everyone knows, with an attack on Plato, specifically on the claim put forward in the *Statesman,* that there is little or no difference (so far as the exercise of authority is concerned) between a large household and a small *polis.*[23] From Aristotle's point of view, this was an extremely dangerous thought. Indeed the whole argument of the *Politics,* the very idea that the *polis* is prior to the individual and that it is the flowering and culmination of nature, depends upon a sharp contrast between actions which take place in an *oikos* or household and actions which take place in the political sphere. In the *Nicomachean Ethics*, one should recall, Aristotle says that practical reason depends upon a distinction between actions which are good for something else (useful actions) and actions which are good for their own sake.[24] Without insight into actions which are simply choiceworthy for their own sake, *phronēsis* or prudence would tumble into an abysmal infinite regress. The basic form which this distinction takes in the *Politics*, in any case, is the split or dualism between household or "economic" actions and public or political actions, or, in Aristotle's terms, between *technē* and *poiēsis* on the one hand and *praxis* on the other. Hannah Arendt has articulated this distinction neatly by contrasting the necessity and constraint of household production with the freedom of political deliberation and action (*The Human Condition*, pp. 28–37). Household production is "technical" in the sense that it has its end or goal (biological survival or mere life) outside itself. Slaves struggle in a repetitive way to satisfy the daily demands of biological nature. Citizens (and Aristotle believes that only those household heads who own slaves should have the franchise) are able to *presuppose* the satisfaction of biological needs. As a result, they can leave behind the realm of necessity or "mere life" and enter into the realm of freedom or "the good life," the domain of citizen-sharing in collective deliberation through language, the domain of happiness, free choice, and noble deeds. The negative side of Greek "freedom," in other words, is release from the repetitive constraints of biological life; the positive side is reciprocity, the chance for peers to rule and be ruled in turn. It is this emphasis on reciprocity or the "partnership in the good life"[25] which explains what Aristotle meant by the "priority" of the *polis* over the individual.[26] If a man lived exclusively in the Peiraeus, surrounded by the whirr of instrumental routines, if he were constantly occupied with activities relating to "mere life," he would never develop those statesmanlike characteristics which Aristotle associated with true humanity. He would not learn, for example, how to rule and be ruled in turn. When Aristotle claims that despots are worse off than citizens who share power (because there is nothing noble in giving orders about necessary things),[27] he is contrasting the unfulfilling nature of instrumental-manipulative action with the "end-in-itself" of communicative partnership and sharing.

An additional factor explaining the "naturalness" attributed to the *polis* is the unique mortality reserved for human beings in colloquial Greek. It we want to explain in Aristotelian terms why only human beings were called *hoi brotoi* or "the mortals," we should recall that for Aristotle all things were made out of a conjunction of form and matter. When an animal died, its form and matter were wrenched apart, but both elements "survived," the matter in a decaying corpse, the form in the species (since there was no evolution). The form or universality of human beings, on the other hand, was thought to be strictly individual. It was the kind of thing which could only be captured in a life story. Its survival was guaranteed by no species, but could at best be achieved by an individual's acting in a memorable way. When Aristotle says that *kala erga* or *kalai praxeis* are the end and purpose of the *polis*,[28] he is suggesting that noble deeds are choiceworthy, in part because they allow men to overcome their mortality and to leave a trace in history—like the heroes of Marathon. According to this line of thought, what makes slavery unendurable is simply the fact that slaves have no chance to leave a trace in history.

Now although this Arendtian claim is quite striking, it should not be allowed to deflect attention from the simpler argument, found throughout Aristotle's practical philosophy, that friendship, partnership and sharing in the good life are worth choosing for their own sakes. It was his supreme concern for *reciprocity,* to be sure, which motivated Aristotle's insistence that a good city be small enough to be "easily surveyed."[29] To this he added the famous demand that all the citizens be able to look at one another, and even to know each other's characters intimately. The "unrealistic" quality of these demands has led numerous historians (following Popper) to dissociate totally the philosophical claims found in the classic texts of Greek political theory from the ordinary life of democratic city-states. Such a dissociation, however, while not entirely unjustified, should not be exaggerated.

5.

The "priority" of the *polis* over the individual, in point of fact, was *not* invented by philosophers. Athens in the classical age, to be sure, did not correspond to the idealized image of a continuous open-air mass meeting. The one thousand square miles of Attica were not "easily surveyable," and its population of sometimes up to 40,000 adult male citizens far exceeded the limit placed on philosophically "ideal" states. Nevertheless, Athens was, like other *poleis,* "a small, homogeneous, relatively closed face-to-face society" (Finley, *Democracy Ancient and Modern* [New Brunswick], pp. 30–31) and its highly integrated character lent a degree of everyday plausibility to Aristotle's rather abstruse philosophical claims.

The colloquial word *politeia,* for example, meant simultaneously the constitution, citizenship, the citizen body, the daily life of the city, administration, a tenure of office, a course of policy, and the general structure of the *polis* (Liddel and Scott, p. 1434). As Victor Ehrenberg summarizes this point:

> The use of the same word for individual participation in the state and for its general structure shows that participation was not in the main a purely legal act between individual and state; it reflected the vital adherence of the individual to the citizen body, as also to the other communities inside the state (*The Greek State*, p. 39).

The *polis,* in other words, was a moral, not a legal, community.[30] Its institutions were commonly said to inculcate virtue and to make the citizens "good." This is why the part was unblinkingly subordinated to the whole, indeed why the whole/part schema seemed applicable to Greek society in the first place. Feeling free, at least after the Greek victory over the Persians, seemed tangibly dependent on political fraternity, solidarity, and collaborative self-government (Pohlenz, *Freedom in Greek Life and Thought*). It carried little connotation of an absence of collective interference in individual lives.[31] The normal democratic polity (and not just Plato's oligarchic dream) guaranteed and encouraged participation in the sense of "vital adherence" of the individual to the community. Democratic institutions such as the lot, short rotating terms of office, and the regular "scrutiny" of officials at end of term all encouraged firsthand participation. In Athens, at least, pay for attendance stimulated citizens to take active roles in the law courts, the council, the magistracies, and the sovereign Assembly (Jones, *Athenian Democracy,* pp. 5–6). By mobilizing public opinion, the city promoted competition by the rich in the financing of public liturgies, the manning and maintaining of war triremes, and so forth. In sum, it told the citizens how best to play their parts.[32] What formal legality there was, moreover, tended to be submerged in the overriding context of moral fellowship. The large popular juries in democratic polities like Athens did not always vote according to standards of codified and predictable legal justice. When a decision like the condemnation and summary execution of the generals in command at Arginusae violated formal procedure, it was justified by appeal to the security and prosperity of the city.[33] Even Aristotle, who explicitly condemns the Athenian tendency to override "law" with "popular decrees," says: "We call those things just which produce and preserve happiness for the political community."[34]

What I want to emphasize here is the fraternal or corporative quality, the *homonoia* which most Greeks (not just "illiberal" philosophers) discerned at the root of political life. *Societas* and *communitas* are the traditional Latin translations of the Greek *koinōnia* or "association." The noun *koinōnia,* in turn, is directly related to the adjective *koinos* meaning "shared in common" (Riedel, *Metaphysik und Metapolitik,* p. 31 ff.; Mulgan, *Aristotle's Political Theory,* pp. 13–17). And according to Aristotle again, what men share in common, holds them together. *A koinōnia*, in other words, was ordinarily understood as an organic association expressing a corporate bond.

Aristotle's whole/part schematization of society, in other words, was not merely abstruse and unrealistic "philosophy." It gained plausibility against the background of an everyday Greek identification of the polity with total society. In the city-state, most spheres of social life had political connotations or overtones. The Periclean building program alone reminds us of the extent to which Greek art was civic art. The conventional Olympian religion, at least, was a civic religion. Indeed, it was almost a self-deification of the *polis*. As a result, impiety was a crime against the state. Law was public and largely nonprofessional. The economy was likewise "submerged" in a surrounding nexus of political and military concerns. Weber referred to the *polis* as a "warrior's guild" (*The City*, p. 220), thinking of Sparta, no doubt—and it is especially true of such cities that even sport and gymnastics had a heavily political tinge. But there seems to have been nothing unusual about the fact that the Athenian Alcibiades' victory in a chariot race at the Olympic games was an integral part of his *political* career (Finley and Pleket, *The Olympic Games*, pp. 104–7).

The claim here is merely that the city-state, as an ideal type, was *relatively* undifferentiated. That it was not completely undifferentiated goes without saying. The fact that the Spartans had to encourage homosexuality, for example, reveals that the family was perceived as a distraction from and threat to the intimacy and coordination of the hoplite phalanx. And of course, the constant reaffirmations of "unity" found in Greek political writings testify to the divisive force of party factionalism and class strife in the ancient city. In any case, the vague politicization of most spheres of social life lent a degree of everyday plausibility to Aristotle's otherwise obscure philosophical claim that all (subordinate) communities are "parts" of the political community. It should now be easy to see what Aristotle meant by his claim that ethics and politics coincide, or that political science is the master or "architectonic" science and studies everything of human value. Everything important in the city-state seemed to go on within the political sphere. Or in Weber's terms: the "total status" (or essential humanity) of the citizen was contained *inside* the single system of the polity. As a result, political "participation" seems to have had the force of a direct moral imperative. It was not justified by any detour of Hobbesian calculation on the part of discrete individuals who longed for security and feared death. It was simply a life worth choosing in and for itself.[35]

Of course, the common Greek practice of enslaving the entire population of conquered cities must have been a factor in the everyday identification of individual freedom with the autonomy of the city. The threat of foreign military power must have made palpable the dependence of all "parts" on the political "whole." This was the case even in Aristotle's "imperfect" polities. Aristotle, one recalls, classified democracy among the "perverse" constitutions, because it granted the franchise to unworthy men. As a consequence, he considered the best democracy to be a democracy of farmers, of men whose continuous labor far from the city would surely impede their daily participation in collective deliberation and policy making.[36] Yet, the possibility of enslavement would have been terrifying enough to transform even such hierarchical half-enfranchisement of "the many" into something resembling total inclusion.

Hegel once wrote in the margin of his own copy of the *Philosophy of Law* (*Grundlinien der Philosophie des Rechts*, p. 417) that "the ancients knew nothing of conscience," perhaps thinking of the fact that when Socrates tried to introduce his private "voice," his daemon who had no place in the public cults, Athens expunged him from its midst. And indeed the modern distinction, so important to Kant, between morality and legality, between inward conviction and outward conformity seems to have had little intelligibility for the Greeks (Kant, *The Metaphysical Elements of Justice*, p. 19). As Aristotle sees it, in any case, ethics is "out in the world," is firmly rooted in *ethos*, in the customs, traditions and institutions of the political community. An education toward virtue is a process of habituation which takes place out in the public domain. You cannot become good by listening to one of Plato's lectures on "the Good," Aristotle warns.[37] You must be habituated into the worldly activities of ruling and being ruled in the political sphere. This line of thought, of course, provided yet another justification for viewing the *polis* as "prior" to the citizens, and thus for conceiving of the polity as an all-encompassing whole made out of citizen parts.

6.

In his *Memorabilia*, Xenophon relates an illuminating conversation about the priority of the *polis* over the individual which supposedly took place between Socrates and his "disciple," the North African voluptuary and sophist, Aristippus. Their exchange begins (as usual) with Socrates trying to convince his interlocutor that self-indulgence is logically absurd, but soon turns to a more interesting discussion of the idea that the only life worth living is the *bios koinōnos*, the collaborative life of citizen interaction within a *polis*. Aristippus, setting an example for the Cyrenaic school which will follow him, repudiates this collectivist ideal. The crippling responsibilities of ruling, he argues, make it a flimsy disguise for slavery:

> For *poleis* claim to treat their rulers just as I claim to treat my servants. I expect my men to provide me with necessities in abundance, but not to touch any of them; and *poleis* hold it to be the business of the ruler to supply them with all manner of good things and to abstain from all of them himself.[38]

The ignoble constraints of being ruled, he goes on to say, are even more unbearable. Political participation, viewed with a cool head, is always self-incarceration. Freedom, he concludes, is incompatible with both ruling and being ruled. It requires us to take a "middle path," the path of the metic, the alien or rootless freeman whose happiness depends on his having no citizenship and no assigned place. "I do not shut myself up in the four corners of a *politeia*," Aristippus gravely announces, "but am a stranger in every land."[39]

To this outburst and before returning to his conventional homilies about virtue being more choiceworthy than vice, Socrates pointedly answers: yes, political life is difficult; but a life without friendship (*philia* in the special Greek sense of a "public virtue" akin to solidarity), without partners or allies is more wretched still. Watch out Aristippus! The highways are dangerous. *Vae soli!* Woe to he who goes alone![40]

I take Aristippus as emblematic for my argument in this chapter for a cluster of reasons, all related to the fact that he is a "part" who (viciously enough) seems to feel no need to be incorporated into the "whole." He is Aristotle's *apolis*, the cityless man said to be either a beast or a god.[41] Significantly, his aloofness from politics does not seem utterly nonsensical to modern readers, even though it was obviously meant to appear outrageous and perverse in its original Athenian context. Indeed, as depicted by Xenophon, Aristippus is exceptionally well-suited for summarizing our argument thus far and for focusing attention on what is at stake in the claim that there is a totalitarian potential inherent in Greek political thought. Because of the evasiveness and self-seeking smallness of his apolitical turn, for example, Aristippus reveals the weakness of Popper's notion that apolitical arguments in ancient Greece were fundamentally liberal, "humanitarian," and pro-democratic. Aristippus also helps us understand that Arendt is right in viewing Aristotle's repudiation of cityless life as merely the obverse side of his affirmation of freedom, happiness, and the partnership in the good life. The Aristotelian *polis* was unquestionably meant to widen the scope and deepen the significance of human life beyond the mechanical satisfaction of biological needs. On the other hand, Xenophon's Aristippus helps us keep clearly in mind the colloquial and pervasive Greek identification of polity with society. *Apolitical* action, even in Periclean Athens, bore the vague stigma (or halo) of being *asocial*. This of course, is no longer the case today. In spite of Arendt's views about the modern privatization of everything, the centrifugal and highly differentiated *communicative* network within which we live and act cannot be adequately depicted as a loose assemblage of dissociated atoms. Just so, our multiple channels of social communication make Strauss's "basic question" ("politics or philosophy?") seem similarly obsolete. We have such a plurality of choices confronting us that the simplistic alternative political/apolitical (whether "apolitical" is taken in its hedonistic-epicurean or in its Socratic-contemplative version) is no longer so overwhelmingly crucial as Strauss seems to have believed. In sum: Aristippus helps us understand that modern liberal sympathy for apolitical ideals is based not so much on philistinism and superficiality of attitude as on a specific set of historical transformations—structural changes which eventually made it unrealistic to conceive of Western societies as civic wholes made out of citizen parts.

7.

The first institutional development to undermine radically the classical whole/part schematization of society was the split between *imperium* and *sacerdotium* which lies at the heart of medieval Christendom. Even the conversion of Constantine and the declaration of Christianity as a state religion did not reverse this differentiation, since Christianity (as Machiavelli lamented) was not well suited for the role of a solidarity—ensuring *theologia civilis.* Behind the *imperium/sacerdotium* dualism, no doubt, we can discern the double heritage of Israel and Greece. Judaic culture, one might say, was marked by a "totalization" of religion parallel to the "totalization" of politics witnessed in Greece. It might not be simplifying too much to say that one of the most striking achievements of Christianity was its successful integration of these two seemingly "contradictory" strands of ancient civilization. This amalgam in turn produced what could well be described as one of the "secrets" of political rationality in the West: the historical unlikelihood of a double totalization.[42] Throughout the Middle Ages people were confronted with two distinct and quite incommensurable realities: the towering stone castle and the towering stone cathedral; Caesar and Christ; sovereignty on the one hand and salvation on the other. The claim to a kind of universality by both politics and religion led, by the end of the fifth century, to the Gelasian doctrine of the "two swords." This doctrine eventually became entrenched as the explicit Western alternative to Byzantine caesaropapism or the Eastern tendency to transform the church into a civil institution. The development of anchorite monasticism might even be understood as a strategy for circumventing the danger, which did arise, of the Church losing its independence and becoming a pliant tool of secular authorities (Parsons, *Societies*, p. 33). It eventually became common in the West to regard any unification of sacred and secular authority as a backsliding into paganism and perhaps as a ruse of the devil.

Such incongruity, as the investiture controversy, the Inquisition, and the revocation of the Edict of Nantes all show, was no comfortable or foolproof solution. Yet it was one of the first and most crucial steps toward the clear *differentiation* between the polity and total society, toward the proliferation of quasiautonomous social domains which eventually made it quite implausible to regard an advanced European society as a political whole "containing" individual human parts. Because individuals participated in both realms, in both faith and citizenship, they could not be incapsulated elements of a single totality. This is why Augustine views the human being as a "social" but not as a "political" animal.[43] In the *City of God,* of course, politics was assigned a strictly limited role *within* the general economy of individual salvation. But this too was a one-sided view.

In sum, because of the "temporal disjunction" between infinity and finitude, there was no longer any noncontroversial *whole* of which individuals (as psycho-organic units) could have been considered the constituent parts. It is this development, perhaps even more than increase in scale, which eventually disqualified modern society from being *eusunoptos* ("easily surveyable") as Aristotle says all good societies must be. Modern ideals of individual freedom and spiritual autonomy seem closely related to this major shift in the infrastructure of society. Located at the intersection of two "autonomous" domains, the individual became (to adapt a phrase of Simmel) a *tertius gaudens.*[44] Thus, the "other-worldly" church could protect an individual from encroachments by the state, while secular authority could defend him or her against the growing power of the ecclesiastics.

With the "bourgeois" differentiation between economy and polity—which started to gain real momentum in the eighteenth century, but had already sparked the beginnings of modern liberalism in the work of John Locke and others—this development was powerfully reinforced.[45] It became even more obvious that the polity could no longer be identified with total society, nor could society itself be conceptualized as an organic entity "incorporating" its various organs.[46] Plato's and Aristotle's emphasis on duties instead of rights, so I have been arguing, depended on the relatively undifferentiated character of the Greek social order. Our highly differentiated society, by contrast, makes Aristippus seem less perverse than Xenophon intended.[47] The ancient question "how can we live best?" is no longer susceptible to a purely political answer. Unlike Aristotle's *hē politikē,* our political science makes no pretence of studying everything of human value. No one considers "government" (our pale replica of *politeia)* to be coextensive with human life. Reasons of scale alone—as well as structural differentiation—make it absurd to hope that modern society could be constructed or "steered" like a conversation. Since politics is now often seen as primarily a conjunction of electioneering, lobbying, and bureaucracy (i.e., large-scale housekeeping), it cannot also be conceived as a whole, much less as a society encompassing whole, which could give moral security and "warmth" to its constituent parts.

8.

Modern citizens, as Giambattista Vico had already noted in the early eighteenth century, "have become aliens in their own nations" (*The New Science*, pp. 378–79). To a society of civic *déracinés,* as I said above, Aristippus' apolitical ideal does not seem entirely unconvincing.[48] Few of us would be shocked or disappointed to hear that we are no longer parts of a political whole but rather, say, occupants of the political system's environment, an environment flatteringly called "the public."[49] In truth, the participation thought necessary for producing legitimacy in pluralistic-constitutional democracies usually boils down to suffrage. The act of voting, however, is just an occasional or periodic choice between competing administrative functionaries and policy makers by a "public" whose life is chiefly and focally *outside politics*, located in other social contexts such as science, religion, economy, family, education, art, law, and so forth. The rational core of modern liberal contractarianism, as a consequence, did not lie in the unbelievable idea that some pre-social Crusoe could (before learning a language and so forth) be articulate about his needs and rationally "choose" to enter society. It lay rather in the historically fitting conviction that an individual who has a complicated life in various nonpolitical social realms can reasonably evaluate different sorts of polity.[50]

In modern society there is no longer any question of morally and humanly fulfilling participation for the mass of citizens inside the political system. As a matter of fact, the right not to participate in politics (part of what "negative freedom" means) is often viewed as a fundamental condition for our being able to live with some degree of happiness and dignity. At least this is what lends credibility to Nietzsche's claim, so shockingly unlike Aristotle's, that politics is "a field of work for the punier heads" (*Morgenröte*, p. 1133). The un-Greekness of such influential and compelling reinterpretations of political participation seems unmistakable. No one can "realize" him- or herself through mass ballot voting. As a result, the ancient ideal of a "full-time voter" sounds either silly or sinister to modern ears (Parsons, *The System of Modern Societies*, p. 105). Such a recognition, needless to say, does not require us to celebrate "voter apathy" as a sure sign of health in a democracy. The consequences of varying degrees of popular participation in political decision-making cannot be safely evaluated in general and in advance. What the foregoing analysis can help us do, however, is to distinguish clearly, as Benjamin Constant did a century and a half ago ("De la liberté des anciens comparée à celle des modernes," pp. 558–60), between the specific and pre-channeled *influence* we want to exert on governmental policy and the much more exorbitant Graeco-totalitarian demand that citizens achieve their total or essential status within the political sphere.

9.

In summary and conclusion: the basic principles of Greek political theory were inextricably coupled to a series of auxiliary claims, most notably to the empirical premise that society can be adequately grasped as a "whole" made out of "parts." This premise, in turn, was rendered plausible by the *relatively undifferentiated* character of the Greek city-state, where art was largely civic art, religion was civic religion, and so forth. With the increase in social differentiation accompanying first the rise of Christianity and eventually the emergence of "bourgeois" capitalism, the whole/part schematization of society became definitively anachronistic. As a direct result, the basic moral claims found in the political writings of Plato and Aristotle (such as the emphasis on duties instead of rights and the subordination of the individual to a single overarching community) lost their initial core of rationality. Thus, liberal "forgetfulness" (not ignorance!) of Greece—or so I want to claim against Arendt and Strauss—is partly justified by the immense increase in structural differentiation characterizing modern society. The same transformation—and here I part company with Popper as well—helps explain how the originally convincing principles of the moral *polis* came to be enlisted in ideological support of what Mill aptly called the moral police.

Notes

1. For one of the earliest and most provocative accounts of how modern attempts to resuscitate ancient liberty unavoidably result in tyranny, see Constant, *De l'esprit de conquête et de l'usurpation*, Pt. 2, Chs. 6–8. Constant's basic insight, which I want to pursue in this chapter, is that the old *res publica* conception of politics, renewed in modern times, only serves to overlegitimate a technically efficient bureaucratic agency with police powers. The idea that only politics provides a "public space" for human self-realization or (what amounts to the same thing) that politics is "man's essence"

makes it nearly impossible to understand why citizens might want to resist the coercive encroachments of a hypertrophic state.

2. No Marxist would openly defend such an "unhistorical" belief. Yet its conservative defenders (and I am thinking here of Leo Strauss and his followers) reveal a kind of "inverted agreement" with the most brashly totalitarian of the leftists. Telling in this regard is Strauss's exchange with Alexandre Kojève (Strauss, *On Tyranny*). Their chief point of consensus, so it seems, is the "alienating" character of post-Copernican and capitalist modernity where human beings have all purportedly become Benthamite atoms (instrumentalizing each other) rather than civic collaborators (harmonizing with each other).

3. The fact that Greek has no precise counterparts to the elementary terms of modem political philosophy should reinforce the point I am trying to make. The Greek terms which perhaps come closest to "legitimate" (as characterizing a justified regime) are *orthos*, right, true, straight or correct, and *kata phusin*, according to nature. Clearly, the modem claim is quite moderate, even "minimalist," in comparison to the Greek. The same will appear to be the case when we turn below to the ostensible Greek analogues of "participation" and "representation."

4. Of course, the best-known recent endeavors to elaborate on the classic sociologists' claim that increasing structural differentiation is the fundamental characteristic of modern society have come from Parsons and his school. (See, for example, Parsons, *Societies: Evolutionary and Comparative Perspectives, The System of Modern Societies.*) For an extremely helpful attempt to reformulate and expand Parsons's theory of social differentiation while abandoning his Durkheimian insistence that all societies require "normative integration," see the numerous (and in Germany, at least, widely debated) works of Niklas Luhmann. For a programmatic statement of his position, see Luhmann, *Soziologische Aufklärung 1, 2.*

5. It should be mentioned here that in the preface to the second edition, written seven years after the original manuscript was completed, Popper refers to liberalism as "a movement which began three centuries ago," thus contradicting the central thesis of his book, *The Open Society and Its Enemies*, p. ix.

6. Havelock's quaint and rambling treatise (*The Liberal Temper in Greek Politics*) suffers from the same defect as Popper's study on which it is based. Neither author betrays any awareness of the decisive linkage between the modern liberal doctrine of the "bourgeois rights of man" and the high degree of structural differentiation unique to modern bourgeois society. For Strauss's criticism of Havelock, see Strauss, *Liberalism Ancient and Modern*, pp. 26–64.

7. For the sake of synopsis, it is possible to locate—following Weber, Parsons, and Luhmann—the basic features of modernity in these nine, historically staggered developments: (1) the privatization of religion, (2) the rise of territorial nation-states with increasingly bureaucratic administrations, (3) the emergence of rational capitalism, (4) the specialization of science on the basis of rigorous quantitatively hypothetical-experimental techniques, (5) the release of art from civic and religious functions, (6) the democratization of mass politics through representative institutions and the eventual stabilization of a universal franchise, (7) the shrinkage of the basic kinship unit to the small and increasingly one-generational nuclear family,

(8) the birth of universal-compulsory education, and (9) the positivization of law or the shift in the basis of legality from immutable "natural law" to formal procedures for changing legal codes in an orderly way.

8. It is Hannah Arendt (*Between Past and Future*, pp. 143–71), and not Popper, who lumps Epictetus together with Mill. Of course, there is some basis for this misreading in Mill's text, since he does echo the Protestant self-deception that reformed religion is purely inward and devoid of a worldly, organizational, and communicative dimension.

9. Although he never seems concerned with the despotic potential inherent in classical Greek political theory, Strauss does at times echo Benjamin Constant. But even when he does so he reveals the extent to which his interest in transformations of attitude overshadows his concern for structural change: "the relative success of modern political *philosophy* has brought into being a kind of society wholly unknown to the classics, a kind of society to which the classical principles as stated and elaborated by the classics are not immediately applicable" (*The City and Man*, p. 11, my emphasis).

10. This is what Strauss has to say about the logical disjunction Weber discerned between descriptive social theory and political partisanship, between stating that different decisions have different costs and actually making one decision and paying its particular costs: "Weber's thesis necessarily leads to nihilism or to the view that every preference, however evil, base or insane, has to be judged before the tribunal of reason to be as legitimate as every other preference." And he goes on to add: "In following this movement toward its end we shall inevitably reach a point beyond which the scene is darkened by the shadow of Hitler" (Strauss, *Natural Right and History*, p. 42).

11. *Pol.* III.1 1274b39–40.

12. As Moses Finley formulates this point: "Classical Greeks and Republican Romans possessed a considerable measure of freedom, in speech, in political debate, in their business activities and even in religion. However, they lacked, and would have been appalled by, inalienable rights. There were no theoretical limits to the power of the state, no activity, no sphere of human behaviour, in which the state could not legitimately intervene provided the decision was properly taken for any reason that was held to be valid by a legitimate authority" (Finley, *The Ancient Economy*, pp. 154–55).

13. Thucydides, *The Peloponnesian War*, Bk. II, 1. 40.

14. This claim must be modified, of course, by consideration of the solitary, almost entranced, quality of Platonic *noēsis* and the small-scale and apolitical character of Socratic *elenchos*.

15. *Rep.* 433B and passim.

16. *Pol.* I.2 1253a25–26.

17. *Pol.* VIII.1 1337a 27.

18. *Rep.* 462C–D; *Pol.* I.2 1253a19–23.

19. For more detailed etymological information, see Cornford, *From Religion to Philosophy.* Since the idea of a *physical* ascription of roles is patently "nonliberal," it was a serious blunder for Donald J. Allen to make it the basis for his defense of Aristotle's underlying "liberalism" (Allen, "Individual and State in the Ethics and Politics").

20. It is crucial to distinguish the generic concept "functional differentiation" from its subclass "division of labor" which is indispensable for analyzing even relatively un-

differentiated societies. Modern social differentiation, as Georg Simmel explains so well (*Conflict and the Web of Group-Affiliations*, pp. 127–95), involves the multiple participation of each individual in incongruous and crosscutting social circles. The distinction between general social differentiation and the differentiation (within the economy) of specific professional groups seems to have been fudged by Durkheim in his otherwise powerful analysis of social differentiation (*The Division of Labor in Society*).

21. *Pol.* I.5 1254a29–31.

22. *NE* IX.8 1168b31–32.

23. *Pol.* I.1 1252a7–20; *Statesman*, 259B.

24. *NE* I.2 1094a18–22.

25. *Pol.* VII.2 1325a7. For the intimate character of this partnership, consider Aristotle's claim that "if the citizens of a *polis* are to judge and distribute offices according to merit, then they must know each other's characters" (*Pol.* VII.4 1326b15–16).

26. The rise of Macedonia (which Aristotle lived to witness) marked the beginning of the end of the Greek *polis* as a significant unit of political and military life. It is in this context, and with some reference to Socrates' daemon, that I want to view Aristotle's evaluation of the life of *theōria* or contemplation as "the complete happiness of man" (*NE* X.7 1177b24). Although he explicitly says in Book I of the *Nicomachean Ethics*, that *autarkeia* (defined as "that which, when isolated, makes life desirable and lacking in nothing" [I.7 1097b15]) is unrelated to the *bios monōtos* or solitary life—the reason being that "man is a political animal" (I.7 1097b9–11)—in Book X, he contradicts this statement by saying that the wise man or *sophos* has more *autarkeia* than others simply because "he is able to theorize all alone" (X.7 1177a32–33). Although this is a contradiction of sorts, it may be explained somewhat by Aristotle's need to find a form of happiness which might survive the imminent collapse of the *polis*. Similarly, the Christian tradition of apolitical inwardness was always able to perceive itself foreshadowed in the ideals of contemplative withdrawal and ataraxia current in Hellenistic times. In one sense, at any rate, Aristotle never swerves from his definition of man as a political animal. He specifically calls *theōria* a divine and not a human *aretē* (X.7 1177b32). For a carefully documented account of Aristotle's less than total commitment to the theoretical life (whose devotees "do not seek those goods which are specific to man" [VI.7 1141b8]), see Cooper, *Reason and Human Good in Aristotle*.

27. *Pol.* VII.3 1325a25–27.

28. "It is for the sake of *kalai praxeis*, beautiful and noble actions, and not for the sake of surviving together, that political associations exist" (*Pol.* III.9 1281a 2–3). See also *NE* VIII.11 1161a34–35.

29. *Pol.* VII.4 1326b25.

30. It was a commonplace in nineteenth-century England that anyone curious about Athens only needed to visit Oxford to discover what it had been like. Perhaps this is what Sir Ernest Barker meant by his not totally inaccurate claim that "the city was not only a unit of government, it was also a club" (*Greek Political Theory*, p. 16).

31. In a book heavily influenced by Constant's understanding of the difference between ancient and modern liberty, we read the following: "The state allowed no man to be indifferent to its interests; the philosopher or studious man had no right to live

apart. He was obliged to vote in the assembly and be magistrate in his turn. At a time when discords were frequent, the Athenian law permitted no one to remain neutral; he must take sides with one or the other party. Against one who attempted to remain indifferent, and not side with either faction, and to appear calm, the law pronounced the punishment of exile with confiscation of property" (Fustel de Coulanges, *The Ancient City*, p. 267).

32. The precise kind of participation encouraged by the state, of course, depended on the relative degree of democratization. Consider, for example, the following: "The Athenians also took part in the Assembly, which had 40 ordinary meetings a year, and public slaves rounded them up from the agora onto the Pnyx for these meetings with the aid of a ruddled rope: anyone found afterwards with red on his clothes was fined" (Webster, *Everyday Life in Classical Athens*, p. 69).

33. Xenophon, *Hellenica*, Bk. I, Ch. vii.

34. *NE* V.1 1129b17–19. Later, after declaring that "friendship holds cities together" (VIII.1 1155a22–23), Aristotle goes so far as to say that "among friends there is no need for justice" (VIII.1 1155a26–27).

35. Many ordinary Greeks, in other words, and not just "totalitarian" philosophers, must have reacted with astonishment to the contractarian attitude which Popper admires in Lycophron (Popper, *The Open Society and Its Enemies*, Vol. I, p. 114 ff.). We can perhaps experience the same sort of astonishment by considering the apparent perversity of Kant's claim that marriage is essentially a relation of contract and exchange (*Die Metaphysik der Sitten*, pp. 91–94). Hegel, Athenian at heart, was absolutely outraged at this suggestion (*The Philosophy of Right*, p. 58). Institutions like the *polis* and the family, he argued, do not simply protect individual rights. Rather, they provide otherwise unattainable possibilities for self-realization in partnership. This explains how, as institutions, they can be said to have "moral" content. They are media for creative collaboration, not mechanisms for manipulative and possessive solitude.

36. *Pol.* VI.4 1318b6–16.

37. *NE* I.3 1095a1–7.

38. Xenophon, *Memorabilia*, Bk. 2, Ch. 1, 1. 9. Aristippus was notorious in antiquity for having been the first of Socrates' disciples to accept payment for his teaching services—an innovation which was commonly thought to signal a betrayal of *both* otherworldly philosophy *and* collaborative politics. See "Aristippus" in Diogenes Laertius, Bk. 2., 11. 65–104.

39. *Memorabilia*, Bk. 2, Ch. 1, 11. 13.

40. I will comment below (though only indirectly) on the curious similarity between Aristippus and Socrates justly stressed by Strauss (*Xenophon's Socrates*, pp. 32–39).

41. *Pol.* I.2 1253a2.

42. With St. Paul's decision that entering the Jewish community and following Jewish law was no longer necessary for a Gentile to become a Christian, Christianity managed to break its ethnic, territorial, and political moorings. It became a *civitas divina.* Thus, it could coexist with temporal powers (you could be a Christian in both Rome and Athens) while resisting integration into political states (Parsons, *The System of Modern Societies*, pp. 30–34).

43. *The City of God,* Bk. 19, Ch. V. It is probably worth recalling that Thomas Aquinas too transformed Aristotle's *zōon politikon* into an *animal sociale. Summa Theologica* Pt. 1, Qu. 96, Art. 4.

44. The "liberal" branch of corporativist theory (and I am thinking, for example, of Maitland and Figgis) focused on the *group* in its status as an intermediary between the individual and the nation-state. Although their main concern was to obviate the tyrannical tendencies of the hypertrophic state, this "medievalism," like the attendant talk of "small religious communities," has never seemed quite convincing. The idea of multiple corporations, at any rate, must be carefully distinguished from the notion of "structural differentiation" developed by Simmel to characterize the basic pattern of modern Western society. (Besides Simmel, *Conflict and the Web of Group-Affliations,* see his *Individuality and Social Forms.*) The point to make against the wistful corporatists is that, in modern societies, the individual cannot be "redeemed" in *any* group, in state, church, guild, or whatever. The "bourgeois rights of man" can be understood as the constitutional correlate of structural developments which rendered obsolete the whole/part schematization of society by reinforcing human individuality at the intersection of several overlapping contexts of social communication. None of these contexts completely encircles or contains the individuals who act within it, and thus none can be considered an "organic corporation." In such a highly differentiated society, individuality begins to seem like an "autogenic" achievement of single persons who, without any socially approved pattern to follow, manage to integrate their diverse roles into coherent life stories.

45. The separation between property ownership and military, political, and ecclesiastical functions only began in the sixteenth century with the "reception" of Roman law (Schlatter, *Private Property: The History of an Idea*). One of the points to make here is that the importance of the economy in modern society depends directly on social differentiation, since capitalism could only "take off" after it had shed its anchorage in the surrounding social and religious nexus (Polanyi, *The Great Transformation*).

46. The modern political arena, in other words, had dwindled to the lowly rank of a subsystem among subsystems. It has become, in Nietzsche's words "the so-little-as-possible state" (*Morgenröte,* p. 1133). Because of this development, human engagement can only be partial and incomplete. This point about politics is just another example of Max Weber's more general claim that, in modern society, the "total status" of the individual is never contained in any single interaction context. For this Simmelian argument, see Weber, *On Law in Economy and Society,* pp. 105 ff.

47. Even in antiquity, of course, and especially after the battle of Chaeronea in 338, there were those who went along with Aristippus' glorification of the *apolis.* Their rejection of *koinōnia,* however, was often tinged with resentment and understandable as a foreshadowing of Christian inwardness.

48. Indicative of modern civic "uprootedness" is the contrast between Aristotle's and Locke's reasons for condemning suicide. For Aristotle, suicide is wrong because it betrays the community; for Locke it is wrong because an individual's survival is "God's property" and hence not to be tampered with (*NE* V.11 1138a 5–14; *Second Treatise of Government,* Ch. 2, Sec. 6). Of course, the classical study of suicide and the difficulty of dealing with it on the basis of the Protestant "ontology of privacy" is Durkheim, *Suicide.*

49. For one of his many attempts to replace the old whole/part schema with a system/environment model for the study of society, see Luhmann, *Funktion und Folgen formaler Organizationen.*

50. Vestigal Aristotelianism may have contributed to a peculiar lack of clarity in early formulations of contract theory. Even that arch anti-Aristotelian Hobbes suggests that the dissolution of government cannot be distinguished from the dissolution of society, thereby in one sense perpetuating the ancient identification of the polity with total society.

2

Aristotle's Social Science

Stephen G. Salkever

THE PURPOSE OF THIS ESSAY is to defend the claim that Aristotle's approach to social science is different from and superior to the two principal approaches characteristic of our time, empiricist and interpretive social science. My defense is not of the specific results of Aristotle's analysis; my claim, in fact, is that the great merit of Aristotle's approach (I avoid the term "method" here for reasons that will become clear) is that it yields, when practiced well, results that are both interesting and open to further discussion. The *Politics* and the *Ethics,* the primary texts to be considered, are not repositories of immutable truths calling for belief or rejection any more than they are oblique reflections of popular Greek opinion. Instead we find in them a discourse made up of arguable judgments of four major kinds: (1) descriptions of general facts or phenomena, the kind of thing that might be referred to as empirical assertions, as, for example, the claims that most human beings consider that any amount of virtue is enough but seek without limit to amass quantities of wealth or possessions or powers or reputation and that the place of deliberation is less powerful in women's lives than in men's;[1] (2) propositions about the efficient causal relationship of several phenomena or variables, which are hypothetical propositions, such as the claim that large cities tend to be freer of internal conflict than small cities;[2] (3) teleological propositions about the place or function of various activities in the lives of human beings, such as the claim that security and friendship are necessary, but not constitutive, conditions of political life;[3] and finally (4) evaluative judgments, both general and particular, such as that the political life is better than the life of war and conquest, and the Spartan culture rests on a mistaken conception of human virtue.[4]

To summarize then, the Aristotelian approach to social science that I propose to defend characteristically weaves together four separate kinds of questions in a particular order: on the basis of descriptions of observed phenomena, propositions of two distinct kinds, hypothetical and teleological, are set out; on the basis of these propositions, action-orienting evaluative conclusions are drawn about institutions, policies, and ways of life. By comparison, an initial contrast with modern social science would suggest that Aristotle's approach is more inclusive than either the empiricist (which culminates in a system of hypothetical propositions) or the interpretive (which culminates in teleological propositions relative to the particular context under study, more or less "from the native's point of view").[5] This much could well be granted by empiricists and interpretive social scientists, who would then go on to challenge Aristotle's procedures by pointing out—quite correctly—that his four types of discussion do not occur in a metaphysical vacuum but presuppose a particular theory of human nature and of nature simply. In order to defend Aristotle's social science, I will have to explain just what that background theory is and how it allows Aristotle to do two things that I believe to be of the greatest value for any social science: to reach conclusions of the sort that can inform practical discussion and to do so in a non-dogmatic language that invites further discussion and revision. My claim will be that the conception of human nature on which Aristotle's social science rests is both more plausible in itself and more likely to result in an adequate social science, one that is both practical and open, than either of the contemporary alternatives.

Before taking this up, however, I need to explain briefly why I am treating Aristotle as any kind of social scientist at all, rather than as a political philosopher or theorist. Aristotle's own name for what he is doing is *politikē*, or "the science of the *polis*." *Politikē* does seem to be the equivalent of modern social science with respect to the subject matter it embraces; Aristotle uses the term throughout the *Politics* and the *Ethics* to refer to the consideration of topics we would today assign to political science, anthropology, sociology, psychology, economics, and history. This substantive equivalence is my primary reason for rendering *politikē* as "social science." The objection may be raised, however, that Aristotle's approach is at odds with the current implications of the term "science." Part of my argument will be an attempt to show that *politikē*, for Aristotle, was indeed a science, and even a kind of natural science. The surface plausibility of this reading is indicated by the way Aristotle uses the word. While *politikē* most frequently in both Plato and Aristotle stands by itself as a noun, its ordinary meaning flows from its adjectival function; it modifies nouns like *technē* ("skill or craft"), *epistēmē* ("science"), and *philosophia*.[6] The question, for Aristotle, seems not to be whether social science is possible, but rather just what kind of a science *politikē* is.

The "social" in "social science" poses a more difficult problem. As Carnes Lord remarks in the introduction to his translation, "the overarching framework of Aristotelian practical science is emphatically a political one."[7] It is surely true that for Aristotle the *polis* is the most important human community or form of relationship, rather than just one among many. But it also is true that his definition of politics and his account of its importance do not simply reproduce standard Greek views on the subject. Briefly, politics according to Aristotle is a kind of human interaction marked by two structural and one functional characteristic. The interaction is structured by *nomoi* ("laws," "customs") rather than by unstructured individual choice; decisions are made according to some procedure for ruling and being ruled in turn, rather than, say, by force, chance, or wisdom; and decisions are motivated by the desire to improve the lives of all the citizens. The reasons for defining politics in this way will be taken up later; here it should be noted that Aristotle is fully aware that Greeks generally use the term *polis* to refer to communities that do not exhibit these features, and further that genuine (in Aristotle's sense) *poleis* are extremely rare. A large part of Aristotle's *politikē*, then, is devoted to explaining why politics is so unusual and how other kinds of interactions (e.g., families, armies, friendships, markets) approximate or distort the looks of Aristotle's sense of politics. Thus the focus of attention is not on the kinds of interactions we call political (as is the case with our "political science"), but on a wide range of human associations and failures to associate, on the advantages and dangers of human relationships of many kinds.

Before returning to the details of Aristotle's views concerning the place of politics in his account of human affairs in general, more needs to be said about why we might want to consult Aristotle in the first place. Why, in other words, is it desirable to look for a third alternative to the claims of empiricist and interpretive social science?

1. Empiricism and Interpretation

The genealogy and general structure of the debate between the proponents of empiricism and interpretation in contemporary social science is too well known to call for extended comment here. The central issue—the question of whether there is an essential difference between methods appropriate to natural science and the methods of the human or social sciences—is one that has a history of several centuries. The empiricist position holds that there is no serious methodological difference and that all science aims at explanations that take the form of propositions connecting separate events or dimensions of variance in a hypothetical way. These propositions, when sufficiently general and sufficiently tested, can be treated as general or covering laws that serve to explain particular events. As far as method and logic are concerned, there is no difference between establishing connections among force, mass, and acceleration and establishing connections among social class, ethnic identification, and political behavior. The purpose of social scientific inquiry understood in this way is the prediction and control of behavioral events; moral quandaries no doubt arise, but this is at least equally true of the natural sciences. For an empiricist there is no strong connection between explanation and evaluation, between giving accurate explanations and deciding how to act in a given situation. As W. G. Runciman observes:

> The difference of subject-matter imposes difference of technique, as it does between one science and another on both sides of the frontier between nature and culture. But this does not impose a requirement on social scientists either to adopt different criteria of validity or to disclaim a capacity to achieve it at all. It is true that there is a difference in the level at which theoretical grounding is to be sought. But again, it is a difference which can be paralleled within the natural sciences as well as between the natural and the social; and it is still a difference within a common mode of reasoning.[8]

It must be remembered, however, that this "common mode of reasoning" of which Runciman speaks has a very definite pedigree and rests—at least historically—on a distinctly uncommon view of the world, to be explained by scientific reasoning. This is the world of Cartesian *res extensa*, within which, according to Thomas Kuhn,

> most physical scientists assumed that the universe was composed of microscopic corpuscles and that all natural phenomena could be explained in terms of corpuscular shape, size, motion, and interaction. That nest of commitments proved to be both metaphysical and methodological. As metaphysical, it told scientists what sort of entities the universe did and did not contain: there was only shaped matter in motion. As methodological, it told them what ultimate laws and fundamental explanations must be like: laws must specify corpuscular motion and interaction, and explanation must reduce any given natural phenomenon to corpuscular action under these laws.[9]

Two features of this program call for comment. First, scientific reasoning thus understood explains natural phenomena by treating them as wholes in need of being reduced to the lawful motion of their smallest parts: real science is in part the search for the smallest element. Scientific sophistication involves unwillingness to treat apparent wholes—such as plants and animals—as if they were real wholes. Thus modern science privileges physics over biology,[10] or rather it implies that the best biology and the best social science will resemble mathematical physics as closely as the awkwardly large and protean quality of their data permit. The second aspect of the project that is relevant here is that historically it takes its bearings from a rejection of Aristotelian physics. This was in many ways a clear gain; overcoming Aristotle's mistakes about the immobility of the earth, circular inertia, and especially his distinction between sublunary (changeable) and celestial (unchanging) matter made extraordinary scientific progress possible.[11] On the other hand, it is not so easy to justify the rejection of another part of the Aristotelian worldview—the idea that living organisms and species were in some respects individuals, wholes that could not be reduced without loss of meaning to an interaction of their elements.[12] What results is the rejection of all teleological explanation as unscientific, methodologically inappropriate. This rules out talk about the relationship between particular traits or behaviors and the way of life of an organism, except insofar as these teleological propositions can be restated as predictive hypotheses. Thus, for example, the teleological hypothesis that the function of politics is to make economic exchange easier would be replaced by the prediction that politics results in easier economic exchange. But the two propositions are not equivalent: the latter is only a claim about the consequences of politics, while the former, the teleological hypothesis, makes the additional evaluative claim that politics is a good thing for human beings *because* it leads to certain economic consequences. In other words, the teleological analysis includes the predictive but adds to it a claim about the relationship of particular phenomena to the whole (in this case, the life of the species) of which they are a part. For modern, anti-Aristotelian, science, on the other hand, there are no universals save universally valid laws. As Thomas Hobbes notes, there is "nothing in the world Universall but Names; for the things named, are every one of them Individuall and Singular."[13]

This rejection of the non-conventional reality of all wholes is historically linked with the rejection of other and manifestly false Aristotelian claims about the world—special ethereal matter and so on—but the modern premise seems much less well grounded in observational necessity. Many biologists would now argue that the reductionist aspect of the modern scientific program was a mistake and that teleological (or teleonomic) analysis is a central part of scientific inquiry, given the reality of organisms and perhaps of species as more than simply a collection of elementary parts.[14] Be that as it may, the first challenge to the extension of modern empiricist science into the study of human affairs came not from biologists but from those contesting the view that human beings could be studied in the same way that natural phenomena can be. Sharing the empiricist view that animals are in no essential way different from machines, critics of a unified natural and social science argued that there was a fundamental difference between human beings and "merely" natural beings. Rousseau is one of the first to adopt this position. As he expressed it, "nature commands every animal, and the beast obeys. Man feels the same impetus, but he realizes that he is free to acquiesce or resist; and it is above all in the consciousness of this freedom that the spirituality of the soul is shown."[15] This assertion of the essential uniqueness of human beings shares with empiricism—against Aristotle—the questionable view that animals are essentially machines. It differs from empiricism in its claim that human action is so different from animal-mechanical behavior as to require an entirely different form of explanation. As elaborated in the nineteenth century, this sense of difference is expressed in terms of concepts like historicity and the historical sense, categories that draw their vitality from the belief that human beings indirectly constitute themselves, create their own significance, through social action.[16]

The twentieth-century heir to the romantic reaction against the Enlightenment ideal of a unified science is interpretive social science. Instead of being, in effect, "laws-and-causes social physics," to use Clifford Geertz's phrase, the study of human affairs should aim at emulating the process of construing a text; societies are to be "read" rather than "predicted."[17] While it would be an exaggeration to say that this method requires a deep empathy or perfect identification with the culture being studied, it is surely very different from the business of providing causal explanations by reference to universal hypothetical laws. It does, however, equally aim at explanation, though teleological rather than predictive, insofar as it attempts both to describe "particular symbolic forms (a ritual gesture, an hieratic statue) as defined expressions," and to place "such forms within the whole structure of meaning of which they are a part and in terms of which they get their definition.[18] But if this is teleology, the limits of its explanatory power are strictly local: the aim is to explain the society in its own terms, given the principle that "societies, like lives, contain their own interpretations."[19]

Interpretation, however, cannot be simply passive, allowing societies or "natives" to speak for themselves. If cultures are texts, then they are texts of a special kind. For Geertz, "doing ethnography is like trying to read (in the sense of 'construct a reading of') a manuscript—foreign, faded, full of ellipses, incoherencies . . . but written not in conventionalized graphs of sound but in transient examples of shaped behavior."[20] For the interpretive social scientist, the meaning of an action is internal to the social context, but it is assumed to be hidden from the view of the actors themselves. Geertz's interpreter does not aim at establishing universal laws, but he seems at least as sure as any physicist (or economist) that his data are not capable of supplying an adequate self-interpretation:

> The ethnographer does not, and in my opinion, largely cannot, perceive what his informants perceive. What he perceives—and that uncertainly enough—is what they perceive "with," or "by means of," or "through" or whatever word one may choose. In the country of the blind, who are not as unobservant as they appear, the one-eyed is not king but spectator.[21]

Just as the physicist ferrets out the laws of the interaction of matter, the interpreter unmasks the hidden categories that inform perception and action; each supplies by science the coherence their data otherwise but mutely display. Indeed, for Geertz, the "study of culture [is] a positive science like any other," no matter what the metaphor of social textuality may suggest.[22] Empiricists aim at universal laws, interpreters at "local knowledge," but both understand their activity as fundamentally disinterested; evaluations are to be avoided in the analysis, and few if any evaluative conclusions can be drawn from the analysis. The function of social science relative to everyday political life thus appears as archival rather than action-orienting, on either account.[23] This situation is characterized by Hans-Georg Gadamer as a "false objectification," falsely treating the subjects of analysis as fundamentally different from the analyst.[24] In interpretive social science, this is achieved by treating the "human"—that attribute shared by analyst and subject—as a property of minimal significance.

The problem with this orientation is that it means that social science can never function as a means of self-criticism, as a way of arriving at conclusions concerning how to change or maintain our lives. To serve this goal, social science must try to do more than "seek and acknowledge the immanent coherence contained within the meaning-claim of the other." What is required in addition is in Gadamer's words, "a readiness to recognize the other as potentially right and let him or it prevail against me."[25] Thus the moral danger posed by cultural relativism is that it leads its adherents not into anarchy—they are a generally civilized lot—but to smugness.[26]

It is his interest in a future- or action-oriented approach to human affairs that leads Gadamer to suggest that Aristotle can supply a language for inquiry that is superior to that of the contemporary adversaries, whether empirical or interpretive.[27] To this it may be added that Aristotle also differs from both varieties of current social science in being open to the possible influence of biological reflection in the study of human affairs. In this way, Aristotle's account of human action rejects both the empiricist assumption that animals are machines (or that nature as such is mechanical) and the romantic dichotomy between the human and the natural.[28]

I believe that an Aristotelian social science begins with a sense of nature, or biological inheritance, as neither determinative of human action nor irrelevant to it, but rather as a potentiating source of problems to be solved and of capacities and inclinations to be shaped. In presenting the Aristotelian possibility, I will consider first his conception of human action and convention and then discuss his notion of the kind of social science that can provide the most adequate account of these actions and conventions.

2. Aristotle and Praxis

Both of Aristotle's great works of social science, the *Nicomachean Ethics* and the *Politics,* begin with observations concerning the intentional character of human conduct: "We see that . . . everyone does everything for the sake of some apparent good"; "Every art . . . and similarly every *praxis* and choice seems to aim at some good."[29] This serves to distinguish human actions from several other classes of events in nature: those that serve a purpose in the life of the organism but are not intentional, like blinks of the eye and the motion of the heart, and those that serve no purpose, like eye color.[30] Human actions are intentional in the sense that they are voluntary (*hekon*). A motion is not identified as voluntary by any prior events (such as internal processes of reasoning or willing) that may have led up to the motion. "Both 'voluntary' and 'involuntary' must be said when the action occurs. An action is voluntary when the source [*archē*] of the motion of the bodily parts is the agent."[31] Voluntary actions are distinguished from other events or kinds of motion by the presence in the agent of the power to act or not at the moment of action. But this power is not the privileged preserve of any uniquely human or transcendent faculty. Other animals are as capable of voluntary action as are human beings, because this internal source of motion is neither reason nor will, but desire (*orexis*), which is common to all animals.[32] Desires are always directed toward some object of desire (some apparent good), and this is an object of sensation or imagination (*phantasia*), a power that is also common to all animals.[33] Thus intentional or voluntary motion can be understood as an interaction of an apparent good, the agent's perception of that good, and the agent's desire for the good in question. Nonetheless, it makes sense to call desire the source or efficient cause of action, because neither the object nor the perception of the object can cause motion in the absence of desire.[34]

Yet it is also possible for Aristotle to say, in response to Democritus' claim for the universality of external efficient cause (a claim shared by modern science), that *all* animals move by choice (*prohairesis*) or intellection (*noēsis*).[35] The reason for the apparent ambiguity here is Aristotle's view that reason and desire are not separate entities but interacting "parts" or aspects of soul (*psuchē*). *Soul* itself, moreover, is not a thing separate from body, but is "a beginning [*archē*] of animal life."[36] That is, to speak of soul, for Aristotle, is to consider the manner in which living things are self-moving and thus distinct from inanimate existence; "of natural things, some have life and some not; we say 'life' where there is nurture, growth, and decay owing to the thing itself."[37] The Aristotelian soul is not separate from the body, but body and soul are properties that exist relative to one another as aspects of the individual animal whose being they define; that is to say that my body is to my soul as the potential of an individual is to its actuality or function.[38] This conception of soul as the definitive activity of a creature is nicely captured in Aristotle's analogy, "If the eye were an animal, sight would be its soul."[39]

Just as soul is not a unique and supernatural immaterial substance for Aristotle, it is also not a peculiarly human property. Even if some kinds of activities, such as deliberation, belong primarily to humans, it is interesting to note that Aristotle explicitly rejects the view that soul and mind (*nous*) are the same. In fact, he attributes such a view to the atomist Democritus and says that it follows from the false relativistic belief that truth and opinion are one and the same.[40]

Thus human actions are not distinct from the motions of animals by virtue of their intentionality or spirituality. Still, there is a distinction to be made. In the *Ethics*, Aristotle says that he wants to reserve the term *praxis* as a characterization of human conduct alone. "There are three things in the soul," he observes, "that are decisive concerning actions and truths: perception, thought, and desire. Of these, perception is in no way the source [*archē*] of *praxis*; for beasts have perception but no share in *praxis*."[41] This is not to say that praxis is *caused* (in the sense of efficient causality) by mind and not desire, since *praxis* is a kind of motion, and "thought by itself moves nothing," at least insofar as actions are concerned.[42] The problem is as follows: the subject of *politikē* is *ta prakta*, matters concerning practice. *Praxis* is uniquely human, but it is not attributable to the existence of any uniquely creative or volitional faculty in human beings,[43] nor can it be said to follow simply from the fact that human beings are capable of thinking in ways that other animals are not. If *praxis* is peculiarly human, it must be as a result of a certain kind of desire.

There can be no desire without imagination, that is, an imagined object of desire, an apparent good.[44] No objects are good or desirable in themselves (and so Aristotle criticizes the Platonic form of the good in the first book of the *Ethics*), but only relative to the animal desiring them: the same object or way of life may be desirable or good for cats, but not for horses.[45] Animals are defined, for Aristotle, by the kind of activity or way of life that is peculiar to them when they are functioning at their best, their *ergon* or *energeia*.[46] Another way of saying this is that a healthy animal is one whose parts or elements are arranged according to the *logos* that defines the animal in question.[47] The *ergon* of an animal is determined by its logos or, in other words, by its soul and is identical with the goal or *telos* it pursues.[48] Things that seem good to an animal, and are thereby desired by it, may or may not actually be good for that animal; the souls of animals are frequently mistaken, so that a certain kind of attractive food may serve either to support or to baffle the way of life of its consumer.[49] In general, though, an animal's pleasures are determined by its *ergon*; most dogs, spiders, and mules take pleasure in the sorts of things that all members of their species accurately desire.[50] Human beings, however, are different. "Among humans there is no small difference in pleasures, for the same things that give enjoyment to some and pain to others are painful and hateful to some and sweet and dear to others."[51] With other animals, pleasures and apparent goods, the starting points of desire, vary mostly by species; with humans, they vary from individual to individual and are the major source of human inequality.

Thus human *praxis* differs in the first instance from other kinds of voluntary motion in its problematic quality and its variability. Aristotle states this difference in the following way in the *Politics:* "Other animals live primarily by nature [*phusis*], and some in a lesser way by habits [*ethos*], but human beings alone live also by reason [*logos*] because he alone has *logos.*"[52] The health (in a sense, the actuality or *energeia*) of nonhuman animals is largely determined by their inherited specific potentiality (*dunamis*) or, as we would now say, their genotype. This is much less the case with human beings, for whom biological inheritance is much less powerful in determining their way of life than is the case for any other species, whether of beasts or gods. To a greater extent than other animals, we desire things as the result of habituation (or "acculturation" or learning) rather than as a direct consequence of biologically inherited responses. As a result, there will be important differences between the goals, and hence the lives, of members of different societies or cultures.

Furthermore, humans can live and desire in a thoughtful way—in a way involving a deliberate choice of goals—whereas other animals cannot.[53] It is at this point that the famous definition of humans as the animals who have *logos,* who have the potential to live by reasoned speech, comes into play. But this is not at all simply to praise human beings, since this capacity for choice (*prohairesis*) is in no way transcendent or divine and since the consequence of having such a capacity is that individuals among us can turn out to be either the best or the worst of animals.[54] It is, rather, to identify a basic problem at the center of human affairs. Our goals as individuals, the shape of our lives, are not set for us by our biologically inherited natures or capacities; still, since we are natural beings defined by a certain definite *telos* or goal, our conception of the good for us as individual human beings can either be correct or mistaken; we can organize our particular capacities and problems relatively well or not.

Therefore, our actions and the customs and thoughts that inform them (that is, our ways of life) can be read and judged as a series of attempts to answer the question, What is the human good?

The judgment that human beings are the rational animals signifies the claim that the structure of our lives is provided by desires that are informed by thought as well as by sensation. But the capacity for thinking well does not actualize itself; rather, it comes into being as the result of the development over time of certain habits over which we initially have no control. As a result, Aristotle should not be understood to claim that human lives are spontaneously, or even usually, happy or flourishing. Instead, his position is that our lives are uniquely controversial answers to the question of how beings like us should live. It is this controversy that provides the central problem for, and the *raison d'être* of, the social scientist.

3. Being a Kind of Animal

In addition to being rational animals, human beings are also said to be the most political animals. But the latter assertion is quite ambiguous, since Aristotle also identifies us as "dualizers," beings whose way of life—unlike that of social insects—is both political and scattered, and perhaps even solitary.[55] This ambiguity is expressed as follows in Book I of the *Politics*: "By nature there is an impulse [*hormē*] in all humans toward such a community [the *polis*], but the first person to establish one was the cause of the greatest good things."[56] The problem is that our biological inheritance includes a number of impulses, not all of them compatible with one another. We also desire our preservation, and this may set us at odds with one another. The point is that there is no single impulse or structure of drives that controls human life. One of the central natural facts about us is that we generally care for one another, or exhibit some aspects of *philia* or friendship, the impulse "to wish for someone else what one thinks to be good, for that person's sake and not for one's own."[57] With this complex of social and asocial impulses, it would appear that if humanity were to be defined by its strongest spontaneous social drives alone, then we should be called familial, rather than political, animals. As we are told in Book VII of the *Nicomachean Ethics*, "friendship between male and female seems to be especially by nature, for the human being is by nature a familial [or pairing], rather than a political animal, inasmuch as the household [*oikos*] is earlier and more necessary than the polis."[58] We have a natural (in the sense of biologically inherited) impulse to live together, but "the purpose of politics is not to make living together [*suzēn*] possible, but to make living well [*eu zēn*] possible."[59] What does this mean? To answer this, it is necessary to consider the second and more important sense in which human beings are political animals.

Aristotle's argument for the proposition that human beings are uniquely political animals is stated in extremely compact form in Book I of the *Politics*.[60] This concision has led to two important misconceptions of the meaning of "political animal" for Aristotle, and it will be useful to consider them before offering my own reading of the passage. The first of these is that in saying we are political animals Aristotle is endorsing the Greek ideal of civic virtue and the superiority of the political life to all others. This is, for example, the view of J. G. A. Pocock, who speaks of "the ancient ideal of *homo politicus* (the *zōon politikon* of Aristotle), who affirms his being and his virtue by the medium of political action."[61] This position suggests that Aristotle is defending the intrinsic value of political life to those who would see it as having only instrumental value (such as Plato or the Sophists,[62] or, prospectively, Hobbes and Locke). But this reading runs afoul of Aristotle's apparent derogation of the political life to a rank below the theoretical life in the concluding books of both the *Politics* and the *Nicomachean Ethics*. As a result, the politics-as-intrinsic-good reading is forced either to ignore these quite prominent passages or to interpret them as a residue of generally overcome Platonism.[63]

The other position I want to contest centers on the claim at *Politics* 1253a29–30 that all humans have an impulse (*hormē*) toward political community. If this is the case, some ask, then why don't human beings seek political life as avidly as beavers build dams or Hobbesian individuals pursue their constant endeavor for power after power? Bernard Williams presents this view in its characteristically critical form:

> In Aristotle's teleological universe, every human being (or at least every non-defective male who is not a natural slave) has a kind of inner nisus toward a life of at least civic virtue, and Aristotle does not say enough about how this is frustrated by poor upbringing, to make it clear exactly how, after that upbringing, it is still in this man's real interest to be other than he is.[64]

The politics-as-spontaneous-drive view leads to the conclusion that Aristotle is hopelessly caught in a contradiction between his biological claim about the human political drive and his ethical and political claims that people do not usually or spontaneously act well.

I want to argue, against both these views, that Aristotle's understanding of the place of politics in human life has an integrity and interest of its own, one that seems to me to be both relatively unusual and plausible. The appeal of the other two views is, however, quite clear. The politics-as-intrinsic-good view allows some modern readers to find in Aristotle a powerful ally against the liberal individualism they oppose, while the politics-as-spontaneous-drive reading permits others to identify Aristotle as a familiar sort of biological student of human affairs—perhaps the biologist of the *polis* in the sense that Freud is called the biologist of the mind. The two interpretations differ most profoundly in their view of the theoretical basis of Aristotle's social science. The intrinsic-good view tends to see Aristotle as making an autonomous ethical argument, and not applying to political issues concepts developed in his biology.[65] The spontaneous-drive view holds that Aristotle is in fact a biological determinist. My contention is that Aristotle's social science is indeed biological, but that it is in no sense determinist—as, indeed, Aristotle's biology is not determinist. For Aristotle, humans inherit a variety of inclinations biologically—toward politics, but also toward living as we please, toward sexual partnership, toward imitation, among others. None of these genetic potentialities should be seen simply as conduct-determining drives; instead, they are potentiating inclinations that can be reinforced or inhibited by any number of experiences as we grow and encounter the world. This is true of animals other than ourselves. What is uniquely human is that our potentialities are many and varied and by no means always compatible or consistent with one another. This lack of strict biological definition is both a strength and a problem for us. Thus for Aristotle, as I will try to demonstrate here, politics—a way of living relative to laws and customs (*nomoi*) and involving both ruling others and being ruled by them—is neither an ethical ideal nor an overwhelming biological drive, neither an end in itself nor an inevitability. It is, instead, the best reasonably possible way of organizing that variety of inclinations and needs that comprise the human biological inheritance, a way that has not arisen either spontaneously from or in opposition to our biological inheritance, but an activity that has developed as the unintended consequence of our attempts to live securely.

Before trying to present the argument about political animals in *Politics* 1253a7–38, I will provide a translation of what I take to be the key portions of that passage, leaving as many of the important terms as possible untranslated. "The reason why human beings are political animals more than the bee or any other herding animal is clear. For nature, as we assert, does nothing in vain, and human beings alone among animals possess *logos*." Other animals have a voice, and so can make significant sounds indicative of pleasure and pain to one another, but *logos* is more than this. "Logos makes plain the *sumpheron* and the *blaberon* [interest and its opposite] and *therefore* [my emphasis] the just and the unjust. For this is unique to human beings as compared with other animals, that they alone have a perception [*aisthēsis*] of good and bad, just and unjust, and other things, and it is a community [*koinōnia*] in these things that makes an *oikos* and a *polis*. And by nature a *polis* is prior to both the *oikos* and the individual." Human beings are unique in having the capacity to perceive what is best for them ("living well") and to order their lives according to that perception. Justice is such an ordering and is, like politics, neither desirable nor natural in itself but only as a way in which "living well" or simply "our interest" (*to sumpheron*) can be brought into being. Differing conceptions of justice are not to be treated as expressing commitment to a moral realm separate from self-interest, but as different judgments about our long-term interests. Polities, the organized communities that assert different views of justice, are neither good nor bad as a whole; rather, they are to be treated as expressing judgments about what our lives require that can be evaluated as correct or mistaken.[66]

Aristotle's claim that our ability to speak reasonably is the human need that explains and justifies the political order is not easy to grasp. The difficulty is caused by the fact that his sense of the function or place of human speech in human life differs radically from conceptions that are familiar to us. In particular, Aristotle holds neither that speech is for the sake of communicating information from one person to another (else it would be the same as "voice") nor that it serves the purpose of expressing or constituting an identity, building up a human world alongside the world of nature. The place of speech in human life is that *logos* makes it possible for us to discover, through argument, conjectures, or narratives, the kinds of goals in terms of which we can most sensibly organize our lives. Errors can of course be made in the process of discovery; as a result, Aristotelian speech is criticizable in a way in which world or identity-constituting speech is not. Our deliberative conclusions about goals are also always uncertain. Nevertheless, some such conclusions are needed if we are not to drift from moment to moment, because they are uniquely not available to us as an immediate consequence of our biological inheritance.

But these reasoned conclusions about our interests do not spring forth spontaneously or by necessity, even though without them we are incapable of becoming flourishing human beings. The capacity of reasonable speech is a potentiality that may or may not be developed; human beings are capable, to a unique degree, of living badly as well as living well. Of no other animal could this be said: "it is sweet for most to live without order [*ataktos*] rather than moderately."[67] Laws and conventions of human construction are necessary to help bring us to an awareness of what is best for us, "for when he has reached his *telos* the human being is the best of animals, but when apart from *nomos* ["law," "convention," "custom"] and justice, the worst."[68] The sense in which we are political animals can now be formulated in this way: human beings are uniquely capable of, *and uniquely in need of*, a reasonable perception of their interest in order to live well, and such a perception (and therefore such a life) is somehow dependent upon the presence of *nomoi*. This statement marks off the tasks of the social scientist, marks a special quality of that science, but requires clarification at three major points. We need to ask, What does "living well" mean? What does it mean to say that this is an object of rational perception? In what way is political life a condition for living well, however defined?

The first of these three questions is taken up in the first book of the *Nicomachean Ethics,* where it is suggested that we live well (or are virtuous—exhibit human *aretē*) insofar as our lives are ordered by the specifically human *telos,* or goal. But strangely enough to our ears, this goal is expressed not in terms of some transcendent ideal or universal rule of obligation, but as a mean,[69] which in turn is defined as an appropriate *logos* or proportion of opposing tendencies. This mean, which indicates the substance or content of human well-being, is said by Aristotle to be a *hexis. Hexis* is a word that turns out to be quite difficult to render in English. It is a key term in Aristotle's social science, and that science becomes inaccessible to us when *hexis* is translated as "characteristic" or "habit" or "trained ability." Perhaps the best way to get at the sense of the term is by example. If I say, "Mary is courageous," or "Mary is a coward," I am describing Mary's *hexis,* making a statement about those relatively stable qualities—desires, feelings, thoughts—that define Mary as an individual. Relative to her biological inheritance, Mary's *hexis* is an actuality or actualization of a particular potentiality; relative to her actions, it is a sort of potentiality.[70] One's *hexis* is of course subject to change over time, but it represents those qualities in a person that are relatively firm and definite at any given moment, those qualities that identify a person as more, or at any rate other, than a bundle of unrealized potentials. The closest English word to *hexis* in this context might be "personality," if by that word we understand those qualities that define a person and distinguish him or her from others. Thus, to live well for Aristotle is to have (or "be") a good personality, and the primary task of the social scientist is to determine as far as possible what such a personality looks like or what sorts of personalities are better than others, in the sense of being better blends or mixtures of those elements (drives and capacities) from which all humans are constituted.

But interpreting *hexis* as "personality" involves real distortion, insofar as "personality" ordinarily refers only to human beings, and so conceals the way in which reference to *hexis* introduces Aristotle's technical language of potentiality and actuality into the discussion of human action (prior to Aristotle, the term was employed in something like his sense by Plato and by the medical writers).[71] For this reason, Terence Irwin's "state" might be the single best translation.[72] At any rate, in the *Categories, hexis* is defined generally as a certain quality (*poion*) "by virtue of which things are what they are."[73] Thus all natural things, insofar as they are composed of elements that are organized in a certain way, can be said to exhibit a *hexis* (or at any rate a *diathesis,* which is simply a less stable, less permanent *hexis*). The term has the function of drawing attention to the way in which individuals are ordered wholes, rather than heaps of elements. Thus health and sickness are said to be *hexeis* of bodies,[74] and stating the *hexis* of a substance is simply another way of describing the actuality (*energeia*) of that substance.[75]

The introduction of the potentiality-actuality distinction for Aristotle's social science indicates that at least some of the key terms of this science are not as radically distinct from the categories of the other sciences of natural things as modern interpretive social science might suggest. Our *psuchē* is analogous to our body in that it can be either well or badly ordered. More precisely, we need to recall here that soul and body are attributes of individuals, rather than separate entities. As Martha Nussbaum says, "the soul is just the functional organization of the entire living body."[76] Each individual has a certain actuality (soul) and potentiality (body) proper to it, and the soul is simply a higher level of organization than the body for that individual, where "higher" refers to nearness to those activities that specifically define the individual as who or what it is. One way to speak of illness in all animals, human beings included, is to say that it is an unnatural condition in which our body rules our soul, when the battle to stay alive effaces the possibility of living well.[77]

Just as the healthy involuntary motions of the body can be identified by reference to a healthy (or normal) physical condition,[78] so healthy voluntary actions are defined relative to a good or healthy personality. Of course, Aristotle is aware that both the elements and the correct blend or proportion are much more difficult to grasp in the realm of action than in that of bodily health,[79] but he can at least begin by asserting that if virtue or excellence is a *hexis*, then good actions are those that are performed by good (*spoudaioi* or *phronimoi*) human beings. Actions cannot be called good or bad by reference to some universally applicable moral rule, like the greatest happiness principle or the categorical imperative. Aristotle and the various schools of modern psychiatry might disagree radically concerning the specific character of a healthy personality, but they are in fundamental agreement that the basis for any understanding of human affairs must be a perception of what constitutes a well-ordered person, just as the practice of medicine must begin with a perception of what constitutes a healthy somatic condition.

4. Political Resolutions and Human Problems

We live well insofar as we perceive what living well is, and act according to that perception. This is also true of physical well-being, but with one important difference: human beings do not always or for the most part spontaneously perceive their interest in becoming good persons or personalities. Our actions and the desires that initiate them can only become informed by a perception of the good human life as a result in the first instance of learning or socialization that is shaped by the laws and customs of our culture.[80] Good human beings act on the basis of rational choice, but in order to reach the possibility of rational conduct we require a very long period of habituation, of a sort of aesthetic education demanded by the relative thinness of our biological inheritance relative to our specific virtue, "for all art [*technē*] and education wish to supply what is lacking in nature."[81] Every culture can thus be seen as implying a solution to the question of the best life, or at any rate the question of the best life under the circumstances. This implicit solution is in fact the meaning or significance of cultural and political organization, even though the most efficient cause or most powerful motivation for the establishment of politics is not the desire to live well but rather the desire to live or to live together. As Aristotle remarks, "the polis comes into being for the sake of living, but is for the sake of living well."[82] The curious fact about human life is that we have a profound biological need for an institution that will shape our desires into healthy patterns, but at the same time we have a relatively weak natural inclination (or *hormē*) for institutions of that sort. Such political inclinations as we do inherit need to be supplemented by our much stronger social inclinations toward institutions that provide security or company rather than *paideia*. Thus it is not surprising that most existing cultures are not well designed for the purpose that justifies them and are instead promiscuous or random heaps of *ad hoc* custom and legislation.[83] Such a city is a *polis* in name only (as a corpse is a human body in name only) and may in fact be nothing more than a concealed form of despotism, the rule of the master over slaves.

Still, we cannot do without political life, without the process of habituation through customs and the practice in ruling and being ruled that are the necessary supports for human rationality. Since we cannot ever become virtuous by our own individual efforts, the shaping or habituating influence of law and custom is a necessary condition for the development of virtuous or flourishing personalities; it is biologically impossible for us to hope to skip over culture or to replace it with a set of rational principles. Thus music education, which trains us to be pleased by and, whenever we can, to emulate the right kind of exemplary characters or personalities, is the most significant, though not the most pressing, part of political life.[84] But this process of socialization is sufficient only to the extent that the conventions that inform it are in turn informed by a true conception of the human good *and* by a solid grasp of local circumstances. Just as a personality or a way of life may be based on a mistaken perception of what it means to live well, so may a *polis* or culture. Thus there may be a difference between a good human being without qualification and a good citizen of a particular city.[85] In spite of these problems, we need politics, and thus the social scientist's task is not that of fashioning an alternative institution. But because of the ever-imperfect character of political life, it is equally not sufficient simply to interpret the internal significance of the conventions of existing cities; rather, the business of the social scientist is to criticize and offer guidance to these cities in the light of an adequate conception of human flourishing or psychic health, a notion that is surely contra the goals of interpretive social science.

But this task of criticizing and reforming cultures is not so easy. It is a difficult and problematic project in part because of the sense discussed above in which politics is an unintended consequence of activity with other ends in view[86] and partly because of the unique importance of individuality and circumstance in human affairs, a fact that cannot be grasped by a social science that proceeds on the basis of strict empiricist assumptions. This essential variability of solutions to the problems posed by human affairs, which results in the peculiar difficulty and imprecision of social science understood as Aristotelian cultural criticism, has two causes: human diversity and the multifunctional character of political organization. The fact of diversity does not simply mean that some humans are in various ways better and worse than others (which is also true for many other species), but refers to the way in which human individuals differ from one another with respect to inherited potentiality (which may fairly be called genetic differences) much more than do individuals of any other natural species or kind. Humans, unlike members of any other species, can be beasts or gods and much else in between. Individuals are each at their best when their elements constitute a mean, but since psychic capacity for action varies at least as much as somatic aptitude for good health, a good personality must be a mean relative to each individual's capacities and circumstances.[87]

The problems caused by the multi-functionality of political life are even more complex, and more interesting for social science. The essential or definitive purpose of politics—its reason for being—is the development of flourishing or virtuous persons. But this defining activity—living well—depends upon the simultaneous presence of two other activities. Before it is possible for individuals to live well, it is necessary for us both to live and to live together—*eu zēn* is the goal, but this presupposes *zēn* and *suzēn*.[88] Both survival or stability and political integration (a low level of *stasis*, or civil disorder) are only necessary conditions, but they are very necessary. Moreover, the relationship between necessary and constitutive conditions of political well-being cannot be viewed as a temporal sequence; so long as we remain the animals that we are, we will not live forever, and we will continue to inherit both sociable and unsociable impulses.[89]

Political organization and authority are not fully justified unless the laws and customs (*nomoi*) of that organization are a reasonable means toward the development of healthy personalities; but that organization cannot continue to exist unless those same *nomoi* are also reasonable ways of providing for the stability and integration of the *polis*. Individuals lead a single life within a single *polis*, but this life is inevitably an ordering of several different, and sometimes conflicting, needs. Now, if those *nomoi* that were best suited to achieving the constitutive aim of politics (virtuous persons) were also in every case those most appropriate for achieving its simultaneous necessary conditions (peace and integration), then social science could in principle provide precise answers to questions concerning the sorts of *nomoi* that could best serve the ends of the *polis*. Unfortunately, the antecedent of this hypothesis is usually not the case; at the heart of the problem of human affairs sits a tension that does not admit of precise theoretical resolution.[90]

This tension emerges in the discussion of who should be admitted to citizenship in the *polis* in Book III of the *Politics*. Citizens, for Aristotle, are those who actively engage in the deliberations of public life, not simply those whose rights are to be protected by public authority.[91] Given this, the question of the appropriate requirements for citizenship seems at first to pose no serious problem for the theorist. Since the constitutive purpose of politics is virtue, only those who are capable of becoming virtuous should be admitted to citizenship, and so those who spend their lives in labor and commerce cannot be admitted without distorting the purposes of the political order. This is so even though labor and commerce (and military pursuits) are conditions necessary for the existence of the *polis*—"for this is true, that not all those without whom the *polis* would not be should be made citizens."[92]

This is all quite straightforward, but only a few pages farther along we are told that the problem of citizenship has not in fact been resolved. "There is an *aporia* ["perplexity" or "puzzle"] concerning who must be sovereign [*to kurion*] in the city."[93] If the sole business of politics were education in virtue, there would be no *aporia* concerning who should rule; the only reasonable claim to citizenship would be made by those who were most virtuous themselves and most capable of recognizing and encouraging excellence in others. But since the *polis* must also provide stability (not to mention civic harmony), it is also reasonable for property holders and, indeed, all free persons to claim the honor of citizenship, "for free people and possessors of taxable property are necessary, since there could be no *polis* composed entirely of the poor, just as there could be none composed of slaves."[94] There is thus no unequivocal theoretical solution to the central question of who should govern (barring the extremely unlikely limiting case of the appearance of a thoroughly godlike human).[95] A determination will have to be made in each case concerning how far to modify the claims of excellence against the subordinate, though indispensable, requirements of stability and integration. The final judgment in each case as to how the balance must be struck will be the work of the wise citizen (the *phronimos*), who has a solid grasp of the possibilities and dangers of local conditions, and not of the social scientists (although there is no reason why a social scientist might not also happen to be a *phronimos* in a given case). General theory based on considerations of human nature is not at all dangerous or irrelevant to political life (as interpretive social science characteristically claims), since it alone can provide a clear statement of the problems that politics must solve; but an adequate social scientific theory reveals its own limitations in showing that the problems it brings to light do not admit of precise theoretical solutions.[96]

The tension produced by the multi-functionality of political order becomes even more evident in Books IV-VI of the *Politics*, as the discussion shifts from the question of what constitutes the best political order simply to the question of the sources of stability and internal tranquility in *poleis*. In outline, the problem is this: leisure is a necessary condition for education in virtues and for political *praxis* generally, but an absence of leisure appears to be an equally necessary condition for the development of that internal stability without which a *polis* cannot exist. Thus in Book IV Aristotle develops the argument that the most stable (and the least unjust) cultures are those in which leisure and hence genuinely deliberative political activity are at a relatively low level, such as those *poleis* in which farmers and small property holders are the preponderant power.[97] In an argument not unlike Madison's praise of the extended commercial republic in *Federalist* 10, Aristotle contends that people who have to work for a living will be the least ambitious, the least likely to oppress one another, and the most likely to live together in friendship.[98] But as soon as we recall that the constitutive goal of politics is not friendship (or integration) but virtue, we are forced to conclude that the hardworking heroes of Book IV cannot be citizens in the best-ordered city. This recollection occurs in Book VII, where Aristotle remarks that "in the most finely ordered *polis* . . . it is necessary that the citizens live neither a worker's nor a businessman's life . . . nor should they be farmers (since leisure is necessary both for the development of *aretē* and for political *praxis*)."[99]

The conclusions of Books III and VII do not contradict those of Book IV; rather, they point to that tension uniquely characteristic of the subject matter of social science, the political order within which human excellence can be formed. The definitive purpose of that order is to shape our perception of our interest (or of what is good for us) so that we may, as expressed in the Aristotelian formula, live well (*eu zēn*). But this project cannot occur unless several important preconditions are satisfied simultaneously, necessary conditions that are summarized by the formulaic terms "living" (*zēn*) and "living together" (*suzēn*). Those *nomoi* best suited to achieving and maintaining the necessary conditions of political life are often not those best suited to developing virtue in those who live and die within their light. This does not mean that politics is an inherently absurd or paradoxical or tragic activity. It does, however, mean that solutions to political problems—or problems about human lives as such—will always (so long as our nature is what it is) be somehow perplexed and imprecise in a way that distinguishes political questions from all others. What will be the character and limits of that scientific or theoretical inquiry that addresses these questions, if indeed such inquiry is possible?

First of all, it is an extremely difficult inquiry. If social science were simply a matter of interpreting the *nomoi* of a particular *polis,* it would not be difficult, "because it is not hard to have understanding concerning those things which the *nomoi* say." But since the purpose of political inquiry is not merely interpretive understanding—not adding to the archives of human political narratives—but evaluation and criticism of cultures in the light of the possibility of better *nomoi,* it is not so easy. *Nomoi* always seem just to those who love them as their own, but in reality they may or may not be just. As Aristotle points out, "these things [the things which the laws say] are not just things, except contingently [*kata sumbebekos*]." Thus "knowing how just things are done and how they are distributed is a greater work than knowing the healthy things."[100] Moreover, hard as it is to determine what a just ordering is, it is even more difficult to persuade people to be just when they have the power to act unjustly—social science must always contend with a rhetorical problem.[101] Nevertheless, difficult and imprecise as the conclusions of social science must be, they are not for that reason indeterminate or arbitrary; although it is not possible to say what the best *nomoi* are in a way that abstracts from the circumstances (possibilities and limits) of each particular culture or *polis,* it is still the case that there is one way of ordering human affairs that will be best for each (as opposed to every) *polis.*[102] This element of determinacy arises from the fact that it is possible to understand what the natural functions of political activity are and to evaluate existing polities in terms of their success or failure in performing these functions. "Human beings combine for the sake of some interest [*sumpheron*], to provide some of the things necessary for life. And the political community seems to be for the sake of interest . . . and this is what lawgivers aim at, and they say that the just is the common interest [*to koinēi sumpheron*] not with respect to a part of life, but concerning life as a whole."[103] Political activity is neither a self-generating end in itself nor an association for the protection of individual rights; its constitutive function is the development of virtuous personalities or ways of life,[104] and social science can criticize and guide this activity although it can never replace it. One can say that social science is, in a sense, continuous with political activity in that it too addresses the basic question, How should we order our lives? But it addresses it from a more universal perspective—that of the human species' good or goods as such, rather than from the necessarily parochial and culturally specific perspective of us political people—the perspective of what is currently good for ourselves and our polity. Thus from an Aristotelian point of view social science cannot simply be an orderly reconstruction of the perspective of the citizen (as it is for Geertz) nor can it replace that perspective with a perfectly adequate general theory (as in the Hobbesian dream of empiricist social science). The goal of this social science is the improvement of local political discussion, rather than the formulation of universal laws or the spinning of narratives based on what the natives think.

5. The Tasks and Limits of the Social Scientist

What, then, are the appropriate questions for the social scientist to address? At the beginning of Book IV of the *Politics*, Aristotle lists four problems that an adequate social science must address. First, the scientist must have a theoretical understanding (*theōresthai*) of the best regime (or ordering of the *polis*), given the most favorable circumstances with respect to the necessary conditions of stability and integration and individual potentiality. In this category fall the discussions of the theorists of the best regimes found in Book II and Aristotle's own suggestions about the institutions of the best possible city in Book VII. Aristotle characteristically prefaces such discussions by saying that he is about to consider how politics should be organized under conditions that are "according to a prayer" (*kat' euchēn*).[105] Such conditions, which seem to be those in which security and civic friendship can be taken for granted, are objects of prayer not in the sense that they are impossible, but rather because their actual occurrence is a matter of chance, rather than a result of conscious planning.[106] Aristotle's best regime in Book VII is not an unfounded dream, insofar as it rests on an adequate human psychology and in particular on a true conception of what constitutes the most desirable life for a human being.[107] But these institutions cannot be a plan or blueprint for legislators or reformers, since the conditions they presuppose can come about only by the remotest of chances.

The second task described in Book IV is that of knowing what sort of culture will be best under less than optimal or providential conditions, when we cannot take stability and integration, the necessary conditions of political activity, for granted. Aristotle's answer for his Greek world is provided in the discussion of the middle-class polity and of farming democracy in Book IV. Third, the social scientist must be able to say how any culture or regime, no matter how imperfect, can be made more stable and coherent. This forms the subject matter of Book V of the *Politics,* with its lengthy and painstaking discussion of how democracies, oligarchies, and even tyrannies can reduce internal conflict. This section of the *Politics* contains the greatest density of predictive explanations of the kind familiar to empiricist social science, but even here the discussion is informed by the evaluative hypothesis that any regime can be made less unjust by being made more stable, even though a stable regime is not necessarily a good or just political ordering. Finally, the social scientist must know the techniques for bringing existing regimes closer to the best, and so must understand the ways and uses of reforms and persuasion. Aristotle is particularly insistent that these four tasks are part of a single science, rather than that they represent different ways of considering human affairs. This insistence is repeated at the end of the *Nicomachean Ethics,* where it is argued that the social scientist must understand both the purpose or function of political life—*eu zēn*—and the ways in which different cultures implicitly carry out that function.

But what kind of a science is this? Are there any other sciences that can serve as paradigms for social scientific inquiry? Clearly, mathematical physics cannot serve as such a paradigm, since there is too much variance from case to case to permit all cultures to be treated as instances to be subsumed under a set of precise general laws (although many lawlike generalizations about political life are both possible and highly informative). Nor can we look to procedures of literary analysis for guidance; social science must indeed "read" the meaning of regimes or cultures, but it cannot take the coherence of their *nomoi* for granted nor assume that every relatively coherent *polis* (such as Sparta) is for that reason, or simply because it understands itself as such, a good *polis.* Yet social science is not *sui generis;* Aristotle has continual recourse to one other science in his discussions of what constitutes an adequate social science and in his arguments about the relation of that science to other kinds of thought. This is the science of medicine.[108] In the first instance, the physician, like the social scientist, must have experience of particular individuals, as well as general causal knowledge.[109] Like medicine (or physical training), an adequate social science requires both an experience of cases and general theory; neither element can satisfactorily replace or be reduced to the other. But why is this true of social science? And why, if it is true, is Aristotle compelled to rely so heavily on medical analogies to illustrate correct social scientific procedure, rather than arguing more directly? I think the best way of approaching these questions is by considering the four characteristics that Aristotle claims (in the first two books of the *Nicomachean Ethics*) distinguish social science from other sciences: the relative imprecision of social science, its dependence on the proper upbringing or habituation of the practitioner, its dependence on his or her maturity, and the fact that social science (unlike other sciences and unlike Aristotle's most frequent characterizations of political activity itself) is not an end in itself, but is an inquiry undertaken for the sake of acting and living well.

The truth or falsehood of all these methodological contentions depends on the nature of the subject matter that defines the project of the social scientist: human conventions and cultures understood and evaluated as attempts to solve the problem that is unique to human beings, the problem of how to live well under a particular set of circumstances. Given the nature of its subject, social science is bound by certain restrictions (imprecision and instrumentality) and dependent upon certain external presuppositions (the good upbringing and maturity of the social scientist).

In Book I of the *Ethics,* Aristotle states that the precision of any art or science depends on its underlying subject matter and that social science is particularly imprecise. "The noble and just things, which *politikē* studies," he says, "have so much variation and irregularity that they seem to be by *nomos* alone and not by *phusis.*"[110] In Book II he amplifies this point, comparing social science to medicine, as follows: "In matters concerning *praxis* and the things that are in our interest [*ta sumpheronta*], there is nothing fixed, just as in matters of health."[111] The good social scientist must know two different kinds of things, both of which can be known, but neither of which (because of the differences among individuals and cultures) can be known precisely. The first sort of thing to be known is the human good, which is the *telos* or function of both individual and *polis.*"[112] This can be expressed variously as flourishing (*eudaimonia*) or as that which is in our interest (*to sumpheron*) or as excellence or virtue (*aretē*). The human good can be known in general[113]—it is a deliberative life, the kind of *hexis* or personality called the mean—but it cannot be known precisely for each individual, given the diversity of biologically and culturally inherited problems we each must solve simultaneously. The second kind of thing to be known (which is logically dependent on the first) are the just things—that is, those laws and customs that tend to promote the human good. Now those *nomoi* that might be just in one place—say, Athens—might not necessarily be just in another—say, the United States. Nevertheless, for each place there will be one set of *nomoi* that are most just relative to human interest and to the peculiar circumstances of that place and time. In the discussion of justice in Book V of the *Ethics,* Aristotle responds to the doubt he earlier raised about whether justice can be said to be by nature (whether *nomoi* can be criticized and evaluated in terms of some determinate natural standard) in the following way: "Among us, some things are by nature even though they are changeable."[114] Social *science* is possible, but its most important findings cannot be presented and transmitted as a set of fixed and precise rules and precepts, as can those of sciences like mathematics and, to some degree, medicine.[115]

The requirement that a good upbringing is a necessary (though not sufficient) condition for the development of a competent social scientist is likely to strike us as hopelessly pre-scientific. But Aristotle is not claiming that only members of the upper class can be good social scientists. The argument is that in order to get a preliminary grasp of the central concept of social science, the human good, it is necessary to have been habituated or socialized in such a way that we are inclined to perceive that there is a human good that is somehow different from our own spontaneous pleasures and pains. This is simply another way of stating the claim that human beings are biologically or genotypically unique in not spontaneously perceiving their own good, their interest in a well-organized life. So in Book I of the *Ethics* Aristotle says, "Thus it is necessary to have been brought up nobly in order to understand sufficiently the noble things, the just things, and the political things as a whole."[116] The indispensable starting point of social science is a sense of the difference between a life (*bios*) or personality (*hexis*) that is flourishing and one that is not. Since, as we have seen, the human good or human interest is so composite and varied that knowledge of it cannot be transmitted by a set of precise theoretical precepts, it cannot be perceived at all except by an observer whose experience and *hexis* are relatively healthy. If poorly brought up, the observer will either have no coherent sense of the human good or be led to misperceive that good by a certain unsoundness of *hexis*.[117] This is not a problem for those sciences that are sufficiently simple to allow teaching by precept, such as arithmetic and geometry. The secondary element of social science, predictive knowledge of what sorts of *nomoi* are likely to produce what sorts of consequences, can to a certain extent be transmitted by precepts or textbooks.[118] But such textbooks (or empirical studies) cannot be adequately employed unless those who study them have (or are) a good *hexis*, since without this basis they are incapable of making the relevant critical determinations. As Aristotle puts it, "those who go through such things without [the appropriate] *hexis* cannot judge them nobly."[119]

In Book I of the *Nicomachean Ethics* (1095a2–13), Aristotle presents two related reasons for thinking that youths (*hoi neoi*) are not prepared to study social science: lack of experience and the tendency to be guided by passive emotion (*pathos*) rather than by active logos. Aristotle explains, "For this reason a youth is not a suitable student of social science, for he is inexperienced in the actions [*apeiros praxeōn*] of life, and the arguments [*logoi*] are drawn from and concern actions. . . . And it makes no difference whether he is young in age or in habits, for his defect is not a matter of time but comes from living according to emotion [*to kata pathos zēn*] and pursuing everything in this way." In order to have a preliminary teleological understanding of human *praxis* as an attempt to solve the human problem of how to live well or according to our interest under particular circumstances—as opposed to, say, *praxis* as a way of maximizing pleasures or as reproductive strategy—experience is required. This experience cannot be replaced by a textbook discussion of the nature of *praxis*, such as is provided by Book I of the *Ethics* and Book VII of the *Politics*.[120] Furthermore, it is an experience of a complex sort, since it cannot be had by those who interpret their own and others' doings through the lenses of passion or emotion. This experience of the human interest, and of the consequent distinction between living and living well, is something that occurs only through the generalizing operations of *logos* (recall *Politics* I.2 1253a14–15), rather than through the senses. If we are incapable of seeing our actions and those of others as subject to criticism and justification, viewing them instead in the context of our passionate likes and dislikes, we will be constitutionally (in other words, because of our *hexis*) incapable of forming an idea of human interest based on our experience of humans *qua* humans, rather than as friends or enemies, good guys or bad guys, which from an Aristotelian point of view is the typically immature way of interpreting the human world.

Thus our experience of the human good or interest is an experience of the possible existence of a fact or a thing, rather than an experience of a relationship.[121] This possible existence is the starting point or *archē* of social science and as such is not something that can be demonstrated or derived from prior principles of that science or from any other science. Aristotle's psychology can never *prove* either that there is a human interest (or a final cause that defines human being) or that the substance of this interest is a deliberative life supported by a variety of moral virtues. What it can do is seek to make our understanding of this interest more precise and secure by setting forth the human capacities and problems that might render such a conception of the human good intelligible.

The human good is thus both a phenomenon and also not immediately visible to the senses, but it is important to note here that it is by no means the only fact that has these characteristics in the Aristotelian universe and that, as a result, maturity and experience are *not* uniquely required of social scientists. That the world of sensible substance is organized into natural kinds (human, horse, and so on) is a fact like that,[122] as is the fact that the same thing cannot both be and not be at the same time.[123] So it makes sense for Aristotle to say that since the *archai* of first philosophy and natural science, like those of social science, come from experience, the young cannot become philosophers or natural scientists, although they can be first-class mathematicians or geometers "because the principles of mathematics come from abstraction, but the principles [*archai*] of the others [natural science, social science, and first philosophy or metaphysics] come from experience."[124]

Thus maturity, like a good upbringing, is a necessary condition for social science, but it is of course not sufficient; else social *science* would be otiose. Nor is the experience of the human good in any way mystical or ineffable; the point, however, is that before the human good can be expressed in theoretical terms (such as Aristotle's theory of the *psuchē* and his account of *praxis* in terms of *orexis* and *prohairesis*) it must be known in some pre-theoretical and relatively inarticulate way. Since theory presupposes this pre-understanding, it cannot establish its own starting point in precise theoretical terms. This is the second aspect of the rhetorical problem, which is inseparable from social science understood in an Aristotelian way (the first being the problem of political rhetoric, of how to intervene in political debate): in order to persuade or remind us of the existence of human interest as a fact, Aristotle has continual recourse to medical analogies, suggesting that just as we all acknowledge the health of the body to be a fact, so we should acknowledge something like "health" to exist concerning human life as a whole.[125] Of course, these analogies prove or demonstrate nothing to someone who is not already disposed to grant the contention that human flourishing or interest exists independently of subjective preferences, but then no such proof is possible—any more than one can prove the law of the excluded middle or that natures exist. Rather, these analogies are metaphoric attempts to render the project of social science plausible by suggesting that social science is to the invisible health of the person as a whole what medicine is to the relatively visible health of our relatively visible bodies. If the subject matter of social science were clearer and less disputed, we could dispense with such analogies; but as Aristotle says after one such comparison, "it is necessary to use visible witnesses for invisible things."[126]

The medical analogy also serves to indicate a secondary sense in which experience is a necessary component of social science. Just as the point of medical science is to cure particular individuals,[127] so the point of social science is to offer criticism of and guidance for particular regimes and cultures, or perhaps more directly to improve the quality of our conversation about our local political life. Some general theoretical grasp of what constitutes health or what constitutes a good *polis* may well be one of the necessary conditions for an adequate pursuit of these goals; however, experience of the particular patient or culture is still required in addition to theory, because the variance among human individuals prevents particular persons or groups of persons from being treated as instances of general laws, as the empiricist model requires. This notion of the unique variability that pertains to human things does not, as we have seen, rest on any romantic notion of individual or cultural creativity; rather, it is perfectly explicable, as far as social science is concerned, in terms of human diversity, the complexity of human need, and the consequent natural multi-functionality of political order.

Perhaps the best-known of Aristotle's statements about the nature of social science, and the one that is frequently cited as evidence of his affinity with the interpretive approach, is his claim that the purpose of studying *politikē* is not the acquisition of scientific theory, but the development of virtue or excellence; in his own words, "the present study is not for the sake of theory, as are the others (for we are not inquiring in order to see what virtue is, but in order to become good individuals, since otherwise there would be no profit in it)."[128] But why would there be "no profit" in a theory of human interest and virtue independently of the consequences of that theory for virtuous *praxis*? It surely cannot be due to any supposed superiority or priority of *praxis* to *theōria*; that much is clear from the surprisingly strong defense of the theoretical or contemplative life that is present in both Book X of the *Ethics* and Book VII of the *Politics.*[129] Then why is it the case that the science of human affairs, unlike other sciences, cannot be considered an end in itself?

The first Aristotelian thought that supports this conclusion about the unique instrumentality of social science is his judgment, strongly at odds with the interpretivist identification of humanity and transcendence, that human beings are not the best things in the cosmos; consequently, social science is not the appropriate field for reflection concerning the primary instance of being. "It would be strange," Aristotle remarks, "if someone thought that social science [*politikē*] or practical wisdom [*phronēsis*] were the most serious [*spoudaiōtatē*] [forms of knowledge], since human beings are not the best of the things in the cosmos."[130] It thus appears that the serious theorist or scientist will not be concerned with human affairs but will look instead to the unchanging entities that in some sense inform all the rest. But strangely enough, it appears that the study of beasts, who are farther from the divine things than are humans, is an end in itself; Aristotle does not say that we should study the parts and lives of animals for the sake of improving agriculture or pharmacology. In the introduction to his *Parts of Animals,* he concedes that animals are indeed very far from the unchanging things, but he adds this in defense of natural philosophy: "Nevertheless, for theory, the nature that fashions animals provides immeasurable pleasures for those who are able to distinguish causes and are philosophers by nature."[131]

Theoretical activity is the constitutive cause of its own being, a self-justifying *telos,* insofar as it provides access to the structure of things, to the articulation of final-formal and efficient-material causality. But human affairs are not a good field of inquiry for such theoretical activity because of their implicit and natural variability and complexity and the resulting way in which the actualization of human potentiality is uniquely problematic. Human affairs are thus peculiarly resistant to the theoretical project and to that desire for understanding that the first sentence of the *Metaphysics* tells us is ours by nature (in other words, by biological inheritance), though not on the romantic ground of a profound separation between humanity and nature.

Thus social science is set apart from the other sciences in that it is not a self-sufficient theoretical activity. Its function is that of an instrumental condition of practical wisdom (*phronēsis*), the excellence at deliberating about particular choices that Aristotle sees as the way to the best of goods for human beings among the practical things.[132] Theorizing about the human things is perhaps best placed as an aspect of practical wisdom, as an inclination toward the universal that can clarify deliberation about our particular lives both by enriching our political vocabulary and by suggesting possible alternatives to political life as such. Aristotle himself provides only one very compressed statement about the relationship between *phronēsis* and *politikē*; he says that they are the same *hexis* but that their essence or being (*to einai autais*) is not the same.[133] The deliberative *hexis*, like nearly everything human, is composite; its primary and constitutive element, *phronēsis*, looks squarely at the particular context at hand, while social science, its complement, looks beyond for the sake of a more adequate particular choice.

The other scientific activity that is similar to social science in this respect is, of course, medicine.[134] The critical judgments of the social scientist vary from case to case just as the judgments of the physician vary from patient to patient, in a way in which the judgments of the natural scientist do not vary from frog to frog or the metaphysician's judgments from unmoved mover to unmoved mover. And yet while social science is in this way analogous to medicine, it is by no means identical with it. The best *hexis* under the circumstances and the *nomoi* that are most likely to encourage and maintain it are the psychic and political analogies of the best somatic *diathesis* and consequent medical treatment. They are analogous for Aristotle in that they both can be expressed as a mean, a certain optimal ordering of the elements of the thing being ordered, whether that thing is a person or simply a body (a subordinate aspect of a person). But the mean that social science has in view is much more difficult to discern than the medical mean, and it is even more subject to case-by-case variation. While we may say that social science as Aristotle understands it is a sort of psychiatry, it by no means follows that psychiatry understood in this way is simply a specialized branch of medicine.[135]

Aristotelian social science is novel in our time in the sense that it cannot be identified with either of the two contemporary approaches to understanding human affairs. But my reconstruction of that social science introduces no exotic new program of social inquiry. Rather, what I think is most valuable about the Aristotelian approach is that it can give us a new way of thinking about human affairs, a way that permits a conversation among various forms of inquiry by freeing social science from its present pervasive concern with the supposed dichotomy between nature and uniqueness and between science and practical discourse. Human beings are both natural and unique, and only the broadest social science, one that is profoundly uneasy about the current academic divisions between moral philosophy, political theory, and the particular social sciences, can continue to understand the ways in which this is so.

While Aristotelian social science yields no rules of method, it is just as surely not a blanket endorsement of everything that claims to be social science. The structure of the Aristotelian approach is a set of questions that define the task of the social scientist. These questions have to do with how, given our specific nature and the various environmental circumstances we confront, particular communities can best solve the three great problems that as simultaneous problems are unique to the experience of human beings: living, living together, and living well. Such a social science may improve political activity, but not by restating or formalizing it. The questions it poses are indeed the same as those raised by prescientific political life. But such a social science may well suggest very different answers to those questions, or perhaps a different attitude about their significance. Recalling Aristotle's remarks about the rank of human beings in the overall scheme of things, we might conclude that the best work of social science would be the development of clearer-headed and less vehemently serious citizens.

Notes

1. *Pol.* VII.1 1323a36–38, I.13 1260a12–13. The claim that democrats tend to identify freedom with unlimited power (V.9 1310a31–32) or that in barbarian cultures women are treated as slaves (I.2 1252b5–6) might also be cited.

2. *Pol.* IV.11 1296a9–10. Another such proposition is that equalizing property will not result in a decrease in some classes of crime (II.7 1267a2–17).

3. *Pol.* III.9 1280b8–1281a3. Or one could cite the proposition that the activities of leisure are more determinative of the quality of a human life than are the activities of occupation and war (VII.14 1333a30–1333b5).

4. *Pol.* VII.14 1333b5–1334a10.

5. Geertz, "From the Native's Point of View: On the Nature of Anthropological Understanding."

6. For its use as a modifier of *technē*, see *Pol.* IV.1 1288b10–1289a25; of *epistēmē*, *NE* I.2 1094a24–29; of *philosophia*, *Pol.* III.12 1282b23.

7. Aristotle, *The Politics*, trans. Lord, p. 7.

8. Runciman, *The Methodology of Social Theory*, p. 221.

9. T. S. Kuhn, *The Structure of Scientific Revolutions*, p. 41.

10. See Mayr, *The Growth of Biological Thought: Diversity, Evolution, and Inheritance*, chap. 2.

11. Cohen, *The Birth of a New Physics*.

12. Mayr's point about the distorting character of reduction in biology is worth noting. He remarks, "One can translate these qualitative aspects into quantitative ones, but one loses thereby the real significance of the respective biological phenomena, exactly as if one would describe a painting of Rembrandt in terms of the wave lengths of the prevailing color reflected by each square millimeter of the painting" (*Growth of Biological Thought*, p. 54). As Mayr says, the case for reductionism in modern biology has been immeasurably strengthened by the widespread acceptance of the false view that the only possible alternative to reductionism was vitalism.

13. T. Hobbes, *Leviathan*, chap. 4, par. b.

14. See Mayr, *Growth of Biological Thought*, pp. 21–82; and Eldredge, *Time Frames: The Rethinking of Darwinian Evolution and the Theory of Punctuated Equilibrium*, pp. 98–218. For an account of a parallel development in social science and moral philosophy—the rejection of Aristotelian practical wisdom and casuistry and the triumph of the "tyranny of principles"—see Jensen and Toulmin, *The Abuse of Casuistry: A History of Moral Reasoning*.

15. Rousseau, *Discourse on the Origin of Inequality*, p. 114.

16. On the centrality of "historicity" in the development of interpretive social science, see H.-G. Gadamer, "The Problem of Historical Consciousness."

17. Geertz, *Local Knowledge*, p. 3. Nietzsche provides the link between Diltheyan historical romanticism and the more recent claims for the primacy of interpretation without any historical ground. See *Beyond Good and Evil*, part 1, par. 22.

18. Geertz, *Negara: The Theater State in Nineteenth-Century Bali*, p. 103.

19. Geertz, "Deep Play: Notes on the Balinese Cockfight," p. 223.

20. Geertz, *The Interpretation of Cultures*, p. 10.

21. Geertz, "From the Native's Point of View," p. 228.

22. Geertz, *Interpretation of Cultures*, p. 362.

23. Ibid., 230–31.

24. Gadamer, *Truth and Method*, p. 280. Gadamer's criticism of Dilthey seems to apply fully to Geertz.

25. Gadamer, "The Problem of Historical Consciousness," p. 108.

26. Geertz, "Anti-Anti Relativism."

27. Gadamer, *Truth and Method*, pp. 278–89.

28. Gadamer appears to deny this, maintaining: "Aristotle sees ethos as differing from phusis in that it is a sphere in which the laws of nature do not operate, yet not a sphere of lawlessness, but of human institutions and human attitudes that can be changed and have the quality of rules only to a limited degree" (*Truth and Method*, p. 279). My argument is that Aristotle's natural science does not aim at the discovery of natural laws and that he is thus able to overcome the reduction/transcendence dilemma.

29. *Pol.* I.1 1252a1–4; *NE* I.1 1094a1–2.

30. *Part. An.* II.13 657a31–b3; *Mot. An.* 11 703b5–6; *Gen. An.* V.1 778a32ff.; cf. V.1 778b11ff.

31. *NE* III.1 1110a14–17.

32. *De An.* III.10 433a32–33. This seemingly different account of the origin of voluntary motion is given in *Metaphysics* XII.7 1072a29–30: "We desire [an object] because it seems [good], rather than it seems because we desire; for thinking [*noēsis*] is the *archē*." These passages can be reconciled if we bear in mind that "desire" and "opinion" are both abstractions; when it comes to action, they are both aspects of a single process, a process that is common to all animals.

33. *Mot. An.* 5 700b15–18.

34. *De An.* III.10 433a15–b1.

35. Ibid. I.3 406b24–25.

36. Ibid. I.1 402a6–7, I.4 408b25–27. Plants are also living things insofar as they are capable of taking in food from the environment (II.2 413a25–28).

37. *De An.* II.1 412a13–15.

38. Ibid. II.1 412a15–21. For Aristotle, "the soul is just the functional organization of the entire living body" (Nussbaum, "Shame, Separateness, and Political Unity: Aristotle's Criticism of Plato," p. 415). This is another instance of the way Aristotle avoids an unfortunate Cartesian dualism. See also Wilkes, *Physicalism,* pp.114–37. Because "soul" in current usage implies the separation of body and soul, it might be best to avoid translating Aristotle's *psuchē* altogether.

39. *De An.* II.1 412b18–19.

40. Ibid. I.2 404a27–31. The problem with Democritus' view is that it cannot account for our experience of making errors. This is fundamentally the same criticism that Socrates makes of Protagoras' *anthrōpos metron* [man is the measure] in the *Theaetetus.* This would be the core of the Platonic-Aristotelian critique of the prevailing relativisms of modern social science, whether individual (the economist's "consumer sovereignty") or communal (the anthropologist's "cultural relativism").

41. *NE* VI.2 1139a17–20.

42. Ibid. VI.2 1139a35–36.

43. Here Aristotle parts company decisively with any hermeneutic or interpretive social science.

44. *De An.* III.10 433b29.

45. While critical of Plato's essentialism here, Aristotle at the same time clearly rejects a nominalist interpretation of the term "good." "Good" is for him an equivocal term whose instances may be related to one another by being derived from one core meaning, by pointing to the same thing, or by analogy (*NE* I.6 1096b26–29). Burnet, *The Ethics of Aristotle,* 29n., suggests that the last proposal (analogy) represents Aristotle's own view. But on the basis of *Metaphysics* 1075a18–23, it seems that "good" is a *pros hen* equivocal. At any rate, Aristotle's opposition to Plato is not nominalist or conventionalist, and so cannot provide grist for the interpretivist mill.

46. *NE* X.5 1176a3–5.

47. *Part. An.* I.1 639b15–16.

48. *Met.* IX.8 1050a22: "For the *ergon* is the *telos,* and the *energeia* the *ergon.*"

49. *De An.* III.3 427b1–2, III.10 433a26–27.

50. *NE* X.5 1176a5. What we call learning and Aristotle calls *ethos* or habit plays a relatively small role in establishing the preference schedules of nonhuman animals.

51. *NE* X.5 1176a10–12.

52. *Pol.* VII.13 1332b3–5.

53. Ibid. III.9 1280a35. For an excellent Aristotelian discussion of the differences between *prohairesis* or choice and mere voluntary action, see Sokolowski, *Moral Action: A Phenomenological Study*, pp. 11–21.

54. *Pol.* I.2 1253a32–34.

55. *Hist. An.* I.1 487b. On the concept of "dualizing," see C. Lord, "Aristotle's Anthropology," pp. 55–56.

56. *Pol.* I.2 1253a29–31.

57. *Rhet.* II.4 1380b35–1381a1.

58. *NE* VIII.12 1162a16–19. With regard to the phrase "more necessary," "necessity" for Aristotle *is* equivocal since "cause" is equivocal. Necessity may refer either to efficient-material causality or to final-formal causality, or it may be used as the antithesis of "natural." Four meanings of "necessity" are given in *Metaphysics* V.5 1015a20–b6. Three types of necessity are distinguished in the first book of *Parts of Animals* (I.1 639b21–640a9, I.1 642a32–b4): simple necessity, characteristic of eternal things; teleological or hypothetical necessity, characteristic of natural things and of the products of art; and elemental necessity, characteristic of the parts of natural things (earth, air, fire, water).

59. *Pol.* III.9 1280b39–1281a4.

60. Ibid., I.2 1253a7–38.

61. Pocock, *The Machiavellian Moment*, p. 550. Pocock's view relies on Hannah Arendt, who is the modern founder of this reading of Aristotle.

62. Nussbaum, *The Fragility of Goodness*, pp. 345–53.

63. Ibid. pp. 373–77.

64. Williams, *Ethics and the Limits of Philosophy*, p. 44. This reading suggests the kind of criticism of Aristotle's "metaphysical biology" made by A. MacIntyre, *After Virtue: A Study in Moral Theory*.

65. Nussbaum's discussion of this view in *The Fragility of Goodness* claims that, for Aristotle, the basic truth about ethical matters is to be sought in "shared human beliefs" (p. 349) or "deeper appearances" (p. 321) rather than in his biological conception of human nature. This would seem to have the questionable advantage of reconciling Aristotle to MacIntyre, in language recalling a similar move to embrace contextualism by Rawls, "Justice as Fairness: Political Not Metaphysical."

66. Ambler, "Aristotle's Understanding of the Naturalness of the City," makes a strong case for treating the first book of the *Politics* as both asserting and calling into question the naturalness of the polity. Part of his argument is the claim that the polis springs more from the "sense (*aisthēsis*) of the good, bad, just, and unjust, than from his ability to explain them in speech" (p. 172).

67. *Pol.* VI.4 1319b31–32.

68. Ibid. I.2 1253a31–33.

69. See Clark, *Aristotle's Man: Speculations on Aristotelian Anthropology*, pp. 84–97. The human good is similarly figured as a mean in several of the later Platonic dialogues: *Statesman* 283E–284C; *Philebus* 66A.

70. Thus it is called a "first actuality" in *De Anima* II.5 417a21–b16.

71. Some Platonic instances are *Theaetetus* 153B and 197B and *Sophist* 247A.

72. Aristotle, *Nicomachean Ethics*, T. Irwin, trans., second edn., p. 349. The term *hexis* is used less frequently in the *Politics*, but at II.6 1265a35 Aristotle speaks of *hexeis hairetai* ("choiceworthy dispositions," in Lord's translation) and at VII.15 1334b19 he uses the word to refer to actualizations of different parts of the soul.

73. *Cat.* 8 8b25–9a13.

74. A blending of hot and cold expressed as a body temperature of 98.6° F indicates a healthy *hexis* as far as the nonvoluntary health of human beings is concerned.

75. *Met.* V.20 1022b4–14.

76. See note 38 above.

77. *Pol.* I.5 1254a39–b4.

78. See Boorse, "Health as a Theoretical Concept."

79. *NE* V.9 1137a13–14.

80. I am using "culture" here as an equivalent of Aristotle's *politeia.* The *politeia* is the form or order (*taxis*) of a given polis (*Pol.* III.1 1274b38–39, III.3 1276b5–10). A *polis* is its particular *politeia* (as a particular game is baseball), and when the *politeia* changes, the *polis* changes, even if people, buildings, and so on remain the same. The best discussion of the meaning of *politeia* is found in Strauss, *Natural Right and History,* pp.135–38. Given present English usage, I think "culture" approximates *politeia* more closely than "regime," but since neither term evokes *politeia* with perfect accuracy, I will use them interchangeably in the text.

81. *Pol.* VII.17 1337a1–3.

82. Ibid. I.4 1253b29–30.

83. Ibid. VII.2 1324b5–6.

84. Ibid. VIII.1 1337a11–12.

85. Ibid. III.4 1276b16ff.

86. It is important to distinguish Aristotle's view from the interpretive conception of human beings as "incomplete animals." As can be seen in the following excerpt from Geertz, *Interpretation of Cultures,* p. 218, such a position derives largely, though perhaps unconsciously, from nineteenth-century German philosophy:

> The tool-making, laughing, or lying animal, man, is also the incomplete—or more accurately, self-completing-animal. The agent of his own realization, he creates out of his general capacity for the construction of symbolic models the specific capabilities that define him. Or—to return at last to our subject—it is through the construction of ideologies, schematic images of social order, that man makes himself for better or worse a political animal.

For Aristotle—as opposed to Geertz and Hegel—*all* animals are the agents of their own realization, and human beings are political animals prior to any human activity. Politics is one of our specific natural potentials, not the royal road out of nature.

87. *NE* II.6 1106b36–1107a1.

88. *Pol.* III.9 1280b30–35.

89. There is no standard Aristotelian formula for expressing this distinction between necessary and constitutive causes or conditions. One clear formulation of the distinction is presented as that between *sunaition* (co-cause or accessory) and *aition*

(cause as such) in *De Anima* II.4 416a12–15: heat is the *sunaition* of growth, while soul is the *aition*. Plato uses the same terms for the same distinction in *Statesman* 281D–E.

90. Leo Strauss presents this tension in these terms: "The political problem consists in reconciling the requirement for wisdom with the requirement for consent" (*Natural Right and History*, p.141). For an interesting, quite Aristotelian account of contemporary American political and judicial deliberation in these terms, see Kronman, "Alexander Bickel's Philosophy of Prudence."

91. Citizenship means participating or sharing (*metechein*) in public offices and decisions (*Pol.* III.1 1275a23–24) and not simply being entitled to protection against unjust acts (III.9 1280b11–13).

92. *Pol.* III.5 1278a2–3. The argument may be stated as follows: (a) *poleis* will be well governed only to the extent that citizens (governors) have or are virtuous *hexeis*; otherwise, the resources of the *polis* are likely to be used for the wrong purposes; (b) leisure is needed for the development of a virtuous *hexis*, and hence for the development of the capacity to act politically; it is not sufficient, but someone whose life by chance or choice is devoted to work or commerce cannot be a good citizen; (c) such unleisurely ways of life are, however, absolutely necessary for the survival of the *polis*—even as they tend to distort political justice; hence, (d) some lives (or careers) that are necessary for *poleis* should as far as possible be excluded from active citizenship if the *polis* is not to be twisted by the pressing claims of private or economic interest.

93. *Pol.* III.10 1281a11.

94. Ibid. III.12 1283a17–19.

95. *Pol.* VII.14 1332b24. If such a person does appear, the only reasonable conclusion is that politics—*nomoi* and the rotation in office—will no longer be necessary for the development of virtue (III.13 1284b30–34). Even then, Aristotle suggests that it would be safer to allow the laws of the *polis* to rule, since "passion perverts even the best when they are ruling" (III.16 1287a31–32). But the possibility itself is so unlikely as to be negligible; even ordinarily virtuous people are a small minority (V.1 1302a1–2).

96. Plato takes up the question of the relationship of the subject matter of different sciences and their relative precision in several dialogues. His conclusion appears to be compatible with Aristotle's: the precision of any science is relative to the intelligibility of the mean that defines that science; see *Statesman* 283D–284D; *Philebus* 55E–56E.

97. *Pol.* IV.6 1292b25–29 and IV.11 1295a25–31.

98. Ibid. IV.11 1295a25ff.; see also VI.4 1318b6–17.

99. Ibid. VII.9 1328b37–1329a2.

100. *NE* V.9 1137a10–14.

101. *Pol.* VI.3 1318b1–5.

102. *NE* V.7 1135a5. This passage has received several readings. I adopt the one defended by J. J. Mulhern, "*Mia Monon Pantachou Kata Physin He Ariste*." As Strauss, *Natural Right and History*, p. 159, argues, for Aristotle, natural right or law resides ultimately in particular decisions, and not in universal rules or principles. Gadamer states the consequences of this: "The idea of natural law has, for Aristotle, only a critical function. No dogmatic use can be made of it, i.e., we cannot invest particular laws with the dignity and inviolability of natural law" (*Truth and Method*, p. 285).

103. *NE* VIII.9 1160a9–23.

104. *Pol.* III.9 1280b6–12.

105. Ibid. I.13 1260a29, IV.1 1288b23, IV.11 1295a29, VII.4 1325b36.

106. Ibid. VII.12 1331b22.

107. Ibid. VII.1 1323a13–15.

108. Lloyd, "The Role of Medical and Biological Analogies in Aristotle's Ethics," and Jaeger, "Aristotle's Use of Medicine as Model of Method in His Ethics," collect and discuss the relevant citations. Clark's analysis (*Aristotle's Man*, pp. 84–97) is especially provocative.

109. *Met.* I.1 981a12–29.

110. *NE* I.3 1094b14–16.

111. Ibid. II.2 1104a3–5.

112. Ibid. I.2 1094b6–7.

113. Social science is imprecise relative to some other sciences, but it is nevertheless determinate. That is, while its subject matter cannot be precisely defined, it does admit of definition in outline: the human good has limits or boundaries and is hence definable. See *NE* II.6 1106b30.

114. *NE* V.7 1134b29–30.

115. Ibid. II.2 1104a7–9; *Pol.* III.16 1287a33–35.

116. *NE* II.2 1104a7–9. Irwin's translation of the passage is a good commentary: "This is why we need to have been brought up in fine habits, if we are to be adequate students of what is fine and just, and of political questions generally."

117. *NE* X.9 1181b9–11.

118. This was the purpose of the Aristotelian collection of regimes or "constitutions," of which the *Constitution of the Athenians*, delineating the movement from moderate to extreme democracy in Athens, survives.

119. *NE* X.9 1181b9–11.

120. For a critical discussion of the attempt by modern empirical social science to escape the maturity requirement, see Bellah, "The Ethical Aims of Social Inquiry."

121. At *Met.* IX.10 1051b22ff., Aristotle distinguishes between taking hold of a substance or entity and asserting a relationship to be the case. Aristotle's conception of experience (*empeiria*) is different from the notion of sensation. To have an experience of a thing means to have many connected memories of the same thing. Thus humans are more capable of experiencing things than beasts, though all animals are capable of sensation. See *Met.* I.1 980b28–981a3.

122. *Phys.* II.1 193a1–6. For Aristotle, as for Newton and Darwin, there is no such thing as an active universal *phusis*, except as a metaphor. This requires argument, however, especially in the light of Aristotle's occasional personification of nature as a craftsman in the statement that "nature makes nothing in vain" (e.g., *Pol.* I.8 1256b21). A good case against ascribing universal teleology to the Aristotelian conception of nature is made by Nussbaum, *Aristotle's* De Motu Animalium: *Text with Translation, Commentary, and Interpretive Essays*, pp. 95–99.

123. *Met.* IV.6 1011a8–13. This same book contains Aristotle's best joke, concerning the problems of talking to people who insist on demonstrations of the indemonstrable (IV.4 1006a11–15).

124. *NE* VI.8 1142a12–19.

125. This is much like Socrates' analogical argument for the existence of human *aretē* at the end of *Republic* I.

126. *NE* II.2 1104a13–14. Aristotle's position concerning the role of metaphor in philosophy is complex. See Arnhart, *Aristotle on Practical Reasoning,* pp. 172–76. Aristotle is sometimes critical of metaphoric speech, as in his discussion of the Platonic notion of participation. Yet he says that analogical metaphors are naturally pleasing as ways of helping us learn about something through seeing its resemblance to something else that is more *clearly* known to us (*Rhet.* III.10 1410b). As Arnhart remarks, this movement may plausibly be said to be, for Aristotle, "the underlying structure of all human reasoning" (p. 175). See also Gadamer, *Truth and Method,* pp. 388–89. At any rate, it would be difficult to imagine Aristotle doing without several of his key analogical metaphors: the physician for the social scientist, nature as creative god for self-sustaining natures in his natural science, language for being in first philosophy, the eye for the soul in *De Anima,* the doctor doctoring himself for nature causing itself in *Physics.* By contrast, empiricist social science aims at being perfectly nonmetaphorical, perhaps in the Hobbesian way, in which "metaphors and senseless and ambiguous words are like *ignes fatui*; and reasoning upon them is wandering amongst innumerable absurdities" (*Leviathan,* chap. 5). At the other extreme, a fully interpretive social science might view metaphor as a way of building a human world separate from natural actuality, without any reference to independent reality.

127. *Met.* I.1 981a12–29.

128. *NE* II.2 1103b26–29.

129. Ibid. X.7 1177a12ff.; *Pol.* VIII.1 1337a27–30.

130. *NE* VI.7 1141a20–22. The word *spoudaios* is a difficult and interesting one; it can mean "eager" or simply "excellent," as well as "serious." As Irwin (Aristotle, *Nicomachean Ethics,* p. 400) notes: "Aristotle regularly uses the term as the adjective corresponding to "virtue," and hence as equivalent to "good." But that sense of the term is clearly different from its meaning in the famous definition of tragedy as the imitation of a *spoudaia praxis* in *Poetics* 6 1449b24.

131. *Part. An.* I.5 645a7–11.

132. *NE* VI.7 1141b13–14. The practical things (*ta prakta*) here may or may not include theory; theorizing is universal and practice not, but for human beings theorizing is surely, for Aristotle, a *praxis*; see *Pol.* VII.3 1325b21.

133. *NE* VI.8 1141b23–24.

134. Ibid. II.2 1104a9; *Met.* I.1 981a18–20.

135. Plato's discussion *of politikē* in the *Gorgias* and the *Laws* also makes systematic use of the medical analogy, but with rather different results. In the *Gorgias* (464B), *politikē* is said to be to the soul what gymnastic and medicine are to the body, namely, the true arts (*technai*) concerned with each. These are contrasted with the sham arts, like sophistry and cosmetics, the difference being that the sham arts are not based on causal understanding but on mere experience (*empeiria*). Hence philosophy is identical with *politikē,* and Socrates is the only true practitioner of the art of politics (521D). Similarly, in the *Laws,* good laws are distinguished from bad via an analogy of two types of medicine: that practiced by the slavish doctors whose skill is

based on *empeiria* alone, on slaves, and that practiced by free doctors, who study nature as do the philosophers, on free people. All existing legislation is said to be comparable to slavish (empirical) medicine (720B–723A and 857C). Among other differences, Plato's use of the analogy downgrades *empeiria* for the sake of showing the unity of the sciences in philosophy, while Aristotle is attempting to indicate the *difference* between *politikē* and philosophy by showing the resemblance of the former to medicine.

3

Political Animals and Civic Friendship

John M. Cooper

ONE OF THE MOST FUNDAMENTAL propositions of both Aristotle's ethical and his political theory is his claim that by its *nature* the human being is a *politikon zōon*—to use the conventional translation, a "political animal," or, perhaps a bit less misleadingly, an animal that lives in cities. This proposition plays an important role in the argument of *NE* I. It is cited at I.7 1097b11 as the ground for holding that whatever a human being's happiness or flourishing ultimately turns out to consist in, it must be something that suffices not just for his own individual good but also somehow includes the good of his family, his friends, and his fellow-citizens.[1] In the second chapter of the *Politica* Aristotle cites it again (at I.2 1253a2–3), this time as a conclusion drawn from his quasi-genetic account of the constitution of city-states from the union of households into villages and villages into the larger social units called *poleis*.[2] Because households and villages, his argument goes, are indisputably natural forms of organized life for human beings—they make it possible for creatures with the natural limitations of human beings to survive relatively easily and comfortably in their natural environment—so also must cities be, since (whatever else cities do) they certainly make more secure and comfortable the means of livelihood already, but less securely, provided by households and villages. Aristotle recognizes that this does not show that everything that civilization in cities brings can be justified as answering to needs of human beings that result from natural and unavoidable facts about their physical make-up and the natural circumstances of human life. But, if true, it does show that the sort of life characteristic of human beings in cities is not governed *simply* by arbitrary and optional conventions originating from nothing more than historical happenstance. To this extent cities can demand the abiding respect of independent-minded persons, as they might not be able to do if they were (and were known to be) merely conventional and not in any way natural habitats for human beings. For, on this view, *some* form of city life is something human beings need if they are to live secure and comfortable lives.

Aristotle goes further, however. In reaching his view that city-life is natural for human beings he says, in a famous phrase (1252b29–30), that though cities come *into* being for the sake of life (i.e., in order to make possible the secure and comfortable life I just referred to)—*tou zēn heneken*—they *are* (they exist) for the sake of "living well," of a good life (*tou eu zēn heneken*). Whatever exactly Aristotle means by *a good life,* it is clear that he thinks it is not normally available at all, not even in a less secure or less complete form, to human beings except in cities. Later on I will say something further about this good life and about how Aristotle intends to link the need for that sort of life to fundamentals of human nature and the natural circumstance of human life. For the moment I simply note that when at the beginning of the *Politica* Aristotle concludes that the city is a natural thing and that the human being is by its *nature* a political animal (1253a1–3), he is thinking not just of the ways in which city life secures the means of livelihood already provided to a human population by household and village life, but of further supposed goods (whichever ones are included in "living well") that (normally) only life in a city makes possible. That the human being is by nature a political animal means that these further goods as well are ones whose status as goods is supposed to be grounded in human nature.

Now in these two passages of *NE* I and *Pol.* I the context makes quite clear what Aristotle means by "political," when he says that human beings are political animals. With one significant exception the same holds good with all the other passages in the ethical and political treatises where Aristotle mentions the political nature of human beings (*Pol.* I.2 1253a7–18; III.6 1278b15–30; *EE* VIII.10 1242a19–28; *NE* IX.12 1162a16–19; X.9 1169b16–22). He means that human nature demands that, in general and as a normal thing, human beings live in *cities* of some sort: cities (*poleis*) themselves or citizens (*politai*) are explicitly mentioned in both of our passages and in all but one of the others,[3] and the etymological connection between *politikon* and *polis* is plainly in the forefront of Aristotle's mind in all of them. To be a *politikon* animal is, he plainly means, to be one suited to live in *poleis.* So Ross's rather picturesque overtranslation of *phusei politikon ho anthrōpos* at *NE* I.7 1097b11 as "man is born for citizenship" does not seriously distort Aristotle's meaning.

But cities are many-faceted social phenomena; moreover, as Aristotle was acutely aware, they can exhibit a variety of social structures and political organizations. Given this complexity and these variations, one wants to know as exactly as possible what it is in and about cities and life in them that Aristotle thinks human beings because of their natures need. What, so to speak, does Aristotle think is essential to city-life as such, that all cities, perhaps with differing degrees of success, give their human inhabitants and that family-life and village-life necessarily do not suffice for? Nothing in the two passages discussed so far addresses this question, particularly when one takes into account "living well," as well as mere "living," as something the city is for. But there are two further passages (one in the *Politica*, the other, perhaps surprisingly, in the *Historia Animalium*) where Aristotle talks about the political nature of human beings that do offer the beginnings of an answer to our question.

Significantly, in these passages, unlike those from which we began, Aristotle introduces a biological perspective. Speaking from the biological point of view he is able to say something appropriately concrete about human nature and so to suggest what it is about city-life that humans most fundamentally need. The two passages in question are, first, *Pol.* I.2 1253a7–18 (the continuation of the passage from *Pol.* I.2 I summarized above). Here Aristotle compares human beings with other (as he calls them) "herding" animals (*agelaia*), such as bees (this is *his* example). Secondly, there is a surprisingly neglected passage near the beginning of the *Historia Animalium* (I.1) which makes it possible to interpret this *Politica* passage correctly.[4] The *Historia Animalium* passage runs as follows:[5]

> There are also the following differences among animals, that depend upon their ways of life and their actions. Of both footed, winged and swimming animals, some herd together and others live solitarily, while others "dualize." And some of the herding ones are political while others live scattered. Now herding animals are for instance (among the winged animals) the pigeon family, the crane and the swan (no crook-taloned bird is a herder), and among the swimmers many kinds of fish, for instance those called migrants, the tunny, the pelamys and the bonito. The human being "dualizes." Political animals are those that have as their function (*ergon*) some single thing that they all do together, and not all the herding animals have that. The human being, the bee, the wasp, the ant and the crane are political animals. Some of these are under leaders and others are rulerless, for instance the crane and the bee family are under leaders while ants and thousands of others are rulerless. And some of both the herding and the solitary animals have a fixed home while others move from place to place. (I.1 487b33–488a14)

The gist of the *Politica* passage is that human beings are political animals in a higher degree (*mallon*) than, e.g., bees or cranes or other similarly herding animals because they possess language.[6] Human beings alone have the capacity to conceive of their own and others' long-term and short-term advantage or good, and so to conceive of justice and injustice as well, since (though Aristotle does not say this explicitly here)[7] in general what is just is what is to the *common* advantage or good of some relevant group. Accordingly, they also have language, which is necessary in order for them to communicate these conceptions to one another: nature gives other animals, which are aware only of what is more or less immediately pleasant and painful, as refined a means of communication as they can use, by giving them the ability to call out to one another by barking, chirping, mooing, etc. As a consequence of having language the kind of work that human beings can do together, in which their being political animals will show itself, is of a much higher order of complexity than that which bees or cranes can manage. Because they can conceive of and communicate their thoughts about their own and others' long-term and future good, and the common good which constitutes justice, human beings can form and maintain households and cities, whereas bees can only have hives and cranes only form elaborate and differentiated migration-schemes.[8] Human beings, then, like bees or cranes, are political animals in what is from the point of view of zoology (though not of course etymology) the fundamental sense of having a work or function that the members of a human group all do together; but because in this case the common work involves maintaining the structure and organization of a *city,* they are political in the further, more literal, sense of being naturally suited to life in cities, to the life of citizens.[9]

There is much of interest in these passages. First of all, as just noted, and surprisingly, when in the *Historia Animalium* Aristotle classifies the human being together with the bee and the crane, etc., as political animals he does not mean, despite the literal meaning of the word, that all these kinds of animals live in cities (*poleis*). There is no reference anywhere in the passage to cities or to citizenship, as there is in all the other passages from the *Politica* and *Ethica* where the political nature of human beings is alluded to. On the contrary, as he himself explains, the criterion being invoked is whether or not an animal species (only herding animals are in question, naturally) is such that it has an essential work that its members all engage in together (with the differentiation of function that goes along with that). If it does, it counts as "political," if not not, and in that case it gets classified as "scattered." (So by this classification oxen, sheep, and cattle are not political but scattered animals: obviously, being scattered is not a matter of how close to or far apart animals of a species typically stand from one another as they go about their daily business of feeding and so on, but whether what they spend their time doing is something that they have to be together to do, because it is something they do in common, as a community.)

So the fundamental point about the nature of human beings that grounds the biological classification is that humans have the capacity for, and are regularly found, taking part in cooperative activities involving differentiation of function. This important point is something that the passages of the ethical treatises and the *Politica* that I first cited, where the political nature of human beings is linked simply to their fitness for life in cities, do not bring clearly to light. What we learn from the *Historia Animalium* theory and its extension in *Pol.* I.2 1253a7–18 is that active participation in a city's life is that single function (*ergon*) which all the human beings belonging to that city perform together, and in the performance of which their character as political animals consists. This counts as a *single* function because, as Aristotle's account of the structure and constitution of a city makes clear, a city is a complex entity having as its ultimate elements not individual human beings as such, but human beings *in* families, households, villages, and other associations, *koinōniai*: the part of a person's active life that is carried out as a family-member or as a farmer in a particular locality, say, is seen as part of the larger complex of activities making up the life of the city of which this family and this locality are parts.[10] Once one brings the biological perspective provided by our *Historia Animalium* passage to bear on the interpretation of the proposition that human beings are political animals, one can see that the fundamental aspect of city life that in Aristotle's eyes marks it as natural for human beings is its involving the cooperative working together of all those who take part in it in an interlocking, differentiated, mutually supporting, single set of activities. What's essential to cities, however they may vary in other respects, is that they involve their citizens in this kind of common activity. In effect, it is by doing that that cities can provide a more secure and comfortable life than households and villages not integrated into a city can do (as we saw earlier Aristotle claims), and we may begin to anticipate that whatever exactly Aristotle means by saying that cities exist for the sake of a good life, and not just for the sake of life, this will turn out to be a life led in some more or less specific version of this kind of cooperative activity.

So far I have left Aristotle's notion of the political activity as an essentially cooperative one rather abstract. In order to begin to flesh it out somewhat, it will be useful to turn to Aristotle's distinction (drawn first in *Pol.* III.6 1279a17–21) between the "correct" (*orthai*) constitutions and the "erroneous" (*hēmartēmenai*) ones or deviation-forms (*parekbaseis*). Since Aristotle says the deviation-forms are contrary to nature (III.17 1287b41), we can examine life in the correct kinds of city to discover what he expects city life to be like if things do go according to nature. That should show us what he includes among the cooperative activities in which the human being's political nature shows itself.

Aristotle's criterion for a "correct" constitution is deceptively simple. A "correct" constitution is one in which the government aims at the common advantage (*to koinē sumpheron*, III.6 1279a17; *to koinon sumpheron*, III.7 1279a28–29); in the deviation-forms the government aims instead at the advantage of the office-holders themselves (and their families) as a group. But to whom is the advantage sought in correct constitutions common, and in what sense is it common?

To the first question the natural answer would seem to be: common to all the citizens, i.e., all the free, native-born residents. In fact, I think this is what Aristotle does intend: it is at least suggested by III.13, 1283b40–41, where Aristotle speaks of "correct" rule as being "for the advantage of the whole city and for the common advantage of the citizens." But if we put Aristotle's view in this way we must recognize that we are using the word "citizen" in a way that departs from his own explicit theory in III.1–2 of who the citizens of a city are. According to this theory, the citizens of a city are just those who have the right to take part in the judicial and/or the deliberative functions.[11] But if we were to use the term "citizen" in Aristotle's official, narrow sense in saying that correct forms of political organization aim at the citizens' common advantage, the result would be that certain correct forms would collapse into their corresponding deviation forms. Thus, under the rule of a king, one of the types of constitution Aristotle counts as "correct," the monarch reserves to himself and his personal appointees both the deliberative and the judicial function—so that, if the aim of a king was the common advantage of what Aristotle *officially* counts as citizens, there would in fact be no distinction between rule by a king and a tyranny, its deviation-form. For in such a monarchy the unique ruler would also be the sole citizen, and so he would rule simultaneously in the sole interest of himself (as ruler) and in that of the citizen body (himself as citizen). Hence such a monarchy would also be a tyranny: rule by the ruler solely in his personal interest. Likewise there would be no distinction between aristocracy and oligarchy, either. (Aristotle's criterion would still separate "polity" from democracy.) So the citizens, whose common advantage is consulted in the correct constitutions, must include the office-holders, jurymen, and assembly-members, but at least in aristocracy and monarchy others besides. How is this larger class of citizens to be determined? Aristotle speaks in this context (at III.7 1279a35–36) of those whose common possession and common activity the city is (*hoi koinōnountes autēs*) as the ones whose advantage the correct governments seek, and by implication he describes a city when correctly constituted as an association in common of its *free* inhabitants (*koinōnia tōn eleutherōn*, III.6 1279a21). This suggests that the citizens in the broad sense include all the free-born native residents, with the presumed exclusion of the nonslave laborers, both urban and agricultural (cf. III.5 1278a6–13). These it is, whether the form of government is a kingdom, an aristocracy or the government in which all the (male) free-born natives participate that Aristotle calls a "polity," whose common advantage is sought in correctly organized cities.

But now we must ask, in what sense is the advantage sought an advantage that belongs to the citizens (i.e., the free-born native residents) *in common*? One way in which this might be conceived is on the model of a joint-stock company. If I own 10 percent of a company's stock and you own 20 percent, then anything that improves the competitiveness of the company or increases its earnings or profits, and so on, is for our common advantage. Here the common advantage can be broken down into the sum of the individual advantages of each of us, and these individual advantages are themselves definable and measurable independently of reference to our jointly owned company and its advantage. If, for example, the company's profits increase a certain amount because of some change in tax rate or tax policy, and my dividend goes from $100 to $200 and yours from $200 to $400, then this act of the government has been to my and your advantage by those amounts, and this advantage, being measurable in such financial terms, is definable without reference to the company and its advantage. The company's advantage is only the causal condition of my and your separate advantages. In a case like this if you and I combine to work for our common advantage we can, and presumably will, each be working for his own single advantage, aiming at this by means of the advantage of the company, which includes our separate advantages as constituent parts. Likewise, if some third party should take an interest in the success of our company this person would be taking an interest in our and the other stockholders' common advantage in this purely additive sense.

In an interesting chapter of *Politica*, Book III Aristotle clearly and explicitly rejects this commercial model for the kind of community a city constitutes, and implies a different account of what the common advantage of its participants consists in. Partisans of an oligarchic constitution, he says (III.9 1280a25–31), think that a city is an association (or common enterprise—*koinōnia*) that came into and continues in existence merely for the sake of possessions (*ktōmata*), that is, for the sake of preserving, exchanging, and increasing possessions for their economic value. And their standard of political justice, which specifies unequal shares in political power, corresponding to the unequal quantity of possessions brought into the common stock by the participating citizens, would be perfectly reasonable if their conception of what a city essentially is were correct. However, on the oligarchic conception a constitution is like a commercial treaty between two separate countries, establishing an agreement as to how trade and other business is to be conducted between their respective citizens, with guarantees for the citizens of each against various forms of cheating by the citizens of the other. And it is plain, Aristotle says, that the kind of common enterprise a city is is badly misrepresented by any such conception of a civic constitution. For, surely, a single city with commercial relations carried on inside it is quite a different thing from two separate cities bound by commercial treaties and carrying on a similarly active and varied trade with one another. One difference Aristotle mentions is important but relatively superficial—the absence in the two-city case of a single, common system of courts and magistracies governing the commercial relations in question (1280a40–b1). But a second difference goes deeper: the people in the two cities carrying on mutual trade and commerce "do not concern themselves about what kind of persons the ones in the other city ought to be, nor are they concerned that no one covered by the agreements *be* unjust (or be vicious in any way at all). They are only concerned that they *do* nothing unjust to one another" (1280b1–5). By contrast, within a single city, people do have this further concern: of course they want not to be cheated or otherwise treated unjustly, in business or anywhere else, but they also care what kind of people their fellow-citizens are. They want them to be decent, fair-minded, respectable, moral people (anyhow, by their own lights).

One should note carefully just how strong a claim Aristotle is making here. He says those in one city who exercise their rights under treaties for mutual commerce have no general concern about the moral characters of those in another city with whom they do business: they do not concern themselves that "no one covered by the agreements *be* unjust (or be vicious in any way at all)." And he implies that civic relations among citizens of a single city, since they are not merely commercial, do involve just these concerns. That is, he holds that in cities we find a *general* concern on the part of those living under the constitution of a city and participating in its civic life for the moral characters of all those similarly engaged—a concern that *no one* taking part in civic life *be* unjust or indeed vicious in any way. This is a concern of each citizen for each other citizen, whether or not they know each other personally, and indeed whether or not they have had any direct and personal dealings with one another whatsoever. The open-ended scope here envisaged for this mutual concern of fellow-citizens for one another's good character is, as we shall see more fully below, a crucially important feature of common life in a city as Aristotle conceives it.

But is it really true that fellow-citizens do have such a concern for one another's good character? No doubt they would in any of the types of state Aristotle himself most favors, since such cities would be governed under a constitution, fully accepted by the citizens themselves, taking as its first aim to make the citizens good.[12] But would they, for example, under the very oligarchic constitution that Aristotle in this passage is trying to show is misguided? Why think that where the constitution was just an elaborate commercial treaty, eschewing all reference to people's characters and any concern for what they are *like* personally, people would differ in this aspect from the citizens of two distinct cities linked by extensive trade relations? On reflection, it turns out to be very plausible that they would, and that Aristotle is right to make this fact a central objection against the oligarchic and in general commercial view of the kind of community a city is.

Even in twentieth-century liberal states, some of which (anyhow in their official ideology) fit the commercial conception rather well, Aristotle's observation seems to hold good (and in Greek city-states the features that make it do so were even more pronounced). There seems no denying that ordinary Americans, for example, are characteristically quite a bit concerned about the moral standards of people prominent in government, business, and industry, and concerned in quite a different way from the concern they presumably also feel about the morality of people in similar positions in foreign countries, even ones with which the United States has extensive trading and business relationships. The typical American when she hears, say, about the attitudes Wall Street brokers and commercial bankers have apparently quite routinely been holding about privileged information that comes their way in their professional work, or about sleaziness in government circles, feels injured in ways she certainly does not feel in hearing similar things said about people in high places abroad. Independently of any way one may expect to suffer financial losses or other direct injuries to one's interests from these people's behavior, one feels injured and diminished simply by there being such people in positions like that. Something is wrong with us, one feels, that among us that sort of person is found in that sort of place. That the same and worse happens in some other country may be reason to introduce special safeguards to protect our financial interests there, or, out of sympathy for the people of that country, to express our moral condemnation of that behavior, or even to join organizations directed toward removing those evils by concerted international financial pressure, etc. But it's nothing to us *personally.* Apart from a legitimate general concern we may feel about immorality wherever it occurs, it's nothing to us *Americans* what, say, French or German or Italian businessmen are like: that's the exclusive concern of the French or the Germans or the Italians, in the sense that *they* are the ones personally injured and diminished by it.

These effects of national feeling are felt more widely, too. Americans take pride in the self-discipline and hard work of the American working force, the inventiveness, entrepreneurial spirit, and skill of American industrialists, the imaginativeness and vigor of American writers, and so on.[13] (That these characteristics may largely be mythical does not matter for the point I am making.)

This is pride not just in accomplishments, but even more in the qualities of mind and character that (are presumed to have) made them possible. Furthermore, it seems that, typically, citizens even of a modern mass democracy feel tied to one another in such a way and to such an extent that they can and do take an interest in what their fellow-citizens quite generally are like as persons; they want to think of them as good, upstanding people, and definitely do not want them to be small-minded, self-absorbed, sleazy. What their fellow-citizens are like matters to them personally, it seems, in ways that the personal qualities of the citizens of a foreign country do not, because they feel some connection to, some involvement with—almost some responsibility for—the former that they do not have for the latter, and this makes them feel that what their fellow-citizens are like, for better or for worse, somehow reflects on themselves.[14]

In this chapter of *Politica* III then, Aristotle decisively rejects the commercial model for the kind of community a city is. What kind of community is a city, then, if it is not to be conceived on the commercial model? Aristotle indicates his own view a little later in the same chapter, when he goes on (III.9 1280b23–1281a2) to explain the nature and source of the special bond between fellow-citizens that grounds their concern for one another's personal qualities. Aristotle says quite explicitly that it is friendship (*philia*, 1280b38) that does this. Friendship, he says, being the deliberate decision to share one's life with another (*hē gar tou suzēn proairesis philia*, 1280b38–39), is responsible for such practices in cities as "connections by marriage, brotherhoods, religious festivals, and the pursuits in which people share their lives" (1280b 36–38). And these, in turn, he evidently means to say, provide the specific sort of connectedness that, in Greek cities, grounds the interest in and concern by each citizen for the qualities of mind and character of his fellow-citizens generally that he has been insisting distinguishes citizenly ties from those provided by contractual agreements for mutual economic advantage.[15] For his purpose in mentioning these more limited contexts for common activity and the role they play in the city is to explain how it comes about that cities differ from commercial partnerships in the way he said earlier in the chapter that they do. Since that involved a concern of each citizen for each other citizen's character, he must mean that these less extensive types of common undertaking give rise to and reinforce the common activity of civic life itself, and the friendship that is specific to that life. In general, even in a Greek city-state, no citizen is bound to each of his fellow-citizens through marriage, or membership of some brotherhood, or one or another other personal relationship of friendship. Hence whatever special concern the members of these associations may come to have for one another's characters will obviously be inadequate for Aristotle's purpose here. So, although Aristotle does not say it here explicitly, the kind of friendship he has in mind is what in the *Ethica Eudemia* he discusses at some length under the name "civic friendship," *hē politikē philia*, and refers to as such four times in the *Ethica Nicomachea*.[16] According to Aristotle, then, a city is a kind of community that depends upon the friendly interest that the citizens take in one another's qualities of mind and character, as well, of course, as upon their common economic interests. In such a community the way or ways in which the government seeks to promote the citizens' good as a *common* good will depend upon the specific character of the friendship that forms the political bond within it, and the ways in which "civic friends" have and do things in common.

In order to see what this is, we must first be clear about the fact that, although Aristotle in the two *Ethics* treats civic friendship as a form of advantage friendship, a friendship based upon the experience or expectation of mutual benefit from the activities in which it is expressed, civic friendship, like other forms of advantage friendship, is really *a friendship*. Aristotle emphasizes in *Pol.* III.9 that whereas mere mutual commerce does not involve any interest in one another as persons, any concern for what kind of people these are that one is dealing with, in civic friendship, even though it is based upon the expectation of mutual benefit just as much as such commercial relationships are, this additional interest is present. That is easy enough to understand if, like all relationships deserving the name "friendship," civic friendship involves mutual good will, trust, and well-wishing, and the mutual interest that fellow-citizens have in one another's characters is part of that good will and well-wishing. Thus what Aristotle says in *Pol.* III.9 confirms what I have argued elsewhere about civic friendship in the *Ethica Nicomachea*[17] where civic friendship characterizes a population there exists, as a recognized and accepted norm, a certain measure of mutual goodwill, and also mutual trust, among the people making up the population. Each expects his fellow-citizens in their dealings with him (political, economic, and social) to be motivated not merely by self-interest (or other private particular interests) but also by concern for his good for his own sake (for his qualities of mind and character, as Aristotle emphasizes in *Pol.* III.9, but also for other elements in his good). And in return each is ready to be so motivated in his dealings with them. This means that in a city animated by civic friendship each citizen has a certain measure of interest in and concern for the well-being of each other citizen just because the other *is* a fellow-citizen. Civic friendship makes fellow-citizens' well-being matter to one another, simply as such.[18]

Here, and not coincidentally, the comparison with a family is instructive. In a family (perhaps a somewhat idealized one—but this idealization is obviously important to Aristotle), the good fortune or success or good character of one member is *experienced* by the others as somehow part of their good as well, and in fact we do think it constitutes a contribution to the good of the other family members. Think of how parents respond to their children's successes, and of how we refer to the character of the children's lives when we intend to be saying how things are for the parents. The members of my family are my people, and any good enjoyed by any of them is shared in also by me, because as members of a family what affects them affects the family, and I too am a member of that. Civic friendship is just an extension to a whole city of the kinds of psychological bonds that tie together a family and make possible this immediate participation by each family member in the good of the others. Civic friendship makes the citizens in some important respects like a large extended family (though they are also, obviously, quite unlike a family in other respects).

Plainly, the common advantage of a civic community conceived as Aristotle conceives it, like that of a family, does not consist wholly (though of course it might well consist partly) of something that can be broken down into a sum of separate advantages belonging individually to the citizens one by one. To the extent that each citizen participates in the good of the others, a good that may belong in the first instance to a single individual (whether a material possession or a good quality of mind or character) becomes a communal good shared in by all who are members in good standing of the community. Insofar as part of the common good of the citizens is thus a set of communal goods, it is not divisible into separate shares at all, but remains indissolubly an "advantage" of the common enterprise itself in which the members of the community are associated. The citizens share equally in the whole of this part of their common good, just because they are associated in the civic enterprise and care about it.

At the beginning of *NE* IX Aristotle says, obviously approvingly, that "friendship seems to hold cities together, and lawgivers seem to be more concerned about it than about justice. For . . . when people are friends they have no need of justice, but those who are just [to one another] need friendship in addition, and the strictest form of justice is found in friendship" (IX.1 1155a22–28). Indeed, Aristotle says that every community (and he explicitly includes here the family as well as the city) carries with it both a specific kind of friendship and a specific set of standards of justice (IX.9 1159b26–27; 1159b35–1160a3). But justice plays a distinctive role in the constitution of civic friendship that so far as I can see it does not play in families.[19] Even if the specific standards of justice appropriate to a family are seriously violated in various ways—if, say, the children are cold and neglectful of the parents, perhaps because earlier on the parents themselves were arbitrary, dictatorial, and selfish—the bonds which tie family members together and make each participate in the good of the others are not entirely destroyed. The parents, however neglected and wronged they may feel and be, are nonetheless affected for better or worse by the successes and good fortune and the good characters of the children (and vice versa). Injustice seems not, of itself, to destroy the relationship (the "friendship") and so it does not do away with the participation by each in the others' good. But this is not so for civic friendship.

Consider, for example, an aristocracy, one conceived according to Aristotle's lights as governed by the morally best people among the citizens. If the virtue of the rulers and their opportunity to exercise it in those most favorable of conditions for the exercise of virtue, the public affairs of a city, is bought at the price of limiting the moral development of the other citizens, or denying them appropriate opportunities to give effective exercise to good moral qualities they possess, then this would not only be an injustice (one recognized even by the aristocratic conception of justice officially countenanced under that form of constitution),[20] it would for that very reason also destroy the friendship existing among the citizens. If those excluded from active participation in the political life of the city recognized their exclusion as an injustice, they would see themselves as being exploited by the rulers for the rulers' own benefit. Their trust would thus have been violated, and a natural consequence of an uncorrected violation of trust is its destruction. Since civic friendship consists in part of the mutual trust of the citizens that they are all effectively concerned for one another's good, the destruction of this trust destroys the friendship too.

Civic friendship, then, requires that those bound together by it (seem to one another to) be behaving justly in their mutual relations (anyhow basically so). Being clear about the role of justice in making civic friendship possible is especially important because it helps one to understand just what it means to say a city is a community (a *koinōnia*) and what would be involved in the "common advantage" of the citizens who make up such a community. In a city animated by civic friendship the citizens are engaged in a common enterprise, an enterprise aimed at a common good, in two different senses. First of all, each regards the others as wishing for and implementing through their actions his individual good (as he also intends in his actions their individual good), as and to the extent justice requires. The good in question certainly includes material interests, but is not limited to that: moral and intellectual good, regarded as individual accomplishments, are included as well. So the common good of the community will consist first of the ways in which, by the organization of civic life, the individuals making it up each severally benefit from it, that is, benefit in ways that are assignable to them each separately *as* individuals. In an Aristotelian aristocracy, for example, the well-born "better" people benefit by the education they receive that helps them to develop good moral and intellectual qualities, and by the opportunity they later enjoy to exercise these qualities in the direction of the community's affairs. The common people benefit, too, because such a group of aristocrats are actively concerned for the good of their fellow-citizens, as justice demands, and make a principle of seeing to the economic well-being of their less well-endowed fellow-citizens and to such moral and intellectual development as they are capable of, so far as providing for that does not unfairly limit the full development of the excellences of the better-endowed.

To this extent, the common advantage of a city is the sum of the advantages of its citizens, separately considered. But where, as in this kind of aristocracy (but also in monarchies and under the more popular governments Aristotle calls "polities"), civic life involves civic friendship, it includes more than this. For where each aims in her cooperative activity at the good of the others, and not just at her own good, the good attained in the first instance by the others becomes, and is conceived of by herself as being, also a part of her own good. In this way the aristocrat participates in the good that comes to the ordinary citizens in their common life, because that is a conscious objective of many of those morally fine activities in which his principal citizenly function is carried out, and of course the attainment of one's conscious objectives (if, anyhow, one is right, as *ex hypothesi* this man is, to adopt them in the first place) makes a direct contribution to one's own good. And the ordinary citizen likewise participates in the moral and intellectual goods achieved directly by the aristocrat. That is because these are good things achieved in the course of a common life the organizing principles of which he endorses and to which he willingly contributes his part. These are, so to speak, *his* aristocrats, so that their intrinsically good qualities and intrinsically good activities are part of the enlarged good that he comes to experience by not just living in this city but being a willing, active part of it.

This account of the common good or common advantage aimed at by the government of a "correctly" constituted city brings into view something important that is easily missed. When Aristotle says that cities exist for the sake of *to eu zēn* (living well)—not just for living, or even for living together, the sharing of life (*to suzēn*)—his official view is that the "living well" in question is that of the households and village-communities that logically preexist the city and from which it is constituted. Sometimes, as in a remarkable passage of *Pol.* III.9, Aristotle is explicit about this: a city is "the common participation in living well by households and families, for the sake of a complete and self-sufficient life" (*hē tou eu zēn koinōnia kai tais oikiais kai tois genesi, zōēs teleias charin kai autarkous*, 1280b33–34). The "living well" aimed at in cities is not, anyhow not immediately, the "living well" of the individual citizens residing in it. What is aimed at is rather the living well of the constituent households and village-communities. Individual citizens' lives are affected just insofar as, in one way or another, the good living of the communities to which they individually belong carries with it the individual citizens' living well too.

But to what extent does the living well of a community imply the living well of its individual members? Plainly, in well-constituted cities of all types, and especially in monarchies and aristocracies as Aristotle conceives them, the city aims through its political and social institutions at providing both for the material well-being and for the fullest possible development and exercise of the highest and best qualities of mind and character of the citizens.[21] The city and its constituent subcommunities cannot live well otherwise than on this condition. But of course in any city, however successful, many, perhaps most, of the citizens will not attain the highest degree of civilized perfection, because of congenital limitations in their natural capacities (if not for other reasons as well). The city itself, however, will live well if those who are naturally capable of a very high degree of mental and moral perfection attain and sustain it through life in the city, and the others attain as high a degree of perfection as they are naturally capable of. So, at a minimum, one could say that in the best, most successful cities an excellent life is provided for those individuals (presumably a small number) capable of leading it, while the others get as nearly excellent a life as they are severally able to manage, given their natural limitations.

But relying on the preceding analysis, we can go further. For according to Aristotle, when civic friendship animates the life of a community, as of course one would expect it to do in any correctly constituted city, each citizen participates in *all* aspects of the good achieved through the common activity that constitutes civic life. This means that even those who are less well-endowed for the excellences of mind and character share in the exercise of the excellences of the better-endowed citizens. In this way all the citizens of a successful city achieve, either directly through their own individual activities, or at second remove through participation in the city's good of which these activities are a prime element, an active, perfected, self-sufficient life.[22]

With this account of civic friendship before us we can now see the full implications of Aristotle's thesis that the human being is by nature a political animal. This means, first, that like certain other herding animals, human beings have a natural capacity and tendency to live together in cooperative communities in which each benefits from the work of the others as well as from his own. But secondly, because human beings can develop conceptions of, and communicate to one another their ideas about, the long-term good both of themselves and others and the common good of a whole group of people living and working together, human beings have the natural capacity and tendency to form communities (and, in particular, cities)[23] in which the life of all is organized in pursuit of a *common good*—a good that is common not just in the sense that each severally gets some part of a sum total of distributable benefit, but in the strong sense that it is achieved in or belongs to the common activity that is the single life they all jointly live by merging their lives with one another's. But this common good is not available to them except on the basis of their all being, and feeling themselves to be, bound together by the bonds of civic friendship. And in the most successful cities, thanks to civic friendship, there is an important sense in which *all* the citizens, even those who individually lack the highest attainments of mind and character, can be said to be living a good and excellent life.[24]

Notes

1. Construed literally, what Aristotle says is that the final good (*to teleion agathon*) for any individual must be *sufficient* both for his own and for his family's, friends', and fellow-citizens' good. I take it, however, that the weaker connection to these others' goods indicated in my summary is what he intends; the datives in *geneusi* etc. 1097b9–10 are to be taken only loosely with *autarkes* (or *arkoun*, understood from *autarkes*) Significantly, these same key expressions (*teleion* and *autarkes*) figure prominently in Aristotle's argument for the naturalness of the *polis* in *Pol.* I.2: at 1252b28–29 he says the *polis* is the *koinōnia teleios, . . . pasēs echousa peras tēs autarkeias.* The two applications of these keywords are connected: the normal human being's final, and in itself sufficient, good depends essentially upon his willing and active participation in a common life together with others in a city, i.e., in a fully-realized, complete human community, which is by itself sufficient to support the *whole* of what human life at its best requires. How this can be so is the main subject of this chapter.

2. I translate *polis* throughout by "city." But it is important to bear in mind that by *poleis* a Greek intended not merely what we call cities, but these taken together with their agricultural hinterland.

3. *NE* X.9 1169b16–22: but even here *othneisi* may be foreigners and not just strangers, so that the connection with cities and fellow-citizens will be clear enough by implication.

4. If this *Historia Animalium* passage is less neglected than it formerly was that is no doubt due to two good recent articles that devote special attention to it: R. G. Mulgan, "Aristotle's Doctrine that Man is a Political Animal"; and W. Kullmann, "Der Mensch als Politisches Lebewesen bei Aristoteles." I have profited from both these discussions, especially Kullmann's. Richard Bodéüs has drawn my attention to his article 'L'Animal politique et l'animal économique' after I had finished this part of my chapter.

5. At I.1 488a2 there seems no doubt that one must bracket *kai tōn monadkēn*, with Schneider and Peck (I translate Peck's text). If one keeps the manuscript reading then Aristotle will be saying that some animals that live in large groups *and some animals that live alone* are political, while others in each classification are scattered or dispersed. One might, of course, attempt on Aristotle's behalf to make sense of the idea that some of the *monadika* animals are nonetheless political. Perhaps some of them live apart most of the year but come together briefly to do some common work; perhaps although the adults of some species live separately from one another the young

continue to live with a parent even after they have become able to feed and defend themselves, so that these species satisfy the condition for living "more politically" that Aristotle refers to at IX.1 589a1 ff.; and other ways of achieving the same result might also occur to one. Aristotle himself, however, offers no encouragement for such speculation. Aside from this passage (i.e., I.1 488a1–14) the term *monadikon* apparently occurs only once in the biological works. That is in I.40 623b10, where Aristotle introduces a long discussion (chs. 40–43) of bees and other (as he says, 623b7) insects that make a honeycomb. He distinguishes nine *genē* of such creatures, six of them *agelaia* and three *monadika*. The three *monadika* are two types of *seirēn* (not subsequently, nor apparently elsewhere, further described by him) and the *boubulios* or bumble-bee. To the bumble-bee he devotes a total of one sentence, in ch. 43 (629a30 ff.): the bumble-bee gives birth under rocks, right on the ground (i.e., without having a hive the way the other wax-producers he has described do), and makes an inferior kind of honey. The bumble-bee is manifestly not by Aristotle's criteria a political animal, and there seems no reason to suspect the *seirēnes* differed in this respect. So far, therefore, as anything Aristotle actually says about any particular ones of the *monadika* animals goes, we have no basis for thinking that *Aristotle* recognized any *monadika* political species at all.

It seems better, therefore, to suppose that at I.1 488a2, having distinguished the *agelaia* (the ones that live in large groups, the "herding" ones) from the *monadika* (those that live alone, the "solitary" ones), Aristotle in fact went on to subdivide the *agelaia* into political and scattered: what he wrote was *kai tōn agelaiōn ta men politika ta de sporadika estin*. This is confirmed below, 488a8–9, where Aristotle gives his criterion for being political and adds, appropriately if the political are intended as a subgroup of the *agelaia*, that not all *agelaia* satisfy it. Moreover, all the examples he gives of *politika* animals are also *agelaia*.

But if this is right, what explains the manuscript corruption? Aristotle has just mentioned that some animals of each of the largest classes he recognizes (the footed, the winged, and the swimming animals) live together in large groups (*ta men agelaia*) while others live alone (*ta de monadika*), while yet others "dualize," i.e., (I take it) are sometimes found in herds and sometimes found living alone. After introducing the subdivision here between the political and the scattered or dispersed animals (*ta men politika ta de sporadika estin*) he returns to the first division, giving examples of both winged and swimming animals that live in herds (he omits to give examples of footed animals, such as sheep and cattle, presumably because herding footed animals are well known to everyone), and having done that mentions that human beings dualize (488a7). In context, coming immediately after these lists of *agelaia*, it seems most natural to take this as saying that human beings dualize between living in large groups and living alone, i.e., dualize between belonging alongside these others among the herding animals, and not doing so but instead being solitary in lifestyle. (The alternative is to understand humans as dualizing between being political and being scattered or dispersed, but the intervention of *agelaia men oun . . . hamiai* makes this difficult, if not quite impossible. Kullmann's suggestion, *op. cit.* 432, that humans dualize between being herding and being *scattered* animals can't be right, since it draws one term of the opposition from the pair herding-solitary and the other from the pair political-scattered: it was perhaps awareness of this anomaly that led him to put it forward only with a query.) So Aristotle belatedly gives humankind as an instance of the dualizers mentioned at 488a1–2, the ones that cannot neatly be classed as either herding or solitary animals. Yet in the next sentence but one he classifies human beings as political animals: for animals to be political is, he says, to have as their function (*ergon*) some single common work, which not all herding animals, but only some—human beings, bees, wasps, ants, and cranes—do. Here human beings are counted among the herding animals. And that might seem to contradict their classification as dualizers. In fact, as I will argue below, there is no contradiction. But if one thought there was, it is easy to see how the text must be corrected to get rid of it: at 488a2 read *kai tōn agelaiōn kai tōn monadikōn*, thus making the division between political and scattered animals cut through the prior division between herding and solitary animals, so that human beings, all of whom Aristotle implies (488a7) either live in herds or solitarily, are after all included as a group in the larger class (which now becomes the union of the herding and the solitary animals) being divided into the two subgroups, the political and the scattered. In that case, when human beings are classified as political just below no contradiction results. The human beings, though as a group political in character, can nonetheless dualize between being herding and being solitary animals, because as Aristotle will now have said, some of each of these larger groups are political in character.

But to make this "correction" betrays a misunderstanding of the way Aristotle employs the notion of "dualizing." He can say that an animal dualizes in some respect (as he says the seal does between being a land-animal and a water-animal because though it has a lung and sleeps and breeds on land it feeds in the sea and spends most of its time there) while nonetheless classifying it as *basically* belonging on one side or the other of the fence in question (as he classifies the seal as basically a water-animal, VII.12 566b31). A revealing passage for our purposes is *Gen. An.* I.4 772b1–6, where Aristotle says both that human beings dualize between having a single offspring and having several or many and that it is most natural for them to have one only; multiple births, being rare, are caused by excess fluidity and heat in the parents' bodies. So in our passage of *Hist. An.* I.1, human beings dualize between living in large groups and solitarily, but the latter arrangement is exceptional and a departure from the norm, so that basically the human being can be classed, as by implication Aristotle goes on to class it, when at 488a10 he says it is a political animal, among the *agelaia*.

Our manuscripts thus result from a misunderstanding of the implications of Aristotle's saying at 488a7 that human beings dualize (between living in herds and living solitarily). That does not in fact count against their being classified as *basically* herding animals, and so does not conflict with the apparent implication of 488a9–10 that, being political animals, human beings live in herds. Hence there was no good reason to alter the text at 488a2, as someone apparently did, to make the political animals something other than a subgroup of the herding ones.

6. I disagree with Bodéüs (*op. cit.*), who insists that by calling the human being *mallon politikon* at I.2 1253a7–8 Aristotle means that human beings have a better claim to the description *politikon* than other animals do (so that by implication he would be counting only the human being and not the bee, etc., as a *politikon zōon* at all), and not that human beings are more *politikon*, *politikon* in a higher degree. On Bodéüs's

interpretation Aristotle would be taking away from the nonhuman "political" animals this description that he had given them in the *Historia Animalium*, in order to avoid the supposed untoward consequence of "masking" under that generic description what is specific to human beings among animals. But the linkage between this *Politica* passage and that from *HA* I.1 is not just close but positive: here again it is with other *agelaia*, including bees, that Aristotle compares human beings, precisely the ones he counted as *politika* in *Historia Animalium*—not with all other animals in general, as would suit Bodéüs's interpretation better. So one cannot reasonably avoid taking Aristotle here to assert that some other herding animals are indeed *politika,* but that human beings are *politika* in a special and distinctive, more complete way. Given the implicit reference to the classification in *Hist. An.* I.1, therefore, *mallon politikon* must be comparative. Compare IX.1 589a1. Had Aristotle wanted here to correct what he says in the *Historia Animalium*, he could easily have written: *dioti de politikon ho anthrōpos monon tōn agelaiōn zōn, dēlon.*

7. But see *NE* IX.9 1160a13–14; *Pol.* III.6 1279a17–19; III.12 1282b16–18; III.13 1283b35–42.

8. On bees, see *Hist. An.* V.21–22 and IX.40. Aristotle does not repeat his classification of bees as political, and does not make a point of mentioning any single special work that bees undertake in common. (They cooperate in many different tasks in the hive and outside it that Aristotle does mention, e.g., at X.40 627a20 ff.) But presumably it is the hive and the differentiated life in it that he has in mind. For cranes see *Hist. An.* X.10 (again no repetition of the classification as political, and no focus on a single activity undertaken by all in common).

Aristotle's distinction towards the end of the *Historia Animalium* passage quoted in the text between political animals that are "under leaders" and those that are "ruler-less" makes it clear that in speaking of "some single thing" the members of a species do together he does not mean something *all* the members of a species cooperate together in doing. He means rather that the political species are naturally found in groups that are defined by the fact that all the members of each group (those, say, which are all under a given "leader") cooperate together in such an activity.

9. *Hist. An.* IX.1 588b30–589a4 (which should be read together with *Gen. An.* III.2 753a7–17) links the "political" character of a species with its members' intelligence (*phronēsis*), on the one hand, and, on the other hand, their tendency to live with and see to the upbringing of their offspring. The *De Generatione Animalium* passage, while not referring explicitly to any kind of animal as political in nature, does say that the more intelligent animals, which also have better memories, and which concern themselves for a longer period with their offspring's upbringing, come to have *sunētheia kai philia* ("intimacy and attachment," tr. Peck) for them even when fully grown. The suggestion is that greater intelligence in animals naturally shows itself in a more intensive and prolonged relationship between parents (or at least mothers) and offspring; this in turn generates ties of affection and friendship (in effect, what in the human case Aristotle calls family friendship, *suggenikē philia, NE* IX.12 1161b16 ff.); and "political" ties, both for human beings and for other animals are in some way natural extensions of these family ties. (On the connection between family friendship and political friendship, see below 244–48 and n.15.)

Although in these passages he makes no mention of a single common work that members of political species, as such, engage in, I assume Aristotle is presupposing, as he says explicitly in *Hist. An.* I.1, that such a common work is the essential mark of a political species. Certainly the emphasis on intelligence fits in very well with this assumption, since the cooperation and differentiation of function involved in such a single work evidently requires a relatively high degree of intelligence. And while rearing broods of offspring to maturity need not involve any work engaged in within a community wider than an immediate family, Aristotle's point seems to be that that kind of cooperative concern is the natural training ground for some more extensive cooperation in which an animal's political nature is more properly exhibited. (This explains why in both passages he seems to take it for granted that the more intelligent, more family-oriented species are all of them herding animals, and not solitary ones: only such could be political in any active sense.)

It is true that Aristotle says at *Gen. An.* III.2 753a14–15 that birds are less family-oriented than "human beings and certain quadrupeds," and that they don't develop "intimacy and attachment" toward their offspring when grown up. Birds are, accordingly, "less political"—because, I take it, the common work they nonetheless do engage in together, not being grounded in a communal family work, is less extensive. There is no reason to interpret Aristotle in either the *Hist. An.* IX.1, or the *Gen. An.* III.2 passage as implying that animals like the crane, which engage in a common work but do not show the extended family concern of such *more* political animals as human beings are not political at all. (In thinking about the implications of these passages about animal intelligence for Aristotle's classification of some animals as political in nature I have profitted from discussions with Jean-Louis Labarrière and from reading his unpublished paper on "La phronesis animale.")

10. Cf. III.9 1280b40–41: *polis de hē genōn kai kōmōn koinōnia zōēs teleias kai autarkous.*

11. As Newman notes, *The Politics of Aristotle,* p. 229 (and cf. 324 and 569–70), Aristotle himself occasionally uses the word *politēs* more widely than his official account permits. Newman refers to VIII.13 1332a32–35, and he might have added III.7 1279a31–32 and III.14 1285a25–29. These passages make it clear enough that Aristotle occasionally employs the word *politēs* in very much the same broad sense that, as I argue in what follows, he needs in order to make clear what he means by aiming "at the common advantage of the citizens." I would maintain, therefore, that even though the interpretation I offer of what this means employs the word "citizen" in a sense different from Aristotle's official one, it is a sense that Aristotle himself not only needs but actually employs on occasion, as well.

12. And it is noteworthy (see Newman *ad loc)* that Aristotle goes on only to say that (not people in general, but only) those who care about *eunomia* do think about how to make people politically good, and that *cities that deserve the name* have to concern themselves about virtue (III.9 1280b5–12). He does not go on to say explicitly, what 1280b1–5 implies, that the citizens in general, under whatever constitution, do (normally) concern themselves about what their fellow-citizens are like as persons.

13. Leaving aside, of course, those who may for one reason or another feel excluded from full participation in American life, or, again, those who may think the potential

good effects of these qualities are seriously compromised by injustices in the social and economic setting in which they operate, or by other contextual factors. On the importance of considerations of justice in this connection, see p. 76 ff.

14. Aristotle's point, then, against oligarchic constitutions is that the official view taken in oligarchic cities of the nature of the civic bond—that it is, or is essentially like, a contract or treaty or other agreement voluntarily entered into for mutual gain—misrepresents the *actual* nature of the citizenly ties that the citizens of the oligarchic city, like all other cities, evince. The constitutions that Aristotle ranks more highly simply take explicit notice of this fact about all cities, the oligarchic ones among the others, and give it the weight in the constitution itself that it deserves to have.

15. One should recall here Aristotle's criticisms (*Pol.* II.2–4) of the plan proposed in Plato's *Respublica* (V 457C–464B) for unifying the ideal city by making each of the rulers speak, think. and feel about each other ruler in the way in which members of a closeknit, harmonious family speak, think, and feel about one another. In effect, Socrates in the *Respublica* proposes doing away with separate families and separate family ties (among the rulers), replacing them with ties of exactly the same kind and strength linking each ruler to each other. He thinks of the civic friendship needed in order to unify and stabilize the city as impossible so long as loyalty to the city can come into conflict with loyalty to one's family. The only effective civic friendship, he thinks, will be one resulting from the extension to the whole ruling group of just those family ties which in other, historical, cities serve to compromise it. This kind of all-inclusive family relationship is impossible in principle, Aristotle thinks (*Pol.* II.4 1262a31)—when you call all of the children of a certain age "my son" or "my daughter," knowing that a large group of your fellow-rulers do the same, you don't and can't think and feel about them in the ways a true parent does. The misguided attempt to achieve this *both* does away with true family ties *and* makes impossible true civic friendship. All you get is a watered-down family friendship. This means that people will neither concern themselves about selected others as their sons, daughters, husbands, cousins, nor about their fellow-citizens in general. Once the family is gone, the use of the words that originally connoted family-relationships to refer instead to fellow-citizens generally, will not carry with it the thoughts and feelings that bind family members to one another (II.4 1262b15–24), and nothing will have been done to encourage the different thoughts and feelings appropriate to fellow-citizens. On Aristotle's view civic friendship must rest upon an understanding of the *special* ways that fellow-citizens are related to one another in a common work, and these do not necessarily compete with, but supplement, the links between family-members. Civic friendship, Aristotle insists, is a specific type of friendship, distinct (e.g.) from family friendship; furthermore, it does not exist at all except where there also exist families, brotherhoods, etc., with their own specific forms of friendship, to which it is added as a natural completion: see *NE* IX.9 1160a9–10; 1160a21–30; *EE* VIII.9 1241b24–26.

16. Oddly, this expression, or a close relative, seems to occur at most only once in the *Politica*. (The *philia tē politeia* referred to at V.9 1309b9 [cf. 1309a34] and II.8 1268a24 is a different thing.) This is at IV.11 1295b23–24, where the run of the argument seems to go best if both *politikēs* is taken with both *philias* and *koinōnias*. Aristotle's point is that it is important to avoid the enmity that exists when a contemptuous

rich class rule over an envious mass of poor people. Aristotle is clearly conceiving of this contempt and envy as being felt by the individual rich and poor persons for the members of the other group en masse: he has in mind a class phenomenon. So, therefore, the *philia* that Aristotle says such feelings preclude, but implies would be achievable if the middle class had power (see 1295b29–32), can only be *politikē philia*—a friendship felt by each citizen for the other citizens en masse, and the only kind of friendship Aristotle recognizes that can be felt quasi-anonymously for a whole group of people. Newman (*ad loc*) says, but without explanation, that "*politikēs* goes only with *koinōnias*, not with *philias*." That, however, is quite unsatisfactory: it is true enough that people who respectively have contempt and envy for one another are not good candidates for friendship of whatever sort, but Aristotle is not talking about contempt and envy in general, but about these feelings as experienced by whole classes for one another, and what that undermines is not friendship in general but civic friendship in particular. So it does seem greatly preferable to take *politikēs* here with *philias* as well as with *koinōnias*.

"Civic friendship" is discussed at length in *EE* VIII.9–10 (see also VIII.7 1241a32), where it is classified as a special form of "advantage friendship," friendship *kata to chrēsimon* (VIII.10 1242b22–23; 1243b4). The references in *NE* are at IX.12 1161b13; X.1 1163b34; X.6 1167b2 and X.10 1171a17. X.6 1167b2–4 makes it clear that in the *NE* too Aristotle classifies *politikē philia* as an advantage friendship, although he nowhere does so explicitly. The same thing is implied by IX.9, where in discussing civic friendship, though not under that name, he emphasizes that the civic community, the kind of community to which this kind of friendship is proper, is formed and survives for the sake of the common advantage of those belonging to it. Aristotle's very lengthy discussions of civic friendship in *NE* IX.9–12 and *EE* VIII.9–10 show clearly that he regarded this kind of friendship, though it is only a form of advantage friendship, as a very important one; he by no means treats it as a minor variation of no fundamental, independent interest. The prominence of civic friendship in the *Ethica Nicomachea* and the importance Aristotle attributes to it there is specially significant, since it seems clear that *NE* IX.9–12 is intended as summarizing central aspects of the political theory developed in the *Politica*. Accordingly, we can claim Aristotle's own testimony that in the *Politica*, too, civic friendship plays a crucial, though as I have noted a somewhat inexplicit, role.

17. See J. M. Cooper, "Aristotle on the Forms of Friendship," especially pp. 642–48 on civic friendship.

18. Civic friendship is therefore a very special kind of friendship, different in important ways from personal friendships (whether of pleasure or advantage, or ones based on character). At *EE* VIII.9 1241b13–17, Aristotle introduces his account of civic friendship by speaking explicitly of kinds (*eidē*) of *philia*, differing among themselves in accordance with the differences in the *koinōniai* (common enterprises) regulating the specific activities of which the *philia* in question consists: *politikē philia* is one of these *eidē*, the one that regulates precisely those activities of which the *politikē koinōnia* itself consists, making them be carried out in the spirit of friendship appropriate to them. In the *Ethica Nicomachea* Aristotle does not use the terminology of *eidē philias* in this connection, but his doctrine is exactly the same: see IX.9 1159b26–31. There is no cause for surprise that this friendship, unlike the personal friendships from

which Aristotle naturally begins his consideration of *philia*, does not require any degree of intimacy nor even any personal knowledge of one another on the part of the "friends." Since the *koinōnia* in question does not require intimacy and personal knowledge, neither, obviously, could the *philia* specific to it. One should bear in mind that in describing in very general terms the conditions that hold good for friendships, of whatever type, in IX.2 Aristotle says only (1155b34–1156a5) that friends must both wish their friends well for the friends' own sake, and know this fact about one another—not that they must be intimate with one another, or even know each other in person. Intimacy and personal knowledge are not the only ways of knowing (or anyhow reasonably coming to believe) that such mutual good will exists, and they are not even the normal way such mutual good will gets communicated in every context where it exists. In the political context, knowledge of the nature of the constitution, of the general level of support for it among the different elements of the population, and of what's generally expected of people in that society is the normal way of knowing about these things, and it is sufficient, sometimes, to establish a reasonable presumption of good will on the part of one's fellow-citizens generally.

Taken together, these considerations show, I think, that Julia Annas was wrong in "Plato and Aristotle on Friendship and Altruism" to think that in seeking to accommodate such "objective" kinds of *philia* as civic friendship, into a common framework with the personal ones Aristotle grossly failed to square his views on the objective with his account of the personal friendships. Annas's bias in favor of the personal friendships (understandable given *our* concept of friendship) prevents her from seeing that Aristotle from the outset of his discussion holds together in his mind—as the Greek concept of *philia* itself did—the phenomena of both the personal and the objective types of *philia*, and sets out to give a comprehensive, systematic account of them all.

19. I do not say that Aristotle was aware of this difference. At IX.11 1161a30–32 he takes note of the fact that in the deviant forms of constitution there is necessarily less civic friendship between rulers and ruled, because of the injustice of the constitutions. Tyranny, being the most unjust constitution, is also the least characterized by civic friendship.

20. See *Pol.* III.17 1287b37–39 for a clear recognition by Aristotle of the ways in which conceptions of justice vary with political constitutions. See also *NE* IX.11, where Aristotle again marks off the conceptions of justice at work in different kinds of constitution, but this time links these differences to differences in the bases of the respective civic friendships.

21. Aristotle does not say much in detail, either in the *Politica* or in the *Ethics*, about how life in a well-run, well-constituted city does encourage the moral improvement of the citizens. One may, perhaps, think first of laws explicitly framed so as to require of the citizens the doing of certain actions (and omission of others) that, if engaged in regularly and in the right spirit, will, Aristotle thinks, lead eventually to the acquisition of the moral virtues. (In *NE* V, as is well known, Aristotle emphasizes that "the law" requires the citizens to do acts of courage, temperance, good temper, and all the other moral virtues: see 1 1129b19–25.) Equally important, however, is the fact that in such a city, animated by civic friendship, the mature citizens care very much about one another's characters and encourage one another and the young in the virtues by showing

what the proper spirit is in which the acts of the virtues are to be done, and by making it clear that in their view acting in that spirit is the central and indispensable part of any human being's own personal good. Life in such a city is a moral education, quite apart from what the laws do or do not *require* the citizens to *do* (or refrain from doing).

22. Aristotle's introduction in *Pol.* VIII.1–3 to his discussion, beginning in ch. 4, of the ideal best city—i.e., the best constitution for a city that enjoys ideal conditions with respect to size and character of population, natural resources, etc.—gives evidence that the analysis just presented spells out implications of Aristotle's theory of friendship that he himself accepted. He begins (VIII.1 1323a17–19) by saying that in general one should expect a constitution which is best (for any population) to be such that those living under it lead the best life available to them in the given external circumstances. Later, again, he says (VIII.2 1324a23–25) that, necessarily, the best constitution will be that arrangement under which anyone (of the relevant group, i.e., of those having a part in the political life of the city) could act in the best way and live happily—the best constitution must not discriminate against any group among the citizens, but must provide the conditions under which (*modulo* the natural wealth of the land, native talents of the population, etc.—the *huparchonta* of VIII.1 1323a18) this life is available to them, if only they do their part. When, accordingly, he raises the question (VIII.2 1324 a 5–7) whether happiness is the same for each individual person and for a city, he is not concerned merely for the question of meaning—whether what it is for a city, as such, to be happy and successful is the same, *mutatis mutandis,* as what is for a single person. (Indeed he settles this question of meaning almost immediately, by VIII.2 1324a13.) A major concern in the subsequent discussion is to see that there really is the coincidence he has declared there must be between happiness for the city and happiness for the participant citizens. (Another major concern is to deal with the threat that cities in pursuit of their own happiness will always seek hegemony or even despotic power over neighboring cities: on this see Carnes Lord, *Education and Culture in the Political Thought of Aristotle*, ch.5.) Against this background I think it is right to attach significance to some of Aristotle's language as he formulates and discusses the relationship between happiness for the city and happiness for the individual. When he first raises this question he asks whether the same life is the most worth choosing for everyone taken in common and taken separately (*koinē kai chōris*, VIII.1 1323a21). In answering that it is the same (1323b40–41; VIII.2 1324a5–8; VIII.3 1325b30–32), viz. the life devoted to the exercise of the virtues both moral and intellectual, he glosses the judgment that it is "best for everyone taken in common" with its being "best for a city" (VIII.2 1324a6) or "best for cities taken in common" (VIII.1 1323b41) or again "best for cities and human beings taken in common" (VIII.3 1325b32). The emphasis in these glosses on the happiness of a city being the common happiness of its people suggests strongly that the virtuous life that a city leads when it is organized into and governed as a true aristocracy is being thought of as a life led *by its citizens* in the broad sense of "citizens" that I have distinguished—the (free) *anthrōpoi* (1325b32) whose common possession or activity it is. If under such a constitution "everyone in common" leads the best life, then even someone who is not himself a virtuous person and so not constantly exercising virtues in his daily life is nonetheless in a secondary way leading a virtuous life, by having his life merged in the

life of the whole city which itself is a virtuous one, by reason (primarily) of the virtues possessed, and exercised in its political and otherwise communal life, by its ruling class.

23. The reason why Aristotle thinks cities in particular, and not merely various, more limited associations for a common life, are needed and naturally pursued by human beings, is that only cities are complete and self-sufficient associations, associations capable of developing to their fullest extent, and giving appropriate scope for the exercise of, the virtues of mind and character which are the core of the natural good for a human being. See above nn. 1, 15, and T. H. Irwin's "The Good of Political Acitivity," esp. 74ff., 84ff.

24. I made extensive revisions to this chapter after the symposium, "Aristoteles' *Politik*," XI. Symposium Aristotelicum (Friedrichshafen/Bodensee 1987), in response to the criticisms contained in Julia Annas's excellent official commentary (especially excellent where she was more firmly in disagreement with my own views), and to written and oral comments of several of the other symposiasts. I made especially substantial additions and changes in reply to questions and criticisms of D. J. Furley and T. H. Irwin. I am indebted also to M. M. Mackenzie for perceptive and, for me, fruitful comments on the original embryo of the chapter, presented to a Princeton Classical Philosophy Conference in December 1983; to John R. Wallach, and to Richard Kraut for discussion and written comments on an intermediate version of the chapter.

4

Ideology and Philosophy in Aristotle's Theory of Slavery

Malcolm Schofield

1. Introduction

ARISTOTLE'S VIEWS ON SLAVERY are an embarrassment to those who otherwise hold his philosophy in high regard. To the modern mind they are morally repugnant. Many find them poorly argued and incompatible with more fundamental tenets of his system, and they certainly contain at least apparent inconsistencies. Worst of all, perhaps, is the suspicion that his theory of slavery is not really philosophy: "No one can doubt that the Aristotelian analysis of slavery—and especially the chapters of *Politics* Book I devoted to it—have an ideological function in the Marxist sense of the word." ("Il ne fait de doute pour personne que l'analyse aristotélicienne de l'esclavage—et surtoux les chapitres qu'y consacre le livre I de la *Politique*—a une fonction idéologique au sens marxiste de mot."[1]) My chapter aims to examine this last claim, and in particular to get clearer about the kinds of evidence which might be offered for or against it, and indeed about what the evidence is evidence of. To my own surprise I conclude that Aristotle's theory is not to any interesting extent ideological.

I operate with a broadly Marxist conception of an ideology, as (i) a widely held body of ideas systematically biased towards the real or imagined interests of a particular sex or social group or class within a society,[2] (ii) believed by its adherents not because of rational considerations which may be offered in its support but as a result either (a) of social causation or (b) of a desire to promote the interests indicated in (i) (or both).[3] Or to put it more briefly (if more vaguely) a set of "views, ideas, or beliefs that are somehow tainted by the social origin or the social interests of those who held them."[4] A philosophical belief, on the other hand, I take to be one which *inter alia* is held because of the rational considerations which are offered in its support. Thus I make the key difference between ideology and philosophy a question of the causation of the beliefs a thinker holds.[5] From my formulation it sounds as though the distinction between rational beliefs and those that are the products of social influences or of ulterior motives is an exclusive one, which would no doubt be a mistake. If it is a mistake, we can expect more or less philosophical ideologies, and more or less ideological philosophies.[6]

Aristotle's theory of slavery perhaps lacks the range or complexity to count as a "body of ideas," although of course the nexus of theses and concepts to which it belongs, for example, those developed in *Pol.* I as a whole, clearly does. Nor have I any interest is asking if the theory was "widely held." What I take as obvious, however, is that in all other respects Aristotle's theory *does* satisfy criterion (i) of ideologies. The question I propose for discussion is: What explains his belief in the theory? Is it [e.g. (ii) (a)] one of those "elegantly presented and well-argued theories" that "rest on certain basic assumptions which . . . turn out to be uncritical reproductions of the most commonplace beliefs of the ordinary members of [its author's] society or class?"[7] Is it [cf. (ii) (b)] the work of a partisan "who chose a side, making a primary commitment to a position and defending it with all the weapons of [his] considerable intellectual armoury?"[8] In other words, is Aristotle's account of the relation of master and slave as natural anything other than an attempt, deliberate [cf. (ii) (b)] or not [cf. (ii) (a)], to articulate an ideological belief, very likely shared widely among well-to-do Athenians and Macedonians, that it was right and proper for most masters to be masters and most slaves (especially barbarian slaves) to be slaves? Or is it simply the outcome of purely philosophical reflection?

To think of Aristotle as the victim or accomplice of ideology in his political theory might seem odd to the reader who remembers the treatment of justice in Book III. That discussion gives grounds for seeing Aristotle as himself the first thinker ever to have identified a set of beliefs as an ideology; or at least—to put the point less anachronistically and in a more appropriately down-to-earth style—he was the first writer we know of to combine in his analysis of an intellectual position diagnosis of social bias [cf. (i)] with a hypothesis about the reason for the bias that includes a non-cognitive component [cf. (ii)], applying in politics as elsewhere his maxim: "We must not only state the true view but also explain the false view" (*NE* VII.14 1154a22–23). The proponents of democracy wrongly suppose that justice is nothing but equality, the partisans of oligarchy no less wrongly assume that it is simply a matter of recognizing inequality. Why do both sides go wrong? Because people are bad judges in their own case (i.e., interest obtrudes), and because they take a partial notion absolutely (precisely the sort of cognitive mechanism Marx saw as characteristic of the ideological distorting effects likely to follow from occupying a particular position in the social nexus): especially for a rich man it is easy (but mistaken) to think that someone who is superior in wealth, for example, is superior in everything (*Pol.* III.9 1280a7–25).

But if Aristotle is uncommonly percipient in Book III, he may yet be vulgarly blind or partisan in Book I. After all, both parties to the disagreement about justice are made up of citizens: "us." What Book I in effect does is define "them"—slaves, women, middlemen—from "our" vantage point. In other words, there is a possible origin—that is, social motivation—for bias in the handling of the topics of Book I, which has no tendency to warp the treatment of justice in Book III.

The blindness [cf. (ii) (a)] and parti pris [cf. (ii) (b)] characteristic of ideological belief are forms of false consciousness: someone holding such a belief will typically labor under a delusion or practice insincerity or both. In prosecuting the enquiry we shall find it useful to employ the category of false consciousness. But in asking whether Aristotle's theory of slavery is a product of false consciousness I assume that we shall not be concerned to be specific about which kind of falsehood—delusion or insincerity—might be in question.

What we shall find more helpful is a distinction suggested by the work of Raymond Geuss. In his book *The Idea of a Critical Theory* Geuss points out that there are different kinds of grounds on which one may attribute false consciousness to someone. Two of the three he distinguishes are of interest to us: consciousness may be ideologically false in virtue of some *epistemic* properties of the beliefs that are its constituents, or in virtue of some of its *genetic* properties.[9] Epistemic vs. genetic is not a contrast we can take over without amendment, since (as Geuss's own treatment of the epistemic category makes clear)[10] the falsehood in epistemic cases is in the end a matter of their origin or casual history, at least insofar as it is distinctively ideological. What Geuss's flawed taxonomy reminds us, however, is that, where we suspect a theory of being ideological, there are at least two different features of it which may give rise to the suspicion: something about the nature, or more specifically the alleged epistemic status, of the theory itself, and something about the methods used in arriving at it.

Thus I first consider the method by which Aristotle reaches the conclusion that for certain sorts of men slavery is just and beneficial. He himself undoubtedly regards his method as a rational philosophical procedure, but we may think that it is largely a reflex of contemporary prejudices or that his belief in the justice of slavery is really the outcome of quite different unavowed influences on his mind. This would be a case of false consciousness that is deluded or insincere because the genesis of the theory is quite other than what Aristotle represents it as being.

After methods we must turn to the issue of epistemic status. Geuss explains:

> By the "epistemic properties" of a form of consciousness I mean such things as whether or not the descriptive beliefs contained in the form of consciousness are supported by the available empirical evidence, or whether or not the form of consciousness is one in which beliefs of different epistemic type (e.g. descriptive beliefs and normative beliefs) are confused.[11]

There are three principal grounds on which one might convict Aristotle's theory of slavery of exhibiting epistemic properties characteristic of false consciousness. First, it may be argued that it suffers from what Marxists would regard as the classic defects of ideology, viz. illegitimate objectification and generalization. Aristotle takes the master–slave relation to be one grounded in nature and of benefit to both parties. In reality this is not an expression of objective, impartial truth, but a projection of the interests and activities of his own class. Second, it is a common complaint among scholars that Aristotle's idea of natural slavery is an anomaly within his philosophical system; certainly inconsistent with his general theory of human psychology, and perhaps even internally inconsistent. It seems not unlikely that the anomaly is due to the influence on his mind of class interest rather than to flaws in purely philosophical ratiocination.[12] Third, it might be granted *argumenti causa* that there are persons who satisfy Aristotle's description of natural slaves, and even that slavery is the appropriate condition for such persons. But (the argument will go)[13] it is a massive error or pretence to assume that in the actual world (for Aristotle, the contemporary Greek world) slaves *are* what he calls natural slaves. Again the obvious explanation of the assumption is wishful thinking.

2. Aristotle's Method

It is easy enough to construct a case for the view that, however Aristotle himself may have thought that he had arrived at his belief in the justice of slavery, it was really little more than the reflex of ordinary Greek prejudices. For it seems likely that most unenslaved Greeks felt at ease with the institution of slavery. In Greek literature down to Aristotle there is precious little evidence of any unease,[14] and it is notorious that Plato felt so little pressure to justify the institution in the *Respublica* that, as is apt to happen where servants are concerned, he barely bothered to acknowledge the unquestionable presence of slaves in his ideal state.[15] The representation of slaves on painted pottery and in comedy, or again the attitude to slaves evidenced in Herodotus and Xenophon, makes it almost as likely that they were usually viewed as inferior, morally, intellectually, physically—whether because they were supposed racially inferior or for whatever reason (enslavement is not calculated to bring out the best in people).[16] Why did unenslaved Greeks hold these views? It is hard to avoid the hypothesis of ideology, albeit a mostly inarticulate and undebated ideology[17] (contrast the treatment of women): the durability and ubiquity of the institution in the ancient Mediterranean world will have made it difficult not to conceive it as part of the proper moral fabric of life, especially for those who had no obvious interest in envisaging any other possibility.

Aristotle makes it clear that his theory of natural slavery is designed to establish an ethical conclusion: "it is clear, then, that in some cases[18] some are free by nature and others slaves: for whom slavery is both beneficial and just" (*Pol.* I.5 1255a1–3). Is it not likely that this ethical proposition is something Aristotle accepted precisely because he too shared the general Greek ideology of slavery, in consequence of the same causes as operated on Greeks in general? Why should he have been exempt from their influence? If he was not, then we should interpret the theory of natural slavery from which he deduces his ethical proposition not as the *fundamental* reason he has for holding the proposition (his acceptance of the ideology is what really causes him to hold it), but as an attempt to justify a belief to which he is already committed and had probably unconsciously absorbed in earliest boyhood. No doubt some elements in the justification articulate ideas other Greeks would readily have shared (e.g., the notion of the psychological inferiority of the natural slave), while others (e.g., the more general notion that all complex systems exhibit hierarchy, 1254a24ff.) are more special to Aristotle although not, or course, lacking in attraction. The key point, however, is that, while Aristotle derives his ethical justification of slavery as natural from these ideas, it is not they that explain his belief in the rightness of slavery but a more deep-seated acceptance of the popular ideology of slavery.

What might Aristotle have said in response to this diagnosis? One fundamental claim one would expect him to have wanted to make is that he is a philosopher and as such committed to examining by *reason* any question proposed for discussion. The assumption underlying such a response is that reason is a powerful source of insight—whether by virtue of its methods or of its scope—independent of common belief and ready to be critical of it. It is an assumption which itself gained the status of a *communis opinio* in Greek philosophical tradition from Heraclitus and Parmenides to Plato.

But if Aristotle shared it, he did so in such a deliberately qualified sense that it may well be doubted whether reason, as he envisages and employs it, can act as a significant counterweight to popular prejudice. The grounds for doubt are supplied by his famous endoxic method:[19] the method has an elective affinity for ideology.

This thesis can be argued in a more or in a less straightforward version. The plainer version takes the endoxic method to embody the view (at least so far as ethics and politics are concerned) that common sense is what ultimately carries authority: reason can correct and refine it but never displace it or depart from it dramatically. It is at any rate very natural to read the celebrated statement of the endoxic method at *NE* VII.1 1145b2–7 in this way:

> We must, as in the other cases, set the things that seem to be the case before us and, after first discussing the difficulties, go on to prove, if possible, the truth of all the reputable opinions about these affections [sc. continence, incontinence, etc.] or, failing this, of the greater number and the most authoritative, for if we both resolve the difficulties and leave the reputable opinions undisturbed, we shall have proved the case sufficiently.

Reputable opinions do not only constitute the starting points and destination of enquiry. They *guide* it, as possessing an independent authority, which it is the business of reason to confirm (if it can: we are in the realm of *to hōs epi to polu* [*what holds for the most part*]; not all reputable opinions are authoritative, but that fact does not undermine the authority of those that are). Of course, Aristotle does not *say* here that the reputable opinions we should be attending to are mostly common or popular opinions (rather than those of the cognoscenti). But in ethics and politics common opinions are what he usually has in mind. He is sometimes prepared to argue that common opinions carry weight because they rest on experience—on what over a long period of time has been found to work (cf. *Pol.* II.5 1264a1–5, *Div. Somn.* 1, 462b14–16) as one would expect of a philosopher who lays such stress on the importance of experience in practical judgment. In fact the beliefs of the majority on matters of ethics and politics all too often constitute ideologies.

In recent years this interpretation of the endoxic method as an elaboration of common sense—at best conservative and at worst parochial—has been called in question by scholars. Barnes has pointed out that "there are remarkably few propositions which Aristotle cannot, in one way or another, include among the initial *phainomena* to be considered."[20] And he suggests that "the process of 'purification,' generously construed, will allow him still greater scope in assembling" the most authoritative ones. He concludes: "The method is not formally vacuous; but it has, in the last analysis, very little content."

Similarly Martha Nussbaum writes:

> The method does not make discoveries, radical departures, or sharp changes of position impossible, either in science or in ethics. What it does do is to explain

> to us how any radical or new view must commend itself to our attention: by giving evidence of its superior ability to integrate and organize features of our lived experience of the world.[21]

I am not persuaded by these revisionist accounts of the method. Barnes may be right that Aristotle's formulations of it are potentially elastic; and there are undoubtedly some texts where reason or argument is put firmly in the driving seat and the *phainomena* relegated to provide supporting evidence and examples (so notably at *EE* I.6 1216b26–28). But at least when he wrote *NE* VII.1 1145b2–7 Aristotle must have wanted to accord more weight to common opinion than that.

Whether the endoxic method is conservative or merely elastic it can offer little resistance to popular ideology. Either way it fails to provide adequate *stimulus* to question whether what we take to be "our lived experience of the world" (e.g., "our" perception of slaves as inferior) is really experience, and even if it is, whether that experience might not be a function of social circumstances which could and conceivably should be different from what they are. The contrast with Plato is striking. Plato expects common beliefs and perceptions to be confused and erroneous, and claims a secure critical perspective from which to exhibit their deficiencies. The proof of the pudding is in the eating. In physics it is Plato who guesses that the elements require a mathematical analysis and are quite other than what appears. In politics, likewise, Plato is the thinker who takes a radical view of the *polis,* from the abolition of the family and the role of women to the education of rulers. Aristotle in these as in so many spheres sticks closer to the *phainomena*—as everyone would acknowledge. Is this not because the endoxic method is either conservative or anodyne? To be sure, the method accords reason a critical role. But Aristotle's discussions of the method leave that critical function theoretically underdescribed and indeed undernourished, so to speak. Is it any surprise that in practice its radical potential (which on a conservative interpretation of the method is in principle more limited in any case than Nussbaum would like) goes largely unrealized?

The endoxic method, then, leaves its practitioners all too prone to succumb to popular ideology.

This truth, however, does nothing to support the view that Aristotle's theory of slavery is ideology. As Victor Goldschmidt pointed out in an important article, Aristotle does not follow the canonical method of *endoxa* in his treatment of slavery.[22] In Book I of the *Politica* Aristotle (1) announces at the outset that he will pursue what is quite evidently an entirely different method: a method of analysis (I.1 1252a17–23); (2) follows this method in his discussions both of slavery and of household management[23]; (3) points out from time to time that he is following it (I.3 1253b1–8; I.8 1256a1–3; cf. I.5 1254a 20ff).[24] Most of the opinions of others on these topics that he cites in the course of the book he rejects as erroneous.[25] For example, he refers dismissively to other views on slavery as ideas "that are nowadays supposed true" (I.3 1253b17–18). It is not in the least surprising that he shows no sign of using them as authoritative guides for investigation (which is what on the conservative reading of the endoxic method *endoxa* are supposed to be). All he attempts to do in this connection is to demonstrate with respect to some (not all) of the opinions he mentions that, with suitable reinterpretation, they can be harmonized with the account of the matter already established by the method of analysis. I suppose that, on an elastic understanding of the endoxic method, this demonstration might count as an application of the method. But the key thing to notice is that it is *not* the method which *guides* Aristotle's enquiry in Book I, but a confirmatory supplement to it. Aristotle himself was surely clear about the division of labor here, which is the same as in *NE* I, where at 8 1098b9–11 he bids us consider the question before us "in the light not only of our conclusion and of the premises of the argument, but also of the things that are said about it."[26]

Is the method of analysis any more resistant to ideology than the endoxic method? Potentially so, inasmuch as it involves an immediate appeal to reason (I.5 1254a20) and to first principles. And if the moral climate in which Aristotle grew up was unquestioningly complacent about slavery, his approach to the issue in the *Politica* shows him well aware that other thinkers rejected it as unnatural and unjust (this view is one of the ideas "that are nowadays supposed true": I.3 1253b20–23). There is clearly a sense in which he treats the question of the morality of slavery as an open one, to be settled by philosophy.[27] Was he self-deceived or insincere in taking this line? The answer to that must largely depend on how powerful a piece of philosophical analysis Aristotle's is: the better it is, the more reason there will be to judge that it is philosophy, not the unavowed but deep-seated assumptions of his boyhood, which brings him to a belief in natural slavery. So it is time now to begin consideration of the more substantive arguments for the charge that the theory is ideology, not real philosophy.

3. Nature and the Projection of Class Interest

We have learned to expect that ethical and political theories which appeal for their premises to human nature will have created "nature" in the image of some contingent, historically situated and conditioned view of man. More particularly, the substitution of nature for history was diagnosed by Marx as a specially characteristic device of ideology:

> The ideologist "justifies" the capitalist society on the ground that it alone is in harmony with human nature. He justifies hard work and attacks the demand for a relaxed social existence on the ground that scarcity is a natural human predicament. He explains overpopulation as an "inherent" tendency in man, and turns "a social law into a law of nature." He presents conflicts between individuals and groups as inherent in human nature and indeed in nature itself. He presents the socially created differences between men and women as natural, and argues that it is natural for women to be confined to homes or to less demanding jobs. He presents the historically created intellectual, moral and other inequalities between men as part of their "natural endowment," and turns "the consequences of society into the consequences of nature." He argues that it is natural for social institutions to be hierarchically organized, for the intellectual skills to be better rewarded than the manual, and so on. As Marx frequently puts it, the ideologist "eternalizes" or "deifies" a given social practice or order, and eliminates history.[28]

Perhaps it seems *prima facie* unlikely that a great philosopher such as Aristotle could have fallen unwarily into the trap of simply assuming that what looks right or wrong must be natural or unnatural. Has any philosopher thought more or harder about nature? But Book I of the *Politica* not only develops the theory of natural slavery, but takes for granted the naturalness of the subordination of women, and goes on to argue the *un*naturalness of trade as a means of acquisition (in contrast to agriculture, hunting, and direct exchange): all within the framework of a conception of the household, and of the *polis* itself, as natural.[29] The longer the book goes on, the more insistent is the reader's suspicion that what Aristotle is really elaborating is the ideology of (or an ideology for) the affluent, slave-owning man of substance whom he sees as the ideal citizen of the *polis.* The claim that slavery is not only natural but beneficial to the slave only reinforces the diagnosis of false consciousness at work. The view that what is in the interest of a dominant class is in the interests of all is a notion even more highly characteristic of ideologies than the appeal to nature.

The complaint is that in *Pol.* I Aristotle projects a particular actual form of society into a general norm. It is a complaint hard to evaluate. On the one hand, it is an attractive suggestion that the theory of slavery comes into proper perspective when we look at its context in *Pol.* I, and see it as just one item in a highly specific recipe for the good life for actual Greek "gentlemen." If you were an Athenian citizen of means, who regarded trade as a matter properly left in the hands of aliens (evidently the standard view),[30] and considered the management of your own household your responsibility (not your wife's, as was often assumed in the fifth century),[31] then *Pol.* I would indeed give you a theoretical justification of what you already believed right and advantageous—but a justification which from our vantage point quite lacks the authority Aristotle's appeal to nature seems designed to lend it. On the other hand, Aristotle is obviously attempting an intellectual project of universal validity. Its focus is man in general as social, autonomous agent, organizing himself and those in his society who cannot organize themselves to secure what is needed by them all for the good life. The ideal Aristotle has in view is not far removed in general character from Marx's own vision of the society we will enjoy when man realizes his potential for self-determined action and so for happiness.[32] Nor is there anything necessarily ideological in thought about what human nature is capable of, or in the concern to secure a harmony of the interests of organizer and organized.

In short, we can come at Aristotle's views on slaves, women, and trade from two directions: from contemporary Greek reality or from his own moral philosophy. If we adopt the first approach, an ideological explanation of these views seems well nigh inevitable. But the second approach allows more scope for argument, and in particular it leaves open the possibility that we need a different story for what Aristotle says about slaves from what he says about women. False consciousness may have eaten its way unevenly into his thinking on these questions.

The key assumption Aristotle makes is that the grip of women and slaves on practical reason is such that they need to have their lives organized by others. He devotes very little energy to arguing this in the case of women. He takes it simply for a fact. And he is mistaken. The obvious reason for this male mistake is an inference from the pliableness of many women reinforced by contemporary social forms: a classic instance of false consciousness.

The treatment of slavery is quite different. It occupies the best part of five chapters of *Pol.* I. As we have seen, Aristotle begins by acknowledging that it is a controversial subject. And instead of accepting from the outset any "facts" about slaves, he so far reverses his normal procedure in scientific enquiry as to discuss first the question What is a slave? before addressing the issue of whether there *are* any slaves properly so called.[33] When he does address it, he works out his answer on the basis of very general considerations about the nature of animals in general and humans in particular. The kernel of his answer—that there are some people better off being ruled than ruling—is a not unreasonable thesis. Above all, at no stage in the central argument of *Pol.* I.4–7 is any use made of an assumption that most of those who in contemporary Greece were enslaved are natural slaves (indeed, the implication of I.6 is that some were unjustly enslaved—those who were slaves only in consequence of the fortunes and conventions of war). Rather the reverse: Aristotle's theory of natural slavery is at least potentially a critical theory. A slave owner who pondered it seriously would have to ask himself: "Is my slave really a natural slave? Or is he too shrewd and purposeful?"

4. Anomaly and Inconsistency

Aristotle's theory of natural slavery is presented as an outwork of his general philosophy of man; it establishes a criterion of who is or is not suited to slavery against which actual cases of enslavement could be judged just or unjust; it is therefore not plausibly explained as ideology. So ran the argument of the previous paragraph. But it can be objected that the theory is in fact inconsistent with Aristotle's general account of man, and constitutes an anomaly within his system. If so, it may then be a sign of false consciousness at work that he advances a positive account of slavery at all.

The very idea that there could be natural slaves might be thought to conflict with a belief firmly rooted in Aristotle's general philosophy, viz. that man is an *infima species* with his own distinctive essence. His natural philosophy recognizes no such species or subspecies as "ensouled tool." The conflict comes close to the surface when Aristotle discusses the question whether a master can enjoy friendship with a slave: insofar as he is a slave, no—for he is merely an ensouled tool; insofar as he is a man, yes—for he can partake in law and contract, and so justice, and so friendship (*NE* VIII.11 1161b3–8). Aristotle's predilection for answering questions "yes and no" is often attractive, and he is often illuminating when he reflects on the different descriptions under which we identify one and the same item. Here the illumination is apparent enough, but the bland "yes and no" extremely uncomfortable. On Aristotle's own finding, "slave" and "man" must be incompatible designations, for the consequences of applying them to one and the same individual are contradictory. The air of compromise is quite bogus.[34]

Consider also the thesis that slavery is beneficial to the natural slave. Aristotle believes that slaves resemble women and children in being incapable of running their own or other people's lives: "the slave simply does not possess the faculty of deliberation [he perceives reason but does not have it]; the female has it, but in her it lacks authority; the child has it, but undeveloped" (*Pol.* I.13 1260a12–14; cf. I.5 1254b22–23). Like women and children, therefore, they need for their own safety to be ruled. For women leadership suffices, but what is right for children is a paternal rule (analogous to that of a monarch). The crucial feature of paternal rule is that its primary concern is the good of the ruled, not as with slavery the ruler's. Why is not paternalism equally the right way to treat the childlike who satisfy Aristotle's description of natural slaves? Is not their psychological condition so similar to children's as to make this the inescapable conclusion, and certainly the one most in their interests? Aristotle notoriously takes a different line. Exploitation, not paternalism, is the order of the day. The childlike are just bodies, sentient tools; they will find more fulfilment in being used—in living out their function—than otherwise. Once again the premise that some people are mere ensouled tools appears to conflict with more widely based tenets of Aristotle's philosophy, in this case his human psychology as adumbrated in Book I of the *Politica* itself. Once again this premise is what he requires to sustain a major doctrine about slavery, viz. that it is in the slave's interest.[35]

The use of the word "childlike" to designate those suited for slavery may appear to conceal an inconsistency of a different kind: one internal to the actual notion of the natural slave. There is much in Aristotle's account of slaves which suggests that they are feeble-minded and brutish. They do not have reason but merely perceive it (I.5 1254b22–23); they are cut out primarily for physical labor, and indeed for the same sort of work as domesticated animals do (1254b12–34). It is in virtue of just such features that their enslavement is held to be justifiable (cf. e.g. I.2 1252a30–34). But while this is the picture that emerges from the main argument in I.5 (with I.2), other comments made by Aristotle later in *Pol.* I point in another direction. I.7, which argues that masters are not masters in virtue of their possession of a relevant science, concedes that there *are* forms of knowledge appropriate both to masters and to slaves. Slaves can be taught their everyday duties of service, and (1255b25–30):

> This kind of instruction might well be extended to cookery and the rest of those kinds of service. For the tasks of the various slaves differ, some bringing more in the way of esteem, others being more in the nature of necessities. As the proverb has it: "slave before slave, master before master."

I.13 adds that they require a form of virtue to withstand temptations that might impede performance of their jobs (1260a33–36), and consequently need not merely instructions but advice or encouragement (more so than children)—and must *not* therefore be denied reason (1260b5–7). Slaves such as these sound not in the least feeble-minded, but like the naturally slavish Asians (III.14 1285a16-22) who are said to be well equipped for thinking and the skills (what they lack is spirit: VII.7 1327b27–29). It is hard to see why on the premises of I.5 they qualify as natural slaves at all.

How has Aristotle got himself into this difficulty? It is tempting to answer: because the ideological roots of his theory could not be concealed for long. In its initial presentation the theory may legitimate only very selective enslavement—of the feeble-minded. But the fact that Aristotle so soon slips in intelligent slaves who practice crafts, not just necessary physical tasks, shows that its real motivation was to justify the actual institution of slavery as he knew it. This hypothesis also suggests an explanation of the anomalous presence of the theory within his system: it is developed because class interest dictates that there should be slaves, not because it fits well with Aristotle's philosophy.

Yet appeal to ideology is not the only reasonable or intellectually respectable way of coping with anomaly and inconsistency. These are phenomena not unknown elsewhere in the writings of great philosophers. And there is at least one other commonly employed strategy for dealing with them: the exercise of interpretative charity. Perhaps that is what we should try in the present case, and hope to show either that these inconsistencies are a sign of a fruitful tension within Aristotle's thought or that carefully considered they turn out not to be inconsistencies after all.

Let us take first the alleged inconsistency in Aristotle's treatment of the all-important issue of the psychology of the natural slave. There is a difficulty in supposing that Aristotle insincerely or self-deludingly forgets later in Book I an earlier characterization of natural slaves as essentially feeble-minded. The faculty in which they are from the outset declared deficient is deliberation or practical reason: the ability "to look ahead in thought" (I.2 1252a31–32). This—the power of deliberation—is once more denied them in I.13 (1260a12). Hence their suitability for slavery: they need someone else to deliberate on their behalf if they are to survive (so for example I.2 1252a30–31). It is because they can follow deliberative reasoning in others (I.5 1254b22) that they are accorded reason at the end of I.13 (1260b5–6); which does not conflict with its denial to them at 5 1254b23—for they cannot deliberate themselves. Now this deliberative incapacity is not for Aristotle incompatible with the intelligent exercise of skills like cookery (I.7 1255b26) or shoemaking (I.13 1260b2): children too acquire such skills without thereby achieving the consistency of purpose and the breadth of reflection needed to look after themselves properly; and it is the comparison with children that Aristotle dwells on most in I.13. It *would* be at odds with the doctrine that slaves cannot deliberate to suggest that they might exercise the architectonic skills of farm managers or bankers. But Aristotle does not suggest any such thing.

In I.2 and 5 he certainly gives the impression that brute physical strength and deliberative incapacity are two sides of a single coin and together supply the rationale of the slave's symbiotic relation with his master. This emphasis on the physical is best seen as expository exaggeration, not unlike the stress put upon habituation of the passions in the initial account of moral virtue in *NE* II, where in order to distance himself from the Socratic identification of virtue with knowledge Aristotle notoriously underplays the role he himself assigns to rational judgment. Maybe the childlike adults of *Pol.* I are usually physically robust, but Aristotle himself observes that this is often not the case (I.5 1254b32–1255a1). We should allow him a similar *hōs epi to polu* (judgment that holds for the most part) with regard to the necessary tasks they are fitted to perform: some may be capable of more than the bare essentials, without significantly altering the general Calibanesque picture, and without moving into the ranks of those who can deliberate.

Aristotle's conception of the psychology of the childlike adult may therefore be seen as a reasonably coherent one, accommodating the possibility of the intelligent exercise of a range of skills. Is the further claim that this psychology equips him to be a living tool similarly defensible within the context of Aristotle's general philosophy of man against the objections we raised? In I.13 Aristotle himself formulates an *aporia* which bears directly on the problem. Does the slave have a virtue (e.g., any of the moral virtues) of greater worth than excellence in service? If yes, how will slaves differ from the free? If no, that is odd (*atopon*—"anomalous," says the Penguin), for they are men and share in reason (1259b21–28).

The resolution Aristotle offers (1260a14–24; 1260a33–36) in effect denies the assumption which the *aporia* comes close to enunciating, viz. that the categories of living tool and human being are incompatible. The excellence of a slave is certainly the fine service of a living tool. But such service will require the exercise of the moral virtues only humans can possess: courage, temperance, and the rest. For without a little of them the slave may fail in his function. He does not need (for example) the administrative courage of a general or statesman, but "subordinate courage" (*hupēretikē aretē*) to cope with the dangers of the job.[36]

So "living tool" is not the name for a distinct species (or pseudo-species) of animal. It is a way of describing a perfectly recognizable sort of human being, so as to pick out what Aristotle regards as the distinguishing mode of activity appropriate to their childlike, but often physically robust, condition.

We might still believe that the correct way to treat such persons is paternalism, not exploitation. It is not clear that we would be right. At any rate Aristotle supplies some materials for an argument to the contrary. The crucial difference, he might say, between a child and a natural slave is that the child can and normally will acquire strategic purposes of his own (even if at present his capacity for deliberation is very undeveloped), but the natural slave never can. This difference may reasonably suggest a difference in rule. We should treat children in such a way as to encourage their development as independent agents. The childlike are best off if prescribed a sensible program of short-term activities that serve our own purposes (as it might be, cooking the lunch, then hoeing the turnips, and then sweeping the yard), since they will never be in a position to construct a program (or at any rate a satisfying sequence of programs) of their own. That way they will share in our life and so have some participation in a full human life, with the possibility of friendship of a sort (I.6 1255b12–15)[37] and the attainment of a kind of excellence (with the self-respect and satisfaction that brings).[38] The only obvious alternative is a passive existence punctuated by desultory activity with no particular purposes at all, as is the fate of many of those we commit to paternalistic institutions (not noted for the liberalism of their regimes) in contemporary civilized societies.

But it is one thing to argue that the doctrine of living tools is a defensible piece of Aristotelian philosophy. It is quite another to understand why Aristotle should have wanted to advance it at all. Until we have a philosophical explanation of that, it will remain very natural to continue to suspect ideological motivation.

5. Slavery and the Argument of the *Politica*

Why does Aristotle include a discussion of slavery in the *Politica* in the first place? This question is harder to answer than one might expect. For example, it is tempting to suppose that Aristotle's main object in Book I is to establish that the *polis* is a natural community; that in order to show this he argues that political life is the fulfillment of a desire for self-sufficiency which finds its first expression in the less developed but no less natural community of the household; and that the need to show that the household is a natural community is what leads him to present at some length a vigorous case for the naturalness of one of its two fundamental component relationships—slavery. (It is then something of a puzzle why he does not supply more argument for the naturalness of marriage, the other basic element in the household, especially given the attack on it in the *Respublica*.[39]) But although Aristotle does not always make the strategy and organization of the argument of Book I as explicit as he might have done, it seems probable that his main preoccupation is not the naturalness of the *polis* and its constituent associations—which is a topic barely mentioned in subsequent parts of the treatise. The issue which appears to dominate his mind right through the book is the question: how many forms of rule (*archē*) are there? And the urge to reply: "not just one but several" is the mainspring of the argument.[40]

This problem about rule is raised right at the beginning of Book I, in ch.1 (1252a7–16):

> It is an error to suppose, as some do, that the roles of a political leader, of a king, of a householder and of a master of slaves are the same, on the ground that they differ not in kind but only in the numbers they rule. For example, they think someone who rules a few is a master, someone who rules more, a householder, and someone who rules still more a political leader or a king, as if there were no difference between a large household and a small *polis*. As to the difference between a political leader and a king, they suppose that when someone is in personal control, he is a king, but when he takes his turn at ruling and being ruled according to the principles of the science they have been specifying, he is a political leader. But these views are false.[41]

The author of the error is not named, but Aristotle's immediate target is clearly a passage in Plato's *Statesman* (258E ff.), which asserts the identities Aristotle denies. What lies behind Plato's thesis is the idea that ruling is essentially a form of knowledge or science (*epistēmē*), and he takes the characteristic Socratic and Platonic view that whether you rule as a king or as a politician, it is one and the same science that you should practice: so despite obvious differences of scale (house vs. city) or constitutional system (monarchy vs. a political form of government) it is one and the same man—the expert in ruling—who is in every case the proper person to exercise rule. Aristotle does not make it clear in I.1 what he most objects to in Plato's account, although later in the book (I.3 1253b18 ff.; I.7 1255b20 ff.) he is contemptuous of the idea that being a master is essentially a matter of *science* at all—it rather consists in a superiority of powers (and preeminence in excellence or virtue, incidentally, is probably what he would say was the key feature which distinguishes or should distinguish a king from a politician). He does suggest immediately, however, that the inadequacy of Plato's position follows (*gar*: 1252a9) from the initial characterization of the *polis* as the most important kind of community, which encompasses all others. The fact of its inadequacy, he goes on (1252a17–23), will become plain if one analyzes the *polis* into its elements. Then we shall see why the roles he has introduced into the discussion differ from each other, and perhaps achieve some expert understanding with respect to each of them. The job of analysis is duly undertaken in chapter 2, where Aristotle develops his argument for natural growth of the *polis* from the household.

That argument, therefore, is launched with a view to refuting Plato's Unitarian conception of rule. How it accomplishes this purpose is not spelled out by Aristotle. But the moral does not need much teasing out. The rule of a master is a *primitive* form of rule, as kingship is the primitive form of government in a state, and it is to be contrasted with what is appropriate to the perfected community of the *polis*; the rule of a master is concerned only with subsistence, politics with the good life. These differences do not in themselves formally disprove Plato's identity thesis. Aristotle must suppose that they are so massive as to make it very implausible.

When he turns to give extended treatment to slavery, he stresses his interest in it as a system of "necessary use" or "essential service," and also the need to achieve a better understanding of it than is supplied by the Platonic identity thesis (I.3 1253b14–20). In I.5, his argument that there is such a thing as natural slavery, he first claims that there is in animals something (the soul) whose nature is to rule and something (the body) whose nature is to be ruled (1254 a28–36). From this he moves straight to the proposition that we can see already in animals the rule of a master and political rule—and see that they are different: the soul is master of the body, but reason exercises political or kingly rule over desire (1254b2–6). Again, after he has completed his statement of the theory of natural slavery and discussed alternative views, he proposes that it is now evident that the rule of master and political rule are not the same. The one is exercised as a monarchy (cf. I.2 1252b19–24) over natural slaves; the other is government of those naturally free and equal (I.7 1255b16–20). Nor is the rule of a master a matter of science (contrast political rule [*NE* I.2; X.9]): someone is a master in virtue of being a person of a certain sort, not because he has a certain kind of skill (*Pol.* I.7 1255b20ff.). The digression on acquisition then intervenes. On his return to discussion of the proper functions of household management in I.12 and 13 it is once again the difference between forms of rule which engrosses Aristotle. In particular, I.13 is a sustained exploration of the sorts of moral excellence that are within the reach of those whose nature it is to be ruled in accordance with one or other of the different forms of rule identified in the examination of the household.

In I.12 Aristotle begins by reminding us of the three "parts" of the household: master and slave, husband and wife, father and children (cf. I.3 1253b 4–12). The job of household management is to exercise the different sorts of rule appropriate to each of these different relationships—it is not just a matter of directing the slaves: the householder has to rule free persons, his wife, and children, as well (1259a37–40). The rest of the chapter is devoted to substantiating the thesis that rule over a wife is different from rule over children. In the one case (wives) the political analogy is *political* rule, and in the other (children) it is *kingship*, for wives need leadership like one's peers, whereas children are junior and not yet fully developed (1259a40–b4). What one might have expected, given the claim of I.2 that the *polis* grows naturally from the household, is some attempt to exploit the political analogy in service of that claim, particularly since elsewhere Aristotle makes a great deal of the parallels in the structure of authority in the household and in the *polis*. Both *Ethics* take the same line (*EE* VII.9 1241b27ff.; cf. *NE* VIII.10 1160b23–1161a9):

> All forms of constitution exist together in the household, both the correct forms and the deviations (for the same thing is found in constitutions as in the case of musical modes)—paternal authority being royal, the relationship of man and wife aristocratic, that of brothers a republic, while the deviation-forms of these are tyranny, oligarchy and democracy; and there are therefore as many varieties of justice.[42]

And both suggest that the household already contains the blueprint or even the seeds of political forms of organization: "resemblances to these—indeed, a sort of pattern of them—can also be found in households" (*NE* VIII.10 1160b23); "hence in the household are first found the origins and springs of . . . political organisation" (*EE* VII.10 1242a40). This style of thought would have well suited the argument of I.2. But Aristotle is apparently not interested in pressing his argument about the household in that direction. My guess is that he has come to feel the schematic analysis of the *Ethics* texts too artificial, and too concerned to interpret the household in terms of the *polis*; and he has of course in a sense located the seeds of the different forms of rule elsewhere—in the psychological structure of the individual (*Pol.* I.5 1254b2–23; I.13 1260a9–14). In any event what we can discern in *Pol.* I.12 and 13 is a greater preoccupation than is perceptible in the *Ethics* with the different forms of *natural* rule found in the household, and with their ethical consequences (*EE* VII.10 had in fact talked as though "natural rule" was a univocal notion [1242a34; 1242b28], effectively equivalent to "paternal rule").

The dissimilarity of the master–slave relation from other forms of rule, then, and especially from political rule, is the focus of Book I in general and of the treatment of slavery in particular. Aristotle introduces discussion of the master–slave relation at a number of later places in the *Politica*. His interest in doing so is once again to distinguish political rule from the rule of the master. Thus in III.4 he argues that political rule is something one learns by being ruled (like military command), whereas the master does not need to learn the "necessities" which are the job of the slave, only how to make use of them (1277a25–b13; cf. I.7 1255b20–35). III.6 holds that the rule of a natural master is essentially concerned with the interest of the ruler, only accidentally with that of the ruled, whereas in politics, like household management, rule is exercised either for the good of those ruled or for the common interest (1278b32–1279a21; cf. VII.14 1333a3–11). Aristotle indicates that the distinction is one he has frequently made in the *exōterikoi logoi* (discourses intended for a wider audience): it is not only the *Politica* that weaves slavery into this pattern of thinking.

Perhaps the most interesting of all the subsequent appearances of the theme occurs in VII.2 and VII.3, where it plays a part in the discussion of the relative claims of the active or political life and a private and inactive life. The passage needs to be read in its entirety. Suffice to say that Aristotle is particularly anxious to expose a premise which he thinks is shared both by those who reject the political life, even though they have a concern for virtue, and by many who admire it, precisely because they have no qualms about committing injustice. Their common mistake is to suppose as "the many" do (VII.2 1324b32) that the rule of a master (or in this context despotism) and political rule are one and the same thing, or that all rule is the rule of masters (VII.2 1325a27 ff.). This is what leads the virtuous to stay out of politics: from their false premise they infer (and would be right to infer) the false conclusion that political life is no life for a free man—for there is nothing impressive in using other people as slaves. It is equally what attracts many people to politics: they have no compunction about dominating (or trying to dominate) neighboring states contrary to justice, and indeed think domination over others is what brings happiness (VII.3 1325a16–27; VII.2 1324b1–22).

Aristotle presents this immoral attitude as a popular one (VII.2 1324b32 ff.), and of course we are put in mind of Callicles and Thrasymachus and of what Glaucon and Adeimantus represent as the common view of justice; or again of the Athenians' line of argument in the Melian dialogue. Aristotle himself associates it with "all the nations that have the power to aggrandize themselves"—the Scyths, the Persians, the Thracians, the Celts (1324b9–12)—and above all with the Spartans (1324b5–9), whose whole system of government is geared to war and conquest, and who do not realize that rule over free men is nobler than despotism and more connected with virtue (VII.14 1333b5–35). Its popularity is no doubt one reason why he is so concerned to undermine the equation of domination and political rule that underlies it. Perhaps it also does something to explain why he gives the attack on Plato's unity thesis such a fundamental strategic role in Book I. Plato's view of all rule as essentially a single form of knowledge does not necessarily entail immoralist consequences. But its obliteration of crucial distinctions is dangerous, for it is just such *apaideusia* (lack of sophistication) that Realpolitik will exploit with a vengeance.

6. Concluding Unscientific Postscript

Except in the context of his preoccupation with the different forms of rule, Aristotle betrays only a very occasional passing interest in slavery in the *Politica*. It is therefore reasonable to expect that this preoccupation will supply us with a vantage point from which to see in proper perspective the problematical features of his theory.

There have to be distinct forms of rule, according to Aristotle, because there is a great variety of deliberative capacities among humans. This makes an equivalent variety appropriate in the kinds of rule exercised over them. Aristotle thus avoids having to lay down by *fiat* his prize thesis that political rule is quite different from despotism and that the one is the right system for a properly thriving human society, the other illegitimate. His distinctions are to be objectively grounded in the nature of things—or rather, of human beings. We modern liberals might have hoped that within this general intellectual framework he would have concluded: some forms of rule are natural, but slavery is unnatural. What he is working with, however, is not a bare division (natural–unnatural), but the richer concept of natural hierarchy. In a hierarchical scheme it was no doubt very tempting to make slavery not something unnatural but the extreme case in a range of cases of natural rule. Certainly it was reasonable to try to identify a specific form of rule appropriate to the childlike.

Does Aristotle's postulation of a natural basis for the difference between slavery and political rule require him to take any stand on contemporary slavery? Does he need to ask whether the slaves in the society of his day were natural slaves? Clearly not. And, of course, he *does* not ask the question. The most economical explanation of the fact that he does not is precisely that it is not a question immediately pertinent to his argument about forms of rule: his concern is with the essential character of the master–slave relation, not with slavery as it actually was in fourth-century Greece.[43]

Unfortunately that is not all that can and should be said about Aristotle's view of contemporary slavery. While his argument does not require him to take a stand on slavery as it actually was in his day, there are points at which he gratuitously expresses or betrays an unargued attitude towards it. The evidence is pretty straightforward. Most Athenian slaves (so the historians tell us) were "barbarians." And Aristotle seems pretty much wedded to the racist idea that barbarians (otherwise Asians) are naturally slavish (I.2 1252b7–9; III.14 1285a16–22; VII.7 1327b27–29), despite having some fun at the expense of double-thinking Greeks who justify enslavement of foreigners by insisting that, although some of them may be well-born, they are so "only at home" (I.6 1255a32ff.). There is no avoiding the conclusion that more or less unthinkingly Aristotle accepted that most slaves in his own society were natural slaves. No doubt his assumption is to be explained in ideological terms, as due ultimately to the bias we might expect in a slave-owning culture which looks outside its own borders and ethnic identity for its supply of slaves.[44]

This is a nasty case of false consciousness. But it does not infect Aristotle's theory of slavery itself. In working out his theory he does not make the supposition that he is describing contemporary slavery or even that what he is saying is applicable to it. The theory does not explicitly or otherwise pretend to be a theory directly or indirectly concerned with contemporary slavery. The false consciousness gets to work when Aristotle stops theorizing.

There is a sort of insulation of theory from reality in *Pol.* I. Aristotle surprisingly does not consider it part of his job as theorist of slavery to comment on existing practice. So when he does allow himself the luxury of an opinion, unsurprisingly it turns out to be uncritical. We have here the same kind of disjunction between thought and practice as is evident in Aristotle's will, which provides that some of his slaves be given their freedom (Diogenes Laertius 5, 14–15). It would be unconvincing to suppose that these were natural slaves. Aristotle simply failed to allow his theory of ownership to exert any pressure on his own practice while he lived.[45]

These are human enough failings. They constitute a form of false consciousness distinct from those identified by Geuss: a sin of omission rather than commission, and a familiar version of *trahison des clercs* (the treason of intellectuals).[46]

Appendix: The Argument of *Pol.* I.6

In I.3 1253b20–23 Aristotle gives a brief indication of a view of slavery which is the very opposite of his own:

> Others say that it is contrary to nature to rule as master over slave, because the distinction between slave and free is one of convention only, and in nature there is no difference, so that this form of rule is based on force and is therefore not just.

He refers to this thesis in the same disparaging terms which he uses of the false Platonic doctrine he has just mentioned (to the effect that being a master is a sort of science, 1253b18–20): it is one of "the things that is nowadays supposed true" (1253b17–18). Does he subsequently discuss this conventionalist view of slavery?

At the beginning of chapter 6 it certainly looks as though he is going to. Chapter 5 has ended with the words: "It is clear, then, that in some cases some are free by nature and others slaves: for whom slavery is both beneficial and just" (I.5 1254b39–1255a2). Chapter 6 begins with what must surely be a reference to the conventionalist view: "But it is not difficult to see that those who say the opposite are in a way correct to do so" (1255a3–4). For the opposite view is presumably that no one is naturally free or slave, and slavery is accordingly unjust, which is precisely what the conventionalist of chapter 3 maintained.

The next lines of chapter 6 (1255a4–7) confirm that it is indeed the conventionalist position Aristotle has in mind. But they also make it clear that he is not going to concern himself with the position as it is conceived by its authors (i.e., by the philosophers referred to at I.3 1253b20–23):

> For *to be in slavery* and *slave* are said in two ways. For there is also someone who is a slave and in slavery *kata nomon* [*in accordance with law*]. For the *nomos* [*law*] is a sort of agreement in which people say that things conquered in war belong to the conquerors.

The reference to *nomos* makes it impossible not to think of conventionalism. The diagnosis of two senses of "slave," the implication that the slave by convention is only one sort of slave, and the restriction of conventional slavery to a category covering only those taken in war are all signs that Aristotle has not the least intention of taking conventionalism seriously as a quite general account of what the basis of slavery is. In effect he is saying: "Chapters 4 and 5 showed that conventionalism is false. But we can extract a useful point from it. *Some* of those called slaves are slaves only as a result of the conventions of war; and such persons are unjustly enslaved." If there were any doubts about this interpretation, the last paragraph of the chapter should allay them (I.6 1255b4–15). Here Aristotle shifts the focus from what is just to what is beneficial (cf. 1255a3), and concludes that where slavery is natural it is beneficial to both master and slave, but the opposite if it is based on convention and force.

In the intervening passage (1255a7–b4), which takes up most of the space and nearly all of Aristotle's ingenuity in the chapter, we are given the actual arguments for the proposition that conventional slavery is unjust. Aristotle proceeds by attacking the contrary thesis, that it is just. But it takes him quite a while to get to the point (at 1255a21 ff.), because he is struck by what is evidently to him a much more interesting thought: that the premises people are or would be prepared to appeal to in debating this issue betray a commitment to the idea that those superior in virtue should rule and be masters (125a20–21; 1255a39–b1)—as being the natural thing (1255a29–32; cf. 1255b1–4).

The train of thought from 1255a7–21 is particularly intricate, and interpretation is complicated by a textual issue. Aristotle begins by implying that the *nomos* [*custom*] making slaves of prisoners of war is taken by many to be something just, and then reports that many of those "versed in the laws," on the other hand, reject it (or rather its claim to justice) as "unconstitutional," so to speak. Their argument is that it would be a dreadful thing if all that was enough to make someone a slave (or in general a subject) were the application of superior force. The reasoning behind this is presumably that the general body of laws do *not* recognize seizure by force as a valid claim to ownership.

There is a similar disagreement, says Aristotle, among philosophers: *tōn sphōn* [*the wise*]. One might expect it to be a disagreement about conventional or legal slavery, but it is pretty clear that it is a more general dispute about whether *rule* based on force is just. (And from 1255a17–19 we can identify the two parties to the dispute as Callicles and Thrasymachus.) The reason for the disagreement, we are told, is a shared premise which provides an element of overlap between the arguments on the two sides: "force is not without virtue"—there is something admirable and excellent and profitable about it. Why does this premise explain the existence of a debate on the question? Aristotle does not say. Presumably his thought is: if there were *nothing* admirable about force, then *everybody* would reject rule based on force as unjust; it is because there is thought to be something good about it that a dispute develops.

Given that both sides agree that "force is not without virtue," it must be something else that they disagree about. Aristotle identifies this as "only justice." I think the context suggests that he means to imply "merely justice": these thinkers have a high regard for force and its virtues—but do not care much about justice. At 1255a17–19 it is explained that each derives from the shared premiss about force (*dia touto*) a different conclusion about justice. One party (Thrasymachus': Pl., *Rep.* I 348 C) considers justice to be nothing but stupidity,[47] as standing in the way of exercising the virtue inherent in force, and therefore, no doubt, they would be willing to say that rule based on force alone is unjust (with the implication: who in their right mind will be troubled at that?). The other party (Callicles': *Gorgias* 483 D) retains the positive evaluation associated with the word "justice," but radically transforms its content: justice simply *is* the principle that the stronger should rule. The rule of force becomes just by definition.[48]

Now follows a difficult *epei* ["since"] in Aristotle's text (*Pol.* I.6 1255a19). I take him to be adducing in conclusion a reason for supposing what has hitherto been merely asserted, that Callicles' and Thrasymachus' arguments do indeed share a premise, viz. the premise he has specified:

> Since although these arguments stand quite apart from each other [sc. they do represent very different views of the justice of rule by force], there is no strength or persuasiveness [sc. so far as Callicles or Thrasymachus is concerned] in the arguments on the other side, to the effect that the superior in virtue should *not* rule or be a master [that is, the arguments which in effect deny the shared premise].

The disagreement between Callicles and Thrasymachus explored at 1255a 11–21 turns out to be something of a digression from Aristotle's main theme, which is the question of the justice of conventional or legal slavery. It is not only that their dispute is about the broader topic of rule by force in general, but its grounds are quite different from those Aristotle seems to indicate in what he says about slavery at 1255a6–11. Those who consider conventional slavery unjust do so because they think it shocking that people should be enslaved by force: Callicles and Thrasymachus are agreed that dominating others by force is admirable. Aristotle himself does not take sides in their controversy, evidently because he finds their shared premise repugnant: but he makes it absolutely clear that in the argument about slavery he takes the side of those who hold that conventional slavery is unjust. So the legal debate (if we may so-call it) and the philosophical debate run parallel only to a rather limited extent. In each case one party thinks a regime based on force just, whereas the other thinks it unjust. And—the thing that really fascinates Aristotle—all parties to both disputes reveal a commitment to the idea that "the superior in virtue should rule." Underlying discussion of force and convention is a more fundamental acknowledgment of natural rule.

This is not an acknowledgment that one would expect to be made by those who believe legal slavery to be just. Aristotle now (1255a21) returns to the dispute about legal slavery—his official topic—and argues that even they are crypto-naturalists beneath the skin (1255a21–32):

> Broadly speaking [*holōs de*] the issue is this: some people take hold, as they would like to think, of a principle of justice of sorts (for *nomos* is something just), and put forward the proposition that enslavement through war is just [sc. because conventional or legal]. But at the same time they deny it. For it is quite possible that the reason for going to war was unjust, and nobody would say that someone who is unworthy of servile status is a slave. Otherwise we should find among slaves and descendants of slaves men of the noblest birth, should any of them be captured and sold: that is why they are not prepared to call them slaves, but only non-Greeks. But when they say that, they are feeling their way towards precisely the principle of natural slavery which we introduced at the beginning of the discussion. For it has to be admitted that there are some who are slaves everywhere, others nowhere.

The passage speaks for itself. Aristotle has a very simple argument against the supporters of the justice of legal slavery: they do not really believe what they say. This emerges in two ways. First, whatever we think of the general idea that laws are just simply inasmuch as they are laws, the legal arrangements which are brought about by an unjust war cannot themselves be just. Aristotle implies that this point is so clear that supporters of legal slavery could not fail to concede it, and thereby to abandon their position (which if valid must by universally valid). Second, Aristotle appeals to usage: no nobleman even if captured and sold would be called a slave. Again, he implies that there is no evidence that supporters of legal slavery would have the tenacity or effrontery to adopt a usage consonant with the position they claim to be defending. His argument is a close cousin of Socrates's initial arguments against Callicles in the *Gorgias* (488B–489E).

Pol. I.6 1255a21–32 presents the sum total of Aristotle's real argument about the topic of the chapter: is conventional slavery just? The fact is that he cannot believe that anyone who answers "Yes" could seriously mean what he says. And he makes little effort to consider what might lead someone to say "Yes"—the reference to the idea that "*nomos* is something just" is his only gesture in this direction. We should not be surprised by his posture. He has no greater interest in the philosophical motivation of the general theory that all slavery is a matter of convention, nor of the sophistic thesis that law is a contract, which receives just one notoriously perfunctory mention in the *Politica*

(III.9 1280b8 ff.). Modern opinion would applaud his belief that legal slavery is unjust while deploring his rejection of the view that all slavery is conventional. His stance on these issues seems to be determined not so much by prejudices about slavery as by a deep hostility, bordering on incomprehension, to conventionalist explanations of anything.[49]

Notes

1. P. Pellegrin, "La Théorie aristotélicienne d'esclavage: tendances actuelles de l'interprétation," p. 350. This paper is the most interesting statement of an ideological interpretation of Aristotle's theory that I know of.

2. Cf. e.g. Parekh, *Marx's Theory of Ideology*, ch. 2.

3. Cf. e.g. Elster, *Making Sense of Marx*, ch. 8.

4. Elster, *Karl Marx: a Reader*, p. 299.

5. Historians are often content to label a set of ideas ideological on the basis of (i) alone. This is no doubt because where such a body of ideas is widely held in a society, it is generally reasonable to assume that (ii) provides the best explanation of the phenomenon.

6. Among English-speaking students of ancient Greek philosophy there has been little discussion of this kind of question. For some pioneering work see G. E. R. Lloyd, *Science, Folklore and Ideology*, and M. Frede, *Essays in Ancient Philosophy*, in his introductory chapter. In his commentary on this chapter at "Aristoteles' *Politik*," XI. Symposium Aristotelicum (Friedrichshafen/Bodensee 1987), Charles Kahn questioned the viability of a definition of ideology in terms of the causation of belief. He would prefer to locate our problem within the theory of interpretation, and to "think of ideology as identifying one particular mode of the more general approach that we call *biographical* interpretation, that is, an interpretation that refers to the life and experience of the author rather than to the logic of his arguments and the systematic structure of his thought." I find this a helpful formulation. But I do not think it excludes the possibility of employing the notion of causation within biographical interpretation; and I doubt whether the arguments for an ideological account of Aristotle's theory of slavery presented in this chapter would need much reformulation or revision if we tried to avoid thinking in terms of causation.

7. Parekh, *Marx's Theory of Ideology*, p. 216.

8. E. M. Wood and N. Wood, *Class Ideology and Ancient Political Theory*, p.1.

9. R. Geuss, *The Idea of a Critical Theory*, p. 13. I have found Geuss's book much the most penetrating treatment of the concept of ideology I have read.

10. *The Idea of a Critical Theory*, p. 69 (cf. p. 14).

11. *The Idea of a Critical Theory*, p. 13.

12. For the idea that anomaly of this kind may prima facie be a sign that a doctrine advanced by a philosopher is ideological I am indebted to Terry Irwin.

13. I am grateful to John Cooper and Martha Nussbaum for pointing out in the discussion of this chapter at "Aristoteles' *Politik*," XI. Symposium Aristotelicum

(Friedrichshafen/Bodensee 1987), that any treatment of the question of ideology in Aristotle's theory of slavery must come to grips with this argument.

14. There are the well-known remarks of Alcidamas: "God left all men free; nature made no one a slave" (schol. on *Rhet.* I.13 1373b18 in: Rabe, ed., *Commentaria in Aristotelem Graeca; Vol.* XXI, pars. II, p. 74); and of Philemon: "Even if someone is a slave, he has the same flesh; by nature no one was ever born a slave" (Fr. 39 ed. Meineke). They presumably reflect sophistic theory, no doubt the conventionalism about slavery mentioned by Aristotle at *Pol.* I.3 1253b20-23; i.e. something rather far removed from common moral reflection. A. W. Gouldner (*Enter Plato,* pp. 24–34) presented a highly a priori argument for the existence of a general disquiet about slavery despite the silence of the sources, but does not seem to have convinced the scholarly world of his case.

15. See G. Vlastos, "Does slavery exist in Plato's *Republic*?" His conclusion is disputed by B. Calvert, "Slavery in Plato's *Republic*," but I think unconvincingly. Calvert omits discussion of the crucial passage *Rep.* V 469B–471C.

16. M. I. Finley, *Ancient Slavery and Modern Ideology*, ch. III. See his illuminating discussion of Herodotus 4, 1–4 (ibid., pp. 118–19 in the Penguin edition, 1983). On Xenophon *Oec. XII* 18–19 see T. Wiedemann, *Greek and Roman Slavery*, p. 61.

17. It is already a drawback to the line of argument developed in this paragraph that it has to rely on the unsatisfactory notion of an inarticulate ideology: how could a body of ideas be inarticulate?

18. In other cases, presumably, enslavement may be contrary to nature: the cases alluded to at *Pol.* I.6 1255b4-5, and discussed at 1255a21 ff.

19. See the classic discussion by G. E. L. Owen, "*tithenai ta phainomena*."

20. J. Barnes, "Aristotle and the Methods of Ethics," p. 510.

21. M. C. Nussbaum, "Saving Aristotle's Appearances," p. 292.

22. V. Goldschmidt, "La Théorie aristotélicienne de 1'esclavage et sa méthode," pp. 149–53.

23. As is clearly shown for household management in Carlo Natali's paper "Aristotle et la chrématistique."

24. His attack on the issue of whether there are natural slaves is professedly launched not from *endoxa* [*reputable opinions*] but from argument or theory (*tō logō*) and the facts (*ek tōn ginomenōn*) (I.5 1254a17-21).

25. As Natali shows with respect to the discussion of household management.

26. I am grateful to Jacques Brunschwig, David Charles, and Terry Irwin for helpful discussions about the endoxic method. Nothing I say about the method implies disagreement with the proposition that in Aristotle's view the first principles of philosophy—and so presumably the natural principles from which he derives his theories of slavery and household management—are ultimately arrived at dialectically by consideration of what is *gnōrimōteron hēmin* [*better known to us*]. But it is one thing to agree that Aristotle would proceed towards his first principles dialectically, and quite another to maintain that that is what he is doing in *Pol.* I. He is not: in *Pol.* I he is arguing *from* first principles.

27. My argument here is congruent with Finley's view (*Democracy Ancient and Modern* [London], p. 66): "In ancient Greece, with its open exploitation of slaves and

foreign subjects, there would be little scope for ideology in the Marxist sense"; or again (*Ancient Slavery and Modern Ideology*, p. 117): "Ideological openness was facilitated by the nakedness of the oppression and exploitation: no 'false consciousness' was necessary or possible."

28. B. Parekh, *Marx's Theory of Ideology*, p. 137.

29. See e.g. G. E. R. Lloyd, *Science, Folklore and Ideology*, Part II, on women; on the household M. I. Finley, "Aristotle and Economic Analysis"; S. Campese, "*Polis* ed economia in Aristotele." All these studies are in different ways alert to ideological dimensions of Aristotle's treatment of these topics.

30. See Finley's classic discussion in "Aristotle and Economic Analysis."

31. See again Carlo Natali's "Aristotle et la chrématistique."

32. See e.g. Stephen Lukes, *Marxism and Morality*, ch. 5.

33. This point is well made by Goldschmidt, pp. 149–53.

34. Aristotle is more willing to admit a real difficulty in connection with the question of the virtue of slaves at *Pol.* I.13 1259b21–28; and his solution is more thoughtful. The strains within his account of slavery are well discussed by R. G. Mulgan, *Aristotle's Political Theory*, pp. 40–44.

35. I am obliged to Charles Kahn for forcing me to consider the issue raised in this paragraph, which I had neglected to do in the original version of the chapter. My formulation of the problem is much indebted to N. D. Smith, "Aristotle's theory of natural slavery." The problem is, I think, crucially one about exploitation, not ownership: are there any humans whom we are justified in using as tools at will? Aristotle actually seems to hold that property simply *consists* in tools whose use one controls (I.4 1253 b30–1254a17). It is worth noting that the idea of treating other humans as tools need not itself be too troubling: Aristotle is prepared to think of friends in this way (*NE* I.8 1099a33–b 2). But friends are not like slaves at one's entire disposal.

36. Mulgan (*Aristotle's Political Theory*, p. 42) observes: "If the slave can be expected to act virtuously even to this extent, he must be capable of independent action and not confined to blind obedience to his master's orders." He seems to think this is inconsistent with Aristotle's view of what a slave is. But we see no incompatibility in recognizing capacities in a sheepdog for independent action in its work with the sheep, while at the same time holding that its function in life is to help its master herd sheep (without itself possessing any sort of strategic deliberative powers).

37. Aristotle would, of course, need to improve on his account in *NE* VIII.11 1161 b3–8 of what makes such friendship—evidently taken to be a form of advantage friendship—psychologically possible. But there is no reason to think the task impossible or even very difficult. What Aristotle has to avoid is the inference: if x is a living tool of y, x is not the friend of y (which he appears to accept in the *Ethics*). That should be easy enough, since it does not look a very plausible inference. Moreover, if life for x involves some rudimentary form of reason (such that x can say, for example: "y gives me food, shelter, and protection in return for my services"), then we could presumably conclude from the living tool premise that x might be the friend of y. In the *Ethics* passage Aristotle gives too much weight to "tool" in constructing his inference; but *Pol.* I.13 shows that he has seen that he has to ponder the consequences of "living" (1260a 33–36).

38. The treatment of the virtue of slaves in *Pol.* I.13 would seem to make a revision necessary in Aristotle's claim (*NE* X.6 1177a8–11) that happiness is not possible for a slave.

39. He does, of course, attack Plato's theory in II 2–4, but makes surprisingly little play with the naturalness of marriage there. He has more to say on the subject at *NE* VIII.12 1162a16–33.

40. My argument for this interpretation has much in common with that developed in C. Natali, "La struttura unitaria del libro I della 'Politica' di Aristotele." H. Kelsen has the main point, although distorted by his preoccupation with monarchy: see "Aristotle and Hellenic-Macedonian Policy," 172–75. He well says: "The whole presentation of the slave problem in this first book of the *Politics* is rather of a political than of an economic character."

41. I adapt the revised Penguin translation (T. A. Sinclair, revised by T. J. Saunders).

42. I cite the Loeb translation of H. Rackham (revised edition).

43. One might have expected that the tacit question motivating Aristotle's theory of slavery was: "Why is slavery so prevalent everywhere?" and that the doctrine of the natural slave was offered as the best explanation of that phenomenon: "Because it is natural." (I am grateful to Julia Annas and Christoph Eucken for pressing this possibility on my attention.) The argument of section 5, however, supplies not only an alternative motivation but one that is much better supported in the text.

44. The acquisition of natural slaves by war is defended as naturally just at *Pol.* I.8 1256b23–26 (cf. I.7 1255b37–39). Aristotle talks there as though he has in mind campaigns—"hunts"—against specifically targeted groups or communities, no doubt "barbarian" communities. He seems to rely once again on a racist premise: e.g., "there are some forms of community so primitive that the natural incapacity of their members for genuine deliberation is thereby apparent to a civilised visitor." I am grateful to Geoffrey Lloyd for drawing attention to the ideological dimensions of this text. Its theme is also the subject of some interesting remarks by Stephen Clark, "Slaves and Citizens," pp. 32–36 (cf. also his *Aristotle's Man*, pp. 106–7), and of a fascinating discussion of a sixteenth-century controversy by Anthony Pagden, "The School of Salamanca" and the "Affair of the Indies," or more expansively in his book *The Fall of Natural Man.*

45. It is true that at VII.10 1330a23-33 he recommends that in the best constitution farm workers will if possible be slaves, and that "it is better to hold out the prospect of freedom as a prize to all slaves." This latter provision has sometimes been thought to conflict with his view that slavery is beneficial for the natural slave, and indeed better for him than freedom. Clearly it does not. All it implies is that natural slaves would usually prefer to be free. That being so, they are more likely to cooperate and to work hard if promised their freedom: that is why it is better to hold out the prospect—better for masters. (I owe this interpretation of this text to Myles Burnyeat.)

46. This chapter has (I trust) benefited greatly from the discussion at "Aristoteles' *Politik*," XI. Symposium Aristotelicum (Friedrichshafen/Bodensee 1987). I have tried to list my main individual debts to symposiasts at the appropriate points in the argument. I owe a more general debt to Charles Kahn, whose commentary encouraged me to scrap some parts of the original version while retaining others, and made me see where I needed to argue a lot harder. Myles Burnyeat kindly read a penultimate draft.

The final versions of sections 4 and 6 have been much influenced by discussion with him. It is more than usually necessary for the author to take sole responsibility for the outcome.

47. I accept Ross's *anoia* for the MSS. *eunoia* at 1255a17; H. Richards's *euētheia*, although implausible as a conjecture, has the merit of drawing attention to the *Respublica* passage Aristotle must have in mind. Against *eunoia*: (1) So far as I know no Greek philosopher ever identifies justice with goodwill. (2) If Aristotle intended something weaker than an identification, he would surely have used a more appropriate locution (like *mē aneu:* 1255a15–16). (3) Aristotle elsewhere associates goodwill with friendship, never mentioning justice (e.g. *NE* VIII.2 1155b27–1156a5; 15 1166b30–1167a21). He is, of course, in favor of goodwill, but he does not think all that much of it: goodwill could be called "inactive friendship" (1167a11). Goldschmidt ("La Théorie aristotélicienne de l'esclavage et sa méthode," p. 155) cites Democritus Fr. 302 (judged inauthentic by Diels-Kranz): *ton archonta dei echein . . . pros de tous hupotetagmenous eunoian.* I do not think there is much mileage to be got from this. (4) "Perhaps Aristotle means that the *element* of justice here (that is, in the enforced enslavement) consists in the *eunoia* of the stronger, who enslaves the weaker instead of killing him. This *moral* superiority gives him a right to be the master." But 1255a13–16 give the impression that it is the use of force itself which is associated with virtue by these thinkers, not restraint in its use. (5) It is hard to understand why the doctrine that justice is goodwill should be conceived as any sort of consequence of the idea that "force is not without virtue." Newman (*The Politics of Aristotle,* p. 156) interprets thus: "One side argues from this, that, force being accompanied by virtue, and virtue attracting goodwill between master and slave, slavery is just only where there is goodwill between master and slave, and that consequently the indiscriminate enslavement of those conquered in war is unjust." This makes the doctrine about goodwill entirely independent of the premise about force (although Newman accepts that *dia touto* (1255 a 17) refers to that premise); nor is the conclusion about the conditions of justice for slavery in any way a consequence of the premise.

48. Cf. D. J. Furley, "Antiphon's case against justice," pp. 81–82.

49. The interpretation of 1255a12–21 has always been much controverted. The most recent full discussion (which like most previous treatments I have found more confusing than instructive) is by T. J. Saunders, "The controversy about slavery reported by Aristotle, *Politics I vi,* 1255 a 4ff." He supplies a good select bibliography of the controversy at 26 n. 8 (to which add V. Goldschmidt, "La Théorie aristotélicienne de l'esclavage et sa méthode," pp. 153–58). It is unlikely that agreement on the passage will ever be reached: a vigorous set of notes on my reading from Jacques Brunschwig, to which I have incorporated some responses, already confirms this judgment. I have tried to be brief and plain (hence the dearth of references to the scholarly literature). I think my treatment is distinctive in its attempt to take as basis for interpretation the impossibility of the MSS. reading *eunoia,* which was universally accepted in the nineteenth century, when most of the scholarly debate took place.

5

Property Rights in Aristotle

Fred D. Miller Jr.

1. Problems of Property

THE MEMBERS OF ARISTOTLE'S POLIS are private individuals with households of their own in addition to being citizens who share in the common life of politics. Although the *Politics* is primarily occupied with constitutional issues, Aristotle is also concerned with the private sphere and its relation to the common or public sphere, as is evident in *Politics* II.1:

> of as many things as it is possible to have in common is it better for the polis that is going to be nobly administered to have them all in common, or is it better to have some [in common] but not others? For it is possible for the citizens to have children, wives, and possessions in common with each other, as in Plato's *Republic*; for there Socrates says that children, women, and property ought to be common. Are things better as they are now or as they are according to the law written in the *Republic*? (1261a2–9)

This chapter focuses on Aristotle's remarks about property, on the grounds that private property necessarily has a central place in any account of the private sphere, since it defines the location and means of private activities. Moreover, the arguments concerning private property parallel the main points which he makes concerning children and wives. He discusses property in several different contexts throughout the *Politics* as well as in other works, most notably the *Rhetoric* and *Nicomachean Ethics*. These discussions, when taken together, provide the basic materials of a theory of property rights. Here I follow the lead of Barker, who refers to "the vindication of the right of private property which appears in the second book of the *Politics*."[1]

I shall begin by indicating in quite general terms how I am using the expression "property rights." Property rights are complex legal or moral relationships involving individuals and objects, concerning different sorts of rights or their correlatives.[2] For example, the right of Coriscus to an object such as a jar of olive oil typically involves both a liberty to possess it and to put it to various uses as well as a claim right imposing duties of non-interference on the part of others with its possession or use. This typically implies the right to compensation or restitution if there is interference or harm to the object by others. It also typically involves the authority to offer the object for sale or to give it away, which changes the legal or moral relationships of others. And it typically involves immunity against others putting the object up for sale or giving it away without the owner's consent. This repeated use of "typically" is deliberate. The various elements into which the relations of ownership and property have been analyzed are not necessarily present in all cases. Thus, although Honoré[3] distinguishes eleven such elements—the right to possess, to use, to manage, the right to the income, to the capital, to security, to transmissibility, the absence of term, the prohibition of harmful use, the liability to execution, and the residual character of property—he contends that while all of these elements are required for full ownership, none is a necessary condition for "owning" something. In ascribing a concept of property rights to Aristotle, I am claiming that such elements play an important role in his normative assertions about property and wealth in the *Politics* and other works. The following section proposes a working concept of property rights in Aristotle's own terms.

A theory of property rights should provide answers to a number of problems about property rights: What sorts of individuals can properly hold rights to property? To what sorts of objects can they have property rights? In what ways are property rights exercised? What is the general moral justification for the thesis that individuals should have property rights? Under what circumstances do individuals justly acquire objects and under what circumstances do they come to possess them unjustly? What specific public policies do property rights imply; that is, in what way should property rights be protected and what constraints, if any, do individual property rights place upon the conduct of government? And in what ways may individual property rights be restricted or regulated by government? In ascribing to Aristotle a theory of property rights, I am claiming that Aristotle offers answers to questions such as these.

The test of this interpretation is whether it does indeed provide a way of connecting Aristotle's scattered claims about property into a more comprehensible whole. Accordingly, this chapter examines his main discussions of property, and Section 8 considers his answers to the foregoing questions concerning property rights.

2. A Working Concept of Property Rights

The ancient Greeks recognized a distinction which is fundamental to the conception of property rights: the distinction between the mere possession of an object and the ownership of it. Socrates acknowledges this juridical distinction in Plato's *Republic* when he says that the goal of the rulers in conducting lawsuits will be "that individuals should neither have [*echōsi*] another's things [*t'allotria*] nor be deprived of their own things [*tōn hautōn*]" (IV 433E6–8).[4] Similarly, the Athenian orator Hegesippus (c. 390–c. 325 BC) states that "it is possible to have [*echein*] another's things; and not all those who have, have their own things, but many have acquired [*kektēntai*] another's things."[5] Again, Theophrastus (c. 320–c. 288 BC) asserts that even if goods for sale have changed hands, the seller remains the owner of the property (*kurios ton ktēmatos*) until he receives the payment.[6]

There were elaborate legal procedures through which property owners could seek protection and compensation; this is especially evident in the Athenian legal system, about which the most is known. Nevertheless, the Greeks did not have an abstract term which unambiguously stood for legal ownership as such.[7] *Ousia*, for example, is used for the concrete property which an individual owns[8] rather than to designate ownership as such. The verbs *echein*, *kratein*, and *kektēsthai* do not have special legal or moral implications. This underscores the importance of Aristotle's attempt in *Rhetoric* I.5 1361a12–25 to offer a *general* treatment of the notion of wealth (*ploutos*). (The argument to which this passage belongs is examined in the following section.) This treatment is of special interest here because it mentions central elements of the concept of property rights.

The treatment begins with an enumeration of the parts (*merē*) of wealth: plenty of money; possession (*ktēsis*) of land and estates; possession of movable objects, animals, and slaves. Since the Greeks typically include with land ownership the buildings and crops on it, Aristotle has enumerated the main types of property recognized by Greek law.[9] In this passage Aristotle states a number of conditions which must be met if one is fully to qualify as being wealthy (*ploutein*):

(1) The properties are numerous, large, and beautiful;
(2) The properties are liberal (*eleutheria*) or useful (*chrēsima*);[10]
(3) The properties are secure (*asphalē*);

(4) The properties are one's own (*oikeia*);[11]
(5) One is actually using the property rather than merely owning it.

The conditions especially important for a right of property are (3) and (4). Aristotle explains what he means by each at 1361a19–23:

> A criterion of "security" is possession [*kektēshai*] in a given place and in such a manner that the use of the objects is up to oneself [*eph' hautōi*]; and a criterion of "being one's own or not"[12] is when the alienation of it is up to oneself; I mean by "alienation" [*apallotriōsis*] giving and selling.

So defined, (3) and (4) differ importantly from (1) which distinguishes wealth from more modest levels of property possession; and from (5) which distinguishes leading an actually wealthy life from being materially capable of doing so. In contrast, (3) and (4) are preconditions not only of wealth but also of ownership in general.

A historian of Athenian law finds it "noteworthy that Aristotle should single out the power to alienate as the true sign of a thing being one's own [*oikeion*]."[13] It is also important to note that (3) and (4) correspond to central elements in the modern Anglo-American concept of property rights.[14] In the light of this parallel, (3) and (4) may be taken to constitute an Aristotelian working concept of property rights, viz.:

> *X* has a property right in *P* if, and only if, *X* possesses *P* in such a way that the use of *P* is up to *X*, and the alienation of *P* (giving *P* away or selling *P*) is up to *X*.

It is reasonable to suppose that this analysis has a force comparable to the conjunction of the following rights claims: *X* has the liberty to use *P* in one way or in another way, and *X* has a just claim against others not to be interfered with in his use of *P*.[15] *X* has the authority to transfer ownership of *P* to *Y* by giving it or selling it to *Y*, and *X* has immunity against others alienating *P*.[16]

The remainder of this chapter argues that good sense can be made of Aristotle's discussions of property in the *Politics* if he is understood as using the working concept of property rights just described.

3. The Eudaimonistic Justification of Property

One important form of justification of property concerns its relationship to happiness (*eudaimonia*). In the context of such a justification, the analysis of wealth discussed in the preceding section occurs. *Rhetoric* I.5 commences with an assertion of the principle of *eudaimonia* similar to the openings of the *Politics* and *Nicomachean Ethics.* Everybody, individually and collectively, has a goal, and this is happiness and its parts. We should understand what happiness is and what its parts are, because all those who try to persuade others presuppose the principle of *eudaimonia*:

> One ought to do the things which provide happiness or any of its parts, or increase rather than decrease it, and ought not to do those things which destroy or hinder it or make those things that are contrary to it. (1360b11–14)

Like the *Politics, Rhetoric* I.5 prescribes happiness as an end for public policy as well as for individual decision-making (1360b4, b31–1361a12). Aristotle then offers an account of happiness:

> Let then happiness be [*a*] doing well with virtue, or [*b*] self-sufficiency of life, or [*c*] the most pleasant way of life with security, or [*d*] a thriving state of possessions and bodies with the power to protect and put them into action. (1360b14-17)[17]

Aristotle is, in effect, treating happiness as a cluster concept, which includes both common notions and philosophical ideas. It is not clear whether these are meant to be necessary or sufficient conditions of happiness. Nevertheless, on the basis of this account, Aristotle infers that happiness has numerous parts,[18] including external goods, such as wealth or property (1360b20, 28).

The eudaimonistic justification is a straightforward application of the eudaimonistic principle of *eudaimonia*:

(1) One should do the things which provide happiness or any of its parts, or increase rather than decrease it, and should not do those things which destroy or hinder it or make those things that are contrary to it.
(2) Wealth is a part of happiness.
(3) Therefore, one should do the things that provide wealth or increase rather than decrease it and should not do those things which destroy or impede its use.

Premise (2) is based on two of the disjunctive conditions of happiness: (*b*) self-sufficiency of life and (*d*) a thriving state of possessions and bodies with the power to protect and put them into action. Moreover, as noted in the previous section, Aristotle states that wealth must satisfy the conditions of being secure and being one's own, conditions which are central elements of property rights: the use and alienation of the possessions are up to the owner.

To be sure, care must be taken with an argument from the first book of the *Rhetoric* which is generally regarded as early in composition,[19] and which is more prone than other Aristotelian compositions to draw uncritically upon commonsense views. Both premises of the above argument seem to be open to objection. Premise (1) speaks of "parts" of happiness, a usage which he avoids in the discussion of happiness in the *Nicomachean Ethics*, I and X.[20] Even more controversially, (2) makes wealth a part of happiness. Not only do the ethical works not treat wealth as a part of happiness, but they also point out a serious mistake which (2) might be taken to commit, of confusing a necessary condition of happiness with a part of happiness (cf. *EE* I.2 1214b24–7; *Pol.* VII.1 1323b24–9; 13 1332a25–7).

Nevertheless, it seems possible to reformulate this argument of the *Rhetoric* in terms of the doctrines stated in Aristotle's ethical works. Wealth is one of the external goods (*ta ektos agatha*) that a human being needs in order to be happy (*NE* I.8 1099a31–4, VII.13 1153b14–19, X.8 1178a23–31; *MM* II.8 1206b33–4; *Pol.* VII.13 1331b41–1332a1). Perhaps the strongest affirmation of this comes in the definition of happiness at *NE* I.10 1101a14–16: "that person is happy who is active in accordance with complete virtue and is sufficiently equipped with external goods not for any chance period of time but for a complete life." The claim that the happy person requires equipment *(kechorēgēmenos)* also occurs at *Politics* VII.1 1323b40–1324a1. Elsewhere Aristotle suggests that the value of external goods derives from that of virtuous activities: "no activity is complete when it is impeded, and happiness is a complete thing; this is why the happy person needs the goods of the body and external goods, i.e., those of fortune, in order that he may not be impeded in these ways."[21] Aristotle thus maintains that wealth, like other external goods, is indispensable for complete human happiness.[22] However, the *Rhetoric*'s justification of property would still need to be corrected to say that wealth is a necessary condition for happiness rather than a "part" of it. And the justification would be restricted to property which plays an essential role in the activities of happiness, e.g., property used in acts of generosity.

4. The Instrumentalist Justification of Property

Politics I.4–10, offers a justification of property rights based on Aristotle's teleological view of nature. This justification is part of a general effort in *Politics* I, to show that the polis arises out of basic natural communities: ultimately, those of master and slave, husband and wife, and parent and child. Hence, his treatment of property is closely bound up with his highly objectionable defense of slavery, but it includes arguments concerning property in general, which can be disentangled from his concerns about slavery. He begins with a loosely structured argument (4 1253b23–1254a17), which I reconstruct as follows:

(1) Just as the specialized crafts need their proper instruments (*organa*) to fulfill their function (*ergon*), the householder needs the proper instruments to fulfill his function.
(2) [The function of the householder is to maintain life.]
(3) A possession (*ktēma*) is an instrument for life, which is separable from the possessor, and property (*ktēsis*) is a number of such instruments.
(4) One cannot live or live well without the necessary things.
(5) Therefore, the householder needs property to fulfill his function.
(6) A part is not only a part of something else but wholly belongs to it, and this is also true of a possession.
(7) [The part belongs by nature to the whole].
(8) Similarly, therefore,[23] property belongs by nature to the household.
(9) [Whatever belongs by nature belongs justly (cf. 1254a17–18).]
(10) [Therefore, it is just for property to belong to the household.]

This justification of property resembles the eudaimonistic justification of *Rhetoric* I.5, in so far as it proceeds from the view of property as a necessary means to the attainment of the natural end of human beings, but it differs in important details. A central role is assumed for the household (*oikia*), the householder (*oikonomikos*), and household management (*oikonomia*), which have the function of fulfilling daily needs. In contrast to the eudaimonistic justification, this argument covers possessions necessary for everyday subsistence. However, the scope of the conclusion is narrowed: it establishes only the property rights of individuals *qua* householders, not *qua* human beings or under any other description.[24] The inference that property is a "part" of the household also seems unwarranted, since on Aristotle's view the fact that *X* is a necessary condition for *Y* does not entail that *X* is a part of *Y*.[25]

The central point, however, is that the householder has a just claim to property because he has it by nature. That this is intended is clear from the immediate context, because *Politics* I.4 defends slaveholding as a form of property ownership, and it follows directly in response to the objection that slaveholding is "against nature" and "not just, for it is due to force" (3 1253b20–23). This argument, of course, rests upon the principle that those human relationships which are by nature or according to nature are just and those which are against nature are unjust. Apart from this, a major difficulty with the argument as it stands is the weakness of the argument for (8) that the household possesses property "by nature." Aristotle has previously argued that the household exists by nature (2 1252b12–14) and he can perhaps infer that its parts belong to it by nature. But even so, it does not follow that *everything* which the household possesses belongs to it by nature. The household might acquire things which it is against nature, and consequently unjust, for it to possess—for example, naturally free human beings. Aristotle must therefore supplement this argument with an account of what the household may acquire according to nature and against nature.

5. Justice and Injustice in Acquisition

Aristotle distinguishes natural (just) and unnatural (unjust) forms of the acquisitive craft (*chrēmatistikē* [*sc. technē*]) in *Politics* I.8–11. This craft is distinct from household management in that it is for the acquisitive craft to supply and for household management to use, because the former studies where possessions (*chrēmata*) and property (*ktēsis*) come from (I.8 1256a10–12, 15–16). The defensible (natural) form of the acquisitive craft is alternatively described as a part of householding (I.8 1256b26–7) or as a subordinate art which provides the resources which the householder uses (I.10 1258a34).

In *Politics* I.8, Aristotle offers a rather loosely organized argument for the conclusion that one form of the acquisitive art is natural. It advances two lines of argument, both of which assume the teleological principle that "nature makes nothing incomplete and does nothing in vain" (1256b20–1). The argument may be summarized as follows: *Part I* (1256a19–b7) There are many kinds of food. It is impossible to live without food. [Nature makes nothing incomplete and does nothing in vain.] Therefore, nature has differentiated the ways of life of animals for their convenience and preference. Similarly, humans have many different modes of life, which involve self-generated (*autophuton*) industry, not exchange or commerce viz., the shepherd, husbandman, brigand, fisherman, and hunter. [Therefore, nature has differentiated these modes of human life.] *Part II* (1256b7–30) Nature makes nothing incomplete and does nothing in vain. The yolks, milk, etcetera needed by the young at birth are given to them by nature. Similarly, [since animals need plants for food,] plants exist for the sake of animals. Humans need animals for food, clothing, and instruments, and as beasts of burden. Therefore, animals exist for the sake of man. The argument as a whole has two major conclusions (1256b7–10, 26–30):[26]

> (C 1) Therefore, such property (*ktēsis*) is given by nature to all both at birth and when grown (cf. 10 1258a34–7).

(C 2) Therefore, one kind of acquisitive craft is by nature a part of household management and must be present (or householding must provide that it be present), and this acquisitive art has to do with those storable things which are necessary and useful for the community of the polis or household.

If Aristotle's teleological principle that "nature makes nothing incomplete and does nothing in vain" is understood to imply that what is needed to make a substance complete exists for its sake and is thus given to it by nature, then his argument appears to be valid.[27] But, unfortunately, this principle would also seem to support the conclusion that human beings exist for the sake of, and are given by nature to, carnivorous beasts or intestinal parasites. However, Aristotle is probably assuming another principle such as that at *Pol.* VII.14 1333a21–4: "The inferior always exists for the sake of the superior, and this is manifest in matters of art as well as of nature. And the superior is that which possesses reason." This principle would postulate a hierarchy of natural kinds along the following lines:

If natural kind K_1 has end E_1 and natural kind K_2 has end E_2 and E_1 *is* superior to E_2 then entities of kind K_2 exist for the sake of, and are given by nature to, entities of kind K_1.

These teleological principles regarding the gift of nature have a place in Aristotle's theory of natural acquisition comparable to the principles underlying Locke's theory: viz., from the view of *Revelation* that God "has given the Earth to the Children of Men" or from the view of *natural Reason* that "Men, being once born, have a right to their Preservation, and consequently to Meat and Drink, and such other things, as Nature affords for their Subsistence."[28]

Natural Acquisition as Limited (1256b30–9)

However, Aristotle wants to establish that the acquisitive craft is natural without establishing too much: he wants to establish that it is a natural art *only in so far as* it provides the necessary means for the natural ends of household management and politics. This argument proceeds as follows: no instrument (*organon*) belonging to any craft is without a limit (*apeiron*) in number or in size. True wealth is the amount of property sufficient for the good life. The householder and politician use property as an instrument for the good life. True wealth is the instrument of household management and politics. Therefore, true wealth has a limit (cf. 9 1257b19–20). The natural acquisitive craft provides true wealth. Therefore, the natural acquisitive craft is constrained by a limit.

Natural acquisition has a limit resulting from its subordination to household management or politics. The basis for the premise that the instrument of a craft has a limit is suggested later at 9 1257b27–8: the end of a craft may be unlimited but not the means, for the end is the limit (*peras*) for all crafts. But the idea of a "limit" as used in this argument is unclear because a limit may be understood as a baseline (minimum) or a ceiling (maximum). Does the end require that a certain baseline of resources be acquired or a certain ceiling? If the end is "the good life" it would seem possible to interpret the limit as a baseline, but Aristotle interprets it as a ceiling as well as a baseline.

His reason for this becomes somewhat clearer in *Politics* I.9 (see also VII 4 1326a35–40). Aristotle contrasts the natural acquisitive craft with another acquisitive craft which has no limit (1256b40–1257a1) and is due to experience and craft rather than to nature (1257a4–5). This unnatural acquisitive craft is one of two arts of exchange (*metablētikē*). It is commerce (*kapēlikē*), "retail exchange," and the other, unobjectionable type of exchange is barter (*allagē*), "simple exchange." The following argument involves three stages: an analysis of the proper use of property, a defense of barter, and a critique of commerce.

(1) Proper Use

He begins by distinguishing two uses of a piece of property such as a shoe: to be worn and to be exchanged. The proper use of a possession is that for the sake of which it came into existence. But such a piece of property did not come into existence for the sake of barter. Therefore, barter is not its proper use (cf. *EE* III.4 1231b39–1232a4).

(2) Defense of Barter

However, activities carried out in order to replenish one's natural self-sufficiency are the result of the natural fact that humans have more or less than what they need. Because barter is carried out in order to replenish the natural self-sufficiency of individuals, it is not against nature.

(3) The Critique of Commerce

Commerce is the art of producing wealth by exchanging things with money. The other crafts (e.g., medicine) have no limit regarding their end (e.g., health). Similarly, this acquisitive craft, whose end is wealth and the possession of things, has no limit to its end. But for the natural acquisitive craft, all wealth has a limit. Therefore, commerce is an unnatural acquisitive craft.

The critique of commerce raises the question: Why is commerce, but not medicine, an unnatural art? It is not that commerce employs a perverted instrument, filthy lucre, because it uses the same instrument as the natural art (1257b35–8).[29] Aristotle attempts to distinguish them by arguing that the unlimited end of commerce is due to a false view of the good life: viz., the unlimited gratification of desires, which requires unlimited wealth. This leads to a vicious disposition towards unlimited acquisition and a tendency to use one's faculties in an unnatural way (1257b32–1258a14; cf. *NE* I.5 1096a5–10). This argument seems open to the objection that the definition of commerce—the art of making an exchange in order to make a profit (1257b4–5)—no more entails that a practitioner must pursue wealth in an excessive manner than the definition of medicine entails that one must pursue health in an excessive manner. Aristotle seems to dismiss without argument the possibility that one could observe the mean while engaging in commerce, or that one might have other motives aside from profit seeking.[30]

Apart from these objections, Aristotle's prescription of a limit for natural acquisition offers an interesting parallel to the Lockian proviso for just acquisition, viz., that there must be "enough, and as good left in common for others."[31] To be sure, Aristotle's arguments in *Politics* I.8 and I.9 for a limit are based upon self-regarding considerations: excessive acquisition will prevent the *agent* from achieving the good life. However, it is noteworthy that when Aristotle sums up his conclusions in *Politics* I.10 he says that commerce or exchange is justly censured "for it is not according to nature but from one another" (1258b1–2). This very brief remark does not obviously follow from the critique and requires considerable speculative unpacking. One way of reconstructing his argument is that commerce is a "zero-sum game," in which there is a loser for every gainer, so that any person can exceed his limit only by taking something which others need in order to attain their natural ends. In this sense people would be making unnatural, hence unjust, gains "from one another."[32]

6. Defense of Private Property

While *Politics* I is concerned with the property rights of a person *qua* householder or statesman, *Politics* II deals with the property of individual citizens. Should property (along with wives and children) be held by all the citizens in common (as Socrates advocates for the guardian class in Plato's *Republic),* or should it be privately owned?

Although *Politics* II.5, aims to defend individual ownership, it is an oversimplification to treat his argument *simply* as a "vindication of private property rights." For he only takes into account three possible property schemes: (i) private property, common use; (ii) common property, private use; and (iii) common property, common use. He omits from discussion another option: (iv) private property, private use. He is not defending a system of unqualified privatization.[33] Hence, we should take careful note of the proviso he adds when he expresses a preference for the "present mode, if improved by custom and correct legal order" (1263a22–3; cf. I.1261a8 where there is no proviso).

Aristotle's way of defending his preferred option is not deductive but is deliberative (seeking the better of three options) and dialectical (appealing to accepted opinions related to property). He offers five different criteria for evaluating a property arrangement:

(1) It does not give rise to quarrels and complaints (1263a8–21, 27–8, b23–7);
(2) It leads to improvement in the care devoted to the property (1263a28–9; cf. 3 1261b33–40; IV.15 1299a38–b1; cf. *Oec.* I.6 1344b35–1345a1);
(3) It facilitates friendship (1263a29–40; cf. VII.8 1328a25–8; 10 1329b41–1330a2);
(4) It fosters natural pleasures, in particular self-love (1263a40–b5);
(5) It makes possible the exercise of virtues such as generosity and moderation (1263b5–14; 6 1265a28–38).

It is noteworthy that criteria (3)–(5) presuppose the moderate-individualistic view that political institutions should promote the advantages of individual citizens, understood to include virtuous activity.

Aristotle's thesis is that these criteria taken together show that mode (i) private property, common use, is better than the other modes. The omitted option (iv) would presumably be ruled out by appeal to criteria (3) and (5).[34] Plato's scheme (iii) is ruled out by all the criteria in Aristotle's view, except perhaps (3). Unfortunately, Aristotle is rather unclear about how these modes differ in practice and what exactly his distinction between "common property" and "common use" comes to. This has to be gathered from the criteria on which he bases his argument. For example, both (ii) and (iii) allegedly fail criterion (i) because conflict is unavoidable under these schemes; but Aristotle does not explain how his own scheme (i) does any better. Why does not the "common use" of slaves, horses, dogs, or crops lead to the same sorts of conflicts as those for which he indicts (ii) and (iii)?

A straightforward and plausible explanation of why Aristotle does not think that this problem will arise for (i) is that he takes for granted the working concept of property rights defined in *Rhetoric* I.5 including the requirements that the use and the alienation of the object are up to the owner. In the case of a piece of property *P* and two individuals, *X*, who wants *P* put to use U_1, and *Y*, who wants to put *P* to use U_2, if U_1 and U_2 are incompatible and if neither *X* nor *Y* has the right to decide in this matter, conflict is the likely result. This is what happens in schemes (ii) and (iii), according to Aristotle. But in his scheme (i) for any object P there is some individual *X* such that it is up to *X* to decide how *P* will be used, so that conflict can be avoided. Thus, although Aristotle recognizes that conflicts can arise in systems of private property, he still maintains that conflict is far more pervasive in common property arrangements.[35]

Criterion (2) should be understood along similar lines. If, as seems plausible, Aristotle is tacitly assuming the property rights concept of *Rhetoric* I.5, his point is that an individual *X* will take better care of object *P* to the extent that the use of *P* is up to *X*; if its use is up to many individuals in addition to *X*, *X* will tend to neglect *P* on the grounds that other people can bear the cost of caring for *P*. Some commentators find a parallel between Aristotle's argument that individuals tend to take better care of their own personal possessions than of common property and explanations by modern economists of the function of private property. In general, privatization gives individuals a much greater incentive to use property efficiently. Also, the costs involved in using resources are more fully taken into account when they are "internalized" in private possessions. Property which is commonly owned tends to be overused, abused, or neglected, resulting in "the tragedy of the commons."[36] However, it should also be noted that Aristotle agrees in *Politics*, VII, that part of the land should be common, to be used for public religious cults and to cover the expenses of common meals for the citizens (10 1330a9–13). Perhaps he thinks these functions are sufficiently circumscribed to avoid the problems associated with criteria (1) and (2).

This interpretation is also consistent with criterion (3) and can be used to explain how he can reconcile a defense of private property with the common use characteristic of friendship. Although private property implies that particular individuals have rights over particular objects, Aristotle also claims that they should place these objects at the disposal of their friends. As long as some individual has the final say over what friend uses what property, criterion (3) is consistent with criterion (i). It is the function of the educational system to habituate individuals to share their property as well as to observe limits on acquisition of the sort discussed in Section 5 (5 1263a38–40, b36–7; 7 1267b5–9). Therefore, this criterion rules out a scheme of (iv) private property, private use, but it is consistent with a scheme like (i) in which educated adults retain property rights.

Criteria (4) and (5) can also be better appreciated from the standpoint of the property rights interpretation. Criterion (4) introduces a new line of teleological argument: a property scheme is according to nature to the extent that it fosters natural pleasures of self-love. True self-love is embodied in persons who act according to their own rational judgment (cf. *NE* IX.8 1168b34–1169a3). True self-love thus requires that persons be able to act according to their own judgment, and the existence of private property provides them the sphere in which they can do so.[37]

Criterion (5) concerns moral virtues such as generosity or liberality, the function of which is in the use of possessions (1263b13–14). Aristotle evidently intends an argument of the following sort: a property scheme should permit the exercise of generosity, which involves the use and alienation of property (cf. *NE* IV.1 11119b23–6). Since one can act generously only if one acts voluntarily and by choice, one can act generously only if the use and alienation of property is up to oneself, and this is the case only in a system of private ownership.

Whether Aristotle's argument based on generosity is sound continues to be debated. Against Aristotle and in defense of common ownership, T. H. Irwin has objected that generosity does not require that agents have resources under their exclusive control.

> Even if we think the practice of generosity requires me to be free to dispose of some resources under my own initiative, it does not follow that the resources must be under my exclusive control. The state might loan them to me, and allow me to dispose of them as I please within certain limits and in certain circumstances; such an arrangement would leave ample room for the exercise of generosity.[38]

Aristotle might regard this as a pallid form of generosity, because the virtue involves actions that cost the agent something and hence it entails giving away something that is the agent's own. Hence, virtuous agents should have a stronger right to property on the grounds that it is nobler to give up something more valuable, for example property that would otherwise be one's own in perpetuity, than an object which one is merely borrowing for a while. However, Irwin responds,

> [T]his objection seems to overlook the virtuous person's attachment to the common good. He will regard the distribution of his friend's resources as a cost to himself, because he regards his friend's resources as his own; and he will take the same view of the community's resources. We might object that such identification of one's own interest with the interests of others is impossible or undesirable; but Aristotle should not be easily persuaded by any such objection, since it would undermine his whole account of friendship.[39]

On Aristotle's behalf, Robert Mayhew offers two objections:

> First, . . . according to Aristotle we will not and indeed cannot attend to common things very well in fact we tend to neglect them. For this and other reasons, I can-

> not feel for the community's resources what I feel for myself and my own things; I cannot really regard the former as my own. Second, I *might* regard the distribution of a close friend's (or family member's) resources as a cost to me, since, in a sense, the goods of such friends are common. But I do not have the same relationship with the community, and thus neither do I view the community's resources in this way.[40]

Mayhew's first point gains support from the aforementioned economists' argument that individuals have more incentive to take care of objects when they own them. The second point is supported by Aristotle's arguments that political friendship falls short of virtue-based friendship and is too diluted to support a genuine identification of interests. Hence, Aristotle would seem to have good reasons for concluding that private property is necessary for full generosity.

7. Citizenship and Property

In *Politics* VII.9–10 Aristotle also discusses property in connection with the best constitution. As we have seen in, the discussion of property is preceded by an account of who the citizens of the best constitution are. In brief, they must perform a necessary function of the polis and must be capable of participating in the common end of the polis. Aristotle argues that citizenship should be confined to those who have the natural capacity, the virtue, and leisure to carry out the military and deliberative-juridical functions of the best polis.

The argument (1329a17–26) for universal property rights may be reconstructed as follows:

(1) The lawgiver should promote the happiness of the polis.
(2) "A polis should be called happy not by viewing part of it but by viewing all the citizens" (1329a23–4).
(3) [Happiness requires equipment (cf. VII.1 1323b40–1324a21).]
(4) Therefore, all citizens have a right to property.

Aristotle's application of this argument is not without difficulty. He claims that "no group partakes of the [best] polis which is not a craftsman of virtue" (1329a20–1) and obviously wants the conclusion to be that property belongs *exclusively* to the soldiers and councillors, but this does not follow from his premises. This would follow only if (4) stated, "Only citizens have a right to property," but that would not follow from (1)–(3). Hence, his premises in fact leave open the possibility that noncitizens could possess property as well (although 1329a25–6 implies noncitizens are slaves).[41]

Aristotle applies conclusion (4), when he argues in favor of a proposal (adopted from Plato's *Laws*, V 745C3–D4) that each person's property should be divided into two lots, one near the frontier and one near the city, "in order that two lots may be distributed to each person and everyone may have a share of both districts. For in this way there is equality (*to ison*) and justice (*to dikaion*) and greater unanimity regarding border wars" (*Pol.* VII.10 1330a14–18). Thus Aristotle argues that property should be distributed not only on the basis of considerations of expediency or security but also on the basis of considerations of distributive justice.[42] Hence, this argument makes it explicit that in the best polis each citizen has a right to a share of property based on distributive justice.

The argument of *Politics*, VII.9–10, also differs from the preceding arguments in the importance that it places upon citizenship as a basis for property rights. For Aristotle here treats political rights as more basic than property rights. The most basic rights are justified directly on the basis of a person's well-being or objective interests, whereas the justification of derivative rights includes the assertion of more basic rights.[43] In *Politics* VII.9–10 Aristotle clearly regards the right to be a citizen and participate in government as a more basic right, because ethical virtues are most fully exercised in political activity. Since citizenship can be exercised only by those who have sufficient property, citizens also have a derivative right to property. [When Aristotle implicitly concludes in *Politics* VII.9 that property should belong exclusively to citizens and not to those who are incapable of political virtue, he may simply be taking it for granted that if property rights cannot be justified as derivative from political rights they cannot be justified at all. This priority of political over property rights in Aristotle is fundamentally at variance with the priority of property to government in Locke[44] and is rooted in the basic principles of the *Politics*—most importantly, that human beings are political animals and that the polis is prior to the individual.

8. Summary and Applications

The first section introduced a number of questions that a theory of property rights might be expected to answer. I take Aristotle's theory to be offering, briefly, the following answers to these questions:

(1) What Sorts of Individuals Have Rights to Property?

He offers two different answers in the *Politics*: it is the citizen of the best polis in *Politics* VII and the householder in *Politics* I. However, in the best constitution every citizen is a landholding householder. In the second-best constitutions, also, the citizens have moderate and sufficient property (IV.11 1295b39–40). Moreover, in democracy he suggests that "the surplus from public revenues should be collected and distributed among the poor, especially if one can collect such quantities as may enable them to acquire a piece of land, or, if not, to make a beginning in trade or farming"(VI.5 1320a35–b1). The focus in these discussions is on land. It is presumably taken for granted, but not stated, that artisans and other lower classes possess movable property.[45]

(2) To What Sorts of Objects Do They Have Property Rights?

The answer given in *Rhetoric* I.5 is land (including dwellings), movable objects, animals, and slaves. Although this answer is accepted in the *Politics,* Aristotle seems to assume an important distinction between land and other forms of property.

(3) What Form Does the Exercise of Property Rights Take?

According to *Rhetoric,* I.5, this consists of two elements: *X* possesses *P* in such a way that the use of *P* is up to *X* and the alienation of *P* (giving it away or selling it) is up to *X.* I have argued that this concept is presupposed throughout Aristotle's treatments of private property in the *Politics.*

(4) What Is the Justification for the Thesis that Individuals Generally Have Property Rights?

I have surveyed four principal strands of argument. These rely upon a number of Aristotelian principles: for example, the principle of *eudaimonia* that happiness and its parts should be protected and promoted, the teleological principle that nature provides all living things with what is necessary for living and attaining their natural ends, and the principle of justice that every citizen should have the things necessary for happiness and the exercise of moral virtue. They also employ Aristotelian dialectic, appealing to accepted opinions. In *Politics* VII.9–10 Aristotle attempts to combine the principles of *eudaimonia* and distributive justice, but he does not indicate what he would say if the two principles came into conflict. Another apparent tension is that the *Rhetoric* argument suggests that property rights are basic rights because the use of property is itself a part of the human end of happiness, and *Politics* II.5 also claims that private property is indispensable for virtuous conduct; but the argument of *Politics* VII.9 suggests that property rights are derivative rights because property is a necessary condition for exercising a more basic right (viz., to membership in the polis). Alternatively, he may mean that membership in a polis is a precondition for entitlement to property because it is a necessary condition for the acquisition and practice of virtue. This might resolve the apparent conflict.

(5) Under What Circumstances Do Individuals Justly Acquire Title to Specific Objects and Under What Circumstances Do They Come to Possess Them Unjustly?

Aristotle recognizes a number of different ways in which property can be justly acquired: original acquisition from nature (hunting, farming, etc.), barter, cash exchange, gifts, inheritance, and distribution by the government. He does not, however, endorse a Locke-style labor theory of acquisition.[46] Although he does not offer a complete set of sufficient conditions for the just acquisition of property, he does indicate some important necessary conditions: an individual *X* can justly acquire object *P* only if (i) the natural end of *X* is superior to the natural end of *P* (if *P* has one), (ii) in acquiring *P*, *X* does not exceed his natural limit, and (iii) *X* does not unjustly take *P* from another person equal to *X*. I see no evidence, however, that Aristotle is committed to the view that *X* owns *P* only if *X* uses *P* to perform a virtuous act or puts *P* to common use (e.g., shares it with a friend). To be sure, Aristotle argues that individuals should be able to acquire property because they need it in order to perform virtuous and friendly acts; and he directs the legislators to institute public education to habituate the citizens to this end. But it does not follow from this that the just acquisition of each piece of property is contingent on the performance of a virtuous and friendly act.[47]

(6) What Are the Implications of the Theory of Property Rights for Public Policy?

As noted in question (1) above, Aristotle's theory has important implications for the distribution of property to the citizens. Property rights also place certain constraints upon the conduct of governments according to Aristotle. In particular, he criticizes confiscation by democratic majorities of the property of wealthier citizens (VI.3 1318a24–6; cf. III.10 1281a17–21).[48] He explicitly rejects the conventionalist argument that whatever law the majority decides to enact is just, objecting that even if the majority wants it, such confiscation is *unjust (adikēsousi dēmeuontes).* Thus, the property owner has a claim of justice, a right against other citizens, which is violated by the law of confiscation. It is implicit that the magistrates in the best constitution will respect the property of the citizens. *Politics* V, especially, is filled with warnings that those with political power should not deprive others of their property.

Aristotle's theory of property rights also allows for the regulation of property. Newman remarks that the defense of private property in *Politics* II.5 is not expressly coupled with qualifications,[49] but Aristotle elsewhere endorses various social policies which limit private property rights. The qualifications upon private property rights should probably be understood in the light of the fact that they are, for Aristotle, subordinate to political rights. His defense of private property is not intended as a case for total privatization. Presumably on similar grounds, he advocates coercive taxation for the purposes of defense and internal needs (VII.8 1328b10–11; III.12 1283a17–18). He also recommends support for needy citizens, as virtuous acts carrying out his policy of "private ownership, common use" (VII.10 1329b41–1330a2; VI.6 1320b2–11). The provisos which he attaches to natural acquisition can explain his advocacy of legal limits on the amount of land any citizen can own (see VI.4 1319a8–10). He also recommends that individuals do not have the liberty to sell and bequeath land however they please (II.9 1270a18–21). He even admits that the ostracism of very rich or powerful citizens may be justified by a sort of political justice (see III.13 1284b15–34; VI.8 1308b19). The point here is probably that the excessive exercise of property and other rights by some persons jeopardizes the political rights of the other citizens, and that the political rights of the latter should override the property rights of the former. Further, the citizens of the best constitution should not be merchants because this is a morally degrading profession (VII.9 1328b39–40) and the "free market" of citizens should be separate from the commercial *agora* regularly frequented by farmers and merchants (12 1331a30–b4). He also recommends market magistrates to supervise transactions. In Athens such officials ensured that commodities were pure and unadulterated, that merchants used fair weights and measures, and that foodstuffs were not unjustly priced *(Ath. Pol.* LI; cf. Plato, *Laws,* XI 917E2–918A1) However, he assumes elsewhere that traders generally have immunity (*adeia*) to set their own terms (*NE* V.4 1132b15–16). In sum, the rationale for these restrictions upon individual property rights involves features of the general theory discussed above: the provisos on the acquisition of property, the precedence of political rights and duties over property rights, and the prescription of "private property, common use."

However, it would be a mistake to ascribe to Aristotle a theory resembling modern socialism or social democracy. For "private ownership, common use" implies that property owners ought to put their property to virtuous uses, thereby benefiting others. He does not mean by this to create entitlements on the part of others to this property. If others have a legally enforceable right to help themselves to one's crops, it is not an act of generosity to permit them to do so.[50] Aristotle holds that no citizen should lack sustenance, and that all of the citizens should be included in common meals (VII.10 1330a2–8). He approves of the Cretan system for providing common meals for everyone including women and children out of the proceeds from common property (II.5 1272a16–21). However, there is no indication that Aristotle advocates a general policy of redistribution of wealth. The rudimentary social safety net for the unfortunate which Aristotle admits is a far cry from the modern egalitarian welfare state.

In conclusion, Aristotle addresses the questions that must be answered by a theory of property rights. His way of developing, justifying, and qualifying his views on wealth and property can be interpreted in terms of a property rights theory, and the policies he recommends for both the best polis and for deviant constitutions are illuminated by this interpretation. Although there are a number of respects in which Aristotle's arguments appear to be objectionable or underdeveloped, and undoubtedly his theory would be unacceptable to many modern theorists (either of a laissez-faire capitalist perspective or of a socialist perspective), his theory of property rights is, nonetheless, comprehensible and worthy of further investigation.

Notes

1. Barker, *The Political Thought of Plato and Aristotle*, p. 248, here, as in many other instances, was following the lead of Newman (*The Politics of Aristotle*, i. pp.167–68). Cf. also Swanson, *The Public and the Private in Aristotle's Political Philosophy*, who argues that Aristotle is concerned to defend a sphere of privacy for the sake of individual virtue. Swanson convincingly criticizes the thesis of Arendt, in *The Human Condition*, that Aristotle depreciates the private (as a realm of violence and necessity) in contrast to the public (as a realm of freedom and virtue). However, as we shall see, property rights do not play as central a role in Aristotle's political theory as they do in Locke's. Nonetheless, I have found it necessary to devote an entire chapter to this topic in order to correct the erroneous view that Aristotle does not recognize individual property rights at all.

2. See Becker, *Property Rights: Philosophical Foundations*, p. 21.

3. Honoré, "Ownership."

4. See Vlastos, "The Theory of Social Justice in the *Polis* in Plato's *Republic*," pp. 4–11.

5. [Demosthenes], VII 26.

6. Stobaeus, *Florileg.* XLIV 22; see Harrison, *The Law of Athens*, i. p. 204.

7. See Jones, *The Law and Legal Theory of the Greeks*, p. 201 n. 4; Harrison, *The Law of Athens*, i. p. 201; MacDowell, *The Law in Classical Athens*, p. 133.

8. See Plato, *Rep.* VIII 551B3

9. See Harrison, *The Law of Athens*, i. p. 202, and MacDowell, *The Law in Classical Athens*, p. 133.

10. I understand *kai* at 1361a15 as disjunctive because Aristotle defines the two conditions so that they are mutually exclusive: useful properties are productive, those from which we derive income or rents; whereas liberal properties are employed in intrinsically valuable activities. All references to Aristotle in this and the following section are to *Rhet.* I.5 unless otherwise indicated.

11. Understanding *oikeia* at 1361a15; cf. a21.

12. On the location of *ē mē* see Grimaldi, *Aristotle, Rhetoric I, A Commentary.*

13. Harrison, *The Law of Athens*, i. p. 202; cf. Jones, *The Law and Legal Theory of the Greeks*, p. 198, on the place of this power in ownership for Greek law generally.

14. Becker, *Property Rights: Philosophical Foundations*, p. 20, argues that among Honoré's elements the right to the capital is "the most fundamental of the elements, if only because it includes the right to destroy, consume, and alienate. (Alienation is understood to include exchanges, gifts, and just 'letting go.')"

15. Cf. 1360b16–17: the defining conditions of happiness include "the power to protect and put to use" one's possessions.

16. See Grimaldi, *Aristotle, Rhetoric I, A Commentary*, p. 112, who remarks that *apallotriōsai* "Aristotle defines immediately as the right to give or to sell (what one possesses)."

17. For (*a*) cf. *Pol.* VII.1 1323b21–3; 3 1325a32–4, b12–16. For (*b*) cf. *NE* I.5 1097b7–21; X.7 1177a27–b4; *Rhet.* I.5 1360b23. For (*c*) cf. *Rhet.* I.5 1360b28.

18. Commentators have remarked that Aristotle's enumeration of these parts is complicated, seemingly redundant, and possibly inconsistent. On the ways of counting and classifying these parts see Grimaldi, *Aristotle, Rhetoric I, A Commentary*, pp. 106–7.

19. See Düring, *Aristoteles, Darstellung und Interpretation seines Denkens*, p. 118.

20. Aristotle indeed speaks in this way in *EE* I.2 1214b26–7; 5 1216a39–40; II.1 1219b11–13; cf. *MM* I.2 1184a18–19, 26–9, 30–1; but he does not use this sort of language in the *Nicomachean Ethics*, except for the common books; e.g. parts of happiness are mentioned in the common books at *NE* V.1 1129b18. Cf. Cooper, *Reason and Human Good in Aristotle*, p. 122.

21. *NE* VII.13 1153b17–19; cf. *NE* I.8 1099a31–b8; X.8 1178a23–b7. Jost, "Moral Luck and External Goods in the Eudemian Ethics," points out a similar treatment of the natural goods (*phusei agatha*), which include wealth, in *EE* VIII.3.

22. The exact significance of this claim is a subject of controversy. Cooper, "Aristotle on the Goods of Fortune," and White, *Sovereign Virtue*, take external goods to be valuable for Aristotle only in so far as they permit virtuous activity; Irwin, "Permanent Happiness: Aristotle and Solon," and Nussbaum, *The Fragility of Goodness*, ch. 11, think that they are intrinsically valuable; and Annas, "Aristotle on Virtue and Happiness," finds Aristotle's account ambivalent on this issue.

23. "Therefore" (*oun*) at 1254a13 implies that (8) is an inference, and I take it to follow from the analogy to parts which precedes it.

24. Aristotle makes another distinction (which I have ignored in the above reconstruction) between property defined as a "practical instrument" and instruments used

for production. A cloak or bed which one uses in one's daily life is an example of the former (because life is action not production), a shuttle an example of the latter. This special sense of *ktēma* and *ktēsis* seems not only unnecessary but also confusing. Note that if (1) were narrowed to practical instruments, the conclusion would not apply to any of the productive implements belonging to the household.

25. See VII.8 1328a21–b37; cf. Newman, *The Politics of Aristotle*, ii. p. 135.

26. See Newman, ii. p. 179. I treat (C 1) as following from both parts because the *men oun* at 1256b7 indicates that (C 1) follows in some way from Part I, and because the *gar* at b10 implies that Part II is also intended to support (C 1). The *men oun* at b26 implies that (C 2) follows at least from Part II.

27. On Aristotle's teleology see Sects. 1.4 and 2.1 above and Sect. 10.2. in my *Nature, Justice, and Rights in Aristotle's Politics.*

28. Locke, *Second Treatise*, V.25.

29. Sinclair's (*Aristotle: The Politics*) suggestion that Aristotle means to contrast commerce with medicine runs afoul of the *houtō kai* at b28 which he infelicitously translates as "but."

30. Aristotle's argument has also been criticized from the Platonist side: Why does not *all* private acquisition have this corrupting influence? In *Pol.* II.5 Aristotle suggests that the acknowledged evils associated with private property such as lawsuits and flattery of the rich are due to moral vice and thus curable through moral education. But this raises such obvious questions as why these evils are curable by education, but those associated with commerce or those associated with Plato's communism are not similarly curable. See Irwin, "Aristotle's Defence of Private Property," pp. 219–20.

31. Locke, *Second Treatise*, V. 27.

32. Cf. *Oec.* I.2 1343a27–30 (perhaps by Theophrastus): "Agriculture is the most just [occupation]; for it does not take from human beings, either voluntarily, as do commerce and wage-earning, or involuntarily, as does military occupation." Although Aristotle's account of commercial exchange certainly reflects ancient Greek popular attitudes (see Dover, *Greek Popular Morality in the Time of Plato and Aristotle*, pp. 172–74), it has been criticized by modern theorists for failing to recognize the mutual gains from voluntary trade and the positive contributions made by profit-seeking entrepreneurs: see Susemihl and Hicks, *The Politics of Aristotle*, pp. 23–31, and Flew, *The Politics of Procrustes*, pp. 148–54. Meikle, "Aristotle and Exchange Value"; Lewis, "Acquisition and Anxiety: Aristotle's Case Against the Market"; and McNeill, "Alternative Interpretations of Aristotle on Exchange and Reciprocity," offer more sympathetic views of Aristotle's arguments. (These articles also include references to the extensive secondary literature.)

33. Cf. Grunebaum, *Private Ownership*, pp. 35–46. References to Aristotle in this section are to *Pol.* II.5 unless otherwise indicated.

34. Cf. Dobbs, "Aristotle's Anti-Communism," pp. 39–40.

35. Similarly, Steiner, "The Structure of Compossible Rights," argues that a system of private property is necessary if individual rights are to be compossibly realizable.

36. See Hardin, "The Tragedy of the Commons"; Machan, *Human Rights and Human Liberties*, p. 206, notes the parallel of Hardin and Aristotle. Also, Aristotle's argument for private property is acknowledged in modern economics texts, e.g., Gwartney and Stroup, *Economics: Private and Public Choice*, pp. 718–19. See also Sect. 10.5 below.

37. Mayhew, "Aristotle on Property," p. 239, also mentions *Rhet.* I.11 1371b12–28 which states that "since everyone is a lover of self, one's things (*ta hauton*) are necessarily pleasant to everyone [individually], e.g. deeds and words," and plausibly suggests that the inference can be extended to physical objects. Cf. also *Pol.* II.4 1262b22–3.

38. Irwin, "Aristotle's Defense of Private Property," pp. 222–23.

39. Irwin, "Aristotle's Defense of Private Property," p. 224.

40. Mayhew, "Aristotle on Property," pp. 814–15.

41. Morrow, *Plato's Cretan City*, p. 112, remarks that Aristotle appears to follow Plato's *Laws* in restricting land ownership to citizens. The issue is further complicated by the fact that the summary in *Pol.* VII.10 describes the previous argument as dealing with "land" (*chōra*, 1329b36–8), prompting the question of whether the earlier argument was intended to be restricted to land rather than to the movable property, including tools of the trade, which might belong to artisans and laborers (cf. Newman, *The Politics of Aristotle*, i. p. 198 n. 3). However, the summary may not be Aristotle's (see Susemihl and Hicks, *The Politics of Aristotle*, p. 516).

42. Cf. VI.3 1318b1–5 where *to ison kai to dikaion* is similarly applied to political rights, viz., voting.

43. Cf. Raz, *The Morality of Freedom*, pp. 168–70, who calls the set of most basic rights "core rights."

44. Cf. Mathie, "Property in the Political Science of Aristotle," p. 17.

45. Cf. Newman, *The Politics of Aristotle*, i. 198 n. 3.

46. See, e.g., Susemihl and Hicks, *The Politics of Aristotle*, p. 28

47. Dobbs, "Aristotle's Anti-Communism," p. 40 n. 9, interprets Aristotle as here maintaining

> paradoxically, only if one shares his property with another can it be said that he has truly acquired it. This is the insight that lies beneath Aristotle's otherwise puzzling use of the verbal and substantive forms of "possession." In other words, it is in a liberal action that it first comes to light that a possession (*ktēma*) can be one's apart from the active possessing (*ktēsis*) or hoarding of it. Thus only the liberal man will feel genuine, natural pleasure in ownership.

Aristotle would agree with the conclusion, but not, I think, with the premises that Dobbs attributes to him. For the uses of *ktēsis* and *ktēma* indicate that liberality or generosity is concerned with both of them. Recall also the definitions at I.4 1253b31–2 which imply that *ktēsis* is a collection of *ktēmata*. Aristotle's point is not that *X* can acquire *P* only if *X* shares it with *Y* but that *X* ought to share *P* with *Y* and that in order to do so *X* must be able to acquire title to *P*.

48. See Jones, *The Law and Legal Theory of the Greeks*, p. 198, who also cites *Ath. Pol.* LVI.2 and Demosthenes XVII.15 for the historical importance of this issue. Aristotle also recommends that confiscation in democracies be discouraged by limiting the uses to which the confiscated property can be put (*Pol.* VI.5 1320a4–11).

49. Newman, *The Politics of Aristotle*, i. pp. 199–200.

50. Nussbaum, "Aristotelian Social Democracy," p. 232, comments on Aristotle's example of sharing one's crops with the needy, "One might fruitfully compare to this housing policies that have been adopted in some socialist and social democratic countries,

giving the homeless certain rights towards unoccupied or luxury housing." Mayhew, "Aristotle on Property," pp. 819–21, argues convincingly that Nussbaum has "failed to grasp the essential nature of Aristotle's view that property should be private generally, but common in use": the policies indicated by Nussbaum would effectively negate the owner's right of use and alienation. Also, her translation (Nussbaum, "Aristotelian Social Democracy," p. 203) of Aristotle's statement that property should have a "common use, in a friendly way (*philikōs*)" (VII.10 1329b41–1330a2) as "common by way of a use that is agreed upon in mutuality" seems in conflict with Aristotle's reasons for rejecting common property.

6

The Wisdom of the Multitude: Some Reflections on Book III, Chapter 11 of Aristotle's *Politics*

Jeremy Waldron

1. Introduction

THERE IS A PASSAGE IN CHAPTER 11, Book III of the *Politics* that has not been given the attention it deserves in modern discussions of Aristotelian political philosophy. My aim in the present article is to exaggerate the importance of a particular passage[1]—to light it up in a way that may go far beyond the intentions of its author—in order to benefit from its illumination of other themes and passages whose importance for the Aristotelian project is, by contrast, indisputable.

The passage I have in mind is Aristotle's attempt to answer the question he poses about political sovereignty at the beginning of chapter 10:

> There is also a doubt as to what is to be the supreme power in the state: Is it the multitude? Or the wealthy? Or the good? Or the one best man? Or a tyrant? Any of these alternatives seems to involve unpleasant consequences.[2]

After reviewing some of these consequences, Aristotle begins chapter 11 by saying that there might be some truth in the principle that the people at large rather than the few best ought to be in power in the polis. He says—and this is the passage I want to focus on—the following:

> For the many, of whom each individual is not a good man, when they meet together may be better than the few good, if regarded not individually but collectively, just as a feast to which many contribute is better than a dinner provided out of a single purse. For each individual among the many has a share of excellence

> and practical wisdom, and when they meet together, just as they become in a manner one man, who has many feet, and hands, and senses, so too with regard to their character and thought. Hence the many are better judges than a single man of music and poetry; for some understand one part, and some another, and among them they understand the whole.[3]

The claim that is made (or at least entertained) here is sometimes referred to as "the summation argument."[4] For reasons explained in section 3, I want to avoid that label. I shall call it by the grander term, the "doctrine of the wisdom of the multitude" (DWM), which has the advantage of begging no questions about the *basis* of the collective superiority of the many.

The thesis seems to be this. If we compare the claim to sovereignty of the people at large (the general body of citizens) with the claim to sovereignty of the individual who happens to be the ablest, best, and wisest, we may want to say that the people's claim prevails. Although, considered individual by individual, each of the people is inferior to the one best man, still, considered as a body which is capable of collective deliberation, the people may make better, wiser, and abler decisions. For they have the benefit of *each person's* knowledge, experience, judgment, and insight—which they can synthesize into collective knowledge, experience, judgment, and insight—whereas the one best man can rely only on his own individual resources. Here, then, is an initial formulation of the doctrine:

> DWM_1: The people acting as a body are capable of making better decisions, by pooling their knowledge, experience, and insight, than any individual member of the body, however excellent, is capable of making on his own.

Actually, DWM_1 is a modest version of the Aristotelian claim. A stronger version would make the case for the multitude not only against kingship but also against aristocracy. That case is harder to make since an aristocratic regime may itself benefit from the doctrine. In considering the rival claims of democratic and aristocratic regimes, the appropriate comparison is not between the people as a whole and individual aristocrats, but between the people acting as a body, on one hand, and an aristocratic subset of them, *also acting as a body,* on the other hand. Just as the people can pool their individual knowledge, experience, and judgment, so the members of the aristocratic subset can pool theirs too. Thus a stronger version of the doctrine offers to make the case for the people against all such subsets.

> DWM_2: The people acting as a body are capable of making better decisions, by pooling their knowledge, experience, and insight, than any subset of them acting as a body and pooling the knowledge, experience, and insight of the members of the subset.

Of the two versions, DWM_2 is politically the more important: the political debates in Athens to which the *Politics* might be taken as a contribution mainly concerned the issue between democracy and oligarchy, the rule of the many and the rule of the few, not between democracy and kingship.[5] For the purposes of abstract discussion, however, I shall focus mainly on DWM_1. A number of the points I want to make concern how we think about the relation between the individual and the polis, and for that purpose the weaker version of DWM is sufficient to bring the important issues into focus. In most of what follows, I shall not be trying to argue that DWM is true in a way that is practically important for constitutional design. Instead I shall consider its theoretical importance for our understanding of certain themes in Aristotle's political philosophy.

2. The Place of the Doctrine in Aristotle's Argument

The doctrine of the wisdom of the multitude is, as I have said, introduced with some hesitation in chapter 11. Aristotle is not sure that it clinches the issue of sovereignty in favor of the many: "Whether this principle can apply to every democracy, and to all bodies of men, is not clear. . . . But there may be bodies of men about whom our statement is nevertheless true."[6]

He says that DWM is conditional on the people not being "debased in character";[7] I shall return to this at end of section 5. He also does not rule out the possibility that there may be in a polis one man or a few men of such outstanding virtue that their ability outstrips even that of the others acting collectively—an elite "so pre-eminently superior in goodness that there can be no comparison between the goodness and political capacity which he shows (or which several show, when there is more than one) and what is shown by the rest."[8] I will discuss this possibility at the end of the chapter.

Despite these qualifications, Aristotle seems happy to apply the doctrine throughout his political theory. He applies it, for example, to judicial as well as legislative and executive functions. The initial question ("[W]hat is to be the supreme power in the state?") arose in chapter 10 after Aristotle had conceded that, although it is best if the laws rule and not men, still we have to ask who is to make and who is to administer the laws. Now, the logic of DWM seems to apply most obviously to legislative assemblies (which is why we treat it as the basis of an argument for democracy); but Aristotle applies it also to the laws' application and to the task of equitable judgment when there are gaps or silences in the law:

> [W]hen the law cannot determine a point at all, or not well, should the one best man or should all decide? According to our present practice assemblies meet, sit in judgment, deliberate, and their judgments all relate to individual cases. Now

> any member of the assembly, taken separately, is certainly inferior to the wise man. But the state is made up of many individuals. And as a feast to which all the guests contribute is better than a banquet furnished by a single man, so a multitude is a better judge of many things than any individual.[9]

He applies the principle also to vindicate the Athenian practice of making state officials accountable to the popular assembly. Though he feels the force of the objection that those with the special capacity to take on magistracies should be selected for that purpose only by their peers ("[a]s, then, the physician ought to be called to account by physicians") and that this election and evaluation can be properly made only by those who have knowledge, he goes on:

> Yet possibly these objections are met by our old answer, that if the people are not utterly degraded, although individually they may be worse judges than those who have special knowledge, as a body they are as good or better.[10]

It is thus striking that what begins as a hesitant speculation quickly becomes "our old answer," a recurring theme, a constant reminder in Aristotle's discussion of institutions:

> For the power does not reside in the juryman, or counsellor, or member of the assembly, but in the court, and the council, and the assembly, of which the aforesaid individuals—counselor, assemblyman, juryman—are only parts or members. And for this reason the many may claim to have a higher authority than the few; for the people and the council, and the courts consist of many persons, and their property collectively is greater than the property of one or a few individuals holding great offices.[11]

Not only this, but DWM is used also as a basis for analyzing the claims of other thinkers. Thus in Book IV, Aristotle says that in democracies,

> the people becomes a monarch, and is many in one; and the many have the power in their hand, not as individuals, but collectively. Homer says that "it is not good to have a rule of many" [*Iliad*, 11 204], but whether he means by this corporate rule, or the rule of many individuals, is uncertain.[12]

It seems, then, not inappropriate to toy with the possibility that DWM occupies a central rather than a peripheral place in Aristotle's overall conception of politics.

3. Aristotle's Grounds for the Doctrine

What grounds does Aristotle give us for thinking that DWM is true? At times he seems to offer little more in its defense than a metaphor: as a "feast to which all the guests contribute is better than a banquet furnished by a single man, so a multitude is a better judge of many things than any individual."[13]

The idea behind the culinary metaphor seems to be that of variety—more contributors will produce a more varied feast, and a more varied feast is better. We shall look at the first of these propositions in section 8, when we discuss the relation of this view to what I take to be Aristotle's pluralism. For the moment, I want to concentrate on the second. As a purely culinary matter, one may contest whether a potluck dinner is better than a carefully planned and organized banquet.[14] And even if it is, is there an appropriate analogy with the kind of decision making a democratic assembly will have to engage in?

One clue is provided by a second analogy that Aristotle uses: that of aesthetic appreciation. "The many are better judges than a single man of music and poetry; for some understand one part, and some another, and among them they understand the whole."[15] This seems to direct us to the multifaceted character of the issues that arise for decision in the assembly. There may be many aspects to a given situation, and no one man, however wise, can be trusted to notice them all. This is obvious enough in the case of policy decisions. The assembly is debating whether to mount an expedition to Sicily—one citizen may be familiar with the Sicilian coastline; another with the military capacities of the Sicilians; a third with the cost and difficulty of naval expeditions; a fourth with the bitterness of military failure; a fifth with the dangers to a democratic state of successful military conquest; and so on. Between them, pooling their knowledge, they can hope to gain the widest possible acquaintance with the pros and cons.

It is interesting, though, that Aristotle relates this point not only to multifaceted policy decisions, but also to equity-based judgments about individual cases:

> [M]atters of detail about which men deliberate cannot be included in legislation. Nor does anyone deny that the decision of such matters must be left to man, but it is argued that there should be many judges, and not one only. For every ruler who has been trained by law judges well; and it would surely seem strange that a person should see better with two eyes, or hear better with two ears, or act better with two hands or feet, than many with many.[16]

The idea here, if I understand it, is that when legislation fails with regard to certain hard cases, it is because their multifaceted character defies the simple categorizations on which the rule of law depends. The cases where general legal rules fail are precisely the cases where one wants a mode of judgment that is sensitive to all aspects of the case, including those which legislation might have overlooked. For that task, one needs many eyes, not just two.

The accounts just given stress the sensitivity of many individuals to many factual aspects of a situation about which a political or legal decision is to be made. However, I think Aristotle's argument is meant to apply to ethical judgments or judgments of value as well.

One possible interpretation, which is not purely a matter of the accumulation of factual knowledge, assimilates Aristotle's view of politics to the utilitarian case for democracy put forward by the earlier Mill and the later Bentham. Maybe what happens when the many come together to make a decision is that they find out from each other how each person's well-being may be affected by the matter under consideration. By this means, they put themselves collectively in a better position to make a judgment of overall social utility. A merchant may not realize how much some measure he is initially inclined to support may prejudice the situation of a farmer until he hears it from the farmer's own mouth.

Or the process may even be cruder than that. Never mind deliberation: each citizen may simply vote his own self-interest, so that it is the collective decision procedure (presumably some form of majority rule) which is "wiser" from the point of view of social utility than any individual member of the collective. Indeed, this crude utilitarian conception of the wisdom of the multitude has the advantage of providing grounds not only for DWM, but also DWM_2. If the criterion of wisdom is social utility, if all groups make their decisions by majority voting, and if all individuals vote their own interests, then obviously the group that comprises everyone will be "wiser" than any subset.[17]

Readers will be relieved to learn that I do not think this was Aristotle's view. There are hints of utilitarian argument, for example, in Aristotle's suggestion that politics is one of those arts whose products are properly judged by the consumer, not just the skilled artist:

> [T]here are some arts whose products are not judged of solely, or best, by the artists themselves, namely those arts whose products are recognized even by those who do not possess the art; for example, the knowledge of the house is not limited to the builder only; the user, or, in other words, the master of the house will actually be a better judge than the builder, just as the pilot will judge better of a rudder than the carpenter, and the guest will judge better of a feast than the cook.[18]

There are two ways of reconciling this suggestion with the generally non-utilitarian cast of Aristotelian politics. It may reflect Aristotle's realistic and moderate view that men come together in society not just in order to live well (i.e., in order to live a life according to virtue), but also to a certain extent simply for the sake of life itself and of life-related interests. Though "a state exists for the sake of a good life, and not for the sake of life only,"[19] still it is true that "mankind meet together and maintain the political community also for the sake of mere life (in which there is possibly some noble element)."[20] Preferring the diners' judgment to the cook's is a way of respecting the importance—partial though it is—of this aspect of political community. For that purpose, the multitude is a better instrument, because by definition it is more widely sensitive to the conditions of life than the one good man.

The other possibility is that, even though Aristotle holds an objective theory of the good life which is not hostage to purely utilitarian or welfarist calculations, nevertheless it is a theory which gives considerable weight to subjective elements—to *what it is like* to live a life of a certain sort. Though the agreeable life is not necessarily the good life, Aristotle does suggest in the *Ethics* that the good life is a pleasant and agreeable life, albeit a pleasant and agreeable life of a certain character.[21] So, discovering that certain political decisions make life disagreeable for many people may be relevant to the assessment of those decisions.

Having said all that, I think that Aristotle, in espousing DWM, is in fact committing himself to the proposition that the many acting collectively may be a better judge than the few best not only of matters of fact, not only of social utility, but also and most importantly of matters of ethics, value, and the nature of the good life—issues which go beyond the mere accumulation of individual experiences. The term traditionally used for the doctrine—"the summation argument"—suggests that all that is going on is *the aggregation* of what each person brings to the argument. But that may be misleading—not only in the way that David Keyt says, because it suggests nothing more than a random and unordered collection of experiences;[22] even the application of a social welfare function is more than *that*. It is misleading because it suggests a merely mechanical ordering, whereas I think Aristotle has in mind something more synthetic or even dialectical. His view is that deliberation among the many is a way of bringing each citizen's ethical views and insights—such as they are—to bear on the views and insights of each of the others, so that they cast light on each other, providing a basis for reciprocal questioning and criticism, and enabling a position to emerge which is better than any of the inputs and much more than an aggregation or function of those inputs.

This is where it really gets interesting. My hunch is that the kind of process that grounds and generates the collective wisdom of the multitude for the purposes of the *Politics* is similar in character to the process represented by Aristotle's own methodology in ethics. Think of the passage about the *endoxa* (reputable opinions) at the beginning of Book VII of the *Nichomachean Ethics*. Introducing his discussion of self-restraint and *akrasia*, Aristotle says,

> Our proper course with this subject as with others will be to present the various views about it, and then, after first reviewing the difficulties they involve, finally to establish if possible all, or if not all, the greater part and the most important of the opinions generally held with respect to these states of mind; since if the

> discrepancies can be saved, and a residuum of current opinion left standing, the true view will have been sufficiently established.[23]

It is an assumption of Aristotle's metaethics that it is better to begin by examining existing views and opinions than to proceed entirely a priori. By taking the *endoxa* seriously, even when they are mutually contradictory, one can see whether they cast light on one another to indicate various aspects of the truth. That this procedure may have (so to speak) a democratic dimension to it—that it is not purely confined to the study of received philosophical opinion—is indicated in Aristotle's remarks about views of happiness (*eudaimonia*) in Book I of the *Ethics*. For after briefly listing the opinions, he writes,

> [S]ome of these views have been held by many men and men of old, others by a few eminent persons; and it is not probable that either of these should be entirely mistaken, but rather that they should be right in at least some one respect, or even in most respects.[24]

The philosopher's job—Aristotle's own job in the *Ethics*—is to consider the common views and use them to cast light on each other, to bring out the respects in which each has something to contribute to the truth. In this way, Aristotle's own philosophical method may be a model of what is supposed to go on when the many act and deliberate collectively.[25]

In a recent discussion of DWM, Mary Nichols has complained that Aristotle overlooks the need for someone who would actually do the synthesizing, someone who (on my account) would do for the various contributing views what the author of the *Nichomachean Ethics* does for the *endoxa:* "A work of music or poetry is more than the sum of its parts. Who is it who judges or appreciates the whole?"[26] In fact, I think, she underestimates the confidence we may have in *genuine* dialectic (as opposed to the fake dialectic of the single author considering "several views" but always on his own terms and in his own formulations). Think, by contrast, of J. S. Mill's suggestions about the synthesis of diverse ideas in *On Liberty.* Some issues, he argued, may not be amenable to being worked out in a dialectic tightly controlled by a single thinker:

> Truth, in the great practical concerns of life, is so much a question of the reconciling and combining of opposites that very few have minds sufficiently capacious and impartial to make the adjustment with an approach to correctness, and it has to be made by the rough process of a struggle between combatants fighting under hostile banners.[27]

On this account, the absence of a master synthesizer may actually be an advantage. Of course, in the end, the view that emerges will end up being held *by* someone (one hopes by all, or by most). There may nevertheless be something to the idea of a consensus "emerging" in open discussion rather than being actively engineered. Though Mill's concerns are no doubt anachronistic in this context, that is no reason to lose sight of the process Mill describes as the kind of possibility Aristotle is contemplating in his model of non-aristocratic politics.

I want to move now to consider the wider significance DWM may have for our understanding of certain central themes in Aristotle's political philosophy.

4. DWM and the Nature of Merit

The first theme is the relation between Aristotle's views on political power and his meritocratic theory of justice.

It is easy to forget that Aristotle's argument in the middle chapters of Book III of the *Politics* is presented as an application of the theory of distributive justice expounded in Book V of the *Ethics*: indeed it is just about the only sustained application of the theory that we have in his work. In the *Ethics*, we are told that "all men agree that what is just in distribution must be according to merit in some sense, though they do not all specify the same sort of merit."[28] In Book III of the *Politics*, Aristotle attempts to apply that doctrine to the distribution of one very important species of good—namely "offices of state," which he says are "posts of honor."[29]

His discussion of what should count as merit for the purposes of the distribution of this good is a fine anticipation of the modern moral doctrine of relevant reasons. "[S]ome persons will say that offices of state ought to be unequally distributed according to superior excellence, in whatever respect," including excellence of wealth and excellence of birth;[30] but Aristotle has no trouble disposing of this view. It is, he argues, like saying that places in an orchestra should be distributed on the basis of beauty and physical courage, whereas in fact they should be distributed only on the basis of those excellences that directly contribute to the purposes for which orchestras are constituted—that is, excellence in playing. Similarly, "the rival claims of candidates for office can only be based on the possession of elements which enter into the composition of a state."

A slightly different problem about the meaning of merit concerns, not its elements or criteria, but the sort of concept it is.[31] Is merit, like our modern concept desert, an essentially backward-looking concept, proportioned to the moral quality of a person's past acts? Is it like the concept of desert that we use, for example, in awarding prizes and honors, and in the retributive apportionment of punishment? Or is merit rather a forward-looking concept for Aristotle, indicating ability in regard to a task to be performed in the future?

The backward-looking view has some support in the *Ethics*. In his discussion of proper pride, Aristotle observes:

> Desert is relative to external goods; and the greatest of these, we should say, is that which we render to the gods, and which people of position most aim at, and which is *the prize appointed for the noblest deeds*; and this is honour.[32]

Honor as "the prize appointed for the noblest deeds" certainly has a backward-looking flavor; and we should not forget that Aristotle explicates the good of political participation as a matter of *honor*.[33]

Even so, I think that it is the forward-looking view that counts in the *Politics*. Certainly that is what the orchestra analogy suggests: one distributes places in the orchestra to people on the basis that they will be able to play well, not on the basis of their having been able to play well in the past. Maybe past performance is evidence of prospective ability. But it is evidence of merit, not merit itself.

Now, if we take this forward-looking view of merit and combine it with DWM, we get a quite striking result. Not only is merit not a backward-looking concept, but it is also not necessarily an individualized concept. The effect of DWM, as David Keyt points out, is to allow the equations of Aristotelian justice to range over groups, not just over individuals.[34]

Take two individuals, Brown and Jones, the former a man of modest virtue and pedestrian judgment, the latter a man of excellence so far as the political virtues are concerned. Considered in terms of their respective individual abilities, Jones merits higher office than Brown; perhaps Brown considered by himself does not merit any office at all. But if DWM applies to a citizenry that includes both of them, then their claims to office may be identical. A group including Brown along with Jones may be collectively wiser than Jones himself or any group comprising only Jones and his peers. It will of course almost certainly be true that a citizen body which included Jones but not Brown (C_J) would be collectively wiser than a citizen body that included Brown but not Jones (C_B). However, if C_J is collectively inferior in wisdom to a body that includes both of them ($C_{J\&B}$), then the difference in merit between Jones and Brown (which grounds the difference in collective wisdom between C_J and C_B) may be of limited relevance so far as political office is concerned. A person's merit is a matter of the collective political capacity of a group of which he might be a member.

Admittedly, this leaves open the question of how $C_{J\&B}$ makes its decisions and how far its procedures may be sensitive to the difference in individual merit as between Jones and Brown.[35] It *may* be the case that $C_{J\&B}$ does better by making decisions on the basis of the equal participation of its members than by any procedure that accords greater weight to the votes of people like

Jones. That need not be the case of course. But the mere fact of the superiority of Jones to Brown, or of C_J to C_B, is not incompatible with its being the case. The dialectical dynamics of $C_{J\&B}$ may be such that the incremental benefits of combining Brown's limited insights with Jones's extensive insights accrue only in the light of a deliberative procedure that treats the two of them formally as equals.

I find this an intriguing possibility, not least for the light it casts on modern discussions about diversity and merit in academic hiring. Many of us support affirmative action because we think that a political science department or a law school will be better able to discharge its mission if it has a diverse membership than if it consists of a pool of similar and similarly talented individuals. On the account I have given of Aristotle's argument, affirmative action can still be regarded as a distribution according to merit—only now, our starting point is the merit of the department or faculty as a whole. The justice claims of particular individuals to a place in the academy are then derived from the merit-based justice claims that can be made on behalf of the groups to which they might belong if appointed, rather than directly on the basis of anything that can be regarded as "their own" merit. Accordingly, when we are choosing between two candidates for a position in a department, we should decide by comparing the merit that *the department* would have if it included one of them with the merit that *the department* would have if it included the other. We may come up with a different result on that basis than we would if we compared their individual merits on the unspoken assumption that each of them would be acting on his or her own.

5. Political Rights as Private Property for Common Use[36]

Though Aristotle talks of "the many" or "the people at large," members of that class are likely to think in terms of *individual* entitlements to participate, based simply on each person's status as a citizen. However, inasmuch as the case for democracy is based on DWM, these individual participatory entitlements must be exercised with some responsibility. There is an interesting analogy here with Aristotle's theory of property.

Aristotle's discussion of property purports to be something of a compromise between a rejection of Plato's communism and an attempt to secure some of the social and ethical advantages that result from sharing:

> Property should be in a certain sense common, but, as a general rule, private. And yet by reason of goodness, and in respect of use, "friends," as the proverb says, "will have all things common." . . . For, although every man has his own property, some things he will place at the disposal of his friends, while of others

> he shares the use with them. It is clearly better that property should be private, but the use of it common; and the special business of the legislator is to create in men this benevolent disposition.[37]

It is not clear what concrete arrangements Aristotle actually has in mind when he talks about private property in common use. His examples mainly involve the sharing of private largesse in a very close circle of friends, and that of course happens in *every* system of private property. Apart from the Lacedaemonian custom of travelers appropriating provisions from fields that they pass by on their journey,[38] there is nothing particularly common in the sense of polis-wide in the examples that Aristotle gives.

But if we turn to *political* property—that is, to the distributable good that consists of the right to participate in politics—we can make perfect sense of the idea of common use. A man's right to participate is in a sense his private property.[39] But the rationale for the distribution of this right requires that each use that property, not just for his own purposes, but in a way that contributes to the excellence in judgment of the group or multitude to which one belongs. Though each has an individual right, the proper use of that right involves an essentially collective exercise. It is possible, of course, that the enfranchisement of the many could be construed by each as purely an individualistic opportunity: "Now I can cast *my* vote. Now I can protect *my* interests. Let everyone else look after themselves." But except on the assumption that DWM is based on purely utilitarian grounds, that attitude will be inappropriate. The individual member of the multitude is required by the logic of his (and their) enfranchisement, not only to use his vote responsibly, but to use it in a way that interacts deliberatively with others, so that the final vote in the assembly reflects a synthesis which is something more than a mere aggregation of its constituent parts.

One way of reading the qualification about corruption, which I mentioned in section 2,[40] is that corruption is the vicious inability to interact deliberatively with others. A person under the influence of money, patronage, or passion, for example, is likely to be someone who will cast his vote without listening to others (except his patron or the one who has bribed him), or who will cast it on the basis of interest or impulse irrespective of what has been said back and forth in the deliberative process. His deafness, so to speak, in deliberation is the mark of his using political property in a narrowly selfish way.[41]

Ideally, then, each will bring his experience and his opinion about the good to the assembly in a form that can be communicated to others, and he must listen to others and reflect on what they say as they contribute their insight and experience. Ronald Beiner in his book *Political Judgment* takes as a motto an interesting comment by Thucydides: "One who forms a judgment on any point, but cannot explain himself clearly to the people, might as well have never thought at all on the subject."[42] The common use of political property requires specific virtues—skill in explaining one's own views, skill in listening to the views of others, skill in bringing the two into relation with one another in a way that highlights their strengths and diminishes their weaknesses, and skill once again in explaining the tentative synthesis that one has arrived at for the benefit of others (who are, of course, engaged in a similar exercise). These are skills of empathy, but they are also, of course, as Beiner reminds us, skills of *rhetoric.*[43] And they bring us to what is perhaps the most important connection I want to draw—between the doctrine of the wisdom of the multitude and Aristotle's conception of reasoned speech—*logos*—as the key to man's political nature.

6. Politics and Speech

There is a suggestion in Rousseau's *Social Contract* that the general will could be expected to emerge even (or perhaps especially) if "the citizens had no communication one with another."[44] For Aristotle, by contrast, the wisdom of which the multitude is capable emerges only "when they meet together"—a phrase he repeats several times.[45] The institution of their meeting together is the assembly (*ecclesia*) and the medium of their meeting together is *speech.*

I have called my approach in this essay one of heuristic exaggeration. However it is, in my view, impossible to overestimate the importance of the connection between DWM and the claim made at the beginning of the *Politics* that the mark of man's political nature is his power of speech.

> Now, that man is more of a political animal than bees or other gregarious animals is evident. Nature, as we often say, makes nothing in vain, and man is the only animal who has the gift of speech. And whereas mere voice is but an indication of pleasure or pain, and is therefore found in other animals (for their nature attains to the perception of pleasure and pain and the intimation of them to one another, and no further), the power of speech is intended to set forth the expedient and the inexpedient, and therefore likewise the just and the unjust.[46]

For one thing the passage immediately undermines any crude utilitarian interpretation of DWM. If collective wisdom amounted only to an aggregation of expressions of individual utility, the multitude could be little more than animals, on this account.

But the connection I want to emphasize works in the other direction. If politics were typically a matter of monarchy, a matter of rule by the one best man, then this power of speech would be largely redundant, except as a vehicle for the expression of decision and command. Speech is the mark of man's political nature because speech is the medium in which politics takes place. And since politics takes place in the medium of speech, it necessarily takes place in a medium of plurality—a context in which there are many speakers, each contributing to a collective decision something that none of the others could have got to by himself.

Thomas Hobbes, infamously, took the human power of speech to be indicative of man's natural unfitness for society. What distinguished men from creatures like bees and ants (which Hobbes mistakenly thought Aristotle regarded as political animals) was, according to Hobbes, that bees and ants

> want that art of words, by which some men can represent to others, that which is Good, in the likenesse of Evill; and Evill, in the likenesse of Good; and augment, or diminish the apparent greatnesse of Good and Evill; discontenting men, and troubling their Peace at their pleasure.[47]

It is tempting to think that the Aristotelian position, in opposition to Hobbes, must be that speech is a medium in which we *share* a view about goodness or justice. Hobbes thinks speech is essentially divisive; Aristotle must think that speech is the natural medium for the expression of the amicable unanimity which is discussed in Chapter 6, Book IX of the *Ethics.*[48] In fact, it would be a mistake to state the contrast between Aristotle and Hobbes in these terms. Between divisiveness and unanimity is debate and complementarity: different views coming together in deliberation to contribute dynamically to a new synthesis. Speech, for Aristotle, is not just the unanimous chanting of accepted truths about justice: it is a matter of conversation, debate in the *ecclesia*, articulate discussion, the sort of dialectic which (as I said) one finds represented in Aristotle's works themselves.

In other words, politics, for Aristotle, is a matter of genuine interdependence. None of us can get by without the others in political life, which we could do if speech were merely a matter of each giving voice to a preordained unanimity. (It is perhaps significant that Aristotle characterizes the individual's dependence on the polis in Book I by asking us to consider what a foot or a hand would be like if the whole body were destroyed[49] and that he characterizes the wisdom of the multitude in Book III with the analogy of a body that has *many* feet, *many* hands, and *many* senses.)[50]

My suggestion then is that DWM stands as a kind of model or paradigm of our nature as *speaking beings.* Each can communicate to another experiences and insights that complement those that the other already possesses, and when this happens in dense interaction throughout a community, it enables the group as a whole to attain a degree of wisdom and practical knowledge that surpasses even that of the most excellent individual member. I don't want to push the exaggeration too far. I do not want to say that the Book I doctrine of speech as the mark of man's political character intimates a direct essentialist argument for democracy. But the passage from Book I does indicate the centrality of the logic of DWM to Aristotle's overall argument in the *Politics:* that people do better in their practical thinking when they work in groups rather than when they rely, one by one, on their individual excellence. What DWM does, in the context of Book III, chapter 11, is pursue that idea to an extreme.

7. Pluralism

I said a moment ago that if we connect DWM with the idea that speech is the mark of man's political nature, we can see that Aristotelian politics cannot just be the unanimous repetition of shared views. Speech is a sign of diversity, a sign that we have something distinctive to learn from one another.[51] DWM thus points us to Aristotle's critique of Platonic unity in *Politics,* Book II, and to his own insistence on difference and diversity. "The nature of a state is to be a plurality. [A] state is not made up only of so many men, but of different kinds of men; for similars do not constitute a state."[52]

Difference here amounts to more than the fact that we each have our own lives to live, our own special needs to be taken into account in any plausible conception of the common good. We are talking here partly about something amounting to a division of labor with regard to knowledge or understanding —a point made prominent in Aquinas's development of these ideas:

> Man has a natural knowledge of life's necessities only in a general way. Being gifted with reason, he must use it to pass from such universal principles to the knowledge of what in particular concerns his well-being. Reasoning thus, however, no one man could attain all necessary knowledge. Instead, nature has destined him to live in society, so that dividing the labour with his fellows each may devote himself to some branch of the sciences, one following medicine, another some other science, and so forth. This is further evident from the fact that men alone have the power of speech which enables them to convey the full content of their thoughts to one another.[53]

In addition, we may also be talking about dialectical difference, as opposed to mere complementarity. My earlier comparison between DWM and Aristotle's way with the *endoxa* indicated that a multitude may be more insightful than one excellent man if its members contrive to spark off each other's dissonant ethical views and sharpen their moral awareness dialectically. Maybe there are some forms of conflict which are so extreme that the proponents of different views (or interests) are just talking at or past one another, not listening particularly, not taking anything that is said by an opponent into account. This extreme of partisan conflict is perhaps itself a form of the corrupt "deafness" I mentioned at the end of section 5. Still, there is a large gap between the moderation of conflict that is necessary to sustain genuine deliberation and the general elimination of diversity of ethical view.

There is therefore some difficulty with Alasdair MacIntyre's claim that Aristotelian political community is "informed by a shared vision of the good."[54] If my hunches bear out, we should expect the citizens in Aristotle's polis to hold views about the good at least as diverse as those canvased as *endoxa* in the *Ethics.* Of course, that's what common sense tells us also. Aristotle did not conjure the conflicting *endoxa* up out of his own imagination. They were views commonly held, some among ordinary people, some among philosophers, some among the elite. He gave no indication that one would expect a good society to exhibit anything less than the diversity of ethical view displayed in the pages of the *Ethics*—the diversity he used as the starting point of his own dialectical wisdom and that I am suggesting forms the basis also of the wisdom of the multitude concocted in political deliberation.

Now Aristotle does say early on in the *Politics* that man alone among the animals has a sense of good and evil, justice and injustice, and that it is the sharing of a view about these things that constitutes a polis.[55] But the fact that that passage immediately follows the discussion of man's power of speech cuts at least both ways. I read it as indicating that our sharing a view about the good or justice is to be understood dynamically, as perhaps the upshot of our talking with one another, talk that presupposes that we come to the conversation from different starting points. So it is misleading for MacIntyre to couch his position in terms of a "form of social order whose shared mode of life already expresses the collective answer or answers of its citizens to the question 'What is the best mode of life for human beings?'"[56] It is wrong, too, for him to suggest that if we ever actually reach new ethical conclusions through deliberation, it can only be because we started from shared premises.[57] Aristotle's own method in ethics intimates no such assumption, and nor, I am arguing, does his politics.

8. A God Among Men

The final connection I want to make stems from Aristotle's discussion in Chapter 13, Book III of the *Politics* where he asks: What if, in a given society, DWM is false? After all, "if the people are to be supreme, because they are stronger than the few, then if one man, or more than one, but not a majority, is stronger than the many, they ought to rule, and not the many."[58] That's predictable enough: we know that Aristotle was prepared to countenance aristocracy or monarchy in certain circumstances.

The striking thing, however, is his assertion a paragraph or two later that the person who provides the counterexample to DWM may justly or properly be regarded as *not a part of the polis*:

> If, however, there be some one person, or more than one, although not enough to make up the full complement of a state, whose excellence is so pre-eminent that the excellence or the political capacity of the rest admit of no comparison with his or theirs, he or they can no longer be regarded as part of a state; for justice will not be done to the superior, if he is reckoned only as the equal of those who are so far inferior to him in excellence and in political capacity. Such a man may truly be deemed a God among men.[59]

You will not be surprised to hear that in my present excited state I cannot resist making a connection between this passage and Aristotle's insistence in Book I, in a sentence immediately preceding the stuff about speech, that anyone who can survive or flourish without the *polis* is either a beast or a god: "[M]an is by nature a political animal. And he who by nature and not by mere accident is without a state, is either a bad man or above humanity."[60] The man who is better than the rest even when they act collectively—the man who is as good without speech, without conversation, as the multitude are with it—has an excellent nature, but not a *political* nature. He is a god among men, for he has no need of the power of speech. From one point of view, he is the ideal absolute monarch; from another point of view, he is (as Hannah Arendt recognizes) as much the antithesis of mundane politics as Billy Budd.[61]

Aristotle does not leave the matter there. Though he says in Book III, Chapter 15 that "the best man must legislate,"[62] the Chapter 13 passage continues, after "a God among men," as follows:

> Hence we see that legislation is necessarily concerned only with those who are equal in birth and capacity; and that for men of pre-eminent excellence there is no law—they are themselves a law. Anyone would be ridiculous who attempted to make laws for them.[63]

It is difficult to know what to make of this. Aristotle's point seems to be about the rule of law—although the "God among men" should legislate, perhaps he should not be bound himself by the rules he makes. The images of divinity and bestiality that Aristotle associates with apolitical natures take another turn at this point—"he who bids the law rule may be deemed to bid God and Reason alone rule, but he who bids man rule adds an element of the beasts"[64]—that I have not been able to figure out.

Even harder to figure out are Aristotle's comments on ostracism. In Chapter 13, he toys with the idea that the ostracism of the truly excellent—their expulsion from the polis over which they tower—"is based upon a kind of political justice."[65] They cannot be subject to law; they are, as Aristotle puts it, a law unto themselves. Yet that will not do for all sorts of reasons, not least that though they are better than the multitude, they are "not enough to make up the full complement of the state."[66] The one excellent man, or the few excellent men, though *morally* self-sufficient, do not have the full self-sufficiency associated with political community:[67] they need to live alongside those with whom they cannot benefit from speaking. And those others in turn would be fools to forgo the benefit of their excellence, even though that may mean denying the efficacy of their own political natures.

And so the discussion in Book III ends with unsatisfactory reassurances: "The best must be that which is administered by the best";[68] "The whole is naturally superior to the part, and he who has this pre-eminence is in the relation of a whole to a part";[69] "Surely it would not be right to kill, or ostracize, or exile such a person, or require that he take his turn in being governed."[70]

Surely? I am not so sure that the preferable conclusion is not the one from Book III, Chapter 16 that perseveres with the power of speech and takes account of the logic of collectivity:

> If, as I said before, the good man has a right to rule because he is better, still two good men are better than one: this is the old saying.
> two going together,
> and the prayer of Agamemnon,
> would that I had ten such counselors![71]

Notes

1. My hermeneutical hero is Michel Foucault, who made this response to someone who quibbled about his interpretation of Nietzsche: "The only valid tribute to thought such as Nietzsche's is precisely to use it, to deform it, to make it groan and protest. And if commentators then say that I am being faithful or unfaithful to Nietzsche, that is of absolutely no interest" (*Power/Knowledge: Selected Interviews and Other Writings 1972–1977*).
2. Aristotle, *Politics* (Jowett-Barnes trans.), III.10 1281a11.
3. Ibid., III.11 1281a43–b9.
4. For example, David Keyt, "Aristotle's Theory of Distributive Justice," p. 270.
5. Either version of the doctrine might also be used as the basis of an exclusionary

claim. We know that when Aristotle talked about the people at large, he—like most Athenians—did not have universal suffrage in mind. The claim made in DWM is made with regard to a body which is itself a subset of all the inhabitants of Athens: women, notoriously, were excluded, as were children, as were those who were enslaved, as were resident aliens, and so on. DWM might be used as a criterion for such exclusion: a person is justifiably excluded from the citizen body if better decisions can be made by pooling the knowledge, experience, and judgment of the members of a citizen body that excludes him, than by pooling the knowledge, experience, and judgment of the members of a body that includes him.

6. *Pol.* 1281b15.

7. *Pol.* 1282a.

8. *Pol.* III.13 1284a.

9. *Pol.* III.15 1286a27–31.

10. *Pol.* III.11 1282a14.

11. *Pol.* III.11 1282a34–41.

12. *Pol.* IV.4 1292a10–14.

13. *Pol.* III.15 1286a29. Indeed, culinary metaphors pervade this part of Book III. We are told that "impure food when mixed with what is pure sometimes makes the entire mass more wholesome" (*Pol.* III.11 1281b36) and that "the guest will judge better of a feast than the cook" (*Pol.* III.11 1282a23).

14. Compare Mary P. Nichols, *Citizens and Statesmen: A Study of Aristotle's* Politics, p. 195, n. 20: "In the background to Aristotle's reference to the feast to which many contribute is the meal described at the end of Aristophanes' *Assembly of Women* (1163–82), a meal made up of so many random foods that the mixture is revolting."

15. *Pol.* III.11 1281a43–b9.

16. *Pol.* III.16 1287b23–8.

17. Bearing in mind that, according to Aristotle, "the whole cannot be happy unless most, or all, or some of its parts enjoy happiness" (*Pol.* II.5 1264b 18).

18. *Pol.* III.11 1282a18.

19. *Pol.* III.9 1280a32.

20. *Pol.* III.6 1278b25.

21. For example, Aristotle, *Nichomachean Ethics,* trans. Sir David Ross, IX.9 1170a. (Unless otherwise indicated, all references to the *Ethics* are to this translation.)

22. Keyt, "Aristotle's Theory of Distributive Justice," p.271.

23. *NE* VII.1 1145b1. For this passage I have used the translation by H. Rackham.

24. *NE* I.8 1098b (Ross translation).

25. I should add that Aristotle uses this method to talk *about* DWM itself—treating this too as a common view that may "contain some difficulty and perhaps even truth." There is nothing either tautological or vicious in this form of self-reference, provided of course that additional grounds for the doctrine are also available.

26. Nichols, *Citizens and Statesmen,* p. 66.

27. J. S. Mill, *On Liberty,* Chap. 2, paragraph 36, p. 58.

28. *NE* V.3 1131a–1131b.

29. *Pol.* III.10 1281a30.

30. Ibid. III.12 1282b23.

31. I am grateful to David Gill for several conversations on the topic discussed in this and the following paragraphs. His view, however, is the opposite of mine.

32. *NE* IV.3 1123b (my emphasis).

33. "Then ought the good to rule and have supreme power? But in that case everybody else, being excluded from power, will be dishonoured. For the offices of state are posts of honour; and if one set of men always hold them, the rest must be deprived of them" (*Pol.* III.10 1281a30).

34. Keyt, "Aristotle's Theory of Distributive Justice," p. 270: "The strategy of the argument is to apply the principle of distributive justice to men taken collectively as well as individually. In terms of our formulation of the principle in modern functional notation, the strategy is to allow the individual variables 'z' and 'y' to reign not only over individual free men but also over groups or bodies of free men."

35. I am grateful to one of *Political Theory*'s referees for pressing this point.

36. My argument in this section owes a lot to many conversations with Jill Frank.

37. *Pol.* II.5 1263a25–35.

38. *Pol.* II.5 1263a35.

39. I know it seems odd to describe it this way, but that is what is implied by Aristotle's treatment of political rights under the auspices of distributive justice.

40. *Pol.* II.5 1282a.

41. I am grateful to one of *Political Theory*'s referees for this point.

42. Thucydides, *History of the Pelopennesian War:* Book II, Chap. 6; quoted by Ronald Beiner, *Political Judgment*, p. 83.

43. Beiner, *Political Judgment*, p. 83.

44. Jean-Jacques Rousseau, *The Social Contract:* Book II, Chap. 3. But "communication" arguably refers to the formation of factions. I am grateful to Paul Thomas for this point.

45. *Pol.* III.11 1281b1 and 1281b5.

46. *Pol.* I.2 1253a8.

47. Thomas Hobbes, *Leviathan,* Chap. 17, pp. 119–20.

48. *NE* IX.6 1167a.

49. *Pol.* I.2 1253a21.

50. *Pol.* III.11 1281b6; see also III.16 1287b26.

51. As Mary Nichols writes, "It is precisely because the members of the multitude have *different* contributions to make that they have a just claim to rule. Aristotle teaches democrats the value of heterogeneity to a defense of their claim to political participation" (*Citizens and Statesmen,* p. 66).

52. *Pol.* II.2 1261a18–25.

53. St. Thomas Aquinas, *On Princely Government*: Book I, Chap. 1, p. 3.

54. Alasdair MacIntyre, *After Virtue: A Study in Moral Theory* (London), p. 146.

55. *Pol.* I.2 1253a18.

56. Alasdair MacIntyre, *Whose Justice? Which Rationality?*, p. 133.

57. Alasdair MacIntyre, *Whose Justice? Which Rationality?*, p. 134.

58. *Pol.* III.13 1283b23–26.

59. *Pol.* III.13 1284a4–11.

60. *Pol.* I.2 1253a2. See also *NE* IX.9: "It would be a strange thing to make the happy man a solitary: no one would choose to have all the good things of the world in solitude: man is meant for political association, and whose nature it is to live with others."

61. See Hannah Arendt, *On Revolution*, Chap. 2.

62. *Pol.* III.15 1286a22.

63. *Pol.* III.13 1284a4–14.

64. *Pol.* III.16 1287a30.

65. *Pol.* III.13 1284b17. See also III.13 1284a19.

66. *Pol.* III.13 1284a5.

67. For the self-sufficiency of the polis, see *Pol.* I.2 1252b30.

68. *Pol.* III.18, 1288a34.

69. *Pol.* III.17 1288a26.

70. *Pol.* III.17 1288a25.

71. *Pol.* III.16 1287b12–15. The quotations are from the *Iliad,* X 224 and II 372, respectively.

7

Citizenship in Aristotle's *Politics*

Dorothea Frede

Preface: The Elusiveness of Aristotle's Political Views

In an evaluation of their basic political ideas, Aristotle usually gets much better grades than Plato. Aristotle's views seem to be much more akin to our modern democratic standards than those of his austere and authoritarian teacher. We only have to recall the most salient features of Plato's political thought to see why this should be so. Plato's state is ruled top-down. There is a class of rulers who determine the state's well-being from start to finish. The third class of citizens, the productive class, has no rights to participate in *any* of the processes of decision-making, legislation, or jurisdiction. These "politically dispossessed" citizens are not just members of the lower classes, by our standards: Plato's third class consists of everyone except for the philosopher-kings and the soldiers—that is, skilled labor, businessmen, doctors, architects, sailors, and so on. The philosopher-kings not only are privileged to run the state, they are also the only ones who enjoy the privilege of higher learning. This learning, which supposedly qualifies them to run the affairs in the Cave, includes ten years of mathematical training and five years of dialectic, the enigmatic highest science. Given our discomfort about handing over absolute power to mathematical and dialectical whizzes, we can leave aside other repugnant features of Plato's ideal state that usually get him even worse grades.[1]

None of those elitist features reappear in Aristotle's politics, or so it seems at first. There are no philosopher-kings; in fact Aristotle is quite determined to keep the philosophers out of politics and to confine them to purely theoretical activities, which they are happy to pursue anyway. Nor are politicians in Aristotle's state required to undergo any special intellectual training. Every able-bodied and -minded adult male is entitled to take part in public affairs in all-important respects. Not only that, Aristotle insists that the citizens should take turns in ruling and being ruled. Given such liberal tendencies we are ready to attribute to the *Zeitgeist* the fact that citizenship is limited to freeborn males, to the exclusion of women, foreigners, and slaves, and that Aristotle's political conception is geared to communities that are smaller than a county by our standards. But apart from such limitations all seems plain sailing. Aristotle was therefore hailed by Newman in the nineteenth century in glowing terms: "Aristotle's dream is of a State, not composed of protectors and protected, but of excellent men of many-sided excellence. . . . His ideal state is one composed of fully developed men. . . . The secret of a State's excellence lies in the fact of its consisting of a large body of excellent citizens organized aright."[2]

My intention is to pour a little vinegar into this sweet wine of Aristotle's reputation by taking a closer look at his conditions for citizenship. We will see that his notion of what it is to be a citizen is actually quite remote from our democratic ideals. If that fact is overlooked by scholars like Martha Nussbaum, who are wont to recruit Aristotle for the modern liberal camp,[3] this is because Aristotle's main political work, the *Politics*, is a text that—even by Aristotle's standards—is not easy to penetrate. The difficulty may in part be due to historical contingencies. There are clear indications that Aristotle's early editors in the first century BC had a disparate bunch of manuscripts on their hands, which they fitted together as best they could under the title *Politika*—"Political Matters."[4] The text presents us with problems great and small. To name just a few: the order of its eight books is still under dispute, and the loose form of presentation often makes it difficult to separate Aristotle's reports of other opinions from his own views, or to distinguish matters of principle from pragmatic considerations.[5] All this leads to seeming inconsistencies that make it hard to pinpoint Aristotle's own position. It is, for instance, easy to overlook the fact Aristotle talks about the "best state" at three levels: (a) There is the best state that one could wish or pray for (*kat' euchēn*). That best form is divulged, albeit incompletely, in his own "utopia" in Books VII and VIII. (b) Then there is the best state "under the *given* conditions"; that is, the best state under the normal circumstances of a Greek city-state. (c) And then there is also the "best state under special circumstances"—making the best of inferior conditions. It takes real vigilance to keep these different perspectives separate in his subsequent discussions.[6]

But keeping track of what Aristotle does in the different parts of this complicated text is not the only problem the student of the *Politics* has to face. The complexities are increased by Aristotle's habit of addressing "difficulties" (*aporiai*) without clearly indicating whose difficulties they are, whether he regards them as serious or not, and how he resolves the issue. Often enough Aristotle presents arguments *pro* and *contra* certain possibilities—without taking a clearly recognizable stance. All these peculiarities account for the great divergence of scholarly opinions concerning Aristotle's *Politics.* For no matter how you proceed, you are forced to treat the text in an "eclectic" fashion by sorting out what is Aristotelian and what is not, what is important and what is negligible. It is easy, therefore, to put together a cocktail of Aristotelian pronouncements that makes him look like a supporter of modern democratic ideas. To name just a few: Aristotle distinguishes proper governments that rule for the common good (*koinē sumpheron*) from flawed and perverted forms that benefit only the rulers.[7] He holds that citizens should rule and be ruled in turn.[8] Being deprived of political rights means dishonor (*atimia*) and is therefore divisive.[9] The judgment of the "many" may actually be superior to that of experts, because many eyes and ears see and hear more than just two.[10] And often enough "a potluck dinner to which everyone contributes is better than a banquet composed by a chef."[11] Furthermore, Aristotle advocates a *mixed* constitution that combines the best features of an aristocracy with that of democracy (IV.7–9); he looks at hereditary kingships with skepticism.[12] And he holds not only that there should be equality among equals, but also that free birth is as good a claim to political influence as is wealth and nobility.[13] In addition, he seems to suggest that his own conception of full citizenship applies most of all to democracies,[14] and that once cities grow they invariably turn into democracies.[15] All this and much more accounts for the fact that Aristotle is often presented as a democrat in good standing. But as an inspection of the chapters 1–5 of Book III that explicitly deal with the principles of citizenship will show, Aristotle's criteria for the assignment of citizenship are far from what we would call democratic and liberal.

Before we take a closer look at that section of the text, I have to add one further preliminary remark. It concerns citizenship in ancient Greece in general. Because Greece was not a nation-state, citizenship was confined to one's native *polis.* And only citizens enjoyed the full protection of its laws and privileges, including their social status. Alien residents depended on a citizen for protection; life in exile therefore usually meant a life of hardship, unless you were very rich and well connected. Hence citizenship was a much cherished and jealously guarded good that was strictly hereditary: inclusion in the "list of citizens" at the age of 18 required proof of legitimate birth and that both father and mother were freeborn citizens. Honorary citizenship could be awarded to aliens and freedmen. But the Athenians were quite reluctant to grant it even to wealthy foreigners or freedmen who had lived in their community for decades. In times of population decrease, citizenship would sometimes be extended to inhabitants with a foreign father or mother, to freedmen of long standing, and to well-to-do foreigners. But every so often, when the native population increased again, those privileges would be revoked.[16] Xenophobia, we may say, started right outside the city walls.

1. The City and the Citizen

With all these reservations in mind, we can finally turn to the text that elucidates Aristotle's own conception of citizenship, *Politics* III.1–5. He addresses the question "what is a citizen" because he wants to establish proper criteria concerning a state's *identity*. As he states, this was a much disputed question because after a change in government the successors often refused to fulfill their predecessors' commitments—most of all, of course, to pay the debts they had incurred.[17] In the United States with its more than bicentennial continuity the question of a state's identity may sound quaint. But if you think of France, which is into its Fifth Republic, and Germany, which would be into its Fourth Reich if it had not given up counting that way, the question of a state's identity is not so outlandish after all.

As Aristotle is anxious to affirm, he is not concerned with whether a state can justify shirking its obligations. What interests him is the *essence* of a state. And that he takes to depend on a state's *constitution* (*politeia*). What the ancient Greeks called "constitution" was not a charter of fundamental laws delineating the citizens' rights and the rules of government; it was directly related to a state's political order. As Aristotle defines it (III.1 1274b38): "The constitution is the order (*taxis*) of the inhabitants of a state." And, as he makes clear in what follows, that "order" is not to include every inhabitant, but only those who *participate* in government (1275a19–23): "The citizen whom we are seeking to define is a citizen in the strictest sense, . . . and his special characteristic (*diorizetai*) is that he shares in the administration of justice (*krisis*) and in offices (*archē*)."

As will emerge, this is *the* decisive criterion in Aristotle's assignation of citizenship. He thereby not only replaces the common concept of citizenship as a hereditary birthright, but also limits citizenship to those men who *actively* participate in government. Given Aristotle's preoccupation with the notions of *form* and *function* when it comes to determining the essence of a thing, such a decision should not come as a surprise. But in the case of citizenship, this resort to "functionalism" has important consequences. A citizen for Aristotle is a person who does the "work" of a citizen. The restrictive character of this injunction does not hit the eye immediately, because the kinds of offices that

Aristotle refers to are those that were common, at least in principle, to all citizens in the Athenian democracy. In fact, at first blush it looks as if Aristotle goes even beyond those democratic principles by extending the title of "office" (*archē*) to all types of political activities.

Traditionally the title of an "*archōn*" was reserved for those kinds of officers in a city that we would call "magistrates."[18] These officeholders were elected individually, mostly for one year, with the possibility of re-election, though some offices could not be held consecutively and some could be held only once in a lifetime. Aristotle deliberately includes the members of juries (*dikastēs*) and the general assembly (*ekklēsiastēs*) among the body of "governors," an unusual move. He acknowledges his innovation by proposing to call them "indefinite offices" (1275a32: *aoristos archē*) and by anticipating objections to his extension of the term "office" (1275a26–29): "It may, indeed, be argued that these are not magistrates at all, and that their functions give them no share in the government. But surely it is ridiculous to say that those who have the supreme power do not govern." Aristotle, thus, includes the representatives of all "three powers," the executive, the legislative, and the judicative, among the offices of government.

Incidentally, the phrase "three powers" is not to suggest that there was a principle of "separation of powers" in ancient Greece; one and the same person could and often did act at the same time as a member of the assembly, as a juror, and as a particular officeholder. But there was at least a functional division of the three powers. I have to add here that none of these functionaries were professionals. There were no trained lawyers, nor were there trained and paid administrators in ancient Greece. Law as a profession and bureaucracy were inventions of the Roman Empire, whose sheer extension made administration so complicated that it could no longer be handled by volunteers.

At first sight Aristotle's broadening of the concept of "office" to include members of the general assembly and of juries among the magistrates seems to be a democratic move. For, as he sums up the result of the first chapter (1275b18–21): "He who has the power (*exousia*) to take part in the deliberative or judicial administration in any state is said by us to be a citizen of that state; and, speaking generally, a state is a body of citizens sufficing for the purposes of life." Though the enormous numbers of citizens nowadays make it impossible that every one of us could make use of the "right" of participation, it is, in principle, still open to every citizen. Hence, as far as entitlement goes, Aristotle's definition of the citizen seems to be quite as liberal as one might hope for.

To see why Aristotle, despite such democratic-sounding principles, is far from being a liberal, we have to inspect some of his further injunctions concerning political participation. For in his criticism of the prevailing system of hereditary citizenship he is ultimately concerned with *competence*, that is, with the competence to exercise the function or fulfill the requirements of an office in the appropriate way.[19] He paves the way to such a distinction with great care. Because he conceives of the state as a partnership of participants, he ties the state's identity to the distribution of their *function*. That the function makes all the difference is illustrated by the example of the chorus in tragedy and in comedy (III.3 1276b1–9). Though the actual members of each chorus may actually be the same, their function differs, and hence comedy and tragedy are different forms (*eidē*) of art. Similarly, in the state (1276b9–13): "It is evident that the sameness of the state consists chiefly in the sameness of the constitution, and it may be called or not called by the same name, whether the inhabitants are the same or entirely different." Thus in the case of the state it is the organization of offices that is crucial. And a citizen is he who performs the functions that make the state what it is.

2. Moral and Political Virtue

If one expects Aristotle to proceed from there directly to determine the citizen's functions by the types of offices that are needed in each governmental order, one will be disappointed. He approaches this topic by a surprising excursion into the sphere of ethics. For he asks (III.4 1276b17–18): "whether the excellence (*aretē*) of a good man and a good citizen is the same or not." This is certainly not the kind of question that would be asked in a modern textbook on political science. Why mix politics with ethics? But this is not what Aristotle has in mind either. If he brings in the conception of "the good man," it is because he wants to compare the *functions* that define a good human being with the *functions* that are characteristic of a good citizen. Now the phrase "good citizen" is quite familiar to us, though the quest for clear criteria would probably provoke some embarrassed hemming and hawing. Preserving law and order? Paying one's taxes? Cooperation? Doing community service? For Aristotle, by contrast, what constitutes the "good citizen" is much more straightforward. His focus is on the functions he has mentioned before; he now wants to see what qualifications they presuppose (1276b18–20): "But before entering on this discussion, we must certainly first obtain some general notion of the *excellence* of the citizen." He resorts to a comparison of the state with a ship. His is not the famous "ship of fools" in Plato's *Republic*, where sailors fight about the ship's control and throw the philosophers overboard as useless stargazers. Aristotle is thinking of a regular ship in order to explain the difference of functions (4 1276b20–24).

> Like the sailor (*plōtēr*), the citizen is a member of a community (*koinōnos*). Now, sailors have different functions (*dynamis*), for one of them is a rower (*eretēs*), another a pilot (*kybernētēs*), a third a look-out man; a fourth is described in some similar way.

Aristotle is concerned with a *division* of labor and with the corresponding division of "virtues" or excellences, which ultimately all contribute to one overall function, namely the safety of the ship.[20]

Aristotle draws several conclusions from his comparison of the state with a ship. Different types of government presuppose different functions, and hence *one* kind of excellence does not suffice for the *different* types of ships; by contrast there is just *one* kind of excellence characteristic of the good man. While there are different types of sailors necessary for the different types of ships, the good man does not fit all of them equally.

More important, as Aristotle continues, not even in the best constitution are all citizens of the best kind. At first one may think that Aristotle is just giving a realistic assessment that human beings are different and that not everyone measures up to the best standards (1276b37–1277a1): "If the state cannot be entirely composed of good men, and yet each citizen is expected to do his own business well . . . the excellence of the citizen and the good man cannot coincide." But when you read on, you realize that Aristotle is not deploring human imperfection. Nor is he concerned with the fact that a good man may find himself in conflict with the actual order of the state—if the order happens to be less than perfect. Aristotle's point is much more practical: no state can consist of good men only. As the metaphor of the ship suggests, there cannot be ships with captains and officers only; there must also be plain deckhands. A state depends on different kinds of work. And for this reason, there are higher and lower functions; there are those in command and those who obey, just as the soul rules over the body (4 1277a5–12). This is the basis of Aristotle's class-distinction that explains his limitation of citizenship.

As it turns out, it is this very distinction of the rulers and the ruled that prompts Aristotle to raise the question whether the excellence of the good man is the same as the excellence of the good citizen. For as Aristotle sees it, only the ruler can at the same time also be a good man (1277a14–16): "To this we answer that the good ruler (*archōn spoudaios*) is the good and wise (*phronimos*) man—the citizens need not be wise." All of a sudden there is a clear dichotomy between rulers and ordinary citizens, with a hierarchy of better and worse, of up and down. As we will see, it is not just their character that justifies the distinction between "better and worse" men, but also their intelligence and education. For Aristotle indicates that there ought to be a special kind of education for those designed to rule (1277a16–20). So we do encounter a kind of elitism that reminds us of Plato, though Aristotle's rulers are not philosopher kings and do not presuppose the kind of philosophical training that Plato deems indispensable.

But if Aristotle turns out to be elitist, he is not exclusivist. For immediately after elevating the ruler to supremacy he puts in some important qualifications that make him sound, once again, like the liberal that many want to see in him (1277a25–27): "But, on the other hand, it may be argued that men are praised for knowing both how to rule and how to obey, and he is said to be a citizen of excellence who is able to do both well." Aristotle does not, however, take such an exchange to be a simple affair. Instead, he holds that ruling and being ruled are two quite different functions, and that ruling is a better activity, superior to that of being ruled (1277a27–29): "Now if we suppose the excellence of a good man to be that which rules, and the excellence of the citizen to include ruling and obeying, it cannot be said that they are equally worthy of praise." Aristotle therefore holds that each citizen must be trained in two quite different ways in order to be able both to rule and to be ruled well. To explain how this is possible, he first distinguishes between two different kinds of obedience (1277a33–b7). There is "slavish" obedience of those who do menial jobs and must obey their masters absolutely; this is not the kind of obedience a citizen has to learn. Instead, there is the obedience between free and equal men. As Aristotle sees it, you learn how to be a citizen only by learning obedience first. He resorts here not to an analogy with a ship, but with a military hierarchy (1277b7–16): "There is a constitutional rule . . . which a ruler must learn by obeying, as he would learn the duties of a general by serving under a general, and a colonel by serving under a colonel, and a captain serving under a captain. Therefore it has been well said that he who has never learned to obey cannot be a good commander. The excellence of the two is not the same, but the good citizen ought to be capable of *both*; he should know how to govern like a freeman, and how to obey like a freeman—these are the excellences of a citizen."

So, all seems to be well again, from a democratic perspective. There are, then, just two different *phases* in the life of a citizen—the phase of learning and the phase of mastery; and once he has learned how to handle the ropes, the full-grown citizen knows how to stand back, at least temporarily, and to let others rule. For if there is to be ruling and being ruled in turn, there must be a periodic change in government. To express it, once again, with the metaphor of the ship: there must be a relief of the watch. A captain must be ready to hand over the ship's command to another officer.

Good as this may sound, things are not as simple as that, in Aristotle's conception of citizenship. He presupposes that such a change is not an easy thing for the good man to accept. Though he does assume that a good citizen must combine the ability to rule and to be ruled, he assumes that exchange presupposes the possession of two different sets of virtues! The good citizen must combine two different kinds of justice and two different kinds of moderation (1277b18–21):

> For the excellence of the good man who is free and also a subject, e.g., his justice, will not be *one* but will comprise distinct kinds, the one qualifying him to rule, the other to obey. They differ as the moderation and courage of men and women differ.

And then Aristotle goes on to specify the differences between the male and the female versions of those virtues. His distinction between the leader and the follower does not stop at the possession of distinct character-virtues. He also extends it to the intellectual virtues; for to our great surprise we learn here that *phronēsis*, "practical wisdom," is the exclusive property of the ruler (1277b25–29): "Practical wisdom (*phronēsis*) is the only excellence peculiar to the ruler: it would seem that all other excellences must equally belong to ruler and subject. The excellence of the subject is certainly not *phronēsis*, but only true opinion (*doxa alēthēs*)."

This distinction between knowledge and correct opinion sounds Platonic, rather than Aristotelian. And, indeed, this relapse into Platonism can be no accident. For Aristotle's justification for this discrimination makes use of a distinction that he clearly borrows from Plato's *Republic* (1277b29–30): "He (the person with opinion) may be compared to the *maker* of the flute, while his master is like the flute-player or the *user* of the flute." It is this very distinction that Plato uses in *Republic* X to explain the difference between the master-science possessed by the user of an instrument and the inferior type of competence of the maker of an instrument. The maker has to obey the instructions of the *user*, because the latter fully understands the object's proper function.[21]

Apart from its Platonic overtones, this limitation of *phronēsis* to the ruler and the dichotomy of the character-virtues like justice and courage seem to fly in the face of Aristotle's entire ethical system. In the *Nicomachean Ethics* everyone is supposed to be endowed with practical reason. It is the necessary complement of the character-virtues.[22] Without reason, none of the "habitual" good conditions are virtues at all—just as practical reasoning without the respective character-traits is not virtue, but mere cleverness.[23] So we may well wonder what is going on here in the *Politics*. In the ethics there is neither a trace of a dichotomy of the character-virtues with a "male" and a "female" version of each virtue, nor a limitation of *phronēsis* to the rulers. Does Aristotle deliberately deviate from his basic ethical principles just to elevate his rulers? And why does he think the rulers need to be so elevated, given that they are to alternate in ruling and being ruled? It seems overkill to equip the citizens with two "moral outfits," one for ruling and one for being ruled—and all that for people who take turns running the public affairs of a community of the size of a county! There is no immediate explanation contained in the text itself. In his conclusion Aristotle treats the matter as settled (1277b30–32): "From these considerations may be gathered the answer to the question whether the excellence of the good man is the same as that of the good citizen, or different, and how far the same, and how far different." In what follows he does not return to the difference between ruling and being ruled.

3. The Exclusion of the Workers from Citizenship

Before we can look for an explanation for this extraordinary elevation of the ruler over the ruled, we first have to take a look at what must look even worse to the modern liberal, namely the exclusion of the "mechanical" workers (*banausoi*) from citizenship that Aristotle presents at the end of his discussion of citizenship in *Politics* III.5. He explains there, in no uncertain terms, that people who have to live by the work of their hands cannot be citizens. To understand what is behind this exclusion we have to remember two things:  Aristotle limits citizenship to *active* participants in government. The right to participate is contingent on the fulfillment of certain standards of "excellence." Only people who have acquired the political virtues are qualified for such offices and thereby can be treated as citizens in the strict Aristotelian sense. Aristotle is well aware that he thereby runs counter to what was customary in Greek states. For even in oligarchies and tyrannies the freeborn inhabitants were called citizens. So Aristotle's injunction that only officeholders should be regarded as citizens runs counter to all common Greek notions of citizenship. He therefore goes to some length to explain why he thinks that hereditary citizenship is a mistake and why he excludes workers *tout court*. We shall briefly look at his justification and then return to where we left off in our discussion of political virtue: why rulers need a different set of virtues and why they alone are entitled to be called "wise" (*phronimoi*).

First of all, who are the workers? Aristotle is not very specific on that point. Most of the time he speaks of *banausoi*, which is usually rendered as "lower craftsmen"; at one point he calls them *technitēs*—which is probably why Jowett uses the expression "mechanic" in his translation. At one point Aristotle also adds the day laborers, the *thētes*, to those excluded. But though it may be somewhat difficult to arrive at a sociologically exact demarcation of this class, it is clear that Aristotle is addressing the part of the population that does hard manual work. For this is his explicit reason for denying that they have the requisite virtues (III.5 1278a8–13):

> The best form of state will not admit a lower craftsman to citizenship; but if he is admitted, then our definition of the excellence of a citizen will not apply to every citizen, nor to every free man as such, but only to those who are freed from necessary services (*tōn anagkaiōn*). These "necessary people" are either slaves who minister to the wants of individuals, or mechanics (*banausoi*) or laborers (*thētes*) who are the servants of the community.

As this quotation makes clear, in Aristotle's eyes such work is slave labor. He would prefer an economic system where such labor was confined entirely to slaves, as he says repeatedly in Book III. Aristotle is not particularly fond of slavery, though he regards the institution as an economical necessity.[24] Here he appeals to it because it would save him an embarrassment as far as his own principles are concerned. For given that there *are* freeborn citizens who do this kind of work, in his scheme there is "a necessary part of the state" of freeborn persons who are excluded from citizenship. His embarrassment is obvious (1277b38–1278a2):

> But if none of the lower class are citizen, in which part of the state are they to be placed? For they are not resident aliens (*metoikoi*) and they are not foreigners (*xenoi*). May we not reply that as far as this objection goes there is no more absurdity in excluding them than in excluding slaves and freedmen (*douloi kai apeleutheroi*) from any of the above-mentioned classes?

As this quasi-excuse shows, Aristotle realizes that his idea of disfranchisement is alien to Greek societies.[25]

Why, if it presents an embarrassment, is he so keen on keeping the lower class out? It is simply a matter of his own principle, that citizenship means *active* participation in government. On this point he is explicit, when he accounts for the political systems that *do* grant citizenship to the lower classes: in that case the citizens are only subjects; that is, they are only among the ruled, not among the rulers. Furthermore in such states the honors are not distributed in accordance with excellence (*aretē*) or merit (*axia*) (1278a20–21): "For no man can practice excellence who is living the life of a mechanic or laborer." Though he acknowledges that his own conception of citizenship is not the one that is accepted in most actual cities, he does not budge (1278a34–36): "Hence, as is evident, there are different kinds of citizens; and he is a citizen in the fullest sense (*malista politēs*) who shares in the honors of the state. . ." And thus he concludes his discussion of citizenship in general (1278a40–b5):

> As to the question whether the excellence of the good man is the same as that of the good citizen, the considerations already adduced prove that in some states the good man and the good citizen are the same, and in others different. When

> they are not the same, it is not every citizen who is a good man, but only the statesman and those who have or may have, alone or in conjunction with others, the conduct of political affairs.

So we see that for Aristotle the good citizen and the good man ought to be one and the same in principle, but this applies only in the case where the rulers fulfill the appropriate conditions. Such participation in Aristotle's eyes not only presupposes sufficient leisure (*scholē*), but also the requisite education (*paideia*).[26]

That Aristotle regards the members of the lower classes as unfit for political offices is, no doubt, due to the nature of labor in his time. In an age where technology did not exceed the sophistication of a pulley, manual work was hard work. People who had to make a living from their handiwork had to work from morning to night to maintain themselves and their families. That Aristotle was aware that these conditions of life put a certain part of the population at a grave disadvantage is confirmed by his list of the "goods of fortune" that are necessary for happiness in the *Nicomachean Ethics*, I.8 1099b3–6. If you are poor, ugly, from a bad family, and friendless, you cannot achieve real happiness. For in that case you will not be able to realize your human potential to the full.

To question the inevitability of the uneven distribution of those "goods of fortune" seems never to have crossed Aristotle's mind. He mentions once in the case of slavery that the conditions may actually be unfair: people who are not "natural slaves" may find themselves in that condition as a result of external misfortune, whereas others who do not have the capacity for leading an autonomous life are born free.[27] Aristotle nowhere suggests that the community might have an obligation to rectify the balance of fortune and to give every talent a chance. In all fairness, we must acknowledge that not only was Aristotle far from being a social revolutionary, but the idea of a general correction of the uneven distribution of "moral luck" was not on anyone's agenda in ancient Greece.[28]

4. The Two Types of Virtues

To get a grip on Aristotle's concept of the "citizen in the full sense," we have to return briefly to his suggestion of a dichotomy of virtues that prima facie seems to clash with the presuppositions of his ethics. To understand what prompts Aristotle to assume such a difference of quality between the rulers and the ruled, we have to resort to Aristotelian *teleology* and its relation to the conception of "happiness" as the good, fulfilling life. As Aristotle sees it, the happy life consists of *activities* in accordance with our best talents. People unable to be active in this way cannot really be happy. This, in a nutshell, accounts for the two sets of virtues and the difference in *phronēsis.* Not only does a ruler need to have the appropriate moral and intellectual virtues; to actively employ those talents is necessary for his happiness. Hence rulers in Aristotle are eager to rule; they are not just motivated by the prospect of "being ruled by their inferiors," like Plato's philosopher-kings. In fact, not to be able to rule curtails their happiness. And that is why they need a different set of virtues that are activated while they submit to the rule of others; by employing those lower virtues they remain active without too much suffering from deprivation. To us this idea sounds eccentric, but it fits well with Aristotle's notion of the connection between the virtues and the happy life.

That he does not mention the need for such a dichotomy of virtues in the *Nicomachean Ethics* is due to the fact that there he is focusing exclusively on human nature in general. But there is at least some indication in the *Nicomachean Ethics* that Aristotle had his eye on the supreme virtue of the communities' rulers. For in *NE* I.2 he mentions that the most "architectonic" form of practical reason focuses not only on the individual's own well-being but on the well-being of the community as a whole (1094b7–10). This is not a fluke, for in what follows Aristotle repeatedly hints at the higher ability to provide for the commonweal.[29] Furthermore, quite early in the *Politics* Aristotle mentions two sets of character-virtues in his discussion of the relationship between husband and wife (I.12). In principle, he states there, the relation between the two is a "political" one, for she is as free as he is and she shares in the same virtues. It is only because of the superiority of his practical reasoning that he rules—and she voluntarily lets him rule.[30] In that connection he also mentions the difference between the male and the female types of character-virtues, which he assigns in Book III to the rulers and the ruled respectively (I.13 1260a14–24). It is this type of virtue and this type of *phronēsis* that is necessary for those ruled—not only because it makes them more obedient, but also because it guarantees them the type of "happiness" that goes along with the mental state of being ruled.

To us, all this must sound rather contrived. But it is actually consistent with Aristotle's basic conception of happiness. Given that the *polis* explicitly serves the purpose of giving the citizens the opportunity to develop and make use of their abilities in full, there is, then, the *right* to rule for those who have a particular talent for ruling. Aristotle mentions such a right in connection with the conception of a political *super-genius.* This phenomenon has puzzled many of Aristotle's readers because, contrary to the general drift of his *Politics,* he once in a while mentions a man of "incommensurably superior political talent," so that there is no way to just integrate him in the political system. In that case, Aristotle suggests, the citizens should relinquish their claim to rule and let him rule as a monarch.[31] What is significant in that connection is not so much that Aristotle regards this as a possibility—for he is in fact not very sanguine about the chances that such a superman could really occur. What is significant is rather the justification he gives for letting that person rule: it would be an *injustice* to such a person not to let him deploy his abilities by ruling the state (III.13 1284a9).

In other words, Aristotle does not just presuppose special talents for ruling, but also a moral *entitlement* to make use of them. And this is quite in keeping with his general principle that man is by nature a "political animal," an animal that finds a self-sufficient (*autarkēs*) life in a *polis*. Only the *polis* gives to human beings the opportunity to develop and to deploy the full range of their talents. And hence for those who have a talent for ruling there is also the entitlement to rule. Thus, if the citizens are to rule and to be ruled in turn, and not to suffer a curtailment of their happiness, they must also possess the virtues and abilities whose activation allows them to live happily while they are ruled over by others—until it is their turn again. The person who has not developed the second set of civic virtues would be dissatisfied by enforced political inactivity. As Aristotle expresses this type of frustration by referring to the tyrant Jason of Pherai (III.4 1277a24–25): "He said that he felt hungry when he was not a tyrant, meaning that he could not endure to live in a private station."

At first blush it must sound bizarre that people should have a "right to rule" or a right to exert any other talent in the society they live in. But in Aristotle's conception of a city, such entitlements are part of the entire scheme. For this is precisely what the *polis* is *for*—to give each person the opportunity to develop and employ his best talent, for to be a political animal in the case of the most gifted means to be a politically *active* animal.

Conclusion: Two Cheers for Democracy?[32]

We still must ask: Why does Aristotle turn a blind eye to the fact that there may be a substantial body of citizens, not just a small elitist group, that is both gifted and willing to rule? Why should not "the many" also be willing and gifted, at least to some degree? I can only make some comments on this issue by way of a conclusion. The answer is, in brief, that Aristotle is not quite as blind to that possibility as I have made him sound so far. The reverse seems indicated by his democratic sounding maxims that I mentioned earlier to explain the favorable evaluation of Aristotle's *Politics* by modern liberals. Admittedly, some of those maxims may represent merely pragmatic considerations, for instance that it is dangerous to exclude the majority from participation in government, because such discrimination causes internal strife and hostility.[33] But in other cases Aristotle seems to view the rule of the majority in a more positive light, though he expresses himself in a tantalizingly ambiguous way (III.11 1281a40–42):

> The principle that the multitude (*plēthos*) ought to be in power rather than the few best might seem to be solved and to contain some difficulty and perhaps even truth (*tacha de k'an alētheian*).

What is that supposed to mean? If it is "solved" then why does it contain a difficulty—and why is Aristotle so cautious about its truth?[34] Aristotle acknowledges that as a body a multitude may be better than the single expert. But, then, who makes up this "body" of citizens? As he nowhere revokes his ban on the participation of the uneducated *banausoi*, the "multitude" must be those who are not quite in the same class as the gifted statesmen, but who are collectively, though not individually, as good as or even better than their superiors.[35] Thus the concession to the notion of a "collective wisdom" and the admission of the risk of disfranchising a part of the population does not make Aristotle a liberal or a democrat.

Aristotle was no friend of the "extreme" Athenian democracy, where offices were distributed by lot and the poor were paid for their service on juries, in the assembly, and in other offices. Nor would we really welcome such a system, though in our most cynical moments we may think that electing politicians by lot is no worse than the present system. What added to Aristotle's negative view of democracy was that in his time there were no professional administrators. All political actors were amateurs. Hence Aristotle's concern for a certain amount of competence and professionalism is intelligible. Even nowadays we may sometimes wonder why we have specialists for everything—doctors, architects, teachers, engineers, lawyers, businessmen—and that the only "amateurs" to whom we trust the most important decisions concerning our lives, both collectively and individually, are our politicians.

If all this makes Aristotle's political views more palatable, we should nonetheless keep in mind two features of his thought that stand in the way of attributing liberalism in a democratic sense to him: (1) He does not think that all people should have a say about what happens in the community they live in; (2) He accepts as inevitable the social distinctions that assign to one class the "necessary labor" that gives the "higher and better" the freedom to develop and employ their talents, be they political or philosophical or artistic. There cannot be a ship without plain oarsmen, and plain oarsmen never act as officers.

I will not consider the question whether the modern economy is really able to overcome the necessity of such a division—and whether modern liberals live in happy blindness if they presuppose that all those who do the heavy work are really not able to do better, and are therefore "happy" with their life's tasks. Life in modern mass-societies has the soothing effect of making all but invisible what every member of the upper crust in a Greek *polis* could not overlook: that their comfort depended on the hard labor of those who were less fortunate than they were themselves.

Notes

This is a revision of my article "Staatsverfassung und Staatsbürger," in *Aristoteles' Politik*, edited by O. Höffe (Berlin: Akademie Verlag, 2001), 75–92.

1. 1. We have to pass over the fact that late in his life Plato changed his mind. In the *Laws* he replaces his aristocracy of the mind with a *nomocracy* and pleads for a mixed constitution: instead of philosopher-kings, the members of a Nocturnal Council act as administrators of the laws. But because Plato's politics are generally associated with the *Republic*, not with the *Laws*, we will leave it at that.

2. W. L. Newman, *The Politics of Aristotle*. Cf. C. Bobonich, *Plato's Utopia*, pp. 79–80.

3. M. C. Nussbaum, "Nature, Function, and Capability: Aristotle on Political Distribution" and "Aristotelian Social Democracy'; O. Höffe, "Aristotele's *Politik*: Vorgriff auf eine liberale Demokratie"; R. Mulgan, "Was Aristotle an Aristotelian Social Democrat?"

4. Aristotle had to leave Athens in haste in 323, because the sudden death of Alexander the Great caused an upsurge of anti-Macedonian feelings that led to Aristotle's indictment for impiety. He probably left behind most of his manuscripts in the hands of his pupils, in the hope of a speedy return to Athens, once things had returned to normal. But his own sudden death in the next year prevented Aristotle's return. He evidently never had time to put the finishing touch to his works and to establish the form in which he intended to leave them for posterity. What we have are—by almost unanimous consent—Aristotle's lecture notes, notes in different stages of elaboration.

5. These difficulties have long prevented a closer study of the *Politics*, as Newman remarks (I, p. 284) and R. Robinson comments on, *Aristotle's Politics* III and IV, pp. viii–x; cf. also D. Keyt's "Supplementary Essay."

6. Cf. *Pol.* IV.1 1288b21–39; 11 1295a25–31; also *Pol.* II.1 1260b27–36; esp. VII.1 ff.

7. On the distinction between proper and perverted governments (*parekbaseis*), cf. III.1 1275b1–3; esp. 6 1279a17–21.

8. *Pol.* I.5 1254a21–24; III.4 1277a25–27; 13 1283b42–1284a3: "And a citizen is one who shares in governing and being governed. He differs under different forms of government, but in the best state he is one who is able and chooses to be governed and

to govern with a view to the life of excellence." (See also *Pol.* VII.14 1333b26–29; 38–1334a2; *NE* V.6 1134b15.)

9. III.10 1281a29; 11 1281b28–31.

10. III.11 1281b4–10; 16 1287b25–29.

11. III.11 1281b2–3.

12. I.2 1252b19–27; 12 1259b10–17; III.15 1286b22–27.

13. III.12 1282b21–22.

14. III.1 1275b5–7.

15. III.15 1286b20–22.

16. Aristotle mentions the extension of citizenship under Cleisthenes (III.2 1275b35–39) and also the revocation of such measures under Pericles.

17. III.1 1274b34–36; 3 1276a8–16.

18. Originally there were nine *archontes*: (1) the *archōn eponymous* was the chief magistrate after whom the year was named, who was the head of the council (*boulē*) and the general assembly (*ekklēsia*), (2) the *archōn basileus*, the chief religious authority, (3) the polemarch, or supreme general, and (4) six *thesmothetai* or chiefs of the courts. Under democracy these offices lost their political power and were reduced to symbolic functions, while the offices of the ten generals (elected annually) and of the treasurer were much more influential. In addition, governments of all kinds relied on services like those of inspectors of the market, walls, roads, buildings, public order (cf. IV.15), all of which Aristotle includes under "government," cf. esp. VI.8 (1321b5 "*archas*").

19. Practical questions, such as that this would not apply to the first generation in a newly founded state, are clearly not his concern (2 1275b22–34), nor is whether offices and citizenship are obtained by legally correct means (1275b37–1276a8). A side issue is also the renewed discussion of what constitutes the *unity* of a state. Aristotle rules out as "superficial" the unity of the territory or the actual citizen-body. The territory may vary—as do the citizens, in a population in a permanent flux of birth and death (3 1276a24–b1).

20. 1276b24–29: "And while the precise definition of each kind's excellence applies exclusively to it, there is, at the same time, a common definition applicable to them all. For they have all of them a common object, which is safety in navigation. . . . Similarly, one citizen differs from another, but the salvation of the community is the common business of them all."

21. This distinction succeeds the distinction between the divine maker, the human craftsman and the artistic imitator of a bed (596A–598D) that starts the critique of art. In what follows Plato unobtrusively replaces the divine maker by the human user who understands the *function* (*chreia*) of the object (601C–602B).

22. *NE* I.13 1103a3–10; II.1 1103a14–18; 2 1103b31–34 *et pass.* The demarcation of *phronēsis* is, however, postponed till book VI.

23. Cf. *NE* VI.12 1144a6–9: "Again the function of man is achieved only in accordance with practical wisdom as well as with moral excellence; for excellence makes the aim right, and practical wisdom the things leading to it." 1144a26–27: "If the aim be noble, then cleverness (*deinotēs*) is laudable, but if it is bad, then cleverness is mere villainy (*panourgia*)."

24. This much-disputed problem will not be addressed here. Cf. M. Schofield's essay in this volume.

25. As a paradigm he refers to children who are not yet citizens to show that there actually are "incomplete citizens" (5 1278a2–6: *ateleis*).

26. Cf. his abortive plan of education in Bks. VII and VIII.

27. *Pol.* I.6 and the distinction between slavery by nature and by convention.

28. Though some thinkers expressed egalitarian tendencies—for example, Euripides' plea for the moral excellence of a poor peasant in his *Electra* (67–70; 253–262) or the sophist Antiphon's claim of a common human nature (DK 87B 44B2)—the upper crust did not suggest serious changes in the whole order of their society.

29. *NE* I.1 1094a14; 2 1094a27; VI.7–8 1141b22–28. Cf. *Pol.* I.12 1260a18; III.11 1282a3–4; VII.3 1325b23.

30. She has *phronēsis*, albeit of a kind that lacks authority (*akuron*), I.13 1260a13.

31. Cf. III.13 1284a3–14; b25–34; 17 1288a15–29; VII.3. On this issue cf. D. Frede, "Der Übermensch in der politischen Philosophie des Aristoteles."

32. Cf. Fred D. Miller, "Sovereignty and Political Rights," esp. pp. 113–15.

33. III.10 1281a28–32: "But then ought the good (*epieikeis*) to rule and have supreme power? But in that case everybody else, being excluded from power, will be dishonored (*atimoi*). For the offices of a state are posts of honor; and if one set of men always holds them, the rest must be deprived of them." In 11 1281b28–30 he mentions the danger of not letting a part of the population participate because a state full of *atimoi* would be a state full of enemies.

34. The text may be corrupt here. Ross accepts the emendation by Richards, changing *luesthai* to *legesthai*, so there would be no question of a "solution"—but even then Aristotle seems unusually cagey.

35. In ch. 11 he argues for collective wisdom (*phronēsis*) and character (*ēthos*) and refers to the collective good taste concerning music and drama (1281b4–10); he concedes the same about a judge trained in the laws and a body of jurymen (III.16 1287b25–29). Though he admits that only experts can select an expert (the doctor, the geometer, the pilot), he concedes that "in some cases" the user can judge the product as well as the producer (III.11 1282a7–23).

8

Aristotle and Political Liberty

Jonathan Barnes

1.

THERE ARE TWO MAIN ISSUES in political philosophy: What questions are political questions? and: How shall political questions be decided?

The second issue is discussed at length in Aristotle's *Politica* under the guise of the theory of constitutions; for a constitution is a political decision procedure. Some may be tickled by Johnson's opinion on the matter: "Sir, that is all visionary. I would not give half a guinea to live under one form of government rather than another."

The first issue is prior to the second. It is an aspect of the problem of political liberty. Anarchists maintain that no questions are political questions. Totalitarians maintain that all questions are political questions. Most theorists are betwixt and between. And one measure of political liberty is fixed by the sort and scope of questions which a State deems to be political.

It is not true that political liberty is the only form of liberty. It is not indisputable that liberty is supreme among the goods to which political philosophy addresses itself. But it is uncontentious that liberty is an indispensable item in political theory and a mighty matter in political practice.

The first main issue in political philosophy is given little attention in Aristotle's *Politica*.

2.

A word on political questions and political liberty (as I here intend the notions).

Some questions are theoretical, others practical. The general form of practical questions is this: Shall x φ? (Here x is any agent: an individual, a couple, a team, a company, what you will.) In deciding the question "Shall x φ?," x normally confronts a range of options, with each of which he associates a cost.

Other agents—in general, other things—can affect x's decision in many ways and by many means. In particular, they may alter the range of his options and they may change the costs he associates with a given option.

External intervention may curtail or enlarge the range of x's options. It may increase or decrease the costs he associates with an option.

Intervention may be direct or indirect. An external agent intervenes directly if it addresses itself explicitly to x's φ-ing or to something of which x's φ-ing is a special instance. Otherwise intervention is indirect. (It is not easy to define direct intervention. Something like this may be on the right lines: y directly intervenes in the question "Shall x φ?" just in case there are propositions P and Q such that (i) P is a component of the proper specification of y's action, and (ii) φx is a component of Q, and (iii) P entails Q.)

States intervene. Let the question be: "Shall Barnes buy a bottle of Glenlivet?" The State may intervene by—for example—(1a) prohibiting the sale of spirits, (1b) imposing an excise duty on whisky, (1c) banning imports from Scotland, (1d) exacting income tax at a punitive level, (2d) offering me a State pension, (2c) subsidising Scotch distilleries, (2b) giving a tax-rebate to alcoholics, (2a) itself distilling a rival malt. (If some of these modes of action seem Utopian, consider a different question: "Shall Barnes go forth and multiply?")

Interventions (2 a–d) enlarge my range of options or decrease my costs. Such interventions raise interesting questions. They are not my interest here.

Interventions (1 c–d) and (2 c–d) are indirect. Indirect State intervention, which normally takes the form of taxation, bears importantly on questions of liberty. (A second measure of political liberty is fixed by the proportion of a citizen's income or wealth which is not removed in taxation. The two measures need not coincide—imagine a Lockean "minimal State" which spends massively on defense. The converse case is possible, but harder to imagine. I suppose that in practice the two measures are usually fairly close to one another.) But I shall say nothing further about taxation, nor, in general, about indirect State intervention. It is a part of the topic of liberty separate from my present concern. And my concern is prior to it in this sense: the State can intervene indirectly in a question of the form "Shall x φ?" only insofar as it intervenes directly in some other question of the same form.

There remains (1 a), which curtails my options, and (1 b), which increases my costs. Both interventions are, I shall say, *restrictive.*

Thus my concern is with direct restrictive State intervention. And I say (quasi-stipulatively) that:

> issues of a kind K are *political questions* just in case the State is entitled to intervene, directly and restrictively, in any question of the form "Shall x φ?" which falls within K,

and that:

> x enjoys *political liberty* with regard to issues of kind K just in case the State does not intervene, directly and restrictively, in any question of the form "Shall x φ?" which falls within K.

Thus the main matter is this: On what conditions and in what circumstances is a State entitled to intervene directly and restrictively in questions of the form "Shall x φ?"

3.

Aristotle never attempts a formal analysis of political liberty, and he barely discusses the substantive question of how much liberty a State may or must allow its citizens. Throughout the *Politica* he speaks of *archein kai archesthai,* of ruling and being ruled. He occupies himself constantly with the question of who should rule whom. He scarcely touches on the question of what the limits of rule should be.

Item: he distinguishes good constitutions from bad, natural from perverted. The good look to the advantage of the ruled, the bad to that of the rulers (e.g., III.7 1279b6–10). The good have willing subjects, the bad unwilling (e.g., III.14 1285a28–30). He never hints that a good constitution might be one which appropriately limits the scope of government, or that one mode of perversion might consist in acting *ultra vires.*

Item: slavery is justifiable in that "ruling and being ruled are not only indispensable [*anagkaion*] but also advantageous; and some things are marked from their very birth for ruling or being ruled" (I.5 1254a22–24). He develops the notion that rule is a natural phenomenon, but his argument does not indicate any natural restrictions on the scope of natural rule. The claim that rule is "natural" is often questioned—at least in its relation to slavery. Yet in the absence of any specification of scope, the claim is worse than questionable—it is unassessably vague.

Numerous other issues in political theory are not raised in the *Politica.* We should not expect to find there a discussion of the problems of multinational corporations. But liberty is not a modern problem. Questions of liberty must impose themselves on anyone who is ruled—and on every decent ruler. As a surplus Aristotle knew of two celebrated fictional incidents: I mean Antigone's demand (in Sophocles' play) that the State may not intervene in certain religious or ritual affairs, and Socrates' confession (in Plato's *Apologia*) that he would not heed the Athenians if they forbade him to philosophize. (If these two examples are—as I have been persuaded—malapropos, then consider Pericles' remarks at Thuc. 2, 37 or Nicias's exhortations at Thuc. 7, 69. And, as Richard Sorabji points out, there were the Cynics.)

Perhaps Aristotle was well aware of the issue, even if the *Politica* does not (as they say) thematize it. At any rate, there are several ideas and various passages in the *Politica* which bear—or seem to bear—on the matter.

4.

First, two red—or at least pinkish—herrings.

There is a familiar theme from the *Ethica.* Roughly: we achieve *eudaimonia* [happiness] only if we act virtuously; we act virtuously only if we act *kata proairesin* [in accordance with decision]; we act *kata proairesin* only if we act *hekontes* [voluntarily]; we act *hekontes* only if we act freely. Hence *eudaimonia*—which is the end of the State no less than of the individual—has freedom as a precondition; and Aristotle must therefore have inclined toward a libertarian, or at least a liberal, position.

This argument depends on a childish confusion. For the freedom which *eudaimonia* requires is not political liberty. More precisely, x can φ *kata proairesin* even if the question "Shall x φ?" is political. And evidently this must be so; for otherwise law-abiding actions could never be virtuous—and that is absurd. Nor can we pretend that Aristotle mistakenly supposed "free action" to demand political liberty. On the contrary, in the *Ethica* and in the *Politica* he regards it as one of the functions of the legislator to outlaw wickedness and enjoin virtue. Whatever may be thought of this view, it is not evidently self-contradictory.

The second herring is Aristotle's attack on "communism." He argues against Plato that women and children should not be "common"; and he argues further that property should not be held in common. Hence one might infer that he is against State intervention in certain areas of life—women and goods do not raise political questions.

The inference is temerarious. Aristotle poses the question: "Is it better for a State which is to be well governed to make common [*koinōnein*] everything that can be made common?" (*Pol.* II.1 1261a2–3). And he answers unequivocally in the negative. But his opposition to communism does not entail, nor does he take it to entail, that questions of property are not in the political domain. On the contrary, he observes that his own preferred economic system will be "improved by character and by the ordinance of upright laws" (II.5 1263a24), and he insists that "it is the peculiar task of the legislator" to see to these matters (1263a40).

A clear analysis of the concept of property is needed in many parts of political theory—not least in Aristotle's own defense of slavery. But Aristotle's view is vague: "it is better for holdings to be private and for us to make them common in their use" (1263a38; cf. VII.10 1329b41–1330a2). In what sense is this Victoria plum tree my private holding if anyone may use its fruit? Property, as the Romans put it, consists in the right to "use and abuse" (cf. Pl., *Euthd.* 301E). It is hard to see how private ownership can be consistent with common use—*horos de asphaleias . . . to entautha kai houtōs kektēsthai hōst' eph' hautō einai tēn chrēsin autōn* [the definition of security . . . is that we possess such things in such a way that the use of them is up to us] (*Rhet.* I.5 1361a19–21). But Aristotle's remarks in the *Politica* are too nebulous to sustain any serious critical discussion. (The Greek legal background will have offered him little help—See A. R. W. Harrison, *The Law of Athens* I, pp. 200–205—but Theophrastus may have done something to fill the gap: see his *Leges* F21 Szegedy-Maszak = Stobaeus, *Anth.* IV 2, 20.)

However that may be, one thing is plain: Aristotle's private property will be closely regulated by public law.

5.

A more plausible starting point is Aristotle's notion of *eleutheria* [freedom]; for *eleutheria* is surely freedom of some sort, and the concept of political liberty is included in the general concept of freedom.

Eleutheria first appears in the *Politica* in contrast with slavery (I.3 1253b4), and the contrast is common, applying not only to individuals but also to States (e.g., V.10 1310b37–38; VII.7 1327b25; 1327b31; 1328a6). A slave is someone who has a master, and who is the possession [*ktēma*] of that master. Hence a man is *eleutheros* [free] just in case he has no master, is no one's possession.

(Or are free men self-possessed? If property is the *ius utendi et abutendi* [right to use and abuse], then a self-owner enjoys the right of self-use and self-abuse—and is not that perfect freedom?)

A master rules his slaves with an *archē despotikē* [rule of a master]. Some people, according to Aristotle, hold that all rule is despotic (cf. Pl., *Statesman*

259C1–4). He dissents, insisting that x may rule y without being master of y (*Pol.* I.1 1252a8; IV.11 1295b21; VII.2 1324b32; VII.14 1333a6). Hence it is possible for there to be rule over free men (III.4 1277b7–10). Indeed, that is the definition of "political" rule, and a State is by definition a fellowship of the free (III.5 1278a3; III.8 1280a5).

(Or rather, an unperverted State is a fellowship of the free: in tyrannies, oligarchies, and democracies the rule is despotic (III.6 1279a21). But can we take this literally? Does Aristotle suppose that citizens in a democracy are all slaves of the State?)

Evidently this general notion of *eleutheria* is not the notion of political liberty. The citizens of an unperverted State are free men: this says nothing whatever about the extent of their political liberties, it does nothing to determine the scope of political questions.

But *eleutheria* is frequently connected in a special way with the notion of democracy. And political liberty may here seem to shamble on to the stage.

Just as the defining mark [*horos*] of oligarchy is wealth and of aristocracy virtue, so the defining mark of democracy is freedom (IV.8 1294a10–11). In other words, the qualification for office in a democracy is *eleutheria*: a constitution (or particular office) is democratic just in case any *eleutheros*—and hence any citizen—is eligible. Every citizen is "equal" in *eleutheria*—and, according to Aristotle, democrats typically and falsely argue that those who are equal in this one thing should be equal in all things (III.9 1280a24; 1281a6; V.1 1301a30; VI.2 1318a9–10).

The connection between *eleutheria* and democracy is thus far trivially definitional. But some people supposed that *eleutheria* and equality were found *especially* in democracies (IV.4 1291b34–35). "A fundamental principle [*hupothesis*] of democratic constitutions is freedom—and some are accustomed to say that in this constitution alone men partake of freedom" (VI.2 1317a40 ff.: construe after Newman; cf. Pl., *Rep.* VIII 562B12–C3).

Such assertions ring familiar. Modern politicians often couple democracy and freedom as though they were Ptolemy and Cleopatra. So it is worth stating that as a matter of logic there is no connection between a democratic constitution and political liberty: if a State is democratic it does not follow that its citizens enjoy a high degree of liberty; if the citizens of a State enjoy a high degree of liberty, it does not follow that the State is democratic. In general, views on the first issue in political theory, "What questions are political?," neither determine nor are determined by views on the second, "How are political questions to be decided?"

As for empirical ties, it is plain from history that more political liberty will be enjoyed under an egocentric monarchy or a self-indulgent oligarchy than under a people's democracy.

Back to Aristotle. He holds that certain oligarchs and democrats make mistakes in their educational programs: they do not educate their citizens *pros tēn politeian* [with a view to the constitution] (*Pol.* V.9 1310a20). In the case of the democrats,

> the reason for this is that they define freedom wrongly. . . . For justice seems to them to be equality, equality to demand that whatever seems good to the mass should be sovereign, and freedom to be a matter of doing whatever you wish. Hence in such democracies each lives as he wishes and "to what end he lists," as Euripides says. But this is dangerous; for one should think it not slavery but salvation to live with an eye to the constitution. (1310a28–36)

The text is uncertain and the argument murky. But it seems clear that Aristotle ascribes to the democrats a definition of freedom as doing whatever you want, and that he regards this as a false definition.

"Doing what you wish"—*ho ti an boulētai poiein, ho ti an doxē poiein*—is alluded to elsewhere in the *Politica* (e.g., IV.8 1294a11–12; V.12 1316b24; VI.4 1319b30; cf. P1., *Rep.* VIII 557B4–6). It was, and remained, with one modification or another, a standard definition of freedom (see Newman's note to *Pol.* V.9 1310a27, and Justinian, *Digest* I *iii* 1, with Moyle's note).

(It is not a contemptible definition. In general, we might suppose that x is free to φ just in case x can φ if he wants to; so that x is free absolutely just in case, for any φ, x can φ if he wants to. ["Absolute" freedom will be incoherent unless some restrictions are put on the possible substituends for φ.] And x is politically free to φ just in case so far as the State is concerned x can φ if he wants to. This is vague; but it deserves more thought than Aristotle awards it.)

A later passage in Book VI repeats the "democratic" definition of freedom and conjoins it with another. Since this is the longest discussion of *eleutheria* in Aristotle's writings, it merits quotation.

> One form of freedom is ruling and being ruled in turn. For democratic justice is having equality according to numbers and not according to worth, and if this is justice, then the majority must be sovereign and whatever seems good to the majority must be the goal and must be justice—for they say that each of the citizens must have equality. (Hence in democracies it comes about that the poor are more powerful than the rich; for they are the majority, and what seems good to the majority is sovereign.) This, then, is one sign [*sēmeion*] of freedom, which all democrats lay down as a defining mark of their constitution.
>
> Another sign is living as you wish. For this is the function of freedom, they say, if it is the mark of a man in slavery that he lives not as he wishes. Now this is a second defining mark of democracy; and hence has come the idea of not being ruled—best of all by no one, but if not then in turn. And it contributes in this way to freedom in respect of equality. (VI.2 1317b2–17)

The passage is opaque, and it requires a more detailed analysis than I can give it.

There are two sorts of freedom. (Or two "signs" of one sort? Aristotle wavers. I assume the vacillation is unimportant, and that we can properly talk of two *sorts* of freedom.) Does *Aristotle* recognize the two sorts? He seems to be speaking *in propria persona*; but given his rejection of the "democratic" definition of freedom at V.9 1310a27–36, it may be that the present passage is in implicit *oratio obliqua*—Aristotle is reporting, and not endorsing, a democratic view.

However that may be, the second sort of freedom is the familiar "democratic" sort: freedom is doing what you want.

The first sort is "ruling and being ruled in turn." This notion is a staple of the *Politica*: in Book I it defines political rule (I.1 1252a16), and in Book VII it turns out to be a fundamental feature of Aristotle's own Ideal State (VII.14 1332b26–27). Every citizen will have a turn in office and a turn out of office. Perhaps this is a pretty idea. But why is it a form of *freedom*? and why should it be dear to *democrats*?

Democratic justice and democratic equality require that each citizen shall count for one. (Votes go to shareholders, not to shares.) Hence—or so Aristotle infers—decisions will be made by majority vote among *all* citizens. (In every constitution, and trivially, they are made by majority vote: IV.8 1294a11–15.) But why should the principle of rule-and-rule-about follow from the principle of majority choice? (And what if a majority rejects the principle, preferring perhaps to pick all *archai* by lot from all citizens?)

An independent argument might lead directly from democratic equality to universal office-sharing: if every citizen is to be equal, then none may rule unless all rule. But this argument does not lead to Aristotle's conclusion—nothing follows about ruling *by turns.* (Why not have all citizens perpetually in office? why not determine all political issues by referendum?)

The connection between ruling by turns and freedom is at first sight equally mysterious.

Perhaps the second paragraph of the quoted text may solve the mystery—and also link ruling by turns to democracy.

> *hen de to zēn hōs bouletai tis. . . . tēs men oun dēmokratias horos houtos deuteros. enteuthen d' elēluthe to mē archesthai, malista men hupo mēthenos, ei de mē, kata meros. kai sumballetai tautē pros tēn eleutherian tēn kata to ison.*

Aristotle's Greek is at least as confused as my English. (The text may be corrupt.) But the general sense peeps through. It is this. The "democratic" definition of liberty suggests that *no one* should rule—and hence, as a *pis aller*, that all should rule in turn. The second sort of freedom is plainly a kind of political liberty and it is avowedly democratic. And in some fashion it leads to "freedom in respect of equality." Hence—or so we might tentatively infer—the first sort of freedom too is both a form of liberty and a feature of democracy.

Then does the "democratic" definition of freedom suggest that no one should rule? It does. According to the definition, I will not be free to φ if my φ-ing is a political question; hence I will not be free absolutely unless there are no political questions; hence only under anarchism will I be free. If democrats hold that the supreme political value is freedom (thus understood), then they have a suicidal goal.

But in any case they cannot dispense with rule altogether (for then, trivially, there would be no *polis* and hence no *dēmokratia*). And the second best option is allegedly ruling by turns.

This allegation ought to seem queer—not because it is false but because it misses the point. If I am theoretically committed to anarchism but recognize that rule cannot be entirely abolished, then I am likely to seek out a "minimal" State, a State which rules as little as possible. I am likely, in other words, to seek to maximize political liberty. Aristotle does not see this. His democrats, anarchists in theory but aware of the need for rule, proceed to ask themselves not *how much* rule there should be but *who* should rule. Their answer betrays no concern, explicit or implicit, for the scope and range of State activities.

The paragraph on democratic freedom tells us nothing positive about Aristotle's attitude to political liberty. But it does confirm a negative point; for just when Dame Liberty beckons, Aristotle shyly diverts the discussion to talk about constitutions.

6.

At IV.14 1297b35–1298a3 he asserts that, in any constitution, there are three elements to which a good lawgiver must pay attention. The second of these is *to peri tas archas* [what pertains to the offices]; and Aristotle explains that *touto . . . estin has dei kai tinōn einai kurias kai poian tina dei ginesthai tēn hairesin autōn*, "what should the offices be—that is, over what should they be competent—and how should officers be selected?" There is a preliminary discussion of the question at IV.15 1299a15–1300a8, and a formal answer at VI.7–8, 1321a5–1323a10. These passages seem to constitute an exception to the general truth that Aristotle does not interest himself in political liberty; for what is the question "*tinōn einai kurias*" [over what should they be competent?] if it is not the question of the scope and range of political power? But tamp down the fires of excitement. When Aristotle answers the question he devotes less than two Bekker pages to it. Moreover, his answer hardly touches on the issue of political liberty.

Archai [offices] are divided into two categories: those which are "indispensable [anagkaion]," in the sense that without them there cannot be a State at all; and those which "bear on good order and decency," without which a State cannot be well governed (VI.8 1321b6–9; cf. IV.15 1299a32; VI.6 1320b24).

The indispensable offices occupy most of Aristotle's brief discussion (VI.8 1321b12–1322b37). They are these: Superintendents of the Market, dealing with contracts and *eukosmia*; Town Superintendents, dealing with public and private buildings, with streets, with boundaries; Country Superintendents, with a corresponding competence in the rural districts; the Treasury, receiving, guarding and distributing public funds; the Record Office, which looks after the registration of all legal contracts and decisions; the Bailiffs, who enforce court decisions, and the Jailers, who guard prisoners; the Military, concerned some with internal security and others with international matters; the Auditors, who scrutinize all public financial dealings; the Council, which prepares business for the sovereign assembly; the Priesthood, in its various forms; and finally the Organizers of Public Festivals. "To sum up, then, the indispensable superintendences deal with the following matters: religious affairs, military affairs, taxes and expenditure, the market and town and harbours and the country, and also law-courts and registration of contracts and collection of fines and custody, and accounts and scrutinies, and examination of the officers, and finally the superintendences concerning the body which deliberates about public affairs" (1322b30–37).

As for the useful but dispensable offices, which are found only in "the more leisured and flourishing States" (1322b38), they are these: Superintendents of Women, Guardians of the Laws, Guardians of Children, Controllers of the Gymnasia, Superintendents of Athletic Games, Superintendents of Cultural Contests. Aristotle concludes that "as for the offices, we have now given an outline account of pretty well all of them" (1323a9–10).

There may seem to be omissions: where, say, is the Ministry of Trade, or the Ministry of Education? The *Politica* itself suggests supplements: a Ministry of Health, perhaps (VII.11 1330a38), or a Ministry of Morals (V.8 1308b20–24). But the catalogue is long enough.

It would not have surprised Aristotle's contemporaries. The various *archai* he mentions are not theoretical inventions: they existed in many Greek States. (Newman's notes supply a rich documentation.) Nor will the list surprise—let alone outrage—any modern politician.

It has not always been so. A hundred years ago, I guess, the reaction to the list might have been very different. Who would then have thought that sporting questions might be political? that a branch of government should be devoted to the conduct of women? that private dwellings should be under the rule of public planners? The Aristotelian and the modern State are relatively similar in the scope and nature of their component *archai.* I find this a noteworthy fact—but I suspect that it is a historical accident.

Why should we accept the Aristotelian list? The indispensable offices are those without which there will be no State at all. Only in the case of two offices does Aristotle explain why this should be so. Here is the more interesting of the two explanations:

> The first of the indispensable superintendences is that concerned with the market. . . . For it is pretty well indispensable in all States that people buy and sell things in relation to one another's indispensable requirements, and this is the nearest path to self-sufficiency, on account of which they are thought to have come together into a single constitution. (VI.8 1321b12–18)

This is mistaken. Perhaps there could not be a State among whose citizens there was no buying and selling. But it does not follow that the State must regulate the buying and selling. There are many relations which will grow up among fellow-citizens: they will play games together, they will form clubs and societies, they will make friendships. It does not follow that the State must—or may—supervise these relations. It is one matter to observe that any society is likely to need a postal service, another to state that the Post Office must be State-controlled and the position of Postmaster General an *archē.* Aristotle fails to see the distinction.

In any event, even if a State must possess (say) law-courts, police and armed forces, *most* of the items which Aristotle lists as indispensable are evidently not so. Why must a State contain supervisors of private buildings? or harbor guardians? or festival organizers? or a priesthood? I can dream up no argument which even *seems* to show that such offices are necessary. And it is quite certain that there is no *good* argument available. For numerous States have as a matter of fact existed without offices of these sorts.

However that may be, what light does the list of *archai* shed on Aristotle's attitude to political liberty? Not much. The passage shows that certain areas of life—sporting events, the behavior of women, the state of the roads—might in Aristotle's view be the locus for political questions. It shows (what hardly needs showing) that he was no adherent to a Lockean or a minimalist conception of the State.

But at every crucial point the passage is vague. The second of the indispensable offices is said to be "that concerned with public and private property in the town—to ensure that there is good order [*eukosmia*] and that dilapidated buildings and roads are preserved and repaired" (1321 b19–21). What exactly is the function of these officials with regard to private houses? May they do no more than (1) order the repair of dilapidated property when it endangers neighbors or passersby? (For example, may they instruct me to mend my tottering chimneys or to prop up my garden wall?) Or may they also (2) regulate any alterations or repairs I make to my house which could in any way affect third parties? (For example, may they require me to paint the external woodwork in a seemly color? May they forbid me to build an ugly garage in my front garden?) Or may they further (3) determine how I deal with the internal affairs of my house, affairs which will affect only its occupants? (For example, may they prohibit me from installing an electric socket in my bathroom? May they require me to fit a damp-course?)

These three possibilities mark out, for any modern thinker, three different attitudes to political liberty. Possibility (1) illustrates an old fashioned liberalism. Possibility (3) illustrates a new fashioned paternalism. Any theorist who interests himself in political liberty must take a stand on these questions. Aristotle takes no stand.

The question "*tinōn einai kurias*" [over what should they be competent?] appears to raise, and directly, the issue of political liberty. The appearance is largely illusory.

7.

But the generous list of *archai* does suggest that he had a tendency towards totalitarianism. And the suggestion is endorsed by the passages, relatively few, in the *Politica* which propose or hint at specific legislation.

There are, for example, revealing *obiter dicta.*

Communication between city and port is advantageous—"and if anything harmful threatens, it is easy to guard against it by the laws, by determining and regulating who may and who may not mingle with one another" (VII.6 1327 a37–40).

"In general the lawgiver must banish foul talk from the State" (VII.17 1336b3–5)—and he must also forbid naughty plays and saucy postcards (1336b13–14). Offenders will be punished, in some cases by flogging.

"That it is particularly incumbent on the lawgiver to concern himself with the education of the young, no-one will dispute" (VIII.1 1337a11–12; cf. *NE* I.2 1094a27–b2). Aristotle perceives no room for debate on an eminently debatable issue.

These passages come from the account of the Ideal State in Books VII–VIII. There are similar passages elsewhere. Aristotle standardly assumes that the State will uncontroversially concern itself with education, with the birthrate, with property regulations, with individual morality, with the decency of women.

The discussion of marriage and procreation at VII.16 1334b29–1336a2 is striking. "Since the lawgiver must from the start see how the bodies of those who are reared attain the best condition, he must first superintend copulation—when and in what state people should have matrimonial intercourse with one another" (1334b29–32). The correct age for marriage and procreation is to be legally fixed. As for the proper time of year, Aristotle is content to follow tradition and opt for the winter months (1335a38). The couples concerned must themselves consult with doctors and scientists to discover the proper meteorological conditions for the event. (But the *kai* [and] in *kai autous* [and they themselves] at 1335a39 suggests that their inquiries supplement the work of the legislator.) Prospective parents must also ensure that their own bodies are in the appropriate condition; and proper care on the part of pregnant women "is easy for the lawgiver to determine, by enjoining them to make a daily journey to worship the gods whose office it is to oversee childbirth" (1335b14–16).

The law will forbid the rearing of any deformed child, and deformed infants must be exposed (1335b19–21). "And on grounds of population, if the rule of custom forbids the exposure of infants, there must be a limit to the number of children a couple may have; and if any are conceived by couples in offence against this," then there are to be compulsory abortions (1335b21–25: I follow Rackham's construe).

Just as the law determines the ages at which couples may begin to breed, "so let it be determined for how long it is fitting for them to do service [*leitourgein*] as child-breeders" (1335b28–29). Men may sire until they are fifty—after that, they may copulate only for the sake of their health "or for some other similar reason" (1335b37–38). And as for extramarital affairs, they are forbidden—at least for husbands—on pain of "the dishonor suitable to the offence" (1336a1–2).

The passage is not as determinate as we might wish. Aristotle never formulates any specific law, and his words sometimes leave it open whether a practice will be legally enjoined or merely recommended. Nonetheless, it is plain that in his Ideal State almost all aspects of child-breeding will be overseen and that numerous detailed laws will determine the sexual conduct of married citizens. Birth, copulation, and—no doubt—death, are political questions for Aristotle.

(They are *political* questions. Issues of population and procreation properly exercise scientists and philosophers and political theorists. There is no doubt that these matters have a public interest and a public importance. That is not at issue. The point is rather that, in Aristotle's view, these things may properly exercise the legislator.)

Nor is there reason to suppose that the passage on copulation and birth is untypical. What we possess of Aristotle's Callipolis—Books VII and VIII of the *Politica*—is only a fragment of a work which was perhaps never completed. But the fragment is uniformly interventionist in its approach to social life.

Here, then, we do find Aristotle taking a stand, in a few particular cases, on questions of political liberty. And his answers encourage us to guess his general attitude to issues of the same kind. We should guess that he inclined to totalitarianism—that he tended to treat a very wide range of questions as political.

But it is misleading to express the matter thus. For he does not opt for totalitarianism as a result of reflecting on general problems of political liberty. He simply *assumes* that child-breeding, for example, is *leitourgia*, a State service, and hence something to be governed by State regulations. Breeding a child is like fitting out a trireme or paying for a tragic chorus.

8.

Why so?

Brentano, whose general adulation for Aristotle did not encompass the *Politica,* offered a methodological explanation. Aristotle was so given to the empirical method that he took his innumerable observations of past and present States to show not only how States are in fact constituted but also how they inevitably and naturally must be constituted. And what must by nature be, ought to be. Having traced, empirically, the natural development of political association, Aristotle inferred from the historically given to the necessary and the ideal.[1]

No doubt there is truth in this. But alongside Brentano's methodological conjecture I should set a metaphysical diagnosis.

The State is a natural phenomenon. It has a goal, namely the welfare or *eudaimonia* of its citizens. The means to this goal include customs and laws. Hence the task of the lawgiver is to legislate for *eudaimonia.* Now *eudaimonia* requires virtuous activity, so that the lawgiver must ensure that his citizens are virtuous (cf. *NE* V.2 1130b23–24). Since the notion of virtue—of excellence, if you prefer—is broad, the lawgiver will be *entitled* to legislate for most aspects of citizen life. For whatever a citizen does or fails to do, his actions and inactions are likely to display virtue or to discover vice. And since most citizens live by their *pathē* [feelings] (X.9 1179b11–16), the legislator will in effect be *obliged* to operate *peri panta ton bion* [with a view to the whole of life] (1180a4; cf. V.1 1129b14f.).

This little argument purports to show how the fundamental axioms of Aristotle's political thought may lead, by a fairly direct route, to a totalitarian political stance. And the argument may thus explain why Aristotle did not see the need to discuss the liberal case.

Its premises might be assaulted—and I, for one, believe that the fundamental theses of Aristotle's political theory are viciously mistaken. But here I urge that even if the premises are granted, the totalitarian conclusion does not follow.

Balliol College exists for the sake of furthering learning in its undergraduates and scholarship in its Fellows. (Or so let us pretend.) Is the College thereby entitled or obliged to legislate in whatever way may promote the achievement of these noble ends? Should it require undergraduates to spend eight hours a day in the Library and oblige Fellows to read at least one book a month? Evidently not, and for two reasons. First, such regulations will never work. You may, as the proverb has it, lead a horse to water; but if you do it won't drink. Secondly, such regulations would be *ultra vires*: they exceed the authority of the College and offend against the rights of its members.

Again, parents are sometimes concerned for the well-being of their children. Every parent knows that legislation for *eudaimonia* backfires. Many parents also recognize that they are obliged to promote but forbidden to enjoin their offspring's happiness.

And so too with the State. Even if the State exists to promote the *eudaimonia* of its citizens, that does not license it to legislate for *eudaimonia*. Such legislation may well be self-defeating. It will certainly be *ultra vires.*

Aristotle's knew that legislation might be self-defeating: witness his arguments against Plato's communism. He does not consider the possibility that his own legislation might be liable to the same objection, that inhabitants of his Ideal State might emerge as less than ideal men.

But the fact that legislation for *eudaimonia* may be self-defeating does not (as Terry Irwin pointed out to me) refute the totalitarian principle: it follows that legislation *peri panta ton bion* would be imprudent (and perhaps therefore not obligatory); it does not follow that the legislator is not *entitled* so to legislate—it is, after all, often irrational for us to do all that we have a title to do.

What, then, of the more powerful charge that such legislation would be *ultra vires*? "He *could* not have considered the charge; for it presupposes some notion of individual rights, and that notion was not packed in his conceptual kitbag." Perhaps. But we can, I think, see how he would have answered the charge had he been able to consider it.

He begins Book VIII by observing that education is the business of the legislator, that it must be the same for all citizens, and that it must be publicly, not privately, arranged. For

> of things common [*koina*] the supervision must be common. And at the same time we should not think that any of the citizens is of himself but that all are of the State—for each is a part of the State, and it is natural that the care of each part should look to the care of the whole. (*Pol.* VIII.1 1337a 26–32)

The first sentence need not detain us: it is an untruism. Either it is trivially true (in that things will be called "common" just in case they should be subject to public supervision) or else it is substantially false (it is a matter of common interest that women should be elegantly dressed, but it is not a fit subject for legislation or public policy).

The rest of the quotation, and the claim that a citizen is a part of the State—there is the nub:

> *hama de oude chrē nomizein auton hautou tina einai tōn politōn, alla pantas tēs poleōs. Morion gar hekastos tēs poleōs. hē de epimeleia pephuken hekastou moriou blepein pros tēn tou holou epimeleian.*

The theme had been announced in Book I. Individuals are posterior to the State insofar as they are parts of the State. A citizen stands to the State as a hand stands to a body (I.2 1253a19–25). Now "a part is not only a part of something else—it is of something else *simpliciter*" [*alla kai haplōs*—or *holōs—allou*] (I.4 1254a10). In this respect the term "part" is similar to the term "possession [*ktēma*]": a slave is not merely a possession of his master—he is of his master *simpliciter.* And Aristotle also observes that a slave is in some sense a part of his master (I.6 1255b11).

(A free man is *hautou phusei* [his own by nature], while a slave is *allou* [another's] (I.4 1254a14–15). A free man is *hautou heneka kai mē allou* [for his own sake and not another's] (*Met.* I.2 982b25–26). If a citizen is not *hautou* [of himself] but *tēs poleōs* [of the State], does it not follow that citizens are slaves, that all rule must, despite his denial, be despotic—and despotic in a literal sense? It is not at all clear to me how he can avoid this conclusion.)

What does it mean to say that a part of x is not merely *a part of x* but also *of x simpliciter?* (The genitive construction comes from Plato, *Laws* VII 804D5–6 and XI 923A6–B1, as Richard Sorabji has reminded me.) The best guess I can make is this: if F's are parts of G's, then F's can only be defined in terms of G; hence F's are of G's *simpliciter* in the sense that to be an F is essentially to stand in some relation to a G (cf. *Cat.* 7, 6a36–b14). Thus a citizen is of a State *simpliciter* in the sense that to be a citizen is to stand in a certain relation to a State. Citizens are, if you like, logically dependent on States.

But men are essentially political animals, that is, they are essentially citizens. Citizens are logically dependent on States. Hence men are logically dependent on States. To be a man is, inter alia, to be of a State. Hence (or so it may seem tempting to infer) any care for the man must look to the good of the State.

If men are essentially of States, what moral or political consequences follow? In particular, does it follow that any care for a man must look to the good of the State? It does not *obviously* follow—and I have yet to find a plausible way of elaborating the inference.

In any event, *are* men of their States? Am I a part of, and am I of, the United Kingdom of Great Britain and Northern Ireland? In a loose enough sense of "part," maybe I am a part of the Kingdom. But I am not a part in any ordinary sense: I do not stand to the Kingdom as my arm stands to my body or as a piece stands to a jigsaw puzzle or as a sparkplug stands to a motor car engine. For I am an independent individual. That, in the end, is the crucial fact about me (and about you), and it is a fact which, in the *Politica*, Aristotle ignores or suppresses.

Aristotle is not the only thinker, ancient or modern, to imagine that people are bits of States. This view, too, is an untruism. In one sense it is trifling and true. In another sense it is substantial and false. Aristotle's implicit totalitarianism rests ultimately on a questionable inference from a metaphysical untruism.

Notes

This chapter is essentially the paper which I presented at the symposium "Aristoteles' *Politik*," XI. Symposium Aristotelicum (Friedrichshafen/Bodensee 1987): section 2 has been largely rewritten, but the remaining sections have been only lightly revised. My thanks to: Annette Barnes, Charles Brittain, and James Leach; at Friedrichshafen to Enrico Berti, Theo Ebert, and Mario Mignucci (for comments on the attempted definition of political liberty); Julia Annas, Jacques Brunschwig, and Carlo Natali (for remarks on property); Charles Kahn, Malcolm Schofield, and Michael Woods (for help with the "democratic" definition of *eleutheria*); Terry Irwin, Wolfgang Kullmann, M. M. Mackenzie, Martha Nussbaum, Gerhard Seel, and Gisela Striker (on various aspects of Aristotle's penchant for totalitarianism); and especially Richard Sorabji, for his constructive Korreferat.

1. See Brentano, Franz. *Über Aristoteles* (Hamburg: Felix Meiner Verlag, 1986), pp. 460–63.

9

Aristotle and Anarchism

David Keyt

1. Anarchism, Ancient and Modern

ARISTOTLE'S INFAMOUS DEFENSE of slavery in the first book of the *Politics* is intended as an answer to a sweeping challenge of the institution. "Some maintain," Aristotle reports, "that it is contrary to nature (*para phusin*) to be a master [over slaves]. For [they argue] it is [only] by law (*nomoi*) that one man is a slave and another free; by nature (*phusei*) there is no difference. Hence it is not just; for it rests on force [*biaion*]" (*Pol.* I.3 1253b20–23).[1] Aristotle does not identify the exponents of this impressive argument. The only writer of the classical period to whom its leading idea can be attributed with certainty is the sophist Alcidamas, a follower of Gorgias. In his Messenian Oration, a speech that Aristotle studied (*Rhet.* I.13 1373b18, II.23 1397a11), Alcidamas is reported to have said that "God left all men free; nature has made no one a slave" (Scholiast on *Rhet.* I.13 1373b18).[2]

The argument challenging slavery that Aristotle preserves has a ramification that its exponents, whoever they were, may not have noticed. It contains the seeds of philosophical anarchism. The conclusion of the argument is inferred from two assertions about slavery: that there is no difference by nature between a master and a slave, and that the rule of a master over a slave rests on force. Now, the very same things can be plausibly maintained about rulers and subjects in a political community: there is no difference by nature between a ruler and a subject, and political rule rests on force. Thus, by parity of reasoning political rule is unjust. A wholesale challenge of political authority is but a short step from the wholesale challenge of slavery.

Philosophical anarchism is simply a generalization of the antislavery argument. Its central idea is that coercion is unjust. The classical statement of the theory is in William Godwin's *Enquiry Concerning Political Justice*,[3] though the use of the word *anarchism* in an ameliorative sense to describe the theory is a later idea. Thus, Godwin claims "that coercion, absolutely considered, is injustice."[4] The phrase "absolutely considered" implies that Godwin might sanction coercion in some circumstances, which in fact he does. He says, for example, that "it is the first principle of morality and justice, that directs us, where one of two evils is inevitable, to choose the least. Of consequence, the wise and just man, being unable, as yet, to introduce the form of society which his understanding approves, will contribute to the support of so much coercion, as is necessary to exclude what is worse, anarchy."[5] As this quotation makes plain, Godwin is a foe of anarchy in the pejorative sense, the false anarchy of disorder and violence. Being opposed to the use of force, Godwin is also a foe of revolution: "Revolutions are a struggle between two parties, each persuaded of the justice of its cause, a struggle not decided by compromise or patient expostulation, but by force only."[6] "Revolution," he remarks, "is engendered by an indignation against tyranny, yet is itself ever more pregnant with tyranny."[7]

The rejection of political authority, which gives anarchism its name,[8] is not a first principle of the theory but a corollary of its view about coercion and force. Thus, Emma Goldman, a twentieth-century anarchist, defines anarchism as "the theory that all forms of government rest on violence, and are *therefore* wrong and harmful, as well as unnecessary"[9] (my emphasis). This is a succinct rendering of a more elaborate argument of Godwin's. The major premise of Godwin's argument is that "[g]overnment is nothing but regulated force; force is its appropriate claim upon your attention."[10] But force, or the threat of force, destroys understanding and usurps private judgment and individual conscience: "Coercion first annihilates the understanding of the subject upon whom it is exercised, and then of him who employs it."[11] Godwin concludes "that government is, abstractedly taken, an evil, an usurpation upon the private judgement and individual conscience of mankind; and that, however we may be obliged to admit it as a necessary evil for the present, it behoves us, as the friends of reason and the human species, to admit as little of it as possible, and carefully to observe, whether, in consequence of the gradual illumination of the human mind, that little may not hereafter be diminished."[12]

The easy transfer of the antislavery argument to the political realm raises the question of whether in the classical period there were any representatives of philosophical anarchism. The answer is that Greek democracy, at least as interpreted by Plato and Aristotle, contains a trace of anarchism, that several of Socrates' ideas are in an anarchistic vein, and that a full-fledged anarchism is implied by some of the sayings attributed to that "Socrates gone mad" (Diogenes Laertius VI.54), Diogenes of Sinope.

Although both Plato and Aristotle find a trace of anarchism in Greek democracy, they find it in different places. Plato finds Greek democracy anarchic in practice. He claims in the *Republic* that in a democracy there is no coercion either to rule or to be ruled (VIII 557E2–4); thus, democracy is *anarchos*, without a ruler (VIII 558C4). By Aristotle's lights, on the other hand, the champions of democracy are anarchists in theory only. As Aristotle interprets their idea of freedom, they recognize the practical necessity of government—democracy is after all one form of government—but would prefer not to be ruled at all (*Pol.* VI.2 1317b14–15).

At least two of Socrates' ideas are in an anarchistic vein. In Plato's *Apology* (25C–26A) Socrates argues that if he corrupts the young, he does so unintentionally. For no one, he reasons, wishes to be harmed; and if a man corrupts those around him, their corruption will lead them to harm him. But if a person corrupts the young unintentionally, he is in need, not of punishment, but of instruction. This is an argument that philosophical anarchists would applaud. Godwin remarks, for example, that "[if] he who employs coercion against me could mould me to his purposes by argument, no doubt he would. He pretends to punish me, because his argument is strong; but he really punishes me, because his argument is weak."[13]

Also in an anarchistic vein is the Socratic idea that the first of the three cities described in Books II and III of the *Republic* is "the true city" and not, as Glaucon characterizes it, "a city of pigs" (372D–E). This first city, an idyllic agrarian community without warriors or rulers whose farmers, craftsmen, traders, seamen, and wage-earners supply the necessities of life but no luxuries, resembles Godwin's anarchist utopia.[14] Even though Socrates is Plato's spokesman throughout most of the *Republic*, this particular idea may reflect a genuine Socratic sentiment. It is of a piece with the argument in the *Apology* opposing punishment and is inconsistent with the Platonic idea expressed later in the *Republic* that the true city is an aristocracy in which the farmers, craftsmen, traders, and other workers of Socrates' first city are ruled by a group of philosopher-kings backed by a military force (*Rep.* IV 445D–V 449A, together with *Statesman* 300D11–301A2).

The seeds of philosophical anarchism are more easily found in Diogenes the Cynic than in Socrates.[15] Diogenes said that "the only correct constitution is that in the cosmos" (D.L. VI.72) and declared himself to be a citizen of the cosmos (*kosmopolitēs*) (D.L. VI.63). The first of these sayings entails that no constitution in a polis is correct (and hence just) whereas the second may be taken, consonant with this, as a disavowal of citizenship in any polis. Diogenes had similar anarchistic ideas about slavery and marriage. "To those who advised him to pursue his runaway slave, he said, 'It would be absurd if Manes can live without Diogenes, but Diogenes cannot without Manes'" (D.L. VI.55). Diogenes implies in this saying that slavery should be a voluntary relation resting on the need of the slave for a master. "He also said that wives should be held in common, recognizing no marriage except the joining together of him who persuades with her who is persuaded" (D.L. VI.72). In this saying, Diogenes advocates free cohabitation and disavows marriage based on coercion.

Aristotle refers to Diogenes only once in his extant works (*Rhet.* III.10 1411a24–25); but since Diogenes was such a prominent spectacle in Athens, it is safe to assume that Aristotle was familiar both with his outlandish behavior and with his ideas.[16]

That Aristotle is addressing the protoanarchism of Diogenes' in the introductory chapters of the *Politics* (I.1–2) has been realized for a long time.[17] The general consensus is that Aristotle is an uncompromising opponent of anarchism. Whereas Diogenes brags about being *apolis*, without a polis (D.L. VI.38), Aristotle claims that "man is by nature a political animal" (I.2 1253a2–3) and that "he who is unable to share in a community or has no need . . . is either a beast or a god" (I.2 1253a27–29). And what could be further removed from anarchism than the total subordination of individual to state that Aristotle seems to envisage (I.2 1253a18–29; see also VIII.l 1337a26–30)?[18]

Aristotle defends the polis against Diogenes' assault. So much is clear. But, it will be recalled, the anarchist's rejection of the state is not a first principle of his philosophy but a consequence of his idea that coercion and compulsion are unjust. So there is a deeper question to consider. Where does Aristotle stand on this matter of the injustice of coercion and compulsion? As a defender of the political community, he must reject the central idea of philosophical anarchism, must he not? The answer is surprisingly unclear. As I shall show immediately, that coercion is unjust is a theorem of Aristotelian philosophy: it follows syllogistically from three basic ideas of Aristotle's ethical and natural philosophy. But whether Aristotle realized this, whether he consciously embraced the central idea of philosophical anarchism, is a further question.

2. Derivation of the Anticoercion Principle

The chief philosophical idea of the *Politics* is that of a link between justice and nature. When Aristotle wishes to justify a certain practice, institution, or form of government, his ultimate appeal is always to nature. He subscribes to two principles relating justice and nature: a positive principle linking the just and the natural (I.5 1255a1–3, III.17 1287b37–39, VII.9 1329a13–17) and a negative principle linking the unjust and the unnatural (I.10 1258a40–b2, VII.3 1325b7–10; and see I.3 1253b20–23). (For both principles together see I.5 1254a17–20 and III.16 1287a8–18.)

These principles are obviously of restricted generality since the sphere of justice is much narrower than the realm of nature. The realm of nature includes all objects that have an internal source of motion—the simple bodies, plants, animals, and the heavens (*Phys.* II.1 192b8–32, *Met.* XII.1 1069a30–b2)—whereas the sphere of justice is restricted to human beings. (The gods are beyond both nature [*Met.* VI.1 1026a13–22] and justice [*NE* X.8 1178b8–12].) Furthermore, many of the movements of human beings such as growth and respiration are natural but outside the field of ethics (*NE* I.13 1102a32–b12). Only voluntary (*hekousia*) actions are praised or blamed (*NE* III.1 1109b30–31). And, finally, among voluntary actions only those that affect others are just or unjust (*NE* V.1 1129b25–27, 1130a10–13, and 11 1138a19–20). The sphere of justice is restricted, in sum, to human conduct that affects others, or, in short, to social conduct.

By Aristotle's theory, the negative principle is not equivalent to the converse of the positive. For although Aristotle holds that everything (within the sphere of social conduct) that is unnatural is unjust, he denies that everything that is just is natural. The people of Amphipolis, for example, passed a law honoring the Spartan general Brasidas, who was killed defending their city (Thucydides V.11). It is just, in Aristotle's view, to obey such a law, once enacted, even though the justice of doing so is legal or conventional only (*nomikon*), not natural (*phusikon*) (*NE* V.7 1134b18–24).

The two principles relating justice and nature are not first principles of Aristotle's philosophy but corollaries of his natural teleology. Consider the positive principle first. According to Aristotelian teleology, "nature makes everything for the sake of something" (I.2 1252b32; *Part. An.* I.1 641b12, I.5 645a23–26; *Phys.* II.8), where this something, the end, or *telos*, of the making, is something good (I.1 1252b34–1253a1; *Phys.* II.2 194a32–33, 3 195a23–25; *Met.* I.3 983a31–32).[19] This view of nature yields the first (or minor) premise in the following quasi[20] syllogism.

1.1 Everything natural is good.
1.2 Everything (within the sphere of social conduct) that is good is just.
1.3 Therefore, everything (within the sphere of social conduct) that is natural is just. (The justice of nature principle.)

That Aristotle subscribes to its major premise, which connects the justice of nature principle with his natural teleology, is clear from his assertion that "justice (*dikaiosunēn*), which all the other virtues necessarily accompany, is social virtue (*koinōnikēn aretēn*)" (III.13 1283a38–40). The justice that all the other virtues accompany is universal rather than particular justice. It is the justice that is the same as complete virtue and whose opposite is lawlessness (*NE* V.1). Since the justice of nature principle applies to every sort of social conduct, this must be the sort of justice referred to in it as well. Furthermore, *dikaios* ("just") is the adjective of the noun *dikaiosunē* ("justice"), and *agathos* ("good") is the adjective of the noun *aretē* ("virtue"). So the relation Aristotle asserts between *dikaiosunē* (justice) and *aretē* (virtue) also holds between that which is *dikaios* (just) and that which is *agathos* (good). Consequently, to say that justice and social virtue are the same is equivalent to saying that in the sphere of social conduct what is just and what is good are the same.[21] Aristotle's statement is thus a bit stronger than the premise he needs, for it entails both the premise and its converse.

The negative principle relating the unjust and the unnatural is derived similarly. If within the sphere of social conduct what is good and what is just are the same, then within the same sphere what is bad and what is unjust are the same. This yields the major premise of a second quasi-syllogism. As for the minor, Aristotle never, to my knowledge at least, asserts straight out that what is unnatural is bad; but his statement that "nothing contrary to nature is beautiful (*kalon*)" (VII.3 1325b9–10) comes close. For the adjective *kalos* applies, not only to physical beauty, but also to moral beauty—the beauty of good character and right conduct. So it seems reasonable to attribute this second argument to him:

2.1 Everything contrary to nature is bad.
2.2 Everything (within the sphere of social conduct) that is bad is unjust.
2.3 Therefore, everything (within the sphere of social conduct) that is contrary to nature is unjust.

It is worth recalling at this point that in Aristotle's philosophy of nature what is forced and what is contrary to nature are identified. Thus, Aristotle says that "what is by force (*biai*) and what is contrary to nature are the same" (*Cael.* I.2 300a23; see also *Phys.* IV.8 215a1–3, V.6 230a29–30; *Gen. An.* V.8 788b27). In Aristotelian physics, for example, fire moves upward toward its natural place by nature but downward only by force and contrary to nature (*Gen. et Corr.* II.6 333b26–30 and elsewhere). This identification of the forced and the unnatural is a feature, not only of inanimate nature, but of the entire natural world (*Gen. An.* II.4 739a4, III.8 777a18–19, V.8 788b27; *EE* II.8 1224a15–30; *Rhet* I.11 1370a9). Thus, Aristotle accepts:

2.4 Whatever is forced is contrary to nature.

When this idea is combined with 2.3, we have an Aristotelian derivation of the first principle of philosophical anarchism:

2.5 Everything (within the sphere of social conduct) that is forced is unjust. (The anticoercion principle.)

That Aristotle was aware of the anticoercion principle there can be no doubt. He chronicles it as a premise of the antislavery argument (*Pol.* I.3 1253b22–23); in an aporetic passage he suggests that certain claims to political power are suspect because they imply its opposite, that rule based on force is *just* (III.10 1281a21–24); and he attempts to mediate a dispute between those who champion the principle and those who champion its opposite (I.6 1255a5–21). Moreover, the fact that it follows from three of his basic ideas—2.1, 2.2, and 2.4—means that he cannot deny it without inconsistency. Since a charitable interpretation strives to preserve consistency, the possibility that Aristotle accepts the first principle of anarchism is worth exploring. I try to show in the remainder of this paper that it is indeed a fundamental principle of his political philosophy.

3. Whose Advantage Is the Common Advantage?

In searching for evidence that Aristotle accepts the anticoercion principle, a good place to begin is with his distinction between constitutions that are correct (*orthoi*) and hence just, and those that are deviations (*parekbaseis*) and hence unjust (III.6 1279a17–20, 11 1282b8–13). The question we need to consider is his basis for inferring that a constitution is unjust because it is deviant. Does the inference rest on the anticoercion principle? But before addressing this question we need to understand the distinction itself. In marking it, Aristotle uses an expression that requires elucidation.

The difference between the correct constitutions (kingship, aristocracy, and polity) and the deviations (tyranny, oligarchy, and democracy) is that the correct constitutions look to the common advantage (*to koinēi sumpheron*), whereas the deviant constitutions look only to the rulers' own advantage (III.6 1279a17–21). Thus, tyranny aims at the advantage of the tyrant; oligarchy at the advantage of the rich; and democracy at the advantage of the poor (III.7 1279b6–9).

Whose advantage do kingship, aristocracy, and polity aim at? Whose advantage is the common advantage? Aristotle does not give a straightforward answer. The common advantage is not the advantage of every inhabitant of a given polis. The common advantage does not include the advantage of slaves

(III.6 1278b32–37). Nor apparently does it include the advantage of resident aliens (*metoikoi*) or foreign visitors (*xenoi*).[22] Aristotle seems to equate the advantage of the whole polis with the common advantage of its citizens (III.13 1283b40–42[23]). As W. L. Newman remarks, "[t]he common advantage . . . which a State should study is the common advantage of the citizens . . , and that of other classes, only so far as their advantage is bound up with that of the citizens. . . ."[24]

In this explanation of the common advantage, who counts as a citizen? The answer is surprisingly complex. By Aristotle's official taxonomy there are four types of citizen. The basic concept is that of a *full* citizen (*politēs haplōs*) (III.1 1275a19–23, 5 1278a4–5). Aristotle defines a full citizen as a man[25] who "is entitled to share in deliberative or[26] judicial office" (III.1 1275b17–19). The group of full citizens is thus the supreme political authority in a polis (III.1 1275a26–29; see also 6.1278b10–14, 11 1282a25–39). The other concepts of a citizen are derivative from that of a full citizen. Thus, a boy or a youth who will in the future be entitled to be enrolled as a full citizen is an *immature* citizen (*politēs atelēs*), and an old man who was a full citizen but is now exempt from political duties is a *superannuated* citizen (*politēs parēkmakos*) (III.1 1275a14–19, 5.1278a4–6). Aristotle also mentions *female* citizens (III.2 1275b33, 5 1278a28) but does not give an account of the concept. A female citizen (*politis*) is presumably a woman or a girl who has the legal capacity to transmit citizenship to her (properly sired) offspring and, in particular, to her sons. The concept of a female citizen is important under any constitution that requires that a full citizen have a citizen mother (I.2 1275b22–24).[27] By this taxonomy the citizens of a polis will normally be the full citizens and the members of their families: their wives, children, and elderly parents.

We are now in a position to notice a problem about Aristotle's explanation of the common advantage that has generally gone unnoticed.[28] On the assumption that a man's advantage is closely tied to that of the household he heads, the advantage of the full citizens of a polis will be the same as the advantage of the totality of its citizens. But, on Aristotle's functional definition of a full citizen, the full citizens of a polis are its rulers. Hence, if the common advantage of a polis is the advantage of the totality of its citizens, a constitution that looks to the rulers' advantage looks to the common advantage, and the distinction between correct and deviant constitutions collapses.

The solution to this problem is to be found in Aristotle's tacit recognition of second-class citizenship. There are several reasons for attributing such a concept to Aristotle. First of all, by Aristotle's definition of a full citizen there is only one full citizen in a kingship—the king himself.[29] Thus, the only citizens in a kingship are the members of the royal family. But in two passages in the *Politics* Aristotle, following the normal Greek practice, refers to other men besides the king himself as citizens (III.14 1285a25–27, V.10 1311a7–8). (In both passages a citizen, a *politēs*, is contrasted with an alien, a *xenos.*) Since these men do not share in deliberative or judicial office, the citizenship they enjoy must be second class. Secondly, in discussing revolution Aristotle twice contrasts a group of men who are "outside the constitution" with the group of rulers (V.4 1304a16–17, 8 1308a3–11). Since these men appear to be neither metics, foreigners, nor slaves, they too must be second-class citizens (compare III.5 1277b33–39). Thirdly and finally, in his essay on the best polis, in a context where only adult males are under discussion, Aristotle uses the expression "citizens who share in the constitution" (VII.13 1332a32–34), which would be pleonastic unless one could envisage (second-class) citizens who do *not* share in the constitution.[30]

Who would these second-class citizens be? Presumably they are individuals who have a moral, though not a legal, claim, based on their free status and place of birth, to be first-class citizens. In short, they are free natives. A second-class citizen, like an immature citizen, is a citizen "under an assumption" (*ex hupotheseōs*) (III.5 1278a5). The assumption in the case of an immature citizen is that he will one day become a full citizen. The assumption in the case of a second-class citizen is that he or she would become a first-class citizen should such citizenship be maximally extended, as in a democracy.

On this interpretation of the *Politics,* Aristotle divides the population of a typical Greek polis into five groups as follows:

1 First-class citizens:
   a Full citizens
   b Immature citizens
   c Superannuated citizens
   d Female citizens
2 Second-class citizens
3 Metics (resident aliens)
4 Foreign visitors
5 Slaves

The solution to the puzzle, then, about the collapsing distinction between correct and deviant constitutions is to take the common advantage to be the advantage of both first- and second-class citizens. The difference between a correct and a deviant constitution is that a correct constitution looks to the advantage of both classes of citizen, whereas a deviant constitution looks to the advantage of first-class citizens only.

But a question remains. By this explanation of the common advantage, shouldn't a democracy, contrary to Aristotle's classification, be a correct, rather than a deviant, constitution? For in a democracy first-class citizenship is maximally extended, and thus in aiming at their own advantage its full citizens aim at the common advantage. The answer is that the definition of democracy that leads to its being classified as a deviant constitution is in terms of social classes rather than free status. By this definition, democracy is essentially rule by the poor and only incidentally rule by the many (that is, by the free) (III.8 1279b34–1280a6). Under such a constitution the poor constitute a majority, vote their own interests in the assembly and in the law courts, and reduce the rich to virtual second-class citizenship. Such a proletarian democracy is as much a deviant constitution as an oligarchy (III.7 1279b8–10).[31]

4. Deviant Constitutions

Aristotle defines a deviant constitution as one under which the rulers rule for their own advantage (III.6 1279a19–20). He goes on to claim that deviant constitutions are characterized by their use of force (III.10 1281a23–24; see also III.3 1276a12–13), that they are contrary to nature (*para phusin*) (III.17 1287b37–41), and that they are unjust (III.1 1282b8–13). Aristotle does not explicitly connect these three claims with each other or with his definition. But the derivation of the anticoercion principle shows how they can be linked together.

That the rulers in a polis with a deviant constitution must use force to maintain themselves in power is a consequence of the nature of their rule. For deviant constitutions are all despotic (III.6 1279a19–21, IV.3 1290a25–29, VII.14 1333a3–6). Under such a constitution the rulers, looking only to their own advantage, treat those outside the constitution, the second-class citizens, as slaves (see III.6 1278b32–37 and IV.11 1295b19–23). Since these outsiders are free men (III.6 1279a21; see also IV.6 1292b38–41), there can be no question of their enduring such treatment willingly (see IV.10 1295a17–23). Thus, under a deviant constitution there is always a group of subjects who obey their rulers only because they are forced to. In a democracy it is the rich; in an oligarchy, the poor; in a tyranny, the free (for tyranny see III.14 1285a25–29, V.11 1314a10–12).

Given the Aristotelian equation of the forced and the unnatural, it follows at once that deviant constitutions are contrary to nature. From this one can infer, by an appeal to nature, that such constitutions are unjust. Thus, we can construct an argument that moves within the same circuit of ideas as the derivation of the anticoercion principle:

3.1 Every deviant constitution rests on force.
3.2 [Whatever is forced is contrary to nature.]

3.3 Therefore, every deviant constitution is contrary to nature.
3.4 Everything (within the sphere of social conduct) that is contrary to nature is unjust.
3.5 Therefore, every deviant constitution is unjust.

Although this argument does not occur explicitly in the *Politics*, it does introduce coherence into the various things that Aristotle says about deviant constitutions. The only premise that Aristotle does not endorse explicitly in the *Politics* is 3.2. But, given its appearance in other treatises, it seems a reasonable one to supply. If this interpretation is on the right track, we have additional evidence for thinking that the anticoercion principle is an operative, though tacit, principle in the *Politics*; for the principle simply telescopes argument 3.

The vast majority of fourth-century Greek cities, it should be noted, had deviant constitutions. Most were democracies or oligarchies (IV.11 1296a22–23, V.1 1301b39–40). Aristotle is hard pressed for contemporary examples of correct constitutions. "Kingships," he remarks, "do not come into existence any longer now, or if they do, they are rather monarchies or tyrannies" (V.10 1313a3–5). Aristocracies are of two main types: true and so-called (IV.7). His favorite examples of so-called aristocracies are Sparta and Carthage (II.9, 11; IV.7 1293b14–18) though he mentions that Thurii and the Epizephyrian Locri were (so-called) aristocracies at one time (V.7 1307a23–29, 34–40).[32] He gives no example of a true aristocracy. The third and last type of correct constitution, polity, seems to have existed for a period at least at Mali (IV.13 1297b12–16), Tarentum (V.3 1303a3–6), Syracuse (V.4 1304a27–29), and Oreus (V.3 1303a18–20);[33] but, like kingship and aristocracy, it "did not occur often" (IV.7 1293a39–b1).

Aristotle's view, then, was that virtually every fourth-century Greek polis was ruled unjustly by a group of men using force to advance their own interests at the expense of a body of second-class citizens. His evaluation of the actual constitutions that people lived under in fourth-century Greece is as unfavorable as that of the protoanarchist Diogenes.

5. Legitimate Force

The anticoercion principle, which links the forced with the unjust, entails that nothing just is forced. Thus, in searching for evidence that Aristotle accepts and tacitly uses the anticoercion principle in the *Politics*, one needs to examine the role, if any, that coercion plays under the constitutions that he regards as correct and hence as just (III.11 1282b8–13). It will suffice to consider only the best constitution, which is a generic constitution with two species: kingship and true aristocracy (III.18; IV.2 1289a30–33, 7 1293b18–19). By the stricter analysis of Book IV, the other correct constitutions, so-called aristocracy and polity, are regarded as deviations from "the most correct constitution," and the three original deviations as deviations from the less correct (IV.8 1293b22–27). The most correct constitution is thus the only one that is absolutely just.

In discussing kingship Aristotle explicitly raises the question to which we want to know his answer. He asks "whether the man who is to rule as king should have some force about him by which he will be able to compel those who do not want to obey" (III.15 1286b28–30). His answer is that the king should have a force stronger than a single individual or small band of individuals but weaker than the many (III.15 1286b34–37). The many referred to here are "the whole body of [second-class] citizens" in the kingdom.[34] If the king had a force stronger than the whole body, he could, if he wished, turn his kingship into a tyranny. This seems to be the rationale for Aristotle's answer. If so, Aristotle is tacitly assuming that coercion of second-class citizens is unjust. The rationale of Aristotle's answer is of a piece with that which lies behind his negative evaluation of deviant constitutions. The passage indicates, however, that Aristotle does not accept the anticoercion principle in an undiluted or unrestricted form. But, then, as we have seen, neither does Godwin.[35]

The true aristocracy sketched in Books VII and VIII[36] has an army, and in two passages Aristotle discusses its proper employment. In the first Aristotle says that "the members of a community must have arms in their own hands also[37] both for purposes of government, on account of those who are disobedient, and with a view to those who try to wrong them from without" (VII.8 1328b7–10). Later in Book VII Aristotle gives a second list of the legitimate purposes of armed force. The armed forces in his best polis, he says, have three purposes: first, self-defense; second, hegemony, or leadership, in foreign affairs exercised, not despotically, but "for the benefit of those who are ruled"; and, finally, "to be master of those who are worthy to be slaves" (VII.14 1333b38–1334a2).

The mention of hegemony (see also VII.6 1327a40–b6) suggests that Aristotle's best polis will adopt an aggressive foreign policy; and, indeed, the great nineteenth-century commentators on the *Politics* believe that this is exactly what Aristotle is advocating, or at least condoning, in the passage just quoted. Franz Susemihl and R. D. Hicks regard Aristotle as a precursor of Bismarck. They remark that "like Athens, Sparta, and Thebes, [Aristotle's ideal state is] to exercise an hegemony; that is, to stand at the head of a more or less dependent confederation, in which union has been achieved, if necessary, with the edge of the sword."[38] Newman, in a similar vein, construes Aristotle's idea broadly enough to accommodate any British imperialist. Aristotle's enumeration of the aims of war, according to Newman, "is wide enough to be accepted by any conqueror, however ambitious, who might be willing to adjust his methods of rule to the claims of the States subjugated by him."[39]

Both comments are misrepresentations. Susemihl and Hicks are demonstrably mistaken in thinking that Aristotle wishes his best polis to emulate the sort of hegemony, or leadership, displayed by Athens or Sparta in the fifth and fourth centuries. Aristotle had no illusions about the Athenian and Spartan empires. He says that, when Athens and Sparta were in positions of leadership, the one set up democracies, and the other, oligarchies, in the cities under their sway, "looking not to the advantage of the cities [they led] but to their own" (IV.11 1296a32–36; see also V.7 1307b22–24). The leadership of Aristotle's best polis is to be the very opposite of this: not despotic, but for the benefit of those who are ruled. In response to Newman's idea that Aristotle's remark about hegemony is wide enough to be accepted by any ambitious but forbearing conqueror, it must be said that one would be hard pressed to cite many historical examples of the sort of hegemony Aristotle envisages. For, as Aristotle points out, cities in a position of leadership, including those that do not tolerate despotism at home, have a propensity for acting despotically toward the cities under their sway (VII.2 1324b22–41 especially b32–36). A city in a position of leadership that looks to the advantage of the cities under its sway would seem to be even rarer than a city with a correct constitution.

The main point for our purposes is that Aristotle evaluates leadership among cities by the same principles he uses in evaluating constitutions. The anticoercion principle, to whatever extent he accepts it, is not abrogated when he turns to a discussion of foreign affairs.

A further question about Aristotle's two lists of the legitimate purposes of armed force is whether the second adds one item or two to the first. In addition to defense against external aggressors, the first list mentions "purposes of government, on account of those who are disobedient." The second list, on the other hand, mentions defense, hegemony, and mastership over natural slaves. Are the disobedient of the first list the natural slaves of the second?[40] If so, Aristotle does not envisage the use of force or the threat of force *within* his best polis.

6. The Best Polis Proper

The polis described in Books VII and VIII has a two-tiered social structure. One tier consists of the proper parts (*oikeia moria*) (VII.4 1326a21) of the polis; the other, of the mere accessories required for its existence. The proper parts, who together hold all the landed wealth in the polis, are hoplites, officeholders, and priests; the accessories, who provide for its material needs, are farmers, traders, artisans, seamen (VII.6 1327b4–9), and day-laborers (VII.8–9). Traders (*agoraioi*) are either merchants (*emporoi*) or shopkeepers (*kapēloi*) (IV.4 1291a4–6).[41]

The proper parts of Aristotle's best polis are citizens; the accessories are not (VII.9 1328b33–1329a2, 17–19). Furthermore, there are no second-class citizens in Aristotle's polis. "A polis is good," Aristotle says, "because the citizens who share in the constitution are good; and for us all the citizens share in the constitution" (VII.13 1332a32–35). To say that all the citizens share in the constitution is to say that all the citizens are first-class citizens.

If farmers, craftsmen, and traders are not citizens, what is their legal status in Aristotle's best polis? Farmers are to be slaves or barbarian serfs (VII.9 1329a25–26, 10 1330a25–31). The status of craftsmen and traders is not indicated, but it can be inferred. They cannot be slaves; for art and trade require a mental capacity denied to natural slaves,[42] the only sort of slaves allowed in a polis that is absolutely just (see VII.2 1324b36–41). Since the population of a polis consists of citizens, metics, foreign visitors, and slaves, craftsmen and traders must be metics or foreign visitors. Foreign trade, the province of the merchant, could all be in the hands of foreign visitors; but craftsmen and shopkeepers would have to be metics.[43] This is their status in the Cretan city of Plato's *Laws* (VII 846D1–847B6, 850A6–D2; XI 920A3–4). Aristotle seems to be silently following in Plato's track.

The regulation and control of foreign visitors and metics is never discussed by Aristotle. This is surprising since he was himself a metic during his long sojourn in Athens (367–357, 335–323)[44] and remarks on the inferior position of a metic (III.5 1278a37–38, *EE* III.5 1233a28–30). Perhaps he thought that rule over metics, from the standpoint either of a ruler or of a metic, did not raise any philosophical problems. From the standpoint of the ruler, the relation of a metic to the polis would be purely economic and contractual. From the standpoint of the metic, the relation would be wholly voluntary since (except for a few involuntary exiles) a metic would have a native polis where he enjoyed the privileges of citizenship and to which he could return whenever the life of a metic became a burden.[45]

Most of the noncitizens in Aristotle's best polis will be natural slaves. A natural slave, in Aristotle's view, is a mental defective who lacks forethought and the ability to deliberate, "shares in reason to the extent of apprehending it but without possessing it," and is capable as a consequence of nothing higher than physical labor (I.2 1252a31–34, 5 1254b16–26, 13 1260a12). Such a person lacks the forethought to provide for tomorrow or next winter and would perish without someone to look after him. If he were not so dim-witted, he would recognize his need for a master and join in a friendly relation with him (I.6 1255b12–15; see also *NE* VIII.11 1161b5–8). But natural slaves do not ordinarily recognize this need and are not willingly enslaved. Consequently, one role of the army in Aristotle's polis is "to be master of those who are worthy to be slaves" (VII.14 1334a2). Aristotle envisages using the army to capture natural slaves (see I.7 1255b37–39, 8 1256b23–26) and to insure that, once captured, they do not revolt. For Aristotle, it seems, what is forced is not always unjust. The anticoercion principle apparently does not apply to natural slaves.

But the matter is not quite as clear and straightforward as this. For Aristotle cannot forget, even while justifying natural slavery, that within his philosophy the forced and the just are polar opposites. The anticoercion principle exerts pressure even on his discussion of slavery. Thus, Aristotle says that "there is an element of advantage and friendship for slave and master in their relation to each other when they merit these things [i.e., mastership and slavery] by nature; but when [those who are enslaved are] not [slaves] in this manner, but *through law and by being forced*, the opposite is the case" (I.6 1255b12–15). Given Aristotle's identification of the common advantage and the just (III.12 1282b16–18), this passage opposes force not only to advantage and friendship but to justice as well.

If, setting the accessories aside, one focuses on Aristotle's best polis proper and the relation of its citizens to one another, what comes into view is a community that approaches the anarchist ideal and where the anticoercion principle is alive and active. The end of Aristotle's best polis is true happiness, a life of virtuous activity, for its citizens (VII.13). And its adult male citizens possess all the cardinal virtues—wisdom, bravery, temperance, and justice (VII.1 1323a27–34, b21–23; 15 1334a11–40). Indeed, Aristotle describes them as "great-souled men" (*megalopsuchoi*) (VII.7 1328a9–10, VIII.3 1338b2–4). Greatness of soul, or *megalopsuchia*, is a magnification and "a sort of adornment (*kosmos*) of the virtues; it makes them greater, and does not come to be without them" (*NE* IV.3 1124a1–3). Aristotle's best polis is thus a virtue state or a moral community.[46] It is no accident, then, that its rulers, being just men (VII.9 1328b37–39), seek the common advantage, the advantage of all the citizens, and not the advantage of some segment of the citizen body only. Furthermore, in such a virtue state, coercion and compulsion will be virtually unknown. For coercion is neither appropriate nor necessary among men of full virtue (see *Rhet.* I.14 1375a16).

This interpretation is borne out by Aristotle's views on corporal punishment. Aristotle does not have much to say about punishment in the *Politics*, but a few ideas emerge. Punishment in Aristotle's eyes, though sometimes just and hence good, is good only conditionally and not absolutely: "just retributions and punishments spring from virtue, but are necessary, and possess nobility [only] in a necessary way (for it would be preferable if neither man nor polis had any need of such things)" (VII.13 1332a12–15). Aristotle would punish those citizens who disobey a law against obscenity in different ways depending upon the age of the offender—a youth with blows and dishonors, an adult with slavish dishonors, but not with blows (VII.17 1336b3–12). He is reluctant, in other words, to inflict corporal punishment on an adult, but is prepared to use it on a minor.

Aristotle certainly believes that coercion has a role to play in the moral education of the many as distinct from the well-bred (see *NE* X.9 1179b4–13). In discussing the moral education of the many, he remarks that "generally passion [which the many live by] seems to yield not to argument but to force" (*NE* X.9 1179b28–29) and that "the many obey coercion more than argument and penalties more than the noble" (*NE* X.9 1180a4–5). But it is noteworthy that coercion plays no role in the education, including the moral education, envisaged in *Politics* VIII, perhaps because all the young men in his best polis will be well-bred (VII.7, especially 1327b36–38). The passions of the young men of Aristotle's best polis yield not to argument but to music (VIII.5–7).

What Aristotle attempts to describe in *Politics* VII and VIII, if the foregoing interpretation is correct, is a political community (= a moral community) held together by the justice of its citizens rather than by the sword, and sustained by a system of moral education that relies on methods subtler than force.

7. Noncoercive Rule

It should be clear by now how Aristotle can embrace both the polis and the anticoercion principle. Coercion is not, in Aristotle's eyes, an essential feature of political rule. It is no more the function of a ruler to coerce his subjects than it is for a physician to coerce his patients or a helmsman his crew: "Nor do we see this [the use of coercion] in the other sciences [any more than in political science]; for it is the function neither of the physician nor of the helmsman to persuade or to compel his patients or his crew" (VII.2 1324b29–31). For someone brought up on Thomas Hobbes[47] this idea can be difficult to grasp.

Just as the anticoercion principle is derivable from first principles of Aristotle's ethical and natural philosophy, the idea that correct political rule is noncoercive is derivable from first principles of Aristotle's metaphysics together with a basic theorem of his political philosophy.

In every unitary entity, Aristotle argues, there is one component that rules and another that is ruled: "For whatever is composed of several parts, whether continuous or discrete, and becomes one common thing, in every case rule and subordination (*to archon kai to archomenon*) may be discerned, and this [rule and subordination] is present in living things from the whole of nature; for even in things that do not share in life there is a ruling principle, for example, of a musical scale" (I.5 1254a28–33). The idea here, an idea firmly rooted in Aristotle's metaphysics, is that what distinguishes a whole (*holon*) from a heap (*sōros*) is the presence of form (or soul)[48] and that the natural relation of form to matter (or soul to body) is that of ruler to subject (I.5 1254a34–36). Not all wholes, in Aristotle's view, have the same degree of unity. Nature is a stronger unifying agent than force: "That which is whole and has a certain shape and form is one [i.e., unitary] even more [than that which is one by continuity], especially if it is one *by nature and not by force* (like a thing made one by glue or a nail or a cord) and has within itself the cause of its being continuous" (*Met.* X.1 1052a22–25).

Aristotle systematically applies these metaphysical ideas to political communities. First of all, since a polis is an organized community and not simply a mass of human beings, it must, like other wholes, have a principle of organization, a form. This form is its constitution (III.3 1276b1–13). Secondly, being a whole, a polis must have a component that rules and another that is ruled. A polis without rulers, Aristotle says, would be an impossibility (IV.4 1291a35–36). Finally, according to a basic theorem of the *Politics*, a polis is a natural rather than an artificial whole (I.2 1252b30, 1253a2, 25; VII.8 1328a21–22) and, consequently, is *not* held together by force when in a natural condition. Thus, coercion is not an intrinsic feature of political rule.

Hobbes and Aristotle differ on the role of force in the life of a political community because they differ about the sort of whole a political community is. For Hobbes a state must be held together by force because it is a product of art rather than of nature: "For by Art is created that great LEVIATHAN called a COMMON-WEALTH, or STATE . . . which is but an Artificiall Man."[49]

As part of his naturalism, Aristotle compares a polis to an animal and identifies its ruling element, which corresponds to the soul of an animal, with those functional groups that preserve it by governing and bearing arms (IV.4 1291a24–28). He never envisages a polis without arms. But for the warriors of a polis to use them against the body politic is as contrary to nature, in Aristotle's eyes, as it is for an animal to use its teeth or its claws against its own body. Aristotle recognizes that even a state that cultivates justice at home is prone to forget about justice when dealing with other states. In their relations with each other, states too often resemble lower animals. But he does not condone such conduct and thinks that a political community, no less than a human being, should strive for a life higher than that of a beast.[50]

Notes

1. Unless otherwise indicated, all references are to Aristotle's *Politics*.

2. On the early critics of slavery, see W. K. C. Guthrie, *A History of Greek Philosophy*, vol. 3, *The Fifth-Century Enlightenment*, pp. 155–60.

3. William Godwin, *Enquiry Concerning Political Justice*, (1976 [1798]). Pages cited within square brackets are those of the 1976 edition.

4. Godwin, *Enquiry*, vol. 2, p. 645 [p. 342]; see also vol. 2, pp. 639–42 [pp. 333–37].

5. Godwin, *Enquiry*, vol. 2, p. 667 [p. 372].

6. Godwin, *Enquiry*, vol. 1, p. 272 [p. 271].

7. Godwin, *Enquiry*, vol. 1, p. 269 [p. 267].

8. One meaning of the Greek adjective *anarchos* is "without a ruler." Thus, Aristotle distinguishes political animals that are under a ruler, such as the crane and the bee, from others, such as the ant, that are *anarcha* (*Hist. An.* I.1 488a10–13).

9. *Anarchism and Other Essays*, p. 50 [repr., p. 56].

10. Godwin, *Enquiry*, vol. 1, p. 242 [p. 230].

11. Godwin, *Enquiry*, vol. 2, p. 639 [p. 334].

12. Godwin, *Enquiry*, vol. 2, pp. 408 [p. 2–3].

13. Godwin, *Enquiry*, vol. 2, p. 641–42 [pp. 337].

14. Godwin, *Enquiry*, vol. 2, pp. 743–47 [pp. 479–84].

15. For Diogenes' relation to the modern movement, see Donald R. Dudley, *A History of Cynicism*, pp. 211–12.

16. But perhaps not with all his ideas, for Aristotle remarks that "no one else [besides Plato] has proposed such an innovation as community of children and women" (II.7 1266a34–35). See W. L. Newman, *The Politics of Aristotle*, ad loc.

17. See Newman, *Politics*, vol. 1, pp. 24–25, and Ernest Barker, *The Political Thought of Plato and Aristotle*, pp. 59, 271–72.

18. On Aristotle's "totalitarianism," see Jonathan Barnes, "Aristotle and Political Liberty" [chapter 8 this volume] and Richard Sorabji, "State Power: Aristotle and Fourth Century Philosophy."

19. In one passage, both points are combined: "We say that nature makes for the sake of something, and that this is some good" (*Somno* 2 455b17–18).

20. It is not a syllogism strictly speaking since the parenthetical expression counts as a fourth term. The argument is of course valid.

21. Aristotle also says that "the political good is the just" (III.12 1282b16–17). Since he goes on in this passage to discuss distributive justice, it is plain that the justice in question here is particular rather than universal justice. This is the reason that the good that is equated with it is the political rather than the social good.

22. For the four juristic categories in a typical Greek polis—citizens, metics, foreign visitors, and slaves—see III.1 1275a7–8, 5 1277b38–39; VII.4 1326a18–20, b20–21.

23. The *kai* in this passage is epexegetical.

24. Newman, *Politics*, vol. 1, p. 119n.

25. That a full citizen will be an adult male is taken for granted.

26. Retaining (contrary to Ross) the *ē* of all manuscripts.

27. It was illegal in Athens after the middle of the fifth century for a citizen to marry an alien. See Douglas M. MacDowell, *The Law of Classical Athens*, p. 87.

28. For one exception, see John M. Cooper, "Political Animals and Civic Friendship" [chapter 3 this volume] pp. 70-71.

29. Newman, *Politics*, vol. 1, p. 230.

30. See Newman, *Politics*, ad loc. and vol. 1, p. 229.

31. Aristotle sometimes defines democracy juristically in terms of free status (see IV.4 1290b1, 1291b30–39, 8 1294a11, 15 1299b20–27; V.1 1301a28–31, 8 1309a2; VI.2 1317a40–41, 1318a3–10). In so doing, he reverses the essential and incidental (the defining and nondefining) properties of proletarian democracy and defines what might be called "egalitarian" democracy. This kind of democracy is essentially rule by the free and only incidentally rule by the poor (since the poor are normally a majority of the free). Contrary to his official definition of democracy, Aristotle remarks in one passage that "in democracies it just happens (*sumbainei*) that the poor are more powerful than the rich" (VI.2 1317b8–9). What "just happens" in such a democracy need not always happen. When it does not—when, for example, property is fairly evenly distributed—the free will not split into rich and poor, and will be able, in theory at least, to rule with an eye to the advantage of all the citizens. If they do, the constitution will be correct rather than deviant. In fact, the best polis described in Books VII and VIII seems to be just such an egalitarian democracy. See the note to 1275b5 in Franz Susemihl and R. D. Hicks, *The Politics of Aristotle*—Books I–V [I–III, VII–VIII] (1894 [repr. 1976]). It should be noted that since egalitarian democracy is defined purely juristically, nothing prevents an egalitarian democracy from also being an aristocracy.

32. See Newman, *Politics*, ad loc.

33. See Newman's note to 1293a39.

34. Newman, *Politics*, ad loc.

35. See the text flagged by note 5 above.

36. The polis of Books VII and VIII is never called an aristocracy. The noun *aristokratia* does not, in fact, occur in Books VII and VIII; and the adjective *aristokratikos* occurs only once (VII.11 1330b20). This has led some scholars to question whether it is really supposed to be an aristocracy. For a recent discussion of this matter, see Charles H. Kahn, "The Normative Structure of Aristotle's *Politics*," pp. 375–81.

37. Newman adds: ". . . as well as in the hands of any mercenaries they may employ or any allies they may possess" (*Politics*, ad loc.).

38. Susemihl and Hicks, *Politics*, p. 55.

39. Newman, *Politics*, vol. 1, p. 328.

40. As Susemihl and Hicks imply in their *Politics*, (note to 1328b8).

41. For the distinction between *emporoi* and *kapēloi* see Plato, *Republic* II 371D5–7 and *Sophist* 223D5–10.

42. The ability to deliberate is an essential property of a craftsman or artisan (see *Met.* VII.7 1032a25–b21; *NE* III.3, VI.4), whereas a natural slave "wholly lacks the deliberative faculty" (I.13 1260a12). Aristotle distinguishes two types of *hired* labor: "that of the vulgar (banausic) arts [retaining *technōn*]" and "that of the unskilled who are

useful for their body only" (I.11 1258b25–27). Since the latter phrase describes the highest work of which a natural slave is capable (I.5 1254b25–26), even the lowest artisan is not a natural slave. For the definition of banausic art, see VIII.2 1337b8–15.

43. This is the standard interpretation. Thus, Susemihl and Hicks write in their *Politics*, that "[o]nly foreigners and resident aliens are allowed to engage in trade, industry, or manual labour [in Aristotle's best State]" (p. 54).

44. See David Whitehead, "Aristotle the Metic," pp. 94–99.

45. David Whitehead, *The Ideology of the Athenian Metic*, pp. 71–72; G. E. M. de Ste. Croix, *The Class Struggle in the Ancient Greek World*, pp. 95, 289.

46. This is true, to some extent at least, of every polis that has a correct constitution (III.7 1279a39–b4, 17 1288a6–15).

47. Thus, Hobbes writes:

> For the Lawes of Nature (as *Justice, Equity, Modesty, Mercy*, and [in summe] *doing to others, as wee would be done to,*) of themselves, without the terrour of some Power, to cause them to be observed, are contrary to our naturall Passions that carry us to Partiality, Pride, Revenge, and the like. And Covenants, without the sword, are but Words, and of no strength to secure a man at all. (*Leviathan*, ch. 17)

48. *Met.* V.6 1016b11–16; VII.16 1040b8–10, 17 1041b11–33; VIII.6 1045a8–10 together with *De An.* II.1 412a19–21, *Met.* VII.10 1035b14–16.

49. Hobbes, introduction to *Leviathan.*

50. The research on this chapter has been aided at critical junctures by that wonderful contribution of modern technology to ancient scholarship, the *Thesaurus Linguae Graecae.*

10

Aristotle's Natural Democracy

Josiah Ober

THE TITLE OF THIS CHAPTER is admittedly paradoxical. Natural democracy seems, on the face of it, impossible in Aristotelian terms: Democracy is defined in the *Politics* as a corrupted (*parekbasis*) regime, and all corrupted regimes exist "against nature" (*para phusin*: *Pol.* III.17 1287b41). Yet I will suggest that certain features of democracy were nonetheless treated by Aristotle as emergent properties of human nature. "Natural democracy" explains otherwise recalcitrant aspects of Aristotle's political philosophy; it reveals unexpected congruities between Aristotelian political philosophy and contemporary work in sociology and political anthropology; and it points to the fulfillment of human political nature as a subject for normative democratic theory.

Aristotle's *Politics* is a philosophical conglomerate, which is part of what makes it such an interesting and frustrating work. One way of making the text less frustrating, and less interesting, is to chop it up into three distinct enterprises. The three standard interpretive silos are: (1) a natural/teleological account of the emergence and characteristics of the community most suited to the lives of humans as political animals, that is, the polis; (2) an empirical/historical account of the variety of institutional arrangements in Greek poleis, along with an account of the effects of internal political change and conflict, and recommendations for stabilizing various sorts of polis regimes; and (3) a detailed description of the best practically achievable polis, that is, the "polis of our prayers," and the educational system by which its youth were to be taught citizenship. My approach seeks to bring the contents of the three silos together in a single comprehensible, if also somewhat paradoxical, whole. The paradox arises from Aristotle's refusal to abandon either history or nature in his philosophical analysis of politics.

1. History and Nature

Oswyn Murray sketches an approach to the co-presence of history and nature in Aristotle's *Politics*, by pointing to "the consequences of history for political theory . . . [and] the disturbances introduced by history in the theoretical picture."[1] Murray argues that the introduction of historical observations of actual political practices into the naturalized account of the polis leads to three philosophical problems. First, the naturalized polis of Book I, which is the natural *telos* of human sociability, has some difficulty in making room for the diversity of types of human political organization, that is for the historical emergence and persistence of non-polis forms of political community. Second, if the polis emerges naturally as a consequence of human political nature, it is not initially obvious why there should be a half-dozen distinct types of polis regime (monarchy, aristocracy, "*politeia*," democracy, oligarchy, tyranny). And finally, the theory does not seem to explain the prevalence of historical regime changes (*metabolai*), least of all changes that come about in the violent context of intrastate conflict (*stasis*).

Now, it is important to keep in mind that nature does not always get its way in the Aristotelian universe.[2] And so, for Aristotle, things and processes may sometimes be natural without being especially prevalent, and they may be quite prevalent without being natural. But there is nonetheless a need to explain the disjunction between the theory of the polis as a unitary natural political entity and the observed sociopolitical diversity of the world known to Aristotle. Murray suggests, I think rightly, that Aristotle can solve the first problem (diversity of types of political organization) by positing a very uneven distribution of political virtue among peoples, Greek and non-Greek. There was, we might add, endoxic authority available to him (preserved for us by, e.g., Herodotus 9.122.3–4 and the Hippocratic tradition: *Airs, Waters, and Places* 12.12–13, 16.3–6, 23.19–21) for assuming that climate and geography affected the development of political virtue. Aristotle himself (*Pol.* VII.7 1327b27–33) points out that Asians and northern Europeans labored under severe disadvantages in respect to the development of political virtue. This left penisular/insular Greeks as the "middling" exemplars of a political nature properly balanced between spiritedness and reasoning ability, and thus as the best candidates for the development of the natural human community (i.e., the polis). The second problem, regarding the different sorts of regimes that emerged in different Greek poleis, was likewise explicable in terms of the differential distribution of political virtue among the members of actual polis communities: in communities in which political virtue was concentrated in one or a few individuals, the natural result would be a monarchical or an aristocratic-oligarchic regime. But, as Murray points out, the third problem, regime change and conflict within a given polis community, remains intractable; it cannot be easily solved on the basis of the "uneven distribution of virtue" hypothesis.

Murray's list of history/nature problems assumes, I think rightly, that Aristotle's natural teleology (e.g., *Pol.* I.2 1252b31–53a1) makes out the polis to be a natural thing more or less in the way that an oak tree is natural: a healthy acorn planted and nurtured under optimal conditions will naturally yield an exemplary oak tree. Likewise, a healthy group of humans, offered the right conditions, should develop into an exemplary polis featuring an exemplary *politeia.* Given the best conditions, no other sort of plant will grow from the acorn and no other sort of community will emerge from the group of humans: both oak tree and polis are natural and final ends (*telē*). But conditions are not always optimal. And so, by analogy, one might well imagine oak trees simply failing to thrive in certain climates, and that in these places much less desirable, even somehow "unnatural" sorts of vegetation might grow up instead (e.g., in Asia and Northern Europe: Murray's first problem). And one might further imagine that some acorns, deprived of certain nutrients or corrupted by disease, might grow into barely recognizable versions of the tree that nature intended (Murray's second problem). But it is very hard to imagine an acorn growing into a tree that first seems to be a poplar, and then suddenly transforms itself into something that appears to be a pine, and then a plane tree, before ever coming into its proper form as an oak (Murray's third problem). It is yet more difficult to imagine that strange series of metamorphoses occurring through conflicts among the tree's several parts.

Murray suggests that this third problem, regarding change and conflict, is ultimately resolved only through the unsatisfactory device of an unlikely assumption: that a *new polis* actually comes into being with each change of regime. He goes on to suggest that this "new regime/new polis" conception was systematically explored in the famous collection of *Politeiai* prepared under Aristotle's direction in the Lyceum. But, as Murray notes, the history of Athens, the one polis for which we happen to have a surviving Aristotelian *Politeia* (hereafter *Ath. Pol.*), ill accommodates the conception of new regime/new polis. In the case of Athens, the democratic regime that pertained before and after the *stasis* situation of 411–403, for example, seems resistant to the new regime/new polis conception: many Athenians clearly clung tenaciously to the conception of themselves as democratic citizens subject to democratic laws throughout these changes, and to say that several distinct poleis emerged and dissolved within this period flies in the face of what a reasonable person could be expected to believe. This is, of course a serious problem for Aristotle in light of his endoxic method.

Does *Ath. Pol.* nonetheless allow us to suppose that a new polis emerged after a regime change? Leaving aside the ephemeral oligarchic regimes, it is certainly true that Athenian democracy in 412 was not identical to the democracy a decade later. There were significant institutional changes made in this period, some of them lasting, notably in the process of lawmaking and in the relationship of fundamental law to statute-law. Some modern historians have suggested that these changes amount to a genuinely profound regime-change—one that might perhaps even give warrant to the conception of the creation of a new polis.[3] But, notoriously, the *Ath. Pol.* takes no special notice of the legal/constitutional changes in *nomothesia* procedure. In the historical account of democratic change offered in the *Ath. Pol.*, democracy in Athens seems to be a continuous (and overall teleological) evolution. That continuous democratic evolution took place both through and in spite of a series of *metabolai.* From the era of Solon to the post-Peloponnesian War settlement, the Athenian *politeia* depicted in *Ath. Pol.* was either explicitly democratic or striving to become so: there was no period of post-Solonian history in which a non-democratic *politeia* achieved a persistent, stable existence: non-democratic interludes either maintained the forms of democratic law (the tyranny of Peisistratus) or failed to gain legitimacy (the oligarchy of the Thirty). The point is that the Aristotelian history of Athenian *politeia* seems to demonstrate the capacity of a democratic regime to survive *stasis* by its ability to change in ways that do not encourage, or even permit us to imagine that a new polis has come into being. Assuming that democracy was in some sense a natural end helps to explain the political teleology of *Ath. Pol.* in ways that are consistent with the account of the natural polis in the *Politics.*[4]

This essay takes Murray's issue of "historical change and conflict in the democratic polis" as a starting point for thinking about natural democracy in the *Politics*, and seeks to show why an Aristotelian political history of Athens need not resort to an improbable "new regime = new polis" explanation for change. Passages in Aristotle's *Politics* offering a positive account of democratic deliberation (see below) are sometimes cited as evidence (along with Plato's *Statesman* and *Laws*) for a moderate revaluation of democracy in mid to late fourth-century Greek philosophical thought.[5] I will argue that Aristotle's revaluation of democracy is more fundamental than is usually supposed, to the extent that the political regime appropriate to the "natural polis" of *Politics* Book I and to the "polis of our prayers" of Book VII (which I take to be the natural polis, fully realized) is, in certain analytically important ways, to be understood as a democracy. The Athenian democracy, on this reading, is an imperfect manifestation of a natural entity: the political counterpart of an oak that has grown up in sub-optimal conditions, and thus is deformed in various ways, but for all that is recognizably an oak.

Democracy in the Athenian style, with its Protean capacity to change and yet remain fundamentally the same, was indeed a contributory part of the interpretive problem identified by Murray. But the political sociology of democracy also supplied the answer to an otherwise intractable problem that arose in the course of Aristotle's discussion of the polis as a community (*koinōnia*) of citizens (*politai*). The imagined political regime I am calling "Aristotle's natural democracy" took (as did actual Greek democracies) the set "actual (i.e., politically active, participatory) citizens" (C^a) to be coextensive with the set "all polis residents culturally imaginable as citizens" (C^i), and (after adding an assumption about inherent political capacity) also coextensive with the set "all polis residents qualified by nature to be citizens" (C^n). Equating actual citizens with imaginable and natural citizens had the effect of removing a primary source of social conflict: The equation $C^a = C^i = C^n$ left no body of persons holding either cultural expectations of citizenship or the natural capacity to exercise citizenship stranded outside the actual citizen body. This eliminated, by definition, a category of residents, present in all non-democratic poleis, who were especially likely to resort to *stasis* in order to gain something they quite naturally regarded of great value and rightfully theirs, that is the status of active, participatory citizenship.

2. The Political *telos* of the Polis

The historical change/conflict problem and its relationship to democracy is in turn related to the question of the polis's political *telos*. In the *Politics* Aristotle argues that despite the fact that there were manifestly several sorts of human community, the political nature of human beings leads ultimately to the polis as the most appropriate form of human community, i.e. the natural social environment for optimal human flourishing. We might then call the polis the social *telos* of human political nature. But that can only be part of the story. Given that the polis is a manifestation of human political nature, it is incomplete (if not unimaginable) without a *politeia*, and given that there are variety of *politeiai* manifest in the histories of the many Greek poleis known to Aristotle, we must also ask: What *politeia* is most naturally conducive to human flourishing? Aristotle states (*NE* V.7 1135a5) that there is only one regime-type that is everywhere best according to nature. This best *politeia* is presumably the political *telos* of the natural polis. But which among the various types of *politeia* discussed by Greek political philosophers is it?

In Book I, Aristotle specifies the developmental steps that lead to the emergence of the "natural polis." It is a progressive process of instrumentally valuable growth in the size and complexity of human communities: the aggregation of individuals into families (for purposes of reproduction), then of families into villages or clans (for mutual defense and in order to achieve conditions of justice), and ultimately of villages and clans into a polis (for the achievement of autarky and, potentially, of *eudaimonia*).[6]

The natural polis having achieved its *telos* in respect to social form, it is ready to take on a political form, a *politeia.* Two possibilities present themselves: First is that the political *telos* is inherently a part of the social *telos* and thus that the "natural *politeia*" of the natural polis will be manifest immediately upon the realization of the polis. In this case all subsequent regime changes are devolutionary, corruptions of the pristine original form. This sort of story is familiar from Books VIII and IX of Plato's *Republic*, where Kallipolis is the original and ideal form, and all other regime-types (timocracy, oligarchy, democracy, tyranny) are devolutions. The other possibility is that, like the polis itself, the emergence of the political *telos* is historical and sequential, requiring a development from one natural stage to the next, until the *telos* is achieved. This second, sequential-emergence, story seems to be what Aristotle has in mind in the *Politics.* So what is the final *politeia* toward which the polis was naturally inclined, and what are the historical stages through which the polis must pass in order to achieve that political *telos*?

Murray suggests that in "an important sense" the final regime of the natural polis should be the hybrid form simply called "*politeia*."[7] That is an attractive suggestion, in that it answers the question of why there should be a *politeia* with the name "*politeia*." But the idea that the hybrid form "*politeia*" was the political *telos* of the polis must account for the historical sequence of regimes alluded to in Book III. The passage is worth citing in full:

> If then the rule of a number of persons who are all good men is to be considered as aristocracy, and the rule of a single person as kingship, aristocracy would be preferable for the poleis to kingship (whether the office be conjoined with military power [*dunamis*] or without it), if it were possible to get a large number of men of similar quality. And it was perhaps because of this that they were ruled by kings in earlier times, because it was rare to find men who were very outstanding in virtue, especially as in those days they dwelt in small poleis. Moreover they used to appoint their kings on account of their public benefactions (*ap' euergesias*), something that is the work of good men. But as it began to come about that many men arose who were similar with respect to virtue, they would no longer submit, but sought some form of commonality (*koinon ti*), and established a "*politeia*." As they became worse and made private profit from public affaris (*tōn koinōn*), it was reasonable that oligarchies should arise as a result; for

> they made wealth a thing of honor. And from oligarchies they first changed to tyrannies, and from tyrannies to democracy; for by constantly bringing the government into fewer hands owing to a base love of gain they made the multitude (*plēthos*) stronger, so that it set upon them, and democracies came into existence. Now that it has happened that the poleis have come to be even larger, it is perhaps not easy for any *politeia* other than democracy to come into existence. (*Pol.* III.15 1286b4–22. Trans. C. Lord, adapated)

Here, the polis is said to experience a sequence of regime changes, in this order: kingship–"*politeia*"–oligarchy–tyranny–democracy. This historical sequence of regimes is offered in the immediate context of Aristotle's discussion of kingship, which is itself part of a complex double debate over whether laws or living persons should be authoritative in the polis, and whether monarchy or some form of collective rule is the optimal form of *politeia.*[8]

The sequence of regimes is obviously related to the canonical Aristotelian list of three uncorrupted regimes (monarchy, aristocracy, "*politeia*") and three corrupted regimes (democracy, oligarchy, tyranny).[9] The first two regime-types in the sequence of regimes passage (kingship, "*politieia*") are from the uncorrupted group. The next three regime-types (oligarchy, tyranny, democracy) are each from the corrupted group. The canonical six-regime list is meant to be rank-ordered in respect to virtue. Aristotle's long and sometimes tortuous discussion of "which regime is best?" in Book III shows that the ranking remains disputed in respect to the uncorrupted regimes: There is a sense in which kingship is best, another sense in which aristocracy is best, and perhaps also a sense in which "*politeia*" is best. But the rank-ordering is clear in respect to the corrupted regimes: democracy is better than oligarchy, which is in turn better than tyranny.

If we were to suppose that kingship is indeed the best of the uncorrupted regimes, then the sequence of regimes passage might indeed support the notion that the political *telos* emerges simultaneously with the social *telos*, i.e. with the realization of the polis. But the notion that kingship is simply the best form of *politeia* is effectively challenged in the course of the discussion of "which regime is best?" Kingship is the ideal form of governance in the event that the virtue of the one individual outweighs the aggregate virtue of all others. But that becomes less likely as poleis grow in size. Kingship is also, as we learn, subject to problems of succession (i.e., when inferior sons succeed superior fathers) and more subject to corruption than collective forms of rule. And so, rather than the political *telos* itself, kingship seems to be a historical way station, and political change will be required if the polis is to achieve a stable political end.

Once we are embarked upon the sequence of regimes, we might expect that the sequence will fit into a developmental scheme based on a progressive change in the distribution of political virtue among the citizens. That is apparently the case in the first change, from kingship to "*politeia*": in the sequence of regimes passage Aristotle says that in early times, when poleis were much smaller, it was difficult to find many virtuous persons. But when "many men arose who were similar with respect to virtue, they would no longer submit [to the king]"; so they sought for some form of *koinon*, and set up a "*politeia.*" We might suppose, on Murray's argument, that with the emergence of "*politeia,*" we have now arrived at the natural political *telos* of the polis. This might seem to be supported by Aristotle's subsequent claim that the three "corrupted" regimes are "against nature" (*Pol.* III.17 1287b41). The emergence of these last three regime-types cannot, therefore, be regarded as a natural consequence of human political nature. The series of post-"*politeia*" regime changes—to oligarchy, then tyranny, and finally democracy—does not fit with a story about systematic changes in the distribution of virtue among the citizens.[10] Rather, the change to oligarchy is said to come about because men became "worse" (*cheirous*) and began making (private) profit out of public affairs (*koina*). The change to tyranny seems to be simply a hypertrophy of oligarchy, with wealth concentrated in ever-fewer hands. This process of concentration in turn results in the many (*plēthos*) becoming stronger, leading to a change to democracy. Aristotle's historical sequence of regimes ends with democracy, which appears to be as far as polis political evolution has got by Aristotle's own time. Immediately after presenting the sequence of regimes, Aristotle suggests that in his own times, now that poleis are even larger, it is "not easy" for any regime other than democracy to arise (*Pol.* III.15 1286b20–22).

Yet we cannot suppose that the polis has, in Aristotle's time, achieved its *telos*, since, as we have seen, democracy is a corrupt regime and in that sense it is by definition "against nature." Albeit, democracy is the least bad of the corrupted regimes. But surely, even though nature does not always achieve what it wants, it cannot be the case that the teleological political development that began with the realization of the polis as a natural form suited not only to the instrumental purposes of human survival and material flourishing but also the potential achievement of philosophical *eudaimonia*, just ends in democracy—or at least in democracy as it is ordinarily understood and as it is manifested in (for example) Aristotle's Athens. This would leave humans with nothing to hope for beyond living in a "not too badly" corrupted political condition.

Obviously, there is more to be hoped for: the "polis of our prayers" described in Book VII. It seems reasonable to suppose that the *politeia* of the polis of our prayers is meant to represent, in a practicable sense, the political *telos* of the natural polis: after all, why would we pray for a regime that fell short of the best and final political end of what nature meant for us as political animals? Thus, if we can characterize the regime-type of the "polis of our prayers" we may suppose that we have arrived at the answer to the riddle of "what regime is the political *telos* of the natural polis?"

There seem initially to be two possible answers to the question, What is the *politeia* of the polis of our prayers?—"*politeia*" or aristocracy. In reference to the sequence of regimes passage, considered above, we will need to choose between a reversion to the regime-type that degenerated into oligarchy, or an advance to a new regime-type. Given that "*politeia*" had failed to resist degeneration, advance to a new regime type seems, on the face of it, a more likely way forward to the political *telos*—even though it may not be easily accomplished. Notably, aristocracy is the "missing regime" in Aristotle's historical sequence of regimes: the only one of the canonical list of six regime-types that is not represented in the sequential history of the polis's political development. And thus, we may guess that political teleology is to be squared with history by a political evolution of the polis through a three-stage political sequence (kingship, "*politeia*," aristocracy), which would correspond to the three-part social sequence (family, village/clan, polis) offered in Book I as leading to the realization of the polis.

Assuming the scenario presented above is correct, in the case of the development toward the political *telos*, there is a sort of hiatus, or detour, between the penultimate ("*politeia*") and ultimate (aristocracy) natural stages: a period (of indefinite duration) characterized by a sub-series of three "unnatural" political regime-types (oligarchy, tyranny, democracy). It is furthermore important to keep in mind that the argument I am developing implies that the teleological process had not been completed by the time of the writing of the *Politics*: the polis of our prayers remains a hope for the future, and thus the polis has not (in Aristotle's day) yet achieved its *telos*.

Aristotle's teleological naturalism demanded that the political *telos* be realizable, even if not yet realized. I have argued elsewhere that the polis of our prayers is not intended as a utopia "laid up in heaven," but rather it is imagined as a real possibility that could be brought into existence within historical time. And moreover, I have argued that Aristotle himself had reason to hope that the polis of our prayers might be brought into existence in the near future, as the consequence of historical developments in his own era.[11] Thus, it seems to me likely that the polis of our prayers is, at least in the first instance, to be regarded as an aristocracy, that it is to be equated with the political *telos* toward which the polis was naturally inclined, and that its appearance was (at least potentially) imminent in Aristotle's own time.[12]

3. Democracy and Nature

Two questions (or sets of questions) remain, which confront us with the paradox of "Aristotle's natural democracy":

First, are we to imagine the sequence of regime changes described in Book III, beginning with kingship, and ending (so I have suggested) with aristocracy, as occurring in a single polis? Or must we, with Murray, suppose that Aristotle was committed to the strange idea that each time the regime changed, so too did the polis? That is to say, when speaking of the sequential changes that antedated the teleological emergence of the best possible *politeia* for the polis, must we imagine that "the polis" in question was actually not a single entity with a continuous existence, but rather a series of conceptually distinct entities? And could the final step—the political *telos*—emerge within an existing polis via regime-change, or does achieving the *telos* entail making a new polis? I hope this set of questions will be answered as a consequence of answering the second question.

The second question sets the agenda for rest of this essay: Is the "hiatus era" of three corrupted regimes sequentially following the degeneration of "*politeia*" into oligarchy to be understood (in Aristotelian terms) only as an unfortunate detour—just a patch of historical bad luck that must, once the political *telos* of the aristocratic polis has been achieved, be mourned as having doomed a certain number of human generations to unnecessary misery? Or was something actually gained from that interlude, such that the final product—a genuinely choiceworthy aristocratic polis, has benefited as a consequence?

Even to ask this last question is to invite the objection that the categories of teleological naturalism and historical development have now become hopelessly muddled: After all, in Aristotelian terms, it hardly seems possible to say that nature can have anything to learn from history. Aristotle's natural polis cannot be analogized to a Darwinian species, "designed" for fitness by a long process of selection driven by historical adaptation to environmental circumstances. I readily acknowledge the issue, but this essay is specifically about the problem of reconciling teleological naturalism and history, a problem with which every reader of Aristotle's *Politics* is confronted as a consequence of the text's "conglomerate" organization and argumentation. Aristotle himself points to the conjunction of human nature and willed human action when he notes that, while "there is in everyone an impulse" to live in a political community, nonetheless he who first brought men together to live in a polis was the cause (*aitios*) of the greatest of goods (*Pol.* I.2 1253a29–31).[13] I suggest that the resolution to the paradox of how nature could learn from history might be discovered by reconstructing Aristotle's thought process, which I would hypothetically restore along the following lines (keeping in mind, of course, that the actual sequence of ideas is unrecoverable and not particularly important).

1. Teleological naturalism is applied to political evolution: starting with the "acorn" of humans as political animals, Aristotle derives the "social form" of the human community in a three-stage sequence—first is the family; next is the village or clan; the third and final stage is the polis.
2. He derives the "political form" of the polis via a three-stage sequence of virtue-based regimes. First is monarchy in which virtue is concentrated in an individual; next "*politeia*," as virtue is distributed more widely among certain residents of the polis; the third and final stage is aristocracy, the point at which virtue is evenly distributed, and maintained at a high level, among all citizens.
3. The empirical data of political history shows that regimes (corrupted as well as uncorrupted) follow one another in a sequence of regime changes and that poleis had become larger over time.
4. Historically, in some cases it appears as if a new polis has emerged as the result of a regime change, but in other cases substantial changes are best understood as evolutionary steps within a single polis and single regime. The development of democracy in Athens, from Solon to Aristotle's own day, is a particularly good example of this latter model.
5. If a real-world example of an aristocratic "polis of our prayers" is to come into being and survive, it will need to be a genuinely new polis—a colonial foundation in which conditions for polis flourishing are optimal. But it cannot exist outside history—which means outside the world of large and successful poleis like Athens. This means that the new polis of our prayers must find a way to borrow from the competences that have made certain existing poleis historically successful in facing external threats: e.g. strong walls and up-to-date defenses against siege.
6. The ideal polis must also be resilient in the face of potential internal conflict. And so, the polis of our prayers must borrow from the sociopolitical factors that made certain poleis (notably Athens) successful in resisting catastrophic *stasis*, and thus in resisting the "metabolic" tendency to change into "another polis." The key factor is the democratic equation of the body of actual citizens with the body of culturally imaginable citizens ($C^a = C^i$).
6. The history/nature circle is squared by allowing the original hypothesis about human political nature to accommodate the thought that in a state of nature, the potential for developing a level of political virtue adequate to participatory citizenship (ruling and being ruled in turns) is innate in virtually all newborn (Greek) males.[14]

8. In existing poleis, innate capacity is frequently squandered, as men corrupt themselves through engagement in bad (that is, slavish, banausic, instrumental) practices. In the polis of our prayers, the socioeconomic (especially land- and slave-holding) and education systems are designed to help nature achieve its purposes by preventing post-natal corruption of innate political capacity in "natural citizens" through precluding their engagement in bad practices. Ergo, under optimal circumstances, $C^a = C^i = C^n$.

Squaring the nature/history circle through this "8-step program" produces one unsurprising result: the political *telos* of the natural polis turns out to be aristocratic in that the citizen-rulers manifest political virtue and share in a standardized education centered on the perfection of that virtue. But it also produces a result that is quite unexpected in light of earlier Greek political philosophizing about the ideal state: The ideal polis is democratic in that no male permanent resident need be excluded *ab initio* from active, participatory citizenship by circumstances other than that of nativity. The unexpected result is, I have suggested, the product of Aristotle's intellectual engagement with the political history of the poleis, and perhaps especially with the history of democratic Athens (as it is presented in the *Ath. Pol.*). Aristotle's ideal state borrows from historical Greek democracy a key sociopolitical characteristic, one that made democracy (in Athens's case, at least) resistant to the corrosive sorts of change engendered by *stasis*. And as a result, the polis of our prayers is an aristocratic democracy (or a democratic aristocracy): a community in which all free native adult males were not only active and participatory citizens, but also highly virtuous citizens. And thus democracy finds a place in the political *telos* of the Aristotelian polis, and it is possible to speak, without irony (if not without paradox), of "Aristotle's natural democracy."[15]

4. Testing the "Natural Democracy" Thesis

My main argument is now complete, but it remains to specify why the formula $C^a = C^i$ (leaving aside C^n, as a distinctively Aristotelian concern) rendered a democracy like Athens historically capable of experiencing change and *stasis* without losing its identity as a unitary polis in the process.[16] As Athenian writers before Aristotle (for example, Ps-Xenophon 3.12–13; Thuc. 6.39.1: speech of Athenagoras of Syracuse) had noted, the equation of the actual citizens with "persons culturally conceivable as citizens" meant that there was no body of disaffected people who might suppose that they were being denied "what they deserved" in terms of political recognition by the fact of being unfairly stranded outside the citizen body. Although this democratic move certainly did not eliminate *stasis*, it removed one of its least tractable sources: So long as there were substantial numbers of noncitizens within the polis who strongly believed themselves culturally entitled to citizenship, there could be no true long-term stability.

Once the Athenian solution was put into place, it proved remarkably successful in creating stable political identities: The account of the *Ath. Pol.* suggests that a key innovation came with Solon's lawcode, which, by forbidding the enslavement of locals, initially defined the Athenian citizen body as "the native adult males."[17] This move was fundamentally important in that it extended the cultural imagination of "who could be a citizen" as far as it would ever be extended in actual Greek practice (if not in Aristophanes' and Plato's imaginations).

After Solon there was a progressive increase in the participation rights of citizens.[18] This progressive augmentation of the participatory aspect of citizenship was not without interruption; there were several oligarchic attempts (in 508: Isagoras and the Three Hundred, in 411: The Four Hundred, in 404: The Thirty) to narrow the definition of citizenship, by restricting the active-citizen body to some subset of the native male population. Each of these attempts failed, because most Athenians continued to act as if $C^a = C^i$, and continued to regard the democratic code of law (which they imagined as dating back to Solon) as continuously valid. The point is that although anti-democratic groups occasionally succeeded in changing the *politeia*, understood as the institutional arrangements by which the city was momentarily governed, they failed to effectively challenge the persistence of a democratic *politeia*, understood as a democratic identity and loyalty to a set of laws. And thus they failed to change the existing polis into a new polis.

Aristotle naturalizes this democratic social/political/cultural solution by defining (implicitly, through an argument about deliberative capacity that excludes natural slaves, women, and children) the "natural citizens" as justly free (i.e., not slave by nature) adult males. Such individuals have, *ex hypothesi*, the potential for developing skills necessary for ruling and being ruled over in their turn. Although the story gets more complicated with the introduction (at the end of Book I: 1260a36–b2) of the idea that voluntary human activity (performance of a trade) can render a free man a sort of "slave by practice," I would suggest that among the most remarkable features of the *Politics* is that it makes "natural democracy" possible by allowing (while never positively asserting) the premise that virtually every Greek male possesses, at birth, the inherent potential for developing the rather high level of political virtue necessary to participate actively in ruling an uncorrupted polity.[19] In no existing polis was the "citizenship potential" of the male population actually realized; Aristotle believed that in actual democracies most of those with participation rights lacked adequate virtue for the proper exercise of citizenship. So the inherent potential of born citizens ordinarily went unrealized in the face of inadequate conditions for its nurture. Yet under the optimal conditions pertaining in the polis of our prayers men's innate political potential could be reliably developed through a standardized system of education and a social system designed to ensure that "natural citizens" do not become "slaves by practice."

We can test this conclusion by a simple contrary-to-fact argument: were the "inherent political capacity" presumption *not* regarded by Aristotle as true—were many of the native-born males of the polis of our prayers expected to be inherently so deficient in virtue as to be uneducable and thus unsuited to ruling in their turn—then some provision would be needed in the polis of our prayers for dealing with them—either for treating them as natural slaves (if they are recognized as such), or for relegating them to a status-group of free yet noncitizen (never-ruling/permanently ruled-over) natives, or for expelling them from the polis. There is no hint of any such provision in the text as we have it. I have suggested above that Aristotle's awareness of the revolutionary tendencies of "native (adult male) non-citizens," whether in residence or in exile, gave him good reason to avoid burdening his best-imaginable polis with a class of such persons.

Can the idea of "natural democracy" stand the test of plausibility? Is it just an inherently absurd idea, one that it would be odd to suppose that Aristotle could ever have entertained?[20] I don't believe it is. Indeed, a recent survey of empirical studies on the comparative anthropology of foraging (hunting-gathering, "pre-agricultural") societies suggests that, in an important sense, the "natural democracy" hypothesis is correct. Something like democracy (or anyway something much more like democracy than oligarchy or tyranny) does indeed seem to be a plausible candidate for the "natural" human political condition.[21] The universal tendency of "simple" human communities to seek to resist the emergence of would-be tyrants or oligarchic cliques suggests that something like a presumption of inherent political capacity, and a commitment to political equality among those manifesting such capacity, emerge from our human nature. Moreover, there is no reason to suppose that our "inherent" preference for democracy is extinguished by the emergence of larger and more complex forms of human community: A methodologically sophisticated "happiness survey," based on 6,000 interviews in Switzerland, demonstrates quite a strong correlation (correcting for other factors) between overall happiness and access to institutions of participatory democracy.[22] A strong reading of these anthropological and sociological studies would suggest that Aristotle's claim that humans are by nature "political animals" is correct; at the least they underline the reasonableness of a presumption that such a nature would tend to lead to a form of political organization that was in some sense democratic.

I have argued, above, that while the political *telos* of the natural Aristotelian polis is in one sense an aristocracy, in another analytically relevant sense, it is a democracy. Aristotle certainly never comes out and states that as a conclusion; it is a thesis that emerges, so I have argued, when we make the attempt at a reasonably comprehensive reading of the *Politics*, i.e. a reading that refuses to split the teleological argument off from the historical/empirical argument, or to split those arguments off from the account of the ideal state. Given that we will not find any simple authorial statement about the role of democracy in the political *telos* of the natural polis, can we test the unexpected conclusion by reference to other passages of the text? It seems reasonable to suppose that if it is true, a "natural democracy" thesis should help explain otherwise difficult-to-interpret passages, in a text that does not lack for passages that resist easy explanation. I offer, as an example, the tricky issues of deliberation and the "summation argument."

If an aristocratic democracy (democratic in the simple sense that $C^a = C^i$) is the most natural form of "Aristotelian" regime, then it should also be the case that democracy allows humans to make best use of certain of their natural human capacities in respect to governance. After speech itself, the most basic and most important human political capacity is deliberation or "deliberative judgment" (*to bouleutikon*). Deliberation is the capacity (as is made clear in the *Rhetoric*) to make reasonable choices about matters relevant to the common good of the community, in the context of meaningful alternatives, and on the basis of prior knowledge (technical and social) and the ability to assess reasoned (but not logically indisputable) arguments.

Deliberation is the very capacity that limits citizenship to adult free males: In a notorious and brief passage (*Pol.* I.13 1260a7–14), Aristotle states that natural slaves lack *to bouleutikon*, that women do not possess it in an adequately reliable way (because it is not the master element in their moral psychology), and (less controversially) that children have yet to fully develop it.

Aristotle does indeed suggest that democratic decision-making processes can (under the right conditions) make optimal use of innate human deliberative capacity through the process sometimes described as "summation."[23] The process is one of aggregation of diverse "knowledge/expertise sets" among the members of a large body of persons who must decide on a matter that cannot be adequately judged by any one of them, or by any small group of experts. The key passage is as follows.

> The many, of whom none is individually an excellent (*spoudaios*) man, nevertheless can, when joined together, be better than those [the excellent few], not as

> individuals but all together [*hōs sumpantas*], just as potluck [*sumphorēta*] dinners can be better than those provided at one man's expense. For, there being many, each person possesses a constituent part [*morion*] of virtue and practical reason, and when they have come together, the multitude [*plēthos*] is like a single person, yet many-footed and many-handed and possessing many sense-capacities [*aisthēseis*], so it is likewise as regards to its multiplicity of character [*ta ēthē*] and its mind [*dianoia*]. This is why the many [*hoi polloi*] judge better in regard to musical works and those of the poets, for some judge a particular aspect [*ti morion*], while all of them judge the whole [*panta de pantes*]. (*Pol.* III.11 1281a40–b10. Trans. C. Lord, adapted).[24]

Aristotle here offers two analogies to explain summation: first the "pot luck dinner," a feast to which each of many diners brings some different dish, resulting in a superior dining experience for everyone. Next is the judgment of "musical and poetic" (certainly including dramatic) performances, an undertaking which demands a variety of sensibilities (in the case of tragedy, this will require an appreciation of the six elements of plot, character, diction, thought, spectacle, and song: *Poetics* 1450a6–10).[25] When the decision-making group is of the right sort, Aristotle claims that this democratic "summation" process in fact yields superior judgments. In order to be of the right sort, the group must be mindful of the common good and sensible to the locus of relevant expertise among its membership. That is to say, the group must not act as a selfish faction, and each of its members must pay attention to the opinions/responses of those who are (in the dramatic example) musically adept in respect to the singing, to those adept at visual art in respect to the staging, and so on.

An important part of the Aristotelian summation argument is that it implicitly acknowledges the issue of democratic diversity in respect to knowledge and judgment-capacity. The large-group decision-making process characteristic of democracy works to optimize the human capacity to deliberate well on matters in which no individual is adequately knowledgeable, only because the group in question is diverse in the right way and not diverse in any wrong way. Once again, there is an unsurprising conclusion and an unexpected conclusion to be drawn.

It is unsurprising (within the usual way of reading Aristotle) to say that if the group is diverse in the wrong way, the summation process will not get off the ground: If the group in question is merely a conglomeration of selfish individuals or selfish factions—each with a preconceived notion of the outcome it desires, then the various members of the group will neither be paying appropriate attention to each of their fellow citizens on the basis of his special knowledge and expertise, nor judging in respect to the common good. The point is that in order to judge well, there must be a certain homogeneity among the membership: each member of the group must possess and manifest at least baseline political virtue, qua group-interest seeking.

The unexpected conclusion is that the group must be diverse in the right way, by which I mean that it must include a diversity of distinctly different knowledge-sets and expertise-sets.[26] If the group were homogeneous in respect to knowledge and expertise, then each would have precisely the same "knowledge/expertise set," and so the decision to be made by the group could be made just as well (and presumably more quickly and efficiently) by any one of its members. By analogy, there would be no culinary benefit in common feasts if each member brought just the same sort of food to the common table—in that case each may as well eat at home. Nor would the dramatic judgment improve if we simply multiply sensibilities that we suppose each individual member possessed in fullness as an individual. It is only when the decision-making group is diverse in the sense that different people bring things that are both different and valuable "to the table" that the process of summation adds value to group judgments.

The summation argument is a test of the "natural democracy" thesis in that it demonstrates that methods of group decision-making strongly identified with democracy as a regime-type do allow, under optimal conditions, for the most effective use of capacities that Aristotle regards as at least potentially inherent in humans as political animals. The summation argument also suggests that a diversity of knowledge and skills among the members of the citizen body could be a source of community strength, and that strength was *not* produced by limiting acts of public judgment to an elite of "the excellent." Unregulated diversity in the context of public decision-making bodies was strongly and negatively identified in the ancient philosophical tradition with democracy as a sociopolitical system (Plato, *Republic* 557C is the locus classicus). Aristotle's discussion of summation opens up a more positive approach to diversity in public decision-making. He suggests that under optimal conditions, the right kind of diversity allowed for better decisions to be reached, as the deliberative capacity inherent in the individual members of groups was conjoined with an aggregated body of knowledge and brought to bear on some object of common concern.

It is important to remember that so long as we stay within Aristotle's conceptual universe, the scope of democracy will remain strictly delimited by the aristocratic frame into which it is put to work. The founder of a "polis of our prayers" can learn from the historical experience of Athenian democracy, but the polis of our prayers is not an option for Athens; it can be realized only by the creation of a new polis under near-optimal conditions. That restrictive aristocratic frame, along with the role of nature in justifying slavery and the exclusion of women from political life on the basis of an improbable and under-theorized moral psychology, renders Aristotle's political theory unsuitable as an "off-the-shelf" model for contemporary democratic theorizing.

Yet when we turn from the project of understanding Aristotle's own political thought to the project of normative democratic theorizing we need not be constrained by classical-era *endoxa* regarding women, slaves, or the effect of labor on the human psyche. The core Aristotelian argument I have attempted to develop here, that democracy is our natural inheritance as political animals and that natural democracy accommodates (even requires) diverse decision-making bodies, is not dependent upon peculiar assumptions about how deliberative capacity is distributed by nature or impaired through practice. If we are willing to expand Aristotle's frame, by assuming that virtually all humans come into the world with the potential to become fully featured political animals in an Aristotelian sense, his core argument could provide the jumping off point for a democratic political theory that moves well beyond the familiar late-twentieth-century frameworks of analytic liberalism and communitarianism.[27]

Notes

1. Murray, "*Polis* and *Politeia* in Aristotle," p. 204.

2. E.g. *Pol.* I.5 1254b26–32. There is, of course, a large bibliography on nature in the *Politics* and its relationship to Aristotelian naturalism elsewhere in the corpus. I have found Lloyd's "The Idea of Nature in the *Politics*," Depew's "Humans and Other Political Animals in Aristotle's *History of Animals*," and Cooper's "Political Animals and Civic Friendship" particularly helpful. In contrast to my fairly conventional understanding of how nature works in Aristotle, Frank, in *A Democracy of Distinction*, argues for "denaturalizing nature," that is, that nature in Aristotle's *Politics* does not constrain humans. This allows her to develop an action-centered model whereby it is not only possible for citizens-by-nature to become slaves through practice, but also possible for "natural slaves" to make themselves into citizens by willfully choosing appropriate activity. While I find this conception *normatively* more attractive than the ordinary way of reading Aristotle on nature, I do not think it it is what Aristotle himself meant. Frank's "denaturalized" reading does not, for example, account for *Pol.* I.8 1256b20–26: the claim that just warfare is acquisitive military action aimed at enslaving those who are slaves by nature; see further, Ober, *Political Dissent in Democratic Athens*, pp. 304–5.

3. E.g. Hansen, *The Athenian Democracy in the Age of Demosthenes*, and Ostwald, *From Popular Sovereignty to the Sovereignty of Law*.

4. I leave to one side, for the purposes of this essay, the question of whether *AthPol*'s Athenian history is, by contemporary historical standards, completely plausible. For the record, I would start the continuous history of democracy with the Athenian Revolution and Cleisthenic reforms of 508/7 BC: Ober, *The Athenian Revolution*, chapter 4.

5. Democracy in *Laws* and *Statesman*: Bobonich, *Plato's Utopia Recast*; Hitz, *Plato and Aristotle on the Failings of Democracy*, pp. 68–88. It is worth noting that Plato's earlier political texts (especially *Gorgias, Protagoras, Republic*) can be read as a "democratic" in the cultural/pedagogical sense of providing readers with both intellectual resources and argumentative method for contesting the apparent (non-democratic) conclusions reached by Plato's Socrates: See Monoson, *Plato's Democratic Entanglements*; Euben, *Platonic Noise.*

6. Although the process is a product of natural impulses, it cannot be accomplished without willed human action, indeed, it requires something like a social contract—although the contract is very different (and based on a very different conception of human nature) than the familiar early modern contract theories (e.g., Hobbes, whose pessimistic conception of humans in the state of nature is radically different from Aristotle's): see Ober, *The Athenian Revolution*, pp. 168–70.

7. Murray, "*Polis* and *Politeia* in Aristotle," p. 201. I identify the hybrid regime-type by putting quotes around the term: thus "*politeia*" is the regime type, *politeia* the general term for constitution, political culture, or literary account thereof.

8. Cf. Ober, *Political Dissent in Democratic Athens,* p. 326. A different account of *metabolai* is offered at V.12 1316a20–39, in the context of an attack on Plato's sequence of regimes in the *Republic.* Here Aristotle suggests that there is no fixed sequence for regime-change, and that the most common form of *metabolē* is from one regime-type to its opposite (rather than its "neighboring type"). Aristotle's argument here is based on empirical evidence of regime-changes in various directions, and the emergence of the political *telos* seems not to be at issue.

9. See for example the schematic diagram, with discussion, in Ober 1998, p. 311.

10. Nor does Aristotle's "oligarchy, tyranny, democracy" sequence reproduce Plato's progression of post-timocracy regimes in *Republic* Books VIII and IX (oligarchy, democracy, tyranny) or Plato's ranking of non-law-abiding regimes in *Statesman* 302B–303B (democracy, oligarchy, tyranny).

11. Ober, *Political Dissent in Democratic Athens,* pp. 339–50.

12. Frank, *A Democracy of Distinction,* offers an account of the relationship between Aristotle's naturalized political teleology and the "polis of our prayers" as an "aristocratic democracy" that is in important respects compatible with the account I offer here, although Frank's activity-centered conception of "Aristotelian political nature" and her conception of the "polis of our prayers" as a possible future for Athens are quite different from my views.

13. See, further, Ober, *The Athenian Revolution,* pp. 168–69 with note 21.

14. At *Pol.* V.12 1316a8–11, again in debate with Plato's *Republic,* Aristotle leaves open the possibility that Plato might be right that some men may be born in a polis who prove uneducable and incapable of developing excellence. We might guess (the text gives us no guidance) that Aristotle would regard such men as slaves by nature. It is unclear, however, whether Aristotle accepts that this category of individual actually exists (other than as sports of nature, see below), or whether he simply allows the possibility in order to show that Plato's understanding of *metabolai* is faulty even granted that unprovable presumption.

15. Given the somewhat contradictory definitions of "*politeia*" as a regime-type in the *Politics*, it is not impossible that this "democratic aristocracy/aristocratic democracy" might be described as both an aristocracy and as a sort of "*politeia*." See, further, the thoughtful discussion of Frank, *A Democracy of Distinction*, chapter 5.

16. The Athenians did indeed "naturalize" their conception of citizenship, but they did it in a very different way than did Aristotle, via legally mandated bilateral nativity requirements for legitimate marriage and procreation and via the development of an autochthony myth and a related ideology of "Athenian character." For a succinct analysis of Athenian naturalized citizenship, see Lape, *Reproducing Athens*, pp. 68–76.

17. Solon's innovation is well analyzed (in explicitly Aristotelian terms) in Manville, *The Origins of Citizenship in Ancient Athens.*

18. For a review of post-Solonian historical development of democratic institutions, see Ober, *Mass and Elite in Democratic Athens,* chapter 2.

19. Cf. above, note 14. One must always account for sports of nature, which might throw up morally defective specimens, just as it threw up individuals with physical deformities. Perhaps a native Greek natural slave, who would of course be excluded from participation, would be regarded by Aristotle as such a sport of nature. The distribution of natural slavishness is a notoriously tricky problem in the *Politics*; suffice it to say here that Aristotle points his reader to Asia as the most obvious place in which slaves by nature were likely to be found: see Ober, *Political Dissent in Democratic Athens*, pp. 304–6. It is not clear how the premise of inherent capacity to develop virtue is to be squared with Aristotle's comment (*Rhetoric* II.15 1390b19–31) that inferior sons are often born to excellent fathers. See other passages cited and discussion in Ober, *Mass and Elite in Democratic Athens*, p. 250 n. 7, 256.

20. Aristotle was quite capable of entertaining implausible ideas, for example natural slavery. But it is surely unfair to saddle him with truly implausible ideas that are not explicitly argued for in the text as we have it.

21. Boehm, *Hierarchy in the Forest* (a project that has a certain conceptual similarity to the collection of *Politeiai* in the Lyceum); cf. Leacock, "Women's Status in Egalitarian Society."

22. Frey and Stutzer, "Happiness, Economy, and Institutions."

23. On the summation argument, see Keyt, "Aristotle's Theory of Distributive Justice."

24. Waldron, "The Wisdom of the Multitude" (chapter 6 in this volume), underlines the importance of this passage, which he discusses under the rubric of the "Doctrine of the Wisdom of the Multitude." Gottlieb, *The Virtue in Aristotle's Ethics*, ch. 13, argues persuasively that Aristotle is neither being ironic nor presenting someone else's argument here. She shows (loc cit. ad fin.) that the optimistic account of democratic decision-making in this and related passages is compatible with the discussion of the unity of the virtues in *NE* and *EE*, because "vices are a disunited lot whereas only the virtues cohere in a unified and coherent way." See Ober, *Political Dissent in Democratic Athens*, pp. 319–24 for further discussion and bibliography.

25. The "summation" passage strongly recalls Aristotle's analysis of tragedy in the *Poetics*, with its discussion of how "parts" make up the whole, and of the essential roles in action and judgment played by *dianoia* and *ēthos*.

26. Cf. *EE* I.6 1216b31: "Everyone has something of his own (*oikeion*) to contribute to the truth." This leads to a question, which cannot be adequately answered here: "What is the origin of diversity in knowledge-sets and expertise-sets?" Suffice it to note that if a community were to take each human infant as a perfect tabula rosa, and submit him (or her) to a perfectly standardized upbringing and education, such diversity would not emerge. The sort of desirable democratic diversity pointed to here assumes either some meaningful differences in inherent abilities, or in the culture to which community members are exposed, or (most plausibly) in both.

27. By "analytic liberalism," I refer to the tradition most strongly associated with John Rawls; by "communitarianism" that associated with Michael Sandel. It is only fair to say that many political theorists, including those working on deliberative democracy, virtue theory, and neo-republicanism, have sought (more or less successfully) to move beyond these paradigms. This essay was first presented as a paper at the Chicago-area Classical Philosophy Conference in April 2004; a revised and expanded version was presented in November 2004 as the Wesson Lectures at Stanford University. For their help at various stages of this chapter's development, I would like to thank Ryan Balot, Richard Kraut, Susan Lape, Sarah Monoson, Barry Powell, and Christian Wildberg. Thanks also to Zena Hitz, Jill Frank, and Paula Gottlieb for sharing their work in advance of publication, and for their valuable comments on Aristotle on democracy.

Bibliography

Editions, Translations, Commentaries

Barker, Ernest. *Aristotle: Politics.* Oxford, UK: Oxford University Press, 1946.

Dreizehnter, Alois. *Aristoteles' Politik.* Munich: Wilhelm Fink, 1970.

Gauthier, R. A. and Jolif, J. Y. *L'Ethique à Nicomaque.* Louvain: Publications universitaires de Louvain, 1959.

Irwin, Terence. *Aristotle: Nicomachean Ethics.* With introduction, notes, and glossary, 2nd edition. Indianapolis: Hackett, 1999.

Jowett and Barnes. *Aristotle: Politics.* Ed. Stephen Everson. Cambridge, UK: Cambridge University Press, 1988.

Lord, Carnes. *Aristotle: The Politics.* With introduction, notes, and glossary. Chicago: University of Chicago Press, 1984.

Newman, W. L. *The Politics of Aristotle*, 4 vols. Oxford, UK: Clarendon Press, (reprinted 1973), 1887–1902.

Nussbaum, Martha. *Aristotle: De Motu Animalium.* Text with translation, commentary, and interpretive essays. Princeton, NJ: Princeton University Press, 1978.

Ostwald, Martin. *Aristotle: Nicomachean Ethics.* New York: Bobbs-Merrill, 1962.

Rackham, H. *Aristotle: Nicomachean Ethics*, rev. ed., Loeb. London: Heinemann, 1934.

———. *Aristotle: Politics*, Loeb. Cambridge, MA: Harvard, 1944.

Reeve, C. D. C. *Aristotle: Politics.* Indianapolis: Hackett Publishing Company Inc., 1998.

Robinson, R. *Aristotle's Politics* III and IV. Oxford, UK: Clarendon Press, 1995.

Ross, W. D., ed. *The Works of Aristotle.* Oxford, UK: Clarendon Press, 1908–1952.

———. *Aristotle: Nichomachean Ethics.* London, UK: Oxford University Press, 1954.

———. *Aristotelis Politica.* Oxford, UK: Clarendon Press, 1957.

Sinclair, T. A. *Aristotle: The Politics.* Rev. T. J. Saunders. Harmondsworth, UK and New York: Penguin Books, 1981.

Susemihl, F. and Hicks, R. D. *The Politics of Aristotle.* Text, introdution, analysis, and commentary to Books I–V (I–III, VII–VIII). New York: Arno Press, 1976 [1894].

Other Works

Allen, Donald J. "Individual and State in the *Ethics* and *Politics*." In *La "Politique" d'Aristote*, Rudolf Start et al. Geneva: Foundation Hardt, 1965.

Ambler, Wayne. "Aristotle's Understanding of the Naturalness of the City." *Review of Politics* 47 (1985): 163–85.

Annas, Julia. "Plato and Aristotle on Friendship and Altruism." *Mind* 86 (1977): 532–54.

———. "Aristotle on Virtue and Happiness." *University of Dayton Review* 19, no. 3 (1988): 7–22.

———. "Comments on J. Cooper." In *Aristoteles' "Politik."* Ed. Patzig, 243–49.

Aquinas, St. Thomas. *On Princely Government.* In *Aquinas: Selected Political Writings.* Ed. A. P. D'Entroves. Oxford: Basil Blackwell, 1959.

———. *Summa Theologica*, Vol. 13. London: Blackfriars.

Arendt, Hannah. *The Human Condition.* Chicago: University of Chicago Press, 1958.

———. *The Origins of Totalitarianism*, 2nd ed. New York: World, 1958.

———. *Between Past and Future.* New York: Viking, 1958.

———. *On Revolution.* Harmondsworth, UK: Penguin, 1973.

Arnhart, Larry. *Aristotle on Practical Reasoning.* De Kalb: Northern Illinois University Press, 1981.

Augustine. *Concerning the City of God Against the Pagans.* Tr. Henry Bettenson. London: Penguin, 1972.

Barker, Ernest. *Greek Political Theory.* London: Methuen, 1918.

———. *The Political Thought of Plato and Aristotle.* New York: Russell & Russell, 1959 [1906].

Barnes, J. "Aristotle and the Methods of Ethics." *Revue Internationatinale de Philosophie.* 34 (1980): 490–511.

Becker, L. *Property Rights: Philosophical Foundations.* London: Routledge and K. Paul, 1977.

Beiner, Ronald. *Political Judgment.* London: Methuen, 1983.

Bellah, R. N. "The Ethical Aims of Social Inquiry." In *Social Science as Moral Inquiry.* Ed. N. Haan et al., 1983, 360–81.

Bobonich, C. *Plato's Utopia Recast: His Later Ethics and Politics.* Oxford, UK: Oxford University Press, 2002.

Bodéüs, Richard. "L'Animal politique et l'animal économique." In *Aristotelica: Mélanges offerts a Marcel De Corte. Cahiers de philosophie ancienne* 3. Liège: Presses Universitaires, 1985, 65–81.

Boehm, C. *Hierarchy in the Forest: The Evolution of Egalitarian Behavior.* Cambridge, MA: Harvard University Press, 1999.

Boorse, C. "Health as a Theoretical Concept." *Philosophy of Science* 44 (1977): 542–73.

Brentano, Franz. *Über Aristoteles.* Hamburg: Felix Meiner Verlag, 1986.

Burnet, John. *The Ethics of Aristotle.* London: Methuen & Co., 1900.

Calvert, B. "Slavery in Plato's Republic." *Classical Quarterly* 37 (1987): 367–72.

Campese, S. "*Polis* ed economia in Aristotele." In *Aristotele e la crisi della politica.* Ed. D. Lanza and M. Vegetti. Naples: Liguori, 1977, 13–60.

Charles, David. "Perfectionism in Aristotle's Political Theory: Reply to Martha Nussbaum." In *Oxford Studies in Ancient Philosophy,* Supplementary Volume (1988), 185–206.

———. "Comments on M. Nussbaum." In *Aristoteles' "Politik,"* ed. Patzig, pp. 187–201.

Clark, Stephen. *Aristotle's Man: Speculations on Aristotelian Anthropology.* Oxford, UK: Clarendon Press, 1975.

———. "Slaves and Citizens." *Philosophy* 60 (1985): 27–46.

Cohen, B. *The Birth of a New Physics.* New York: Anchor Books, 1985.

Constant, Benjamin. *De l'esprit de conquête et de l'usurpation.* In *Oeuvres.* Paris: Pléiade, 1957 [1814].

———. "De la liberté des anciens comparée à celle des modernes." In *Cours de politique constitutionelle,* Vol. 2. Ed. E. Laboulaye. Paris: Guillaumin, 1861 [1819].

Cooper, John. *Reason and Human Good in Aristotle.* Cambridge, MA: Harvard University Press, 1975.

———. "Aristotle on the Forms of Friendship." *Review of Metaphysics* 30 (1977): 619–48.

———. "Aristotle on the Goods of Fortune." *Philosophical Review* 94 (1985): 173–96.

Cornford, F. M. *From Religion to Philosophy.* New York: Harper, 1957.

Cranston, M. *Freedom.* London: Longmans, 1953.

Depew, D. "Humans and Other Political Animals in Aristotle's *History of Animals.*" *Phronesis* 40 (1995): 156–81.

de Ste. Croix, G. E. M. *The Class Struggle in the Ancient Greek World.* London, Duckworth, 1981.

Diogenes Laertius. *Lives of Eminent Philosophers.* Tr. R. D. Hicks. London: Loeb, 1972.

Dobbs, D. "Aristotle's Anti-Communism." *American Journal of Political Science* 29 (1985): 29–46.

Dover, K. J. *Greek Popular Morality in the Time of Plato and Aristotle.* Berkeley: University of California Press, 1974.

Dudley, Donald R. *A History of Cynicism.* London: Methuen, 1974 [1937].

Düring, I. *Aristoteles, Darstellung und Interpretation seines Denkens.* Heidelberg: Winter, 1966.

Durkheim, Emile. *The Division of Labor in Society.* New York: Macmillan, 1933.

———. *Suicide.* Glencoe, IL: Free Press, 1951.

Ehrenberg, Victor. *The Greek State.* New York: Norton, 1964.

Eldredge, N. *Time Frames: The Rethinking of Darwinian Evolution and the Theory of Punctuated Equilibrium.* New York: Simon & Schuster, 1985.

Elster, J. *Making Sense of Marx.* Cambridge, UK: Cambridge University Press, 1985.

———. *Karl Marx: A Reader.* Cambridge, UK: Cambridge University Press, 1986.

Euben, J. P. *Platonic Noise.* Princeton, NJ: Princeton University Press, 2003.

Feinberg, Joel. *The Moral Limits of the Criminal Law,* vol. 3, *Harm to Self.* Oxford, UK: Oxford University Press, 1986.

Finley, M. I. "Aristotle and Economic Analysis." *Past and Present* 47 (1970): 3–25.
———. *The Ancient Economy*. London: Chatto and Windus, 1973.
———. *Democracy Ancient and Modern*. London: Chatto and Windus, 1973.
———. *Democracy Ancient and Modern*. New Brunswick, NJ: Rutgers University Press, 1973.
Finley, M. I. and H. W. Pleket. *The Olympic Games: The First Thousand Years*. New York: Viking, 1976.
———. *Ancient Slavery and Modern Ideology*. London: Chatto and Windus, 1980.
Flew, A. G. N. *The Politics of Procrustes*. Buffalo, NY: Prometheus Books, 1981.
Foucault, Michel. *Power/Knowledge: Selected Interviews and Other Writings 1972–1977*. New York: Pantheon, 1980.
Frank, Jill. *A Democracy of Distinction: Aristotle and the Work of Politics*. Chicago: University of Chicago Press, 2005.
Frede, Dorothea. "Der Übermensch in der politischen Philosophie des Aristoteles." *Internationale Zeitschrift für Philosophie* 2 (1998): 259–84.
———. "Staatsverfassung und Staatsbürger." In *Aristoteles' Politik*. Ed. O. Höffe. Berlin: Akademie Verlag, 2001, 75–92.
Frede, M. *Essays in Ancient Philosophy*. Minneapolis: University of Minnesota Press, 1987.
Frey, B. S. and A. Stutzer. "Happiness, Economy, and Institutions." *Economic Journal* 110 (2000): 918–38.
Furley, D. J. "Antiphon's Case against Justice." In *The Sophists and Their Legacy*. Ed. G. B. Kerferd. Wiesbaden: Steiner 1981.
Fustel de Coulanges, Numa Denis. *The Ancient City*. New York: Doubleday, 1956.
Gadamer, H.-G. "The Problem of Historical Consciousness." In *Interpretive Social Science: A Reader*. Ed. Rabinow and Sullivan, 1979, 103–62.
———. *Truth and Method*. New York: Seabury Press, 1975.
Geertz, C. *The Interpretation of Cultures*. New York: Basic Books, 1973.
———. "Deep Play: Notes on the Balinese Cockfight." In *Interpretive Social Science: A Reader*. Ed. Rabinow and Sullivan, 1979, 181–224.
———. "From the Native's Point of View: On the Nature of Anthropological Understanding." In *Interpretive Social Science: A Reader*. Ed. Rabinow and Sullivan, 1979, 225–42.
———. *Negara: The Theater State in Nineteenth-Century Bali*. Princeton, NJ: Princeton University Press, 1980.
———. *Local Knowledge*. New York: Basic Books, 1983.
———. "Anti-Anti Relativism." *American Anthropologist* 86 (1984): 263–78.
Geuss, Raymond. *The Idea of a Critical Theory*. Cambridge, UK: Cambridge University Press, 1981.
Godwin, William. *Enquiry Concerning Political Justice*, 3d ed., 2 vols. Ed. Isaac Kramnick. Reprint (2 vols. in 1). Harmondsworth: Penguin, 1976 [1798].
Goldman, Emma. *Anarchism and Other Essays*, 3d rev. ed. New York: Dover, 1969 [1917].
Goldschmidt, Victor. "La Théorie aristotélicienne de l'esclavage et sa méthode." In *Zetesis: Melanges É. de Strycker*. Antwerp: De Nederlandsche Boekhandel, 1973, 147–63.

Gottlieb, P. *The Virtue in Aristotle's Ethics* (forthcoming).

Gouldner, A. W. *Enter Plato.* London: Routledge & K. Paul, 1967.

Grimaldi, W. M. A. *Aristotle, Rhetoric I: A Commentary.* New York: Fordham University Press, 1980.

Grunebaum, James. *Private Ownership.* London: Routledge & K. Paul, 1987.

Guthrie, W. K. C. *A History of Greek Philosophy*, vol. 3, *The Fifth-Century Enlightenment.* Cambridge, UK: Cambridge University Press, 1969.

Gwartney, J. D., and R. L. Stroup. *Economics: Private and Public Choice*, 5th ed. San Diego: Harcourt Brace Jovanovich, 1990.

Haan, N. et al., eds. *Social Science as Moral Inquiry.* New York: Columbia University Press, 1983, 360–81.

Hamburger, Max. *Morals and Law, the Growth of Aristotle's Legal Theory.* New Haven, CT: Yale University Press, 1951.

Hansen, M. H. *The Athenian Democracy in the Age of Demosthenes: Structure, Principles, and Ideology.* Oxford, UK: B. Blackwell, 1991.

Hardin, G. "The Tragedy of the Commons." In *Exploring New Ethics for Survival.* Ed. G. Hardin, Baltimore: Penguin, 1973.

Harrison, A. R. W. *The Law of Athens*, 2 vols. Oxford, UK: Oxford University Press, 1968 and 1971.

Havelock, Eric. *The Liberal Temper in Greek Politics.* New Haven, CT: Yale University Press, 1957.

Hegel, Georg W. F. *Grundlinien der Philosophie des Rechts.* Hamburg: Felix Meiner, 1955 [1821].

———. *The Philosophy of Right.* Tr. T. M. Knox. Oxford, UK: Oxford University Press, 1952.

Heinimann, Felix. *Nomos and Physis.* Basel: F. Reinhardt, 1945.

Hitz, Zena. *Plato and Aristotle on the Failings of Democracy.* Unpublished Ph.D. dissertation in philosophy. Princeton, NJ: Princeton University, 2004.

Hobbes, Thomas. *Leviathan.* Ed. Richard Tuck. Cambridge, UK: Cambridge University Press, 1991 [1651].

Höffe, O., ed. *Aristoteles' Politik.* Berlin: Akademie Verlag, 2001.

———. "Aristoteles' Politik: Vorgriff auf eine liberale Demokratie." In *Aristoteles' Politik.* Ed. O. Höffe, 2001.

Honoré, A. M. "Ownership." In *Oxford Essays in Jurisprudence.* Ed. A. G. Guest Oxford, UK: Oxford University Press, 1961, 107–47.

Hurka, Thomas. *Perfectionism.* New York: Oxford University Press, 1993.

Irwin, Terence. "Permanent Happiness: Aristotle and Solon." In *Oxford Studies in Ancient Philosophy*, 3. Ed. J. Annas. Oxford, UK: Oxford University Press, 1985, 89–124.

———. *Aristotle's First Principles.* Oxford, UK: Clarendon Press, 1988.

———. "The Good of Political Activity." In *Aristoteles' "Politik."* Ed. Patzig, 1990, 73–98.

———. "Aristotle's Defence of Private Property." In *A Companion to Aristotle's* Politics. Ed. Keyt and Miller, 1991, 200–25.

Jaeger, W. "Aristotle's Use of Medicine as Model of Method in His Ethics." *Journal of Hellenic Studies* 77 (1957): 54–61.

Jensen, A. R. and S. Toulmin. *The Abuse of Casuistry: A History of Moral Reasoning.* Berkeley: University of California Press, 1988

Jones, A. H. M. *Athenian Democracy.* Oxford, UK: Blackwell, 1957.

Jones, J. W. *The Law and Legal Theory of the Greeks: An Introduction.* Oxford, UK: Clarendon Press, 1956.

Jost, L. "Moral Luck and External Goods in the Eudemian Ethics." unpublished.

Kahn, Charles H. "The Normative Structure of Aristotle's *Politics.*" In *Aristoteles' "Politik."* Ed. Patzig 1990, 369–84.

Kant, Immanuel. *Die Metaphysik der Sitten.* Ed. Karl Vorländer. Hamburg: Felix Meiner, 1922 [1797].

———. *The Metaphysical Elements of Justice*, trans. John Ladd. New York: Bobbs-Merrill, 1965 [1797].

Kelsen, H. "Aristotle and Hellenic-Macedonian Policy." In *Articles on Aristotle*, vol. 11. Ed. J. Barnes et al. London: Duckworth, 1977, 170–94.

Keyt, David. "Aristotle's Theory of Distributive Justice." In *A Companion to Aristotle's* Politics. Ed. Keyt and Miller, 1991, 238–78.

———. "Aristotle and Anarchism." *Reason Papers* 18 (Fall 1993): 133–52.

———. "Supplementary Essay." In *Aristotle's Politics* III and IV. Tr. R. Robinson. Oxford, UK: Clarendon Press, 1995, 125–48.

Keyt, David and Fred Miller, eds. *A Companion to Aristotle's* Politics. Oxford, UK: Basil Blackwell, 1991.

Kraut, Richard. "Are There Natural Rights in Aristotle?" *The Review of Metaphysics* 49 (1996): 755–74.

Kronman, A. T. "Alexander Bickel's Philosophy of Prudence." *Yale Law Journal* 94 (1985): 1567–1616.

Kuhn, T. S. *The Structure of Scientific Revolutions*, 2d ed. Chicago: University of Chicago Press, 1970.

Kullmann, W. "Der Mensch als Politisches Lebewesen bei Aristoteles." *Hermes* 108 (1980): 419–43.

Lape, S. *Reproducing Athens: Menander's Comedy, Democratic Culture, and the Hellenistic City.* Princeton, NJ: Princeton University Press, 2004.

Leacock, E. "Women's Status in Egalitarian Society: Implications for Social Evolution." *Current Anthropology* 19, no. 2 (1978): 247–75.

Lewis, T. J. "Acquisition and Anxiety: Aristotle's Case Against the Market." *Canadian Journal of Economics* II (1978): 69–90.

Liddell, H. G. and R. Scott. *A Greek-English Lexicon*, rev. ed. Oxford, UK: Oxford University Press, 1940.

Linz, Juan. "Totalitarianism and Authoritarian Regimes." In *Handbook of Political Science*, Vol. 3. Ed. Greenstein and Polsby. Reading, MA: Addison-Wesley, 1975.

Lord, Carnes. *Education and Culture in the Political Thought of Aristotle.* Ithaca, NY: Cornell University Press, 1982.

Lord, Carnes and D. O'Connor, eds. *Essays on the Foundations of Aristotelian Political Science.* Berkeley: University of California Press, 1991.

———. "Aristotle's Anthropology." In *Essays on the Foundations of Aristotelian Political Science.* Ed. Carnes Lord and D. O'Connor, 1991, 49–73.

Lloyd, G. E. R. "The Role of Medical and Biological Analogies in Aristotle's Ethics." *Phronēsis* 13 (1968): 68–83.

———. *Science, Folklore and Ideology.* Cambridge, UK: Cambridge University Press, 1983.

———. "The Idea of Nature in the *Politics.*" In his *Aristotelian Explorations.* Cambridge and New York: Cambridge University Press, 1996, 184–204.

Luhmann, Niklas. *Funktion und Folgen formaler Organizationen.* Berlin: Duncker und Humbolt, 1965.

———. *Soziologische Aufklärung 1,* 3rd ed. Opladen: Westdeutscher Verlag, 1972.

———. *Soziologische Aufklärung 2.* Opladen: Westdeutscher Verlag, 1975.

Lukes, Stephen. *Marxism and Morality.* Oxford, UK: Oxford University Press, 1985.

MacDowell, D., ed. *Andokides on the Mysteries.* Oxford, UK: Clarendon Press, 1962.

———. *The Law in Classical Athens.* Ithaca, NY: Cornell University Press, 1978.

Machan, T. R. *Human Rights and Human Liberties.* Chicago: University of Chicago Press, 1975.

MacIntyre, Alasdair. *After Virtue: A Study in Moral Theory.* London: Duckworth, 1981.

———. *After Virtue: A Study in Moral Theory.* Notre Dame, IN: University of Notre Dame Press, 1981.

———. *Whose Justice? Which Rationality?* Notre Dame, IN: University of Notre Dame Press, 1988.

Manville, P. B. *The Origins of Citizenship in Ancient Athens.* Princeton, NJ: Princeton University Press, 1990.

Mathie, W. "Property in the Political Science of Aristotle." In *Theories of Property: Aristotle to the Present.* Ed. A. Parcel and T. Flanagan. Waterloo: Wilfrid Laurier University Press, 1979.

Mayhew, R. A. "Aristotle on Property." *Review of Metaphysics* 46 (1993): 803–31.

Mayr, E. *The Growth of Biological Thought: Diversity, Evolution, and Inheritance.* Cambridge, MA: Belknap Press, 1982.

McDonald, L. M. *Western Political Theory.* New York: Harcourt, Brace & World, 1968.

McNeill, D. "Alternative Interpretations of Aristotle on Exchange and Reciprocity." *Public Affairs Quarterly* 4 (1990): 55–68.

Meikle, S. "Aristotle and Exchange Value." In *A Companion to Aristotle's* Politics. Ed. Keyt and Miller, 1991, 156–81.

Mill, J. S. *On Liberty.* Ed. Carragheen V. Shields. Indianapolis, IN: Bobbs-Merrill, 1956.

Miller, Fred D. Jr. "Aristotle on the Origins of Natural Rights." *The Review of Metaphysics* 49 (1996): 873–907.

———. *Nature, Justice, and Rights in Aristotle's Politics.* Oxford, UK: Oxford University Press, 1995.

———. "Sovereignty and Political Rights." In *Aristoteles' Politik.* Ed. O. Höffe, 2001, 107–19.

Monoson, S. S. *Plato's Democratic Entanglements: Athenian Politics and the Practice of Philosophy.* Princeton, NJ: Princeton University Press, 2000.

Morrow, G. R. *Plato's Cretan City: A Historical Interpretation of the Laws.* Princeton, NJ: Princeton University Press, 1960.

Mulgan, R. G. "Aristotle's Doctrine that Man is a Political Animal." *Hermes* 102 (1974): 438–45.

———. *Aristotle's Political Theory.* Oxford, UK: Clarendon Press, 1977.
———. "Was Aristotle an Aristotelian Social Democrat?" *Ethics* 111 (2000): 93–106.
Mulhern, J. J. "*Mia Monon Pantachou Kata Physin He Ariste.*" *Phronēsis* 17 (1972): 260–68.
Murray, O. "*Polis* and *Politeia* in Aristotle." In *The Ancient Greek City-State.* Ed. M. H. Hansen. Copenhagen: Munksgaard, 1993, 197–210.
Nagel, Thomas. "Equality." In *Mortal Questions.* Cambridge, UK: Cambridge University Press, 1979, 106–27.
———. *Equality and Partiality.* Oxford, UK: Clarendon Press, 1991.
———. *The Possibility of Altruism.* Oxford, UK: Clarendon Press, 1970.
Natali, Carlo. "Aristotle et la chrématistique." In *Aristoteles' "Politik."* Ed. Patzig 1990, 296–324.
———. "La struttura unitaria del libro I della 'Politica' di Aristotele." *Polis* 3.1 (1979–1980): 2–18.
Neumann, Franz. *The Democratic and Authoritarian State.* New York: Free Press, 1957.
Nichols, Mary P. *Citizens and Statesmen: A Study of Aristotle's* Politics. Savage, MD: Rowman & Littlefield, 1992.
Nietzsche, Friedrich. *Morgenröte.* In *Werke.* Ed. Karl Schlecta. Munich: Carl Hanser, 1966 [1881].
Nussbaum, Martha. "Aristotelian Social Democracy." In *Liberalism and the Good.* Ed. B. Douglas, G. Mara, and H. Richardson. New York: Routledge, 1990: 203–52.
———. *The Fragility of Goodness.* Cambridge: Cambridge University Press, 1986.
———. "Nature, Function, and Capability: Aristotle on Political Distribution." In *Oxford Studies in Ancient Philosophy,* Supplementary Volume (1988): 145–84.
———. "Reply to David Charles." In *Oxford Studies in Ancient Philosophy,* Supplementary Volume (1988), 207–14.
———. "Saving Aristotle's Appearances."In *Language and Logos.* Ed. M. Schofield and M. C. Nussbaum. Cambridge, UK: Cambridge University Press, 1982, 267–93.
———. "Shame, Separateness, and Political Unity: Aristotle's Criticism of Plato." In *Essays on Aristotle's Ethics.* Ed. Rorty, 1980, 395–435.
Ober, Josiah. *The Athenian Revolution: Essays on Ancient Greek Democracy and Political Theory.* Princeton, NJ: Princeton University Press, 1996.
———. *Mass and Elite in Democratic Athens: Rhetoric, Ideology, and the Power of the People.* Princeton, NJ: Princeton University Press, 1989.
———. *Political Dissent in Democratic Athens: Intellectual Critics of Popular Rule.* Princeton, NJ: Princeton University Press, 1998.
Ostwald, M. *From Popular Sovereignty to the Sovereignty of Law: Law, Society, and Politics in Fifth-Century Athens.* Berkeley: University of California Press, 1986.
Owen, G. E. L. "*tithenai to phainomena.*" In his own *Logic, Science and Dialectic: Collected Papers in Greek Philosophy.* Ed. M. Nussbaum. London: Duckworth, 1986, 239–51.
Pagden, Anthony. "'The School of Salamanca' and the 'Affair of the Indies.'" *History of Universities* 1 (1981): 71–112.
———. *The Fall of Natural Man.* Cambridge, UK: Cambridge University Press, 1982.
Parekh, B. *Marx's Theory of Ideology.* London: Croom Helm, 1982.

Parsons, Talcott. *Societies: Evolutionary and Comparative Perspectives.* Englewood Cliffs, NJ: Prentice-Hall, 1966.

———. *The System of Modern Societies.* Englewood Cliffs, NJ: Prentice-Hall, 1971.

Patzig, Gunther, ed. *Aristoteles' "Politik": Akten des XI. Symposium Aristotelicum.* Göttingen: Vandenhoeck & Ruprect, 1990.

Pellegrin, P. "La Théorie aristotélicienne d'esclavage: tendances actuelles de l'interprétation." *Rev. Philosophique* (1982): 345–57.

Pocock, J. G. A. *The Machiavellian Moment.* Princeton, NJ: Princeton University Press, 1975.

Pohlenz, Max. *Freedom in Greek Life and Thought.* Dordrecht: D. Reidel, 1966.

Polanyi, Karl. *The Great Transformation.* Boston: Beacon, 1957.

Popper, Karl. *The Open Society and Its Enemies*, rev. ed. Princeton, NJ: Princeton University Press, 1966.

Rabe, Hugo, ed. *Commentaria in Aristotelem Graeca; Vol. XXI, pars II.* Berolini: Typis et impensis Georgii Reimeri, 1894.

Rabinow, P. and W. M. Sullivan, eds. *Interpretive Social Science: A Reader.* Berkeley: University of California Press, 1979.

Rawls, John. "Justice as Fairness: Political Not Metaphysical." *Philosophy and Public Affairs* 14 (1985): 223–51.

———. *A Theory of Justice.* Cambridge, MA: Harvard University Press, 1971.

Raz, J. *The Morality of Freedom.* Oxford, UK: Oxford University Press, 1986.

Riedel, Manfred. *Metaphysik und Metapolitik: Studien zu Aristoteles und zur politischen Sprache der neuzeitlichen Philosophie.* Frankfurt am Main: Suhrkamp, 1975.

Rorty, A. O., ed. *Essays on Aristotle's Ethics.* Berkeley: University of California Press, 1980.

Ross, W. D. *Foundations of Ethics.* Oxford, UK: Clarendon Press, 1939.

———. *The Right and the Good.* Oxford, UK: Clarendon Press, 1930.

Rousseau, Jean-Jacques. *Discourse on the Origin of Inequality.* Tr. J. R. Masters and R. D. Masters. New York: St. Martin's, 1964.

———. *The Social Contract and Discourses.* Tr. G. D. H. Cole. London: J. M. Dent, 1973.

Runciman, W. G. *The Methodology of Social Theory.* Cambridge, UK: Cambridge University Press, 1983.

Saunders, T. J. "The Controversy about Slavery Reported by Aristotle—*Politics I vi,* 1255 a 4ff." In *Maistor: Classical, Byzantine and Renaissance Studies for Robert Browning.* Ed. A. Moffatt. Canberra: Australian Association for Byzantine Studies, 1984, 25–36.

Sayre, Farrand. *Diogenes of Sinope.* Baltimore: J. H. Furst, 1938.

Schlatter, R. *Private Property. The History of an Idea.* New Brunswick, NJ: Rutgers University Press, 1951.

Simmel, Georg. *Conflict and the Web of Group-Affliations.* New York: Free Press, 1955.

———. *Individuality and Social Forms.* Chicago: University of Chicago Press, 1971.

Skemp, J. B. *Plato's Statesman.* London: Routledge & K. Paul, 1962.

Smith, N. D. "Aristotle's Theory of Natural Slavery." *Phoenix* 37 (1983): 109–22.

Sokolowski, R. *Moral Action: A Phenomenological Study.* Bloomington: University of Indiana Press, 1985.

Sorabji, Richard. "State Power: Aristotle and Fourth Century Philosophy." In *Aristoteles' "Politik."* Ed. Patzig, 1990, 264–76.

Steiner, H. "The Structure of Compossible Rights." *Journal of Philosophy* 74 (1977): 767–75.

Strauss, Leo. *The City and Man.* New York: Rand McNally, 1964.

———. *Liberalism Ancient and Modern.* New York: Basic Books, 1968.

———. *Natural Right and History.* Chicago: University of Chicago Press, 1953.

———. *On Tyranny.* Ithaca, NY: Cornell University Press, 1968.

———. *Xenophon's Socrates.* Ithaca, NY: Cornell University Press, 1972.

Swanson, J. A. *The Public and the Private in Aristotle's Political Philosophy.* Ithaca, NY: Cornell University Press, 1992.

Thucydides. *The Peloponnesian War.* Tr. Rex Warner. London: Penguin, 1954.

Vico, Giambattista. *The New Science.* Tr. T. Bergin and M. Fisch. Ithaca, NY: Cornell University Press, 1968 [1744].

Vlastos, G. "Does Slavery Exist in Plato's *Republic*?" In his *Platonic Studies.* Princeton, NJ: Princeton University Press, 1973, chap. 6.

———. "The Theory of Social Justice in the *Polis* in Plato's *Republic*." In *Interpretations of Plato.* Ed. H. North. Supplementary vol. of *Mnemosyne* (1977): 1–40.

Weber, Max. *On Law in Economy and Society.* New York: Simon & Schuster, 1954.

———. *The City.* New York: Free Press, 1958.

Webster, T. B. L. *Everyday Life in Classical Athens.* New York: Putnam, 1969.

Westermann, W. L. "Slavery and the Elements of Freedom in Ancient Greece." In *Slavery in Classical Antiquity.* Ed. M. I. Finley. Cambridge, UK: Cambridge University Press, 1960.

White, S. A. *Sovereign Virtue: Aristotle on the Relation between Happiness and Prosperity.* Stanford, CA: Stanford University Press, 1992.

Whitehead, David. "Aristotle the Metic." *Proceedings of the Cambridge Philological Society* 21 (1975).

———. *The Ideology of the Athenian Metic.* Cambridge, UK: Cambridge University Press, 1977.

Wiedemann, T. *Greek and Roman Slavery.* London: Croom Helm, 1981.

Wilkes, K. V. *Physicalism.* Atlantic Highlands, NJ: Humanities Press, 1978.

Williams, B. *Ethics and the Limits of Philosophy.* Cambridge, MA: Harvard University Press, 1985.

Wood, E. M. and N. Wood. *Class Ideology and Ancient Political Theory.* Oxford, UK: Blackwell, 1978.

Xenophon. *Hellenica.* Tr. C. L. Brownson. London: Loeb, 1918.

———. *Memorabilia.* In *Memorabilia and Oeconomicus.* Ed. E. C. Marchant. London: Loeb, 1923.